Sport and Social Exclusion

Tackling social exclusion is a key aim of the social policy of any government. *Sport and Social Exclusion* assembles a vast array of evidence from a range of global sources to demonstrate how the effects of social exclusion are as evident in sport as they are in any area of society.

The book uses sport as an important case study for reflecting critically on existing social policy, and addresses sport's role as a source of new initiatives for tackling exclusion. It covers key topics such as:

- What we mean by 'social exclusion'
- How social exclusion affects citizenship and the chance to play sport
- How exclusion from sport is linked to poverty, class, age, gender, ethnicity, disability, and involvement in youth delinquency
- How exclusion is linked to concepts of personal and communal social capital.

Sport and Social Exclusion includes a wealth of original research data, as well as a range of important new studies of social exclusion policy and practice in the UK and elsewhere. Drawing upon this research, the author offers important recommendations on how exclusion from sport and society should be tackled in the future. By relating current policy to new research the book provides a foundation for students, academics and policy makers to examine their own understanding, studies and practices.

Mike Collins is Senior Lecturer in Sport and Leisure Management at Loughborough University. He was Head of Research at the Sports Council and has conducted and managed research on behalf of the Sports Council, the Department of Culture, Media and Sport and many other organisations.

Sport and Social Exclusion

Michael F. Collins
with Tess Kay

London and New York

First published 2003
by Routledge
11 New Fetter Lane, London EC4P 4EE

Simultaneously published in the USA and Canada
by Routledge
29 West 35th Street, New York, NY 10001
Routledge is an imprint of the Taylor & Francis Group

© 2003 Michael F. Collins

Typeset in 10/12pt Times by Graphicraft Limited, Hong Kong
Printed and bound in Great Britain by Biddles Ltd, Guildford and King's Lynn

British Library Cataloguing in Publication Data
A catalogue record for this book is available from the British Library

Library of Congress Cataloging in Publication Data
A catalogue record has been requested

ISBN 0-415-25959-2 (pbk)
      0-415-25958-4 (hbk)

Dedication

This book is dedicated to three people: two friends and colleagues who have been models of intellectual integrity in social research and policy application – Allan Patmore and the late Sue Glyptis; and my wife Sue, who has loved, fed and watered, and supported me for nearly forty years, and who is my severest critic!

Contents

Figures

Tables

Foreword

Michael Collins has been at the heart of sports policy in Britain for more than thirty years, first as Head of Research and Planning at the erstwhile Sports Council, and then, since 1989, at Loughborough University as founder Director of the Institute of Sports Planning and Management and a lecturer and researcher. His impact has been immense, far more than any simple record of publication might suggest. At the Sports Council, not only was he the inspiration and mentor behind a huge body of research projects (over 500), but he also used his legendary energies to see research concepts tested in the field and become an inherent part of the delivery of national sports policy and funding. At Loughborough, his energies have been undiminished, as much in the stimulation of others as in purely personal achievement. Generous almost to a fault with his time, he is so often the first point of contact of any writer and researcher with ideas to test and explore.

It is due in no small measure to Mike Collins that British sports policy has been deeply concerned with so much more than the simple provision of sports facilities or the financial support of elite athletes and their coaches. For him, the slogan 'Sport for All' has been a tenet of belief – not just a belief springing from simple emotion, but one founded on a practical concern with tested outcomes. He is clear that sport should never be funded only as an adjunct to greater national prestige and national glory; he is far more concerned with the deep-rooted benefits widespread participation in sport can bring to health, enjoyment and well-being across the whole of society.

He is not alone, of course, in this belief, but he has long felt that there should be an accessible but uncompromising review of the evidence for the social impact of sport, as a firmer foundation for formulating sports policy at both national and local levels. This volume is that foundation, the happy outcome of the urgings so many have made of its author. Its range and grasp are magisterial. The bibliography alone will be a treasure for contemporary workers. Almost all references are to material less than a decade old and he ranges with easy familiarity over British, American and European sources. But this book is not simply – or even primarily – an evidential review. The evidence is used, carefully and convincingly, to test the links between the benefits of sport and the well-being of those who have less than average economic and social capital, to challenge much contemporary thinking, and to leave – as ever – a legacy of fresh ideas in the spending of hard-won public resources.

At the heart of the book lies the contemporary concept of social exclusion. The term is itself of French derivation (Tunstall et al., 2002) and is perhaps best described in the Social Exclusion Unit's 1997 words as 'a shorthand term for what can happen when people or areas suffer from a combination of linked problems such as unemployment, poor skills, low income, poor housing, high crime environments, bad health and family breakdown'. The concept is more fully explored in Chapter 2, but this description will suffice the present purpose. It is a complex phenomenon with complex roots: the essence of the debate in this book is to explore how far such exclusion may be ameliorated, or even overcome, by sports participation and sporting provision.

Inevitably, the answers – or perhaps the pointers towards answers – are much more complex than the definition. Social exclusion, as both concept and phenomenon, has many facets, facets explored in succeeding chapters. It is not the purpose of this foreword to anticipate arguments or conclusions, but from the very beginning it is clear that the evidence for the impact of sport on differing themes within social exclusion varies greatly both in extent and quality. The variation may perhaps be most simply expressed in the length of the successive chapters of the book, but it still on occasion surprises. Compare, for example, the very full discussion in relation to education and young people's sport (Chapter 5) with the necessarily meagre debate on sport's relation to older people (Chapter 6), which is a greater and growing segment of the population as a whole.

The messages from the debates within the book are complex. But in wrestling with them a couple of cautious notes may be helpful from the outset. The first, of course, is that sport, or provision for sport, is no panacea in itself for the problems stemming from social exclusion. It must not be forgotten that a prime characteristic of sport, as with all other leisure activities, is the element of choice. Even when all barriers to participation have been removed by the public purse – or the private and voluntary sectors – the individual has the obvious personal right to refuse to participate. Indeed the right to accept, whatever the evidence of benefits, remains a right and not a duty!

It is beyond the remit of the book, in considering how to tackle social exclusion, to weigh the relative worth of investment in sport with investment in other forms of recreation, or indeed with far more basic programmes of health, housing and education. But the comment is made only to keep the whole issue of sport in necessary perspective and not to suggest in any way that the debate on the role of investment in sport in all its facets is neither worthy nor worthwhile!

The second comment is one of equal but differing caution. Accepting that initiatives in the field of sport may have a valuable – even a vital – role to play in helping to overcome social exclusion, it is dangerous to move too far in the

other direction, to pursue a wide range of differing (if equally valuable) initiatives, yet to pursue none long enough for its significance and effects to be fully
and fairly assessed. As politicians and managers change, each in turn locked
into a personal quest for distinctive policies 'to make a difference' and to carry
their individual stamp for wider approbation, so programmes are all too often
terminated long before their impact or success can be perceived or measured.
The tendency to indulge in what Mike Collins calls 'initiativitis' is dangerous
and counter-productive in trying to tackle social exclusion. 'Sustainability'
should be an exhortation to funders as much as to the funded.

These points are basic to profiling the riches of this study, for sport alone
can never be a panacea to countering social exclusion, and programmes need
time as well as funds and staff to become effective. But with these cautions in
mind, there remains a great range of concept, of policy, of theory and of practice
to be explored before truly sound funding decisions can be made. In this context, academics and pragmatists, policy makers and practitioners owe Mike
Collins a great debt for having done so much of their thinking – and reading –
for them. But though the intended audience may be diverse, the heart of this
book is simple and clearly focused: that in sport there is a suite of powerful
tool to tackle and ameliorate some of the varied and painful ills of social
exclusion in the developed societies of the twenty-first century. It is rooted in
a profound, and overt, belief that sport can become an agent rather than a
mirror of change in society.

Allan Patmore

Reference

Tunstall, R. et al. (2002) *Targeting social exclusion: CASE report to the New Opportunities Fund* London: CASE, London School of Economics.

Preface

After seventeen years of fascinating and challenging work as Head of Research, Planning (both town and strategic) and sometimes Information at the Sports Council, now Sport England, I came to Loughborough, first as founder Director of the Institute of Sport Planning and Management (now the Institute of Sport and Leisure Policy) and subsequently as a lecturer in sport and leisure management. Here the research has been almost as varied as the more than 500 projects I managed in London.

Since 1972 I have seen several major switches of politics, five different directors and seven chairmen of the Sports Council/English Sports Council/ Sport England and even more different sports ministers with varying levels of energy, imagination and competence, considerable professionalisation of sports occupations, the rapid growth of sponsorship and then of commercial operations in sport, and three transformations of how sport is delivered through local government.

The two overriding lessons I learned from my Sports Council work was first that one had to find ways of making real the policy challenges to all the parts of the fragmented sports system; and second that there are two roles that the public agencies cannot duck and which they must carry out to serve the citizens whose taxes pay for their salaries and operations – that of co-ordinating all the parts including voluntary and commercial partners, and that of serving those who have less than average economic and social capital. For these lessons I have much to thank Walter Winterbottom, Gordon Cherry and Allan Patmore for, and George Walker, secretary to many Council of Europe committees for sport, with whom it was a pleasure to work over that same period.

In my other guises as a Methodist preacher and youth leader, school governor, Community Health Council chairman, and secretary to various professional and voluntary bodies, I had long been aware of the often-hidden phenomenon of inequality of resources and opportunities in British society. This was driven home in a new and graphic way when I was commissioned by the Department for Culture, Media and Sport to review social exclusion in sport for the Policy Action Team 10. I am grateful to Paul Bolt, Director of

Policy and Information, and to Phyllida Shaw who shared the work in focusing on the arts, and gave me new insights into that facet of leisure.

I am especially grateful to colleagues and PhD students who have shared the burden of working with me on the four case studies in the book – Guy Jackson, Chris Kennett, Fiona McCormack, and Jim Buller. Likewise, I thank Tess Kay whose great experience in gender and sport issues made her a better author of Chapter 6 than I could be, and whose friendship is a week-by-week pleasure. I acknowledge with thanks permission to reproduce Figure 3.1 by Aston Business School, Figures 12.1 and 12.2 by Professor Ken Roberts, and Figure 12.3 by Sport England.

That too-rapid review of what I knew and gathering much new material convinced me that this issue needed a book to set it out; I am grateful to my Department and Faculty for the sabbatical which enabled me to get into the work, if not completely out of it! Throughout the writing, I am grateful to the many people, too many to list, in the UK, Europe, North America and other parts of the world who have given me information and advice, especially through the spate of social exclusion and inclusion publications of the last eighteen months. I hope I have made good and accurate use, quotation, summary and reference to what you told and sent me. Errors and omissions are mine, and not yours.

Michael F. Collins
Shepshed, April 2002

Glossary

APS	Anti-Poverty Strategy
CA	Countryside Agency (formerly Countryside Commission)
CCPR	Central Council of Physical Recreation
CIPFA	Chartered Institute of Public Finance and Accountancy
CLR	Centre for Leisure Research (Edinburgh University)
DCMS	Department for Culture, Media and Sport
DETR	Department of Environment, Transport and the Regions (now Department for Transport, Local Government and the Regions)
DfEE	Department for Education and Employment (predecessor to DfES)
DfES	Department for Education and Skills
DNH	Department of National Heritage (predecessor to DCMS)
DSS	Department of Social Security (now Department for Work and Pensions)
EC/EU	European Commission/European Union
ESC	English Sports Council (preceded by the Sports Council)
HEA	Health Education Authority (now the Health Development Agency)
HSC	Hampshire Sports Counselling
ILAM	Institute of Leisure and Amenity Management
ISRM	Institute of Sport and Recreation Management
LC	Leisure Card (or Passport to Leisure)
LGA	Local Government Association
NPFA	National Playing Fields Association
NSTS	Nottinghamshire Sports Training Scheme
ONS	Office for National Statistics
PAT 10	Policy Action Team 10 (on sport, arts and social exclusion)
SAZ	Sport Action Zone
SE	Sport England (successor to ESC)
SEU	Social Exclusion Unit (in the Cabinet Office)
SS	Street Sport, Stoke on Trent
UKS	UK Sport

Chapter 1

Introduction

This book is intended for both academic and professional audiences. It is not a cook book, nor even a guide to good practice. As I discuss in Chapter 12, several of these have appeared, more than one from government, long before evidence-based conclusions can be drawn. These are based on professional and journalistic anecdotes, often on great experience, and are not to be altogether dismissed.

The intention of this book is to issue a clarion call to researchers and policy makers to:

- alert them to the scale and deep-rootedness of inequality and exclusion issues, and the slowness of change to which politicians will often not admit;
- warn them of the dangers of succumbing to 'initiative overload' from government and its agencies, or to 'compassion fatigue', and of convincing themselves and their executive committees, councils and boards of management that current actions are sufficient which in most cases they are not;
- persuade them to be committed to policies and practices to increase inclusion despite the whims of politics, the changing winds of financial and human resources, the waywardness of colleagues and partner organisations, and the sporadic interest of the media and general public, more often looking for scandals and bad news than good.

It seeks, for each facet of exclusion, to summarise the evidence of it in society generally, to draw together coherently the scattered research evidence from the UK and elsewhere of how it is manifested in sport and leisure, to describe the current policy context and actions to combat exclusion, and to outline initial research results where these are available. In four chapters, I provide summaries of case studies I have been able to complete with colleagues in recent years on four issues – discount shemes and poverty, inequality manifested in children's sport, disability, and youth delinquency. These are attempts at evidence-based work, imperfect because they were done in hindsight and so depend on recall stimulated by postal and telephone questionnaires and interviews, with incomplete corroboration from records not gathered for monitoring and evaluation purposes. They were also done with no national agency or research council or foundation funding, which would have provided more money and 'person power'.

The thread of the book unrolls as follows. In Chapter 2, I show how the concepts around poverty have developed from a simple measure of the basic staples of life – *absolute* poverty – through the ideas of the poverty of some groups in twentieth century society *relative* to what the majority have and expect in terms of a wider range of goods and services including leisure and culture, to the wider idea and process of exclusion from the main sphere of involvement in contemporary society. The chapter ends with a debate about different forms of equality and a view of what an inclusion policy might seek to achieve.

Chapter 3 provides an overview of two substantial literatures that form a background to the main debates in the book. It is clear that everyone is constrained to a degree in the range and intensity that they can commit to their leisure pursuits, but some are multiply constrained. These tend substantially to be people with poorer education, low skills and income, poorer housing and health – a nexus of disadvantage and exclusion. This clearly needs attacking through a coherent group of policies and a network of agencies. So far as the wide range of personal and social benefits claimed for taking part in sport by politicians, managers, medics and educationalists is concerned, it is clear that much evidence is patchy and small-scale, situation-specific and based on no baseline or longitudinal data, and on participants' self-reports. But even if only part of such claims, on top of sport's intrinsic values of enjoyment and personal achievement, are real and can be substantiated for the sceptics, why should a substantial minority of citizens and taxpayers have substantially poorer opportunities?

Chapter 4 focuses on poverty, which I believe underpins the exclusion experienced by people because of other factors like age, gender, disability, ethnic grouping, or location. I illustrate it with a case study of the introduction of systematic discounts through leisure cards, contrasting an early example in the city of Leicester and a more recent one in Oxford. The reality of a quarter of adults and a third of children being poor is generally linked to the basics of life (housing, income from jobs or welfare, education and health), but is underplayed by central and local government when related to leisure. This was true in PAT 10's report, and in the Department for Culture, Media and Sport (DCMS) reviews of PAT 10 and general progress on social inclusion, and many local anti-poverty strategies do not see culture and leisure as part of the opportunities, if not rights, of citizenship.

Chapter 5 examines the differing chances of children from their early experiences of sport and physical education (PE), mediated in primary and secondary school and in clubs through gender, disability, ethnicity and location. The case study is of the differential access and take-up of opportunities to try new sports and develop skills in Nottinghamshire.

In Chapter 6 Tess Kay looks at the evidence from perhaps the longest lasting and most studied of exclusions – that of gender. From its inception sport has been organised by men and overwhelmingly seen until recently as a pursuit for men. Women have been trying to equalise opportunities to play, teach, coach and administer, but as she shows, are still some way from that position despite equal opportunity laws. Women are, however, slowly finding ways to empowerment.

In Chapter 7 I look at how opportunities to partake in sport diminish with age, except for the richest and best educated people, but how other countries engender more inclusion, whether because of history, sports structure and finance, or a different philosophy of active citizenship through sport.

Chapters 8 and 9 cover aspects where Britain has enacted legislation to bolster and encourage equal opportunities for two minority groups – people from ethnic minorities and people who are disabled. The majority of people from ethnic minorities are indisputably multiply deprived to a degree that threatens to ghettoise them, even in their second and third generation's residence in Britain. Many people with a disability are dependent on welfare and are thereby poor because of the modest level of payments in the UK compared with much of north and west Europe. Both groups have been allocated priority programmes by both the DCMS and Sport England, and there is a new English Federation of Disability Sport which may become a source of real empowerment. Meantime football, cricket and rugby are seeking to root out racism from both players and spectators.

Chapter 10 delves into the growing mountain of reviews and studies of sport and recreation being used for preventive or rehabilitative means. Using a case study of primary (preventive) recreational work amongst young teenagers in Stoke on Trent and of rehabilitative work amongst young adult offenders in Hampshire, it attempts to unravel the problem of the impoverished childhood of many 'at risk' or offending youngsters, and to show the methods and limitations of such interventions, often ridiculed by the popular press as 'holidays for hooligans', which deters politicians from supporting them. The limitations are notably their under-funded and short-term nature when trying to combat years of poor and crime-ridden environments, broken families, and educational failure.

Chapter 11 shows that social exclusion manifests itself equally in town and country, giving the lie to Power's (1998: 1) strong averrance that it is *almost entirely an urban problem* and *an urban agenda*. But it *is* much more strongly concentrated in cities and correlated with manifestations of poor housing, poor health and crime. Consequently exclusion has been much more studied and attacked by grant aid and public policy programmes in cities, than in the countryside, where Slee, Curry and Joseph's (2001) overview is the first related to leisure and sport.

Explicit governmental social inclusion policies and programmes are very new, too new to yield reliable accounts of best practice let alone researched and considered critiques of outcomes, so Chapter 12 draws together two threads:

a number of suggestions as to how to make them more effective in delivery and outcome, mainly through less novelty, better resourcing, more commitment, a closer focus, and less impatience; and a consideration of the role of sports clubs as a form of civic action and social capital in the mixed economy of modern governance. But I believe the government's aspirations will not be met, even if the autonomous club movement concurs and forms partnerships, unless the historic structural and organisational weakness of local fragmentation is substantially remedied.

After summarising the findings of previous chapters, Chapter 13 draws some conclusions:

- Participation does not equal exclusion, but time and time again the poor have a low level or narrow range of participation not only in sport but in a much wider range of leisure, and this is even more true if they are female, non-white and disabled. Is it credible to believe that they repeatedly restrict their leisure in this way by choice? Exclusion is widespread, established early (see the gendered attitudes to sport by the age of 9 or 10 exhibited in Chapter 5), persistent and difficult to overcome. Its core is poverty. Moreover, such differences are repeated in other European countries and the USA, even though they are nuanced by different income and class gradients.

- Evaluation has been rare, skimpy and under-resourced. Difficult as it is, politicians, the media and the public expect, and are being led increasingly to look for, evidence that relates not to the more easily measured outputs, but to the broad, complex, overlapping, slippery and sometimes contradictory outcomes. But these take time to develop and neither officials nor politicians show any understanding of this in exercising patience, or resisting jumping between programmes at the first sign of positive news of take-up or popularity.

- Evidence for benefits to cardiovascular health from vigorous exercise and to other ailments from moderate exercise, and to self-confidence and self-esteem are unquestionably confirmed; but for most other claims evidence is patchy, anecdotal or open to question in methodology. Researchers have to be more clever and determined, and funders more generous and patient, for above all longitudinal data is needed.

- On the one hand, sport can rarely yield economic, environmental, health, safety or social benefits acting alone; it needs to be a partner, often a minor one, with those promoting other policies; but it will, I believe, betray its potential if it fails to strive and colludes with sustaining the current unequal status quo. On the other hand, DCMS and Sport England among others must beware of making claims that cannot be supported by good evidence, and be open to claims of exaggeration or prematurity.

Chapter 2

From absolute poverty to social exclusion

From absolute and relative poverty to social exclusion

Poverty is a contested concept; as Alcock (1997: 3) commented, 'there is no correct, scientific, agreed definition because poverty is inevitably a political concept, and thus inherently is a contested one.' Documented studies of poverty started at the end of nineteenth century, with Booth (1882) and Rowntree (1901) who set a threshold below which people were said to be *absolutely poor*. Rowntree distinguished those in 'primary' poverty, not having the basic food, clothing, housing or warmth for 'physical efficiency', and others in 'secondary' poverty, caused by waste or lack of knowledge. Booth was scathing about the latter, calling them loafers, feckless, near-criminals. Both arguments have developed a tradition. Booth's line was followed by Charles Murray's (1990) denigration of an 'underclass' in the US and Britain, and by John Moore (Secretary of State for Social Security) in 1989 (cited in Levitas, 1998) and John Lilley (1996), who all denied the existence of (absolute) poverty in 'affluent' Britain.

There are two flaws to the absolute poverty definition. First its determination, according to the architect of the British Welfare State, is *a matter of judgement* (Beveridge, 1942), and levels of subsistence change over time, as do people's expectations; second, it takes no account of socio-cultural needs, whereby an item can be seen as a luxury in one era, but as a necessity in another (Donnison, 1982).

So emerged a *relative* definition, going beyond subsistence and defining poverty in relation to the accepted standard of living in a society, or 'the custom of the country,' as Adam Smith (1979) called it as long ago as 1812. This was echoed by Townsend (1979: 60) in writing that people are poor when 'they lack the resources to obtain the types of diet, participate in the activities . . . which are customary, or at least widely encouraged or approved, in the societies to which they belong.' He recognised leisure as part of this – 'deprivation can arise . . . in different spheres of life, such as at work, at home, in travel, and in leisure time activities' (1979: 271). Apart from housing and food, he included the following items in his Deprivation Index:

- no holiday away form home in last year
- no visit to or from a friend or relative for a meal in last month (adults)
- no friend to play or to tea in last month, no party on last birthday (children under 15)
- no afternoon or evening out in last two weeks.

Thus in terms of a broader look at lifestyle, Townsend (1987: 125) summarised what he called deprivation as 'a state of observable and demonstrable disadvantage relative to the local community or the wider society or nation.' Holman (1978) and Oppenheim and Harker (1996) follow this relative line, as did the EU Poverty I and II grant-aid programmes, though few projects had a leisure element.

Critics of this approach have claimed it is subjective, but Townsend had stated in 1979 that subjectivity was inevitable in social scientists' definitions. A more substantive criticism is that the numbers seen as poor would not change if living standards fell evenly (Roll, 1992), and it takes the moral element from poverty (McGregor, 1981), likening those who go to Butlins on holiday to those who go to an upmarket villa in Tuscany, while others starve.

Lister (1990) and Scott (1994) developed Townsend's arguments to say that poverty can be understood as *exclusion* from aspects of citizenship. The European Commission's Poverty III programme was concerned to integrate the 'least privileged' into society, and before its completion, the rhetoric had moved to a concept of 'social exclusion'. It had become an accepted term, according to Tricart, an officer in the European's Commission's DGV, responsible for social affairs:

> Today, the concept of social exclusion is taking over from poverty, which is more static . . . and seen far more often as exclusively monetary poverty. . . . Social exclusion does not only mean insufficient income, and it even goes beyond participation in working life.
>
> (European Commission, 1994: 12)

The term originated in France, and is usually attributed to René Lenoir, Secretary of State for Social Action to the Chirac government, who published in 1974 *Les Exclus: Un Français sur dix*, concerned with the breakdown of structural, cultural and moral ties (Levitas, 1998: 21) and a *contract d'insertion*, focused on job-seeking but also including other forms of social participation. Room (1994) said this involved three social shifts – from income to multi-dimensional disadvantage; from a state to a process; and from a focus on individuals or households to local communities. Berghman (1995) argued that both terms could be process *and* outcome, suggesting using 'poverty and deprivation to denote the outcome . . . and impoverishment and social exclusion to refer to the process.' Room (1995) suggested that whereas poverty is *distributional*, exclusion is *relational*, a reason for needing 'joined-up' (integrated) policies to tackle it.

Commins (1993), focusing on Ireland, further suggested that social inclusion has to involve belonging to four of society's systems:

- the democratic and legal system, which promotes civic integration
- the labour market, which promotes economic integration
- the welfare system, which promotes social integration
- the family and community system, which promotes interpersonal integration.

He argued (1993: 4) that 'when one or two (of these) are weak, the others need to be strong. And the worst off are those for whom all systems have failed.' Berghman (1995: 19) spoke of a 'denial or non-realisation of citizenship rights.'

In the most intensive study of exclusion Europe-wide to date, exclusion is seen as a consequence of unemployment and low income (Roche and Annesley, 1998), leading to exclusion from a fair share of social goods and capital in the forms of recognition, income and work. The UK was seen as a liberal welfare regime, following Esping-Anderson's (1990) classification, who identified three main causes of social change in welfare: mass unemployment and insecure employment; family restructuring with a rapid growth of one-parent families and workless households; and a growing inequality, with a group of really poor separated from the rest – an economic underclass. The groups most at risk are the young, unskilled, lone parents, the jobless, and children (who live disproportionately in poor households). In terms of inclusive policies, in the UK:

> welfare provision is increasingly contractual, emphasising rights and duties of the providers and recipients . . . and welfare provision comes from an increasing mixed range of resources It operates through a lightly regulated labour market (in European terms), a mild form of workfare in the New Deal, and targeting in terms of the Jobseeker's Allowance involving evidence of willingness to work.
>
> (Roche and Annesley, 1998: 98)

The argument against this line, which in many ways the Blair Government has followed since 1997, is that employment is not the answer to many people's exclusion, and this is an argument I shall return to later in this chapter and in the conclusions.

Room et al. (1993) suggest that Anglo-Saxon, liberal concepts of poverty have become fused with conservative, European concerns with moral integration and social order, and so no single discourse has emerged. Levitas (1998) clearly laid out under three headings the main forms of discourse and related policy responses: RED (redistribution); MUD (moral underclass); and SID (social inclusion).

RED: Social exclusion, redistribution and critical public policy

The roots of this are in Britain, and in Townsend's analysis of deprivation and his preferred solution of redistribution through benefits given as of right, rather than through means-testing. In the eighteen years of Tory government following his analysis, inequality, unemployment and poverty increased, with the only redistribution being to the richer citizens (see the Rowntree Commission and HBAI statistics discussed below, pages 11 and 127), and no evidence of the 'trickle-down' effects that were supposed to benefit those on lower incomes. Tories attacked redistribution discourse as immoral, a totalitarian imposition of uniformity, a brake on economic growth through unnecessary taxation, and evidence of a 'nanny' state.

In 1997 the Child Poverty Action Group published *Britain divided: The growth of social exclusion in the 1980s and 1990s* (Walker and Walker, 1997), and hopes were raised when Shadow Chancellor Gordon Brown recognised the need to reduce inequality in his John Smith Memorial Lecture. Building on T.H. Marshall's 1950s model of citizenship, Goodin (1996) argued that this idea was more egalitarian in terms of belonging than the insider/outsider aspects of inclusion, though Marshall was criticised for overlooking aspects of gender and ethnic inequalities. Lister (1990: 68) related poverty, social exclusion and citizenship thus: 'poverty spells exclusion from the full rights of citizenship in each of these [civil, political and social] spheres and undermines people's ability to fulfil the private and public obligations of citizenship.'

MUD: A dependent underclass

The Conservative Government responded to rising unemployment by reducing and tightening the eligibilities for benefits, and eventually blaming the poor for their circumstances, while reducing public expenditure, mainly that of local authorities. 'Benefits dependency,' 'giro culture,' and 'the underclass' became commonplace terms, but this rhetoric was linked with a neo-Conservative policy line of strengthening the moral order. So the poor were either deserving and needful of help, or 'feckless/scroungers' and undeserving. The American Charles Murray (1990: 23), invited by the right-wing Institute of Economic Affairs, described himself as 'a visitor from a plague area come to see if the disease [of people who rejected the ethics of work and family] is spreading.' He supported the underclass idea on the basis of illegitimacy, crime and dropping out from the labour force. Later (Murray, 1994) he was even more extreme, including gender in his labelling – delinquent males are wilfully idle and criminally antisocial, while delinquent women are sexually irresponsible single parents who should have their benefits cut.

Table 2.1 The three discourses of social exclusion

Redistribution	Moral underclass	Social Insertion
• emphasises poverty as the prime cause • implies better benefits as the solution • could valorise unpaid work • if inclusion=citizenship, not a minimalist model • goes beyond materialism in addressing social/cultural/political spheres • focuses on processes of impoverishment • implies radical redistribution of power and resources	• underclass are seen as distinct from mainstream society • focuses on behaviour of individuals, not structures • implies benefits encourage dependency, and are bad for recipients • inequalities in the rest of society are ignored • gender-stereotyped argument about young male criminals and immoral single mothers	• narrows definition to paid work • neglects why people not in paid work are poor • obscures inequalities between employees • ignores women's low pay/poorer jobs • neglects differences between workers and those with capital • fails to address unpaid work, and undermines its legitimacy

Those espousing a redistribution discourse reacted strongly to what they saw as an argument without the foundation of evidence, which blamed the poor for their poverty and supported policies that are punitive rather than supportive (Oppenheim and Harker, 1996). But the concept of an underclass allowed the persistence of poverty to be recognised, while absolving the government of at least some of the blame, and it became a term used in the media and by politicians, including Tony Blair, and Labour MP Frank Field (1990). Also, it gave moral expression to the distancing and alienation of the poor from the rest of society (Duffy, 1995; Adonis and Pollard, 1997).

SID: social exclusion and integration in Europe

SID is distinguished from the two earlier versions by its emphasis on exclusion from paid work. Throughout the European discourse social exclusion and exclusion from work are used as interchangeable terms, as in Roche and Annesley's (1998) report. Part of this rhetoric, however, is to include ideas of recognition and non-financial income. Recognition involves status and respect and trust (as in the ideas of Giddens, 1991 and Beck, 1992). Income means primarily money, but may include goods and services provided through the welfare state, informal work or volunteering. Levitas (1998: 26) commented that SID 'reduced the social to the economic.'

Table 2.1 is based on Kennett's (2002) summary of the three discourses, which do overlap. Levitas' criticism of all three is that they neglect unpaid work, so disadvantaging women in their non-employed roles. All have a moral element, especially MUD, but all differ on what the socially excluded need: in RED they have no money, in MUD they have no morals, and in SID they have no jobs (Levitas, 1998). MUD neglects the social and political, SID largely ignores the political and cultural, RED is broader, but the discourses overlap.

The 'new contract for welfare', said the Department of Social Security (1998: 20), should provide 'public services of a high quality to the whole community, as well as cash benefits.' So, what is exclusion about? It is more than the simple condition of being equal. In any case even equality is slippery and can be defined in several ways (Palfrey et al., 1992). Is the interest in equal use, equal opportunities or equal outcomes? People are not equally endowed – neither with intellect, physique nor the world's goods; as a result, the New Right could claim 'inequality is seen as an inevitable and tolerable result of social freedom and personal initiative' (Nankivell, 1988). Unequal treatment of equal access to resources will not lead to equal use. In 1985 the World Health Organisation did seek a simple outcome: the narrowing of the gap between the most and least healthy countries by 25 per cent by 2000. But few equity targets can be so simply specified.

The philosopher Rawls (1971) sought a different aim: to provide the best possible position for the poorest (the principle of 'maximin'), and many public policies in health, employment, education, housing, crime prevention, and sport and leisure have sought something like this, while accepting that there will still be diversity. In the context of physical education, Penney spoke eloquently and idealistically of equity being:

> concerned with giving value to, and celebrating social and cultural difference of individuals and society . . . as a source of enrichment to all. To be concerned with equity is thus to be concerned with social justice, and specifically, the matters of dignity, privileges and power that all individuals are entitled to.
>
> (Penney, 2000: 60)

More pragmatically, Sport England has produced guidance for sports governing bodies in writing their equity plans in the following terms:

> 'sports equity' is about fairness in sport, equality of access, recognising inequalities and taking steps to address them. It is about changing the structure of sport to ensure that it becomes equally accessible to all members of society, whatever their age, gender, race, ethnicity, sexuality, or socio-economic status.
>
> (Sport England, 2001: 4)

Equity and exclusion are slippery concepts, and measurement is approximate and contended. But governments have tried, more or less depending on their ideology, to use taxes on income as a means of closing the financial gaps between the richest and poorest. In recent years the edge of this weapon has been blunted by a move to indirect taxes on services and transactions, which tend to be regressive, penalising the poor. In the following chapters I examine the reality of the gaps regarding sport for various social groups.

Measuring poverty and social exclusion

We have seen above that Townsend developed a set of indicators of deprivation in 1979; Mack and Lansley (1985) extended his twelve to thirty-five; but arguments continued amongst researchers and policy makers about the value of such relative as opposed to absolute measures. The Blair Government's new Social Exclusion Unit (SEU) defined exclusion as:

> a shorthand label for what can happen when individuals or areas suffer a combination of linked problems such as unemployment, poor skills, low incomes, poor housing, high crime environments, bad health and family breakdown
>
> (Social Exclusion Unit, 1998)

'Households below average income' is a frequent measure of poverty, used by the SEU and the Child Poverty Action Group as a main indicator, one with the advantage of enabling comparisons with other EC states. The measure describes income for those below 50 per cent of average household income after housing costs, which translated to £166 a week for a single parent, £272 for a pensioner couple and £292 for couples with children in 1999–2000 (Department of Social Security, 2001). By this measure, 23 per cent of the UK population was poor in 1992–93, a stark increase from 9 per cent since the Conservative Government took over in 1979. Despite government efforts since then, the levels have not reduced overall. In 1998 the Statistical Program Committee of the European Union suggested that the 0.6 threshold (individuals receiving below 60 per cent of median income after housing costs) should be used for international comparisons. Table 2.2 uses both the 0.5 and 0.6 (50 and 60 per cent) thresholds, and Table 2.3 uses 0.6. Table 2.2 shows that a higher proportion of children than adults are poor, because poor households, and particularly those composed of ethnic minorities, contain more children.

Table 2.3 looks at who the poor are, by type of household and family status, and their risk of falling into poverty. While couples with children were the largest group at 37 per cent of all households, the others were roughly of similar magnitude. But while lone parents make up only 1 in 7 of all households, they had a 63 per cent chance of being poor in 1999–2000; given the multiple roles such parents have to play, it is clear that their time and money for leisure are particularly limited. Table 2.3 also shows that a large percentage of people not currently poor nevertheless are at risk of becoming so. Those aged over 60

Table 2.2 Poor adults and children, 1979–2000 (percentage below 0.5 and 0.6 of contemporary median income after housing costs)

	Adults		Children	
	0.5	*0.6*	*0.5*	*0.6*
1979	9	19	10	20
1981	11	22	16	27
1987	19	29	24	35
1994–5 (FES)	23	32	32	41
1994–5 (FRS)	24	33	31	41
1999–2000 (FRS)	25	33	34	41

Sources: Family Expenditure Survey, Family Resources Survey, DSS, 2001

(and mainly with no resources other than the State pension) and families with one or both partners out of work make up largest group of poor, but that these are now equalled by families with one in part-time work. Table 2.3 shows how the risk of poverty clearly grows when a household has no second income.

Figures for households below average income provide more details regarding children, gender and ethnic minorities:

- 33 per cent of children were in poor households, a 23 per cent increase since 1979; 71 per cent lived in households with no full-time worker in 1992–3.
- 58 per cent of lone parents were poor in 1999–2000.
- Women were more likely to be poor than men (19 per cent compared with 16 per cent in the poorest fifth of the population in 1999–2000).
- Ethnic minorities were overwhelmingly more likely to be in the poorest than the richest fifth of the population than whites (48 per cent versus 11 per cent, compared with 18 versus 21 per cent for whites in 1999–2000), but especially Pakistani/Bangladeshi groups (61 per cent versus 4 per cent).
- Three-quarters of disabled people were estimated to be dependent on benefits and hence likely to be poor (Martin and White, 1998).

There are also subjective measures of poverty, identifying people who feel they are poor; concensus measures for the whole population can be seen by poor people as stigmatising (Kempson, 1996). Policy measures that require poor people to produce evidence of eligibility for discounts, as they often still have to in appearing at leisure venues, can also be seen as stigmatising, unless operators have moved to swipe/smart cards where the confidential data can be hidden in the magnetic strip or chip (see Chapter 4).

The dynamics of poverty are important. From 1979 to 1994–5, the poorest tenth of the population suffered a fall in real income of 8 per cent, while the

Table 2.3 The composition and risk of becoming poor, by family and economic status in 1994–5 and 1999–2000 after housing costs and including self-employed, percentage of individuals below 60 per cent of median income in real terms, 1994–5

Family type	% of poor		% risk of becoming poor	
	1994–5	1999–2000	1994–5	1999–2000
Pensioner couple	36	26	23	15
Couple, no children	16	13	12	10
Single pensioner	51	37	31	15
Single, no children	29	25	23	19
Lone parent	71	63	55	47
Couple with children	31	25	23	17
All types	33	27	24	18
Millions	18.2	15.1	13.1	10.2

Economic status	% of poor		% risk of becoming poor	
	1994–5	1999–2000	1994–5	1999–2000
Single/couple in FT[a] work	5	5	2	3
One FT, one PT[b] worker	9	7	3	3
One FT, one not working	26	23	15	14
Self-employed	32	27	26	23
Head/spouse over 60 yrs	46	34	29	18
One/more in PT work	41	37	28	25
Head/spouse unemployed	80	79	72	69
Other inactive	72	68	58	52

Source: Family Resources Survey, DSS, 2001, tables E1, E2, 11, 12

Notes:
a FT = full time
b PT = part time

average income had increased by 40 per cent, and those of the top tenth by 68 per cent. The Joseph Rowntree Inquiry into Income and Wealth commented that the poorest three-tenths of people had failed to benefit from economic growth. It strikingly claimed that while the richest fifty people in the UK are worth £3.4bn, it took 3.4m of the poorest to accumulate the same amount (Barclay, 1995).

Duration of poverty is an important issue, only recently researched. The British Household Panel Survey demonstrated a core of people with persistent low income – 6 per cent being in the lowest tenth of income for all five years between 1991 and 1995, and 12 per cent in the lowest three-tenths. These were more likely to be lone parents and single State pensioners, living in public rented housing, to be in workless households, and without qualifications (Walker and Park, 1997). The SEU advocated using Income Support and Housing Benefit data that shows duration and can also be disaggregated to electoral ward level.

Tony Blair promised to eliminate child poverty, but stated that it would take twenty years. Piachaud (*Guardian*, 1 Sept 99) sought to summarise the effects of New Labour policies in their first three years of operation:

Reduced poverty
- improved child allowance (550,000 parents and 800,000 children)
- Surestart programmes to benefit care and education for 5 per cent of children under 4 years old
- reduced unemployment (394,000 adults)

Static or worse
- pensions, apart from winter heating allowances (a small increase was given in 2001)
- eligibility for disability benefits (because of concern that their cost had quadrupled over twenty years)
- reduced Income Support for people on the margins of eligibility (300,000).

The net effect was to reduce people defined as poor from 14 million in 1997 to 12 million in 1999, still twice that of twenty years earlier (Department of Social Security, 1998), comprising:

Group	%	Millions
Adult women	24	5.3
Children	35	4.5
Adult men	20	4.2
Older people	31	3.0
Lone parents	63	2.9
Unemployed	78	2.3

By late 2001 the effects of Chancellor Gordon Brown's Children's and Family Tax Credits (FTC) had helped increase the incomes of the bottom fifth of the distribution by over £30 a week (12 per cent), compared with only £3 for the top half. One and a quarter million people received FTC, twice the number who had received its predecessor, Family Credit (Elliott and Davey, *Guardian* 21 Nov 01). As Atkinson (2000) commented, one of the problems of using income as a proxy for exclusion is that it is easy to neglect the relational and spatial aspects. Only recently have small-area analyses of incomes and welfare payments begun.

The geography of exclusion

Exclusion can be experienced by persons or groups and by places, neighbourhoods or communities (Healey et al., 1998; Walker, 1995). Interventions are aimed at both levels – welfare payments at the first, City Challenge and Single Regeneration Budget schemes, etc., at the second, and the SEU's Neighbourhood Strategy implies intervention to be spatially targeted at the 3,000 worst areas. But not all Policy Action Teams used a common definition of social exclusion or poverty (for example PAT 9, Community Self-Help, was concerned with the 3,000 worst neighbourhoods according to the English House Condition Survey, whereas PAT 7, on unpopular housing, used a different definition). Alcock and Craig (1998) recorded sixty-three local surveys of poverty but no common definition, and only one local authority in three with a strategy had any form of evaluation, so being *data rich but information poor.*

One of the major debates regarding deprivation and poverty has been how far area-based strategies are relevant. Is there an independent effect of living in an area, or is this merely a concatenation of different societal/national trends and influences? Rowntree's and Booth's early studies described in graphic Dickensian terms the differences in the lived experience of poverty between various neighbourhoods. Marx and Engels did likewise, and so did Stedman-Jones in his careful study of Victorian 'outcast [socially excluded?] London':

> as the Webbs later admitted, the first World War showed that the existence of the casual poor had not been the effect of some mutation induced by the degenerating effects of city life. The casual poor were shown to have been a social and not a biological creation . . . once decent and regular employment was available, the 'unemployables' proved impossible to find.
>
> (Stedman-Jones, 1971: 336, Peregrine edition)

Glennerster et al. (1999: 3) commented that 'this could be taken as a classic Keynesian view as well as a New Left one. A high enough tide of full employment will float off all poverty stricken areas. Get the macro economy right and area policy will look after itself.'

In 1979 Townsend was positive that there was no area effect, after studying four especially poor areas in Glasgow, Salford, Neath and Belfast:

> however we try to define economically or socially deprived areas, unless we include over half the areas in the country, there will be more poor persons or poor children living outside them than in them . . . the pattern of inequality is set nationally.
>
> (Townsend, 1979: 560)

This has been repeatedly found since, whether the measures have been of income, poor housing, unemployment or poor health. Townsend did, however, speak of 'cardinal' policies needing to be national, leaving space for secondary, area-based ones.

Economists argue that cities have areas of growth and decline, and trying to intervene to slow or stop the downward spiral of the latter will merely trap communities in a low but subsidised existence. Some American sociologists (for example Park in 1952, and Burgess in 1967) have argued that such areas are needed to provide transition zones where newcomers can find cheap housing, low-paid starter jobs, and cheap premises for the new and innovating businesses any city needs.

But in recent decades the growth of poverty has resulted in more evident and frequent concentrations of urban poverty. This has led politicians and social and physical planners to pragmatically devise area-based policies to attack the problems, typified in the SEU's description of social exclusion and its focus on the 3,000 worst areas in the country. Thus arose the Urban Programme, the Single Regeneration Budget, and under the Blair Government the proliferation of Action Zones – for Health, Employment, Education and even for Sport. There was never adequate recognition of the equivalent rural problem (see Chapter 11), because though the levels were no less, the absolute numbers were smaller and scattered, and never commanded the same political response. The Rural Development Areas were based on narrower, mainly economic criteria, and consequently were more tightly drawn.

But some will now argue strongly that while city-wide employment changes may trigger these differences, once set in motion they become self-reinforcing, with better-skilled and better-paid workers choosing to move out of declining areas. This was Wilson's (1997) thesis, based on studying Chicago, and Jargowsky's in Milwaukee (1996). The latter concluded that one-fifth of the poverty could be attributed to area effects. In the UK, recent economic theory suggests that one reason that the economy cannot run at full capacity is because there are pools of people who are not part of the labour market (Layard, 1997), and that the Bank of England chooses to exercise anti-inflationary checks on economic growth before it reaches a level that would involve these people.

Poor management of public housing, and the sale of council houses under the Thatcher regimes also meant that public housing increasingly became a refuge of people who are old, disabled, mentally or physically ill, ex-prisoners, and the very poor (Power, 1997). There is little data available and have been few attempts yet to explain how these factors interact. Despite evidence that area-based policies do not hit the majority of the poor (Oatley, 1998) and may not have long-term benefits, the Blair Government has introduced separately defined Education and Health Action Zones, and Sport England has followed suit, with thirty-five Sport Action Zones, based on the Department of Environment, Transport and the Regions index (DETR, 1998).

Back in the late 1970s and early 1980s there was much debate and an Economic and Social Research Council programme on transmitted deprivation (where successive generations remain locked in poverty), and while there were intergenerational effects, there was also scepticism about a cycle in which people become trapped (Brown and Madge, 1982). More recently, however, analysis of a cohort of people born in 1958 and studied regularly until they were 33 years old clearly shows that poverty, family disruption, and contact with the police result in lower earnings which are also influenced by lower social class and poor school performance:

> Thus there is little doubt that social exclusion, as captured by the adult outcomes and childhood factors used here, is transmitted through the generations and through the life-course. . . . But it is essential to emphasize that all these associations capture here are just aggregate tendencies observed and in no sense determinist. . . . Thus, there is huge scope for many, if not most, individuals to escape from the patterns and tendencies observed.
>
> (Hobcraft, 1998: 95)

Hobcraft therefore argued strongly for better investigation of those who 'get out of the trap'. In the same way Glennerster et al. (1999) at the London School of Economics have set up new studies in twelve poor areas (inner London and similar, coastal industrial, manufacturing, coalfield and others) where they will interview 200 people every six months over five years. The area effects and particular exclusion problems and attempted remedies for both urban and rural areas will be examined in Chapter 10.

Sport and social class

Debates rage in sociology as to whether social class boundaries have dissolved such that 'we are all middle class now', or whether the process of individualisation is breaking up the identity of social classes so that inequalities, like other differences, are becoming personal, with the result that non-class coalitions are formed (often briefly) as and when threats appear (Beck, 1992: 100–1; see also Savage, 2000). Roberts concurred with this view, saying that currently there is a:

leisure democracy in the sense that members of all social strata do similar things in their leisure, but democracy is not the same as equality: the privileged classes are distinguished by their ability to do more, which they exercise in virtually all areas of out-of-home leisure. Money is now at the root of the main differences between the use of leisure in different social strata, and the leisure differences between them are basically and blatantly inequalities rather than alternative ways of life.

(Roberts, 1999: 87)

Marshall (1997: 16) refuted such arguments as 'no less premature than their predecessors' and, using data from the International Social Justice projects, showed the chances for working class children in Britain of becoming a member of the 'salariat' as 5–6 to 1, compared with 3–4 to 1 in the USA, and 4–5 to 1 in West Germany. Adonis and Pollard (1997: ix) went further, stating that Britain's class system 'separates its people as clinically today as it did half a century ago – far from diminishing, class divisions are intensifying as the distance between the top and bottom widens and the classes at both extremes grow in size and identity' and later (1997: 244) suggested that 'far from leisure being in the vanguard of the classless society, the way we live our lives is a daily, hourly testament to our place in Britain's class structure.'

Other sociologists of sport also doubt the disappearance of class. Bourdieu (1978, 1985) argued for early socialisation in structuring individual choices and preferences, and then of the social environment, which he calls 'habitus', in shaping youth and adult practices. Kew (1997: 149) spoke of Bourdieu providing 'compelling evidence for the saliency of social class in structuring if not determining a person's choice and preferences in sport'. Elsewhere Sugden and Tomlinson said:

For Bourdieu, then, sport . . . acts as a kind of badge of social exclusivity and cultural distinctiveness for the dominant classes; it operates as a means of control or containment of the working or popular classes; it is represented as a potential source of escape and mobility for talented working-class performers . . . it articulates the fractional status distinctions that exist within the ranks of larger class groupings; and it reveals the capacity of the body to express social principles and cultural meanings, for physical capital to connect with forms of economic and cultural capital.

(Sugden and Tomlinson, 2000: 319)

For Bourdieu sport is a social arena where, as Jarvie and Maguire argued (1994: 197), 'different classes derive different kinds of profit from sport in terms of health, slimness, relaxation and social relationships,' according to the 'capital' they possess, which is 'not just economic but is also cultural (e.g. education, knowledge of high culture and art) and symbolic (presentation of self-demeanour)' (1999: 201). Social capital in personal terms comprises the education and skills they possess, not just for work but for political participation and social participation in sport and leisure, and also the confidence to seek out opportunities, and the ability to organise one's time, friends and companions, childcare and transport to make participation real. Scores of site surveys and some home interviews make it clear that these attributes are not equally distributed. Horne, Tomlinson and Whannel (1999: 107) said, 'in contemporary sports cultures class categories . . . continue to influence participation and activity,' and they confirm Tomlinson's view from over a decade earlier about 'issues of access and exclusion . . . still at the heart of British sports cultures' (1986: 109).

Exclusion, sport and citizenship

Marshall (1950) provided the foundation for modern concepts of citizenship, and defined it as having three areas of rights: to equality before the law, to universal franchise in politics, and to access to services and welfare benefits. Liberals have interpreted citizenship as the right to control one's own activities and own property in leisure as much as in other life spheres – what Byrne (2001) called *possessive individualism*. In the USA it led to 'blaming the poor' for their poverty, a version of the 'moral underclass' discourse (Hurst, 2001; Marger, 2001). Conservatives interpreted it as status-based control, in leisure and other public services as benevolent paternalism in providing what the leaders thought citizens should have. Socialists saw it as solidarity, leading to Keynesian provision, including leisure, to offer citizens choices, what Coalter (2000) called a 'welfarist approach'.

Coalter attributed a 'strong' version of welfarism to Ravenscroft (1993), who opined that the state has a social responsibility, regardless of its dominant economic ideology, to provide for the basic leisure needs of society. Ravenscroft described the shift from a basic welfare view of sports services under the Thatcher Government as a response to scepticism about what he called (1993: 35) 'the overplayed and unsubstantiated' external/social benefits long claimed for sport. Glyptis (1989: 42) listed them as 'containing urban problems, building a sense of community, and overcoming class and other social conflicts', while the matters of enjoyment were to be left to the market. With a bias to male and middle-income users (Audit Commission, 1999) and as one of only a few face-to-face charged municipal services, sports services were ripe for marketisation under compulsory competitive tendering (see Chapter 4).

Ravenscroft (1993: 42) argued that in sport the higher order individual human needs for esteem and self-actualisation had become emphasised over the lower order communal ones of consumption for health, quality of life and social benefits through affiliation, and yet access had been restricted, by ability to pay, to 'the "good" citizen at the expense of deprivation, rejection, and suppression of the "deviant" citizen,' who were respectively leisure 'gainers' and 'losers'. The losers were supplied only through legal necessity or social expediency, and represented a policy shift from local democracy in which the politics of choice has been replaced by the politics of means. Subsequently Ravenscroft argued (1996: 171) that sport and leisure as a form of consumption and experience was central to the New Right politics.

But while compulsory competitive tendering improved efficiency in reducing costs, through breaking the unionisation of labour, and promoted popular, revenue-earning activities, it almost certainly held down or reduced usage by poor and already under-represented groups like people with a disability, ethnic minorities, and one-parent families for whom such public services were intended (McIntosh and Charlton, 1985; Taylor and Page, 1994). More (2000) made the same arguments about US National and State Parks in relation to extended charging. Thus the introduction of Best Value by the Blair Government retained the efficiency objective but added that of quality and customer satisfaction through involving citizens in planning and monitoring the provision. Ravenscroft (1999: 149–51) doubted whether it would change the political map and hoped that local authorities and their professional officers would 'remain committed to the needs of the community rather than embracing euphemistic notions of consumer focus.'

Coalter (1998) described Roberts' (1978) approach as a 'weak' version of welfarist ideology when he suggested the state might be interested in distributive justice, though 'recreation . . . interests are too diverse to make their satisfaction into rights of citizenship' and, within a pluralist view, felt the market was an effective participatory mechanism. Coalter argued that leisure professionals have failed to produce output and, even more, outcome measures, and leisure researchers have failed to define needs and to show how citizens' obligations and responsibilities are delivered. Earlier Coalter had said (1989: 127) there was 'a lack of a coherent philosophy or politics of "recreational welfare" with which to resist consumerist definitions and managerialist practices.' Veal (1998) concurred. This is clearer for those in clubs and governing bodies than for individuals and consumers. In the case studies in Chapters 4, 5, 9 and 10 I make a small step toward doing some of the empirical rather than theoretical work.

The European Foundation for the Improvement of Living and Working Conditions (1995: 14) wrote, 'improving access and increasing consumer involvement in public services is not a substitute for promoting equal rights, treatment and opportunities for users of welfare services.' But in the context of local government, Fenwick argued that consumerism could be 'a potent force . . . not containable within a market-based conception of the consumer or an ideology which equates the range of local government services with commodities.' Coalter (1990) thought such a view might be a strong defence and political justification for public leisure services. In 2000, he developed the idea that leisure studies had been too pro-public and anti-commercial in its views, blaming it on a loose mixture of Marxism and Methodism (Coalter, 2000: 164)! He set out various perspectives:

- *Pessimistic Marxism*, represented by Clarke and Critcher – consumerism as false consciousness, where the ability to produce sport as a series of products is its political validation, and it develops a hold over its customers. Constant innovation is needed to maintain consumption.
- *Pessimistic elitism*, represented by Tomlinson, who spoke of shallow products and exchanges pandering to the *whims* of consumers in contrast to the [unexplained] *interests* of citizens.
- *Optimistic Marxism*, in which ever-widening desires can never be adequately met and consumers always want for more, or where some, often youths, seek to subvert the market.
- *Productionism*, a weak version of the alienation in pessimistic Marxism, where some value is gained but consumers are passive (as argued by Parker, 1997) or where serious leisure is like work (according to Stebbins, 1997).

He went on to argue that if there is anything in the concept of social citizenship, exclusion needs to be theorised in terms of which groups are being excluded and on what basis. We come back to this argument in Chapter 12.

Sport was seen by the Labour Government of the 1970s as 'part of the fabric of the social services' (Department of the Environment, 1975), and Coalter et al. (1986) spoke of a policy shift from 'Recreation as Welfare' (of participants) to 'Recreation for Welfare', as instrumental benefits of health and self-esteem, and constructively using the time of unemployed youth. In the 1980s and 1990s economic concerns overrode social ones, and sport, like the arts, became a means of regenerating towns, and of creating income and jobs. Then, as critiques of these approaches grew, a wider concept of citizenship appeared, and Ravenscroft (1993) argued for access to leisure and recreation to be seen as part of 'inclusive citizenship' (Healey et al., 1998; Roche and Annesley, 1998), reflecting Commins' (1993) systems mentioned above.

Veit-Wilson distinguished between weak and strong concepts of social exclusion:

> in the weak version, the solutions lie in altering the excluded people's handicaps and character and integrating them into the dominant society; [the stronger form involves identifying] the role of those who are doing the excluding and therefore aim for solutions which reduce the power of exclusion.
>
> (Veit-Wilson, 1998: 45)

Social inclusion has become one of the mantras for the Blair Government; but, as several commentators have remarked, it is repeated against a background of shifting views about the role of the welfare state, from being a prop to passive recipients in need of help, to a springboard for improving conditions of life and, especially, work. Thus *A new contract for welfare: New ambitions for our country* said:

> The new welfare state should help and encourage people of working age to work where they are capable of doing so. The government's aim is to rebuild the welfare state around work.
>
> Our ambition is nothing less than a change of culture among benefit claimants, employers and public servants – with rights and responsibilities on all sides. Those making the shift from welfare into work will be provided with positive assistance, not just a welfare payment.
>
> (Department of Social Security, 1998: 23–4)

Chancellor Gordon Brown drove this home in a 1996 speech:

> For far too long we have used the tax and benefit system to compensate people for their poverty rather than doing something more fundamental – tackling the root causes of poverty and inequality . . . the road to equal opportunity starts not with tax rates but with jobs, education, and the reform of the welfare state and redistributing existing resources more efficiently and equitably.
>
> (quoted in Powell, 1999: 18–19)

Consequently, Giddens argued that New Labour equates equality as inclusion and inequality as exclusion (1998: 102) and Levitas (1996) and Lister (1998) stressed that the inclusive mechanisms for Blair are education and employment. Also, the new politics changes the view of citizenship from 'dutiless rights' to 'conditional welfare' (Powell, 1999: 19) or, in Giddens' words (1998: 65) again, 'a prime motto for the new politics, no rights without responsibilities.' The 1998 Labour Conference document stated 'work for those who can; security for those who cannot' (p. 67). Since the number of working age households where no-one was working had increased from 8.2 per cent in 1979 to 20.3 per cent in 1996–7 (Department of Social Security, 1999: 83), this priority is not to be wondered at.

What inferences can one take from this set of policy attitudes and aspirations?

- The belief that work will provide the income, status and self-esteem and thereby make recipients into active citizens, exercising their political and consumer rights, cannot be achieved quickly.
- It will also depend on the jobs being decently skilled and paid.
- Meantime, secondary support from welfare payments will be necessary.

It is also worth remarking that the Government's early rhetoric did not mention sport and leisure (other than fleetingly in the SEU's *Bringing Britain*

Together, 1998: 49, 58, 70), nor did the major discussion papers (Levitas, 1999, Lister 1998, Powell, 1999). Nonetheless, there has been stress on building up community capacity and social capital, this time in the communal rather than the individual sense, particularly in areas needing economic regeneration. This is seen as strengthening: civic networks and infrastructure; a sense of local/neighbourhood identity; a level of participation and solidarity; and, in Putnam's use of the term, also trust and reciprocity between citizens and their civic institutions.

Several studies have suggested that more egalitarian societies are healthier because of their social cohesion (Wilkinson, 1998), and that they grow faster economically (Glyn and Miliband, 1994). Indeed there are signs that greater equity is good for growth (Osberg, 1995), which would make sense intuitively; a human analogy is that inequities cause tensions and friction in a body politic as much as in families or friendship circles.

In this chapter we have looked at the concepts of poverty, deprivation and social exclusion, at measures of poverty and exclusion in general, and at the role of social class in sport. In Chapter 3 I look at what I consider the core of exclusion from sport and leisure as well as many other aspects of life-poverty, and in subsequent chapters the themes of gender, age, ethnicity, disability, involvement in crime while young, and urban or rural location. These issues also are picked up in the conclusions.

Chapter 3

Constraints on and benefits of playing sport

Both main parts of this chapter are brief, because each is a summary of a small mountain of studies. The first part reviews the issues of constraints on taking up, playing, lapsing and re-introducing leisure and sports activities. The second outlines the benefits claimed for playing sport, which comprises both research reviews and a growing number of policy and advocacy documents from several countries which draw not only from this research, but also include anecdotes and reviews of current schemes.

Constraints on playing sport

Goodale and Witt (1989) and Jackson (1988) reviewed research into the barriers faced and constraints experienced by people seeking to take part in recreation. In 1991 Jackson edited special issues of the *Journal of Leisure Research* (23.4) and *Journal of Leisure Sciences* (13.4) devoted to this topic. In his editorial review he criticised this earlier research for: being limited to barriers to using public recreation resources; being concerned with those groups the authors subjectively identified as constrained; and being limited to *rudimentary* item-by-item analysis (Jackson, 1991). In newer work, he identifies a move from recreation to leisure, and focuses on a wider range of activities and groups, and a diversification of interest in points of constraint other than initial take-up – in particular, lapsing preferences and satisfactions. He also distinguished (Jackson, 1990, a, b) between *antecedent* constraints (those that influence the formation of preferences, divided into intrapersonal and interpersonal) and *intervening* or *structural* ones (those that affect which preferences are turned into participation). Later (in Jackson and Scott, 1999) he also criticised North American constraints research for being too positivist, quantitative, dominated by social psychology, and focused on individuals rather than groups. Kay and Jackson (1991) reported high levels of constraint on the lower social groups in their sample in Stoke on Trent, but also constraints on affluent groups who wished to participate in more activities or more frequently. Virtually everyone is constrained in some way relative to the ideal lifestyle of their dreams.

Having reviewed these studies and over fifty more that affect particular groups, Collins et al. (1999) produced Table 3.1, since modified in terms of detailed weightings in the light of further studies reviewed for this book. Here a distinction is made between three groups of constraints. The first, comprising rows 1 to 4 of the table, identify *structural/environmental* factors – the nexus of economic, physical and social factors that lead to identifying 'problem estates' and neighbourhoods in cities so graphically described in *Bringing Britain Together*, but which is much more dispersed and concealed in rural areas, as spelled out in Chapter 11. At the other end of the scale are the personal, internal, psychological factors – seeing some activities as 'not for me' because of feelings of powerlessness and unfit, 'unsporty' self-image, or lacking the money, skills or educational and social capital to take part. These are shown in the lower six rows of Table 3.1. As Harland et al.'s study (nd) shows, these are just as effective as poverty, lack of transport, and managers who are blind to or prejudiced about some particular clients. Between these two groups are the mediating factors of 'gatekeepers' like facility managers, coaches, sports development officers, teachers, or club officers who select who is 'in' and who is 'out' of groups, and society's representatives who label people as 'different', an issue I explore in Chapters 8 on ethnic groups and 9 on disabled people in sport. This arrangement has some echoes in the structure and agency issues in sociology. The columns of Table 3.1 cover the main groups in society that may be considered excluded, and about whom the evidence is displayed in Chapters 4 to 10.

The number of plus-signs indicates the estimated importance of a particular factor for a particular group. Presenting this material in this manner illustrates that:

- Large numbers of people are affected by one or more of these factors (looking across the rows). Thus improving the design of buses and buildings for access for wheelchair users also benefits others with mobility problems, like older people using walking sticks, and mothers with pushchairs, toddlers and lots of shopping bags.
- Many groups are multiply constrained (looking down the columns). So implementing an inherently good single policy to attack a particular constraint, like leisure/loyalty cards with discounts to combat poverty or adaptations for physical disability, have no effect on exclusion if managers do not proactively market and make their facilities or services known to particular groups, or if the target population feel threatened by going to certain venues (as we know female, ethnic minority, aged and disabled citizens do at night and in secluded places). Releasing one constraint merely gives another prominence. Here is the permanent ground and justification for better partnerships and 'joined-up' thinking, and client-centred policies.

Table 3.1 Constraints and exclusion in sport and leisure

Group excluded	Youth			Poor/ unemployed	Women	Older people	Ethnic minority	People with disability/ learn difficulty
	child	young people	young delinquent					
Structural factors								
Poor physical/social environment	+	+	+	++	+	+	++	+
Poor facilities/ community capacity	+	+	++	++	+	+	+	++
Poor support network	+	+	++	++	+	+	+	++
Poor transport	++	++	++	++	++	++	+	+++
Mediating factors								
Managers' policies/ attitudes	+	+	++	++	+	+	++	++
Labelling by society	+	++	+++	+	+	+	+++	++
Personal factors								
Lack of time structure	+	+	++	+++		+		+
Lack of income	+	+	++	+++	+	++	++	++
Lack of skills/personal social capital	+	+	++	++	+	+++	++	++
Fears over safety	++	++	++	++	+++	+++	++	++
Powerlessness	++	++	+++	+++	++	++	+++	++
Poor self/body image	+	+	++	++	+	+	++	++

Note: The number of +s represent the severity of particular constraints for particular groups

Poverty adds an extra intensity to each of the other factors in terms of 'locking people in' and accentuating their feeling that they are not autonomous agents, capable of bringing change to their lives. Even for the community as a whole, money is listed as the most significant constraint; the second, time, is quoted by rich and poor alike, even by retired people; the chronic unemployed (including the young) is the group with the greatest problems of time structuring (Kay and Jackson, 1990, 1991). As we see in much of the rest of the book, there are combinations of aspects of exclusion that can be fairly said to lead to double deprivation – for example, being elderly or from an ethnic minority and in lower social groups.

As evidence in Chapter 5 and elsewhere shows, if exclusion is prolonged in youth, it tends to affect the rest of the life trajectory, and only a few determined people break through, often for short periods, while some can also slide down the social ladders, especially during unemployment or single parenthood (Walker, 1995). It can affect opportunities to play recreationally and to socialise through sport, and also, despite sponsorship and Lottery grants, chances of competing and achieving at elite level (see pages 80–3).

Benefits claimed for playing sport

The number of reviews of the benefits of sport has grown (Table 3.2), beginning with Driver, Brown and Peterson (1991) in the US and its update, where Driver and Bruns (1999) listed 105 different benefits for individuals, some for the whole community, and some for particular groups. They argued for using it practically in Benefits-Based Management (BBM), whether for generic benefits to communities or specific ones for specific groups. It was adopted by the Parks and Recreation Federation of Ontario in a condensed form, which is used in Table 3.2 as a basis for comparison. Allen et al. (1998) and Huertes et al. (2000) reported on specific applications to help at-risk youth in a series of site studies in several states (see also Chapter 10). In New Zealand, Sullivan (1998) used a range of evidence for sport aiding national, community, family and personal cohesion, and again combating youth delinquency. More recently the Council of Europe (Vuori et al., 1995, Dorricott, 1998) undertook a similar review.

Crompton and colleagues drove forward the idea of claiming benefits, arguing that, in the USA at least, recreation services had been downgraded in the public's eyes to no more than another utility, and the wider benefits to society on which the professional parks and recreation movement had been founded in the late nineteenth century had been forgotten. Thus, a conscious marketing and information effort was needed to 'reposition' the services and the profession (Crompton and Witt, 1997). Such a move was made in the UK in 1999 by Sport England in collaboration with the Local Government Association (LGA) through a review and consultation process on the value of sport, produced as a summary report and in versions aimed at partner agencies – local

Table 3.2 Benefits of sports participation: coverage of selected reviews

Form of benefit	PRFO review[a]	HC review[b]	SpE review[c]	LGA review[d]
Personal				
1 Aiding a full/meaningful life	*	*	*	
2 Ensuring health	*		*	*
3 Helping stress management	*		*	*
4 Giving self-esteem/image	*	*		*
5 Offering balance/achievement/ life satisfaction	*		*	
6 Play and human development	*	*		
7 Positive lifestyle choices	*	*		
8 Open spaces and quality of life	*			
9 Better academic performance			*	*
Social				
1 Strengthening communities	*	*	*	*
2 Reducing alienation/loneliness/ antisocial behaviour	*	*	*	*
3 Promoting ethnic/cultural harmony	*	*	*	
4 Strengthening families	*	*		
5 Community involvement/ownership/ empowerment	*	*	*	*
6 Access for disabled/disadvantaged	*		*	
7 Promoting community pride	*	*		*
8 Protection for latch-key children	*			
9 Ethical behaviour models (cheating/ drugs/violence)		*		
Economic				
1 Cost-effective health prevention	*		*	*
2 Fitness for productive workforces	*		*	
3 Small sums/large economic returns	*			
4 Attracting new/growing businesses	*			
5 Reducing cost of vandalism/crime	*		*	
6 Catalyst for tourism	*			
7 Funding environmental protection	*		*	
8 Regeneration of jobs/communities			*	*
Environmental				
1 Aiding environmental health	*		*	
2 Protecting/rehabilitating environments	*		*	*
3 Increasing property values	*			
4 Ensuring a sustainable environment	*		*	
National				
1 Integration/cultural cohesion		*		
2 Pride		*	*	
3 Trade balance/marketing		*		
4 International influence/representation			*	

Sources: Parks and Recreation Federation of Ontario, 1992; Sullivan, 1998 for the Hillary Commission; Sport England, 1999 a, b; Coalter, 2001c

Notes:
a Parks and Recreation Federation of Ontario
b Hillary Commission
c Sports England
d Local Government Association

Table 3.3 Potential benefits of sport as perceived by local authority staff (percentage citing as 'very important')

	Leisure departments (%)	Leisure centre managers/ Sports development officers (%)
Personal development		
Improving self-esteem and self-confidence	96	91
Cohesion and social benefits		
Improving community identity and cohesion	66	53
Improving the health of the community	66	59
Diverting young people from crime and vandalism	57	53
Empowerment and capacity		
Empowering disadvantaged groups	51	19
Improving the capacity of the community to take initiatives	40	16
Economic benefits		
Improving young people's prospects of employment	23	16
Developing local enterprise around sports activities	17	13

Source: Long and Sanderson, 2001

authorities, health authorities (Sport England, 1999 a-d). Subsequently the LGA commissioned Edinburgh's Centre for Leisure Research to review the evidence of benefits in the form of outputs and outcomes, and to illustrate it with case studies, not only for sport (Coalter, 2001c) but for the other sectors of cultural services – libraries, museums, arts, parks and open spaces, children's play and tourism (Coalter, 2001 a, b, d, e, f, g) – see Table 3.2.

Long and Sanderson (2001) decided to see how far local authorities believed such evidence, surveying leisure departments and officers nearer 'the coal face' in leisure centres and sports development sections; Table 3.3 shows the results. Clearly the central department staff gave greater credence to all four forms of benefit, but especially the first three. When asked for personal experience many sought to underplay them unless they underpinned the claims of Sport England. Long and Sanderson admit the difficulty of obtaining better evidence, but reinforce the necessity of having evidence over and above that of the enjoyment of recreation and winning medals, to convince hard-headed (if not cynical) councillors and sponsors to invest in sport.

Bovaird, Nichols and Taylor (1997) tried to devise a theoretical model that would link some inputs in terms of improved provision and time spent

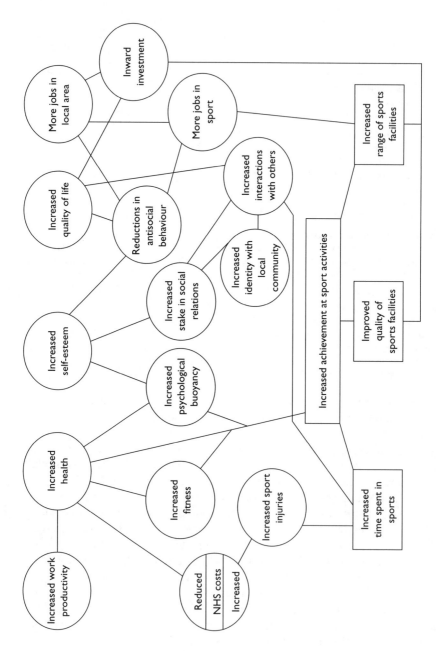

Figure 3.1 Model of relationships between sport and wider social and economic benefits

on sport to many of these benefits as intermediate or final outputs (see Figure 3.1). Even this is a great simplification of the interactions, and would require a mass of aggregate and personal or household data to test such links as between:

- time and effort spent on sport and the resulting fitness benefits to individuals and society (which the Brodie and Roberts (1992) six cities study and the Allied Dunbar National Fitness Survey (1992) both showed to be complex)
- fitness and reduced absenteeism from work, and consequent lowering of NHS costs – work done so far only for overseas samples and mainly white collar workers
- the cost of reduced production due to poor fitness and health (a very difficult task)
- the total benefit of reduced NHS costs and increased productivity.

It might be thought that the overwhelming benefits definitively confirmed between exercise and health (for example, the Allied Dunbar National Fitness Survey, 1992) and the equally definitive link between poor health, poor diet, and poverty which afflicts groups who are generally low participant in sport (HEA, 1999, Purdy and Banks, 1999) would have led to more joint programmes. That was the plan until in 1995 Ian Sproat, Minister for Sport, broke an established partnership between the Health Education Authority (HEA) and the Sports Council, saying it was not the latter's business. This is the area of benefit where research evidence is most systematic and strongest, but it relates mainly to physical activity and not sport per se. Coalter (2001c) was strongly influenced by Brodie and Roberts' findings about 7,000 residents in six UK inner cities, that;

> Sport participation was certainly not the sole determinant of these people's health, but however favourable or unfavourable their other circumstances and living habits, playing sport was leading to measurable gains.
>
> (Brodie and Roberts, 1992: 138)

It has to be said, however, that their health measures looked mainly on cardiovascular, muscle and lung benefits rather than the numerous benefits to joints, asthma, osteoporosis, mild depression and general coping which can be got from moderate exercise, as now promoted by the American College of Sports Medicine and the HEA in Britain. Waddington came to a conclusion qualified along a different parameter:

> It is probably reasonable to suggest that in the case of rhythmic, noncompetitive exercise where body movements are, to a relatively high

degree, under the control of the individual participant, the health benefits substantially outweigh the costs. However, as we move from non-competitive exercise to competitive sport, and as we move from non-contact to contact sport, so the health costs, in the form of injuries, begin to mount. Similarly, as we move from mass sport to elite sport, the constraints to train longer and more intensively and to continue competing through pain and injury also increase, with a concomitant increase in the health risks.

(Waddington, 2000: 419)

It has long been said that Britain's National Health Service concentrates on treatment to the neglect of prevention; Gratton and Taylor (2000: 107) comment that this 'may be an expensive mistake.'

Coalter (2001: 21) stressed the importance of social groups and friendship networks in sustaining participation and adherence. Wilkinson made even stronger claims relating social life and health in communities:

An essential part of the socialisation of life involves expanding the areas of working life and life on the streets which are egalitarian and socially mediated. This includes not only areas like health services ... but a huge range of voluntary work. It is not simply a matter of an intimate cocoon of social relationships for each of us; it is also a matter of social inroads into the public life of society, of finding ways of making the public space more of a social space. . . . The quality of the social environment is clearly the next big project facing developed societies.

(Wilkinson, 1998: 83–4)

Although the overwhelming majority of studies refer to the benefits of recreation, some sources do refer to possible disbenefits or downsides, for example:

*   for nations and communities, of dividing them along ethnic or cultural boundaries, or vilifying minorities through racism
*   for the economy, of losing money and image through poor investment, as in the mismanagement of transport and tickets at the Atlanta Olympics
*   for the environment, of damage by the poor siting of winter sports facilities, or allowing disturbance of wintering and breeding wildfowl
*   for families, of excessive concentration on a gifted youngster at the cost of neglecting his/her siblings
*   for individuals, of isolating them through prejudice, pricing poor people out of choices, or exposing them to chronic injuries and heavy stress of elite competition at ages when they struggle to cope.

Sport England (1999 a-d) was also upfront about aspects of social exclusion from English sport because of disability, gender, social disadvantage and

Table 3.4 Inequalities in participation in sport by social class: from the 1960s to the 1990s

	Visiting sport and leisure centres (%)		Any sport in last four weeks (%)	
	1960s	1990s	1987	1996
A (professional)	20	40	65	63
B (managerial)		52	52	52
C1 (junior non-manual)	44	33	45	47
C2 (skilled manual)	27	20	48	45
D (semi-skilled manual)	7	8	34	37
E (unskilled manual)			26	23
Total			45	46
Difference between professional and unskilled	13	32	40	40

Sources: English Sports Council, 1997; Sport England, 1999

ethnicity and referred to its equity policy and programmes for its twelve Sport Action Zones. It also uses lottery capital money for Priority Areas covering 29 per cent of England's population, and revenue for Community Action projects. It also runs 'showcase' projects, which I refer to in Chapter 12. Collins et al. (1999) and Coalter (2001) summarised the quality of evidence as:

• patchy and often situation-specific
• dependent often on small, sometimes self-selected samples
• often *post hoc* and dependent on uncorroborated self-report
• often lacking baselines, longitudinal and control group data, and
• often concerned with intermediate outputs, of the sort that interest and influence politicians, media and the general public, rather than final outcomes.

But, even if only part of such claims on top of sport's intrinsic values of enjoyment and personal achievement are real, why should a substantial minority of citizens and taxpayers have substantially poorer opportunities? Table 3.4 sets out the current social inequalities in playing sport, and in using public facilities, built with the encouragement and grant aid of the Sports Council/Sport England to promote access/sport for all (Collins, 2002). The gaps are great, and have not substantially closed over the generation since the 1960s. How far this is due to misguided policy, how far to implementation failures (lack of resources, low priorities, etc.), and how far to wider social pressures is hotly debated and not fully researched. But the gaps are real.

In each of the following six chapters I examine the evidence for exclusion and its significance for a major group in society, before looking at geographical manifestations in town and country in Chapter 11.

Chapter 4

Poverty

The core of exclusion

Jesus is recorded as saying 'the poor you will have among you always, and you can help them whenever you like' (Mark 14.7 Revised English Bible).

Introduction: Why we know so little about the economic gradient in sport and leisure

We have seen in Chapter 2 that social exclusion has many aspects and many faces, and that unemployment, disability, single parenthood, and race have strong influences on exclusion. But for me, poverty *is* the core of exclusion, as a factor in itself and compounding the others just mentioned. In this section I look at why we have so little data on leisure and poverty and often use social class as a surrogate measure. In the next section I set the context for policy since the 1970s.

I review evidence of the influence of price and cost on sports and recreation participation, then examine the growth of local authority anti-poverty strategies and leisure cards/passports to leisure. The operation of one of the early and successful Leisure Cards in Leicester and one of the recent re-launched smart cards at Oxford are compared as case studies. In conclusion, I argue that leisure/loyalty cards have the potential for being the most flexible and comprehensive mechanism so far devised that local authorities can use to combat not only poverty but other aspects of exclusion, if properly managed. Byrne suggests that 'although income is only a proxy for exclusion [by examining its distribution and sources] we can get a grip on processes that are central to exclusion in relation to exploitation' (2001: 10).

Leisure studies as a new academic field has been criticised as having many shortcomings, but curiously not yet for ignoring poverty. Four features made this chapter difficult to write. First, leisure studies have produced only a handful of items discussing income and poverty, and mainstream poverty studies have ignored or neglected leisure issues. The reasons for this lie in a lack of income data in most of the main sources of population-wide data – the Family Expenditure Survey produces a slender summary of some leisure expenditures, but the General Household Survey, the UK Day Visits Survey and the UK surveys of incoming and domestic tourism do not ask questions about income, perhaps because asking such questions increases the cost of surveys, encounters respondent resistance and leads to higher non-response.

Second, lack of income data means that major sociological texts on leisure and sport have focused on the more difficult to define concept of class (for example Horne et al., 1999; Sleap, 1998; Polley, 1997; Kew, 1997). With the growth of social mobility, Roberts (1999) did mention income, while then going on at greater length to discuss class. He wrote:

> Pay has always been the most plausible explanation of why the higher occupational strata do more. Income is the source of the clearest, widest, and most consistent leisure contrasts . . . income effects are so powerful that they override what, all other things being equal, would presumably be the negative leisure effects of relatively long work hours. These effects are long-standing and show no signs of diminishing.
>
> (Roberts, 1999: 95–6)

Thereafter, however, he neither presented nor discussed any data.

Third, most data analyses of sports and leisure participation are by socio-economic group or social class (as used by the market research industry), which relate to income in a very loose fashion. Fourth, none of the 'mainstream' poverty analyses discuss impacts on sport and leisure patterns. For example, in the first five years of the specialist newsletter *Anti Poverty Matters* (Local Government Association, 1994–9) there was no item on this issue. Even the Department for Culture, Media and Sport's (DCMS) Policy Action Team (PAT) 10 (1999: 65–6) report on *Sport and Arts* (in social exclusion) mentioned gender, but concentrated on ethnic groups and disability, saying only about economic disparities, 'people from lower socio-economic categories tend in general to participate less in the arts/sport and therefore to benefit less from Government support for the arts/sport.' A review of PAT action plans (Social Exclusion Unit, 2001a) focused on housing, jobs, and crime, with only a line about sport and arts.

The context of anti-poverty policies and leisure

Chapter 2 charts the movement from the concept of absolute poverty through relative poverty to that of social exclusion. The post-war Keynsian economy was paralleled by the development of a welfare state based on virtually full employment and free health and pension systems. While public agencies were set up for broadcasting, national parks and the arts, it was not until the early 1970s under the direction of the newly formed Sports Council that local authorities were urged and grant-aided to make a minimum provision of sports facilities in all areas. Urban deprivation, however, only became an issue after urban unrest late in the decade. Townsend and Abel Smith had been reminding society that poverty had not gone away, suggesting in 1960 that 14 per cent of people were poor. In the USA, Kaplan (1975) suggested that 'the poor' included the 'leisure poor', comprising low-paid workers, the long-term unemployed resulting from structural change, and unskilled young people who could not forge a career. Townsend (1979) and Mack and Lansley (1985) included leisure activities in definitions of poverty.

During the 1970s, local authority leisure services grew in range and number. While sports halls and swimming pools had encouraged middle-income people to participate more than poor people (Grimshaw and Prescott-Clarke, 1978; Collins, 1979 cited in Henry, 1993), across-the-board concessions were intended to keep prices low and encourage participation, especially among children and old age pensioners. Gratton and Taylor (1985) argued they benefited the higher socio-economic groups who were well informed and mobile enough to make use of them without social barriers, that is, that many were what economists call 'free riders' in no need of subsidy.

As crises developed in capitalism and unemployment grew, government grants became focused on old urban areas. Sports policy followed suit, Houlihan (1991) suggesting that by the turn of the 1980s the Sports Council's Sport for All campaign had been transmuted into 'sport for the disadvantaged' and for 'inner city youth', or as Coalter (1989) described it, sport as welfare. In its next annual report, the Sports Council (1981: 4) recorded that it would 'continue to work on the social front in relation not only to the unemployed, but also areas of urban and rural deprivation and with schemes for the ethnic minorities and the retired.' In its strategy *Sport in the Community*, the same Council (1982) identified several target groups, none of which were specifically poor, though the Action Sport schemes were aimed at promoting involvement amongst inner city youngsters. Glyptis (1989: 42) commented on a duality of purpose for public leisure provision, of enjoyment, and a belief that it could 'contain urban problems, build a sense of community and . . . overcome class and other social inequalities.'

In the late 1980s, with a Tory party in power determined to reduce public spending and increase efficiency, public leisure services looked like a candidate for compulsory competitive tendering, with its emphasis on marketing and direct delivery to customers. However, obsession with reducing costs and maximising income, rather than quality and equity, meant encouraging popular activities and regular users at the cost of protecting social/sports development objectives of serving deprived and low-participation groups (Collins, 1997). As a discretionary service, municipal sport and leisure took disproportionate cuts in finance. In those urban areas where they held sway, the urban New Left reacted by producing anti-poverty strategies (see pages 543–4). It also used sport, arts and leisure first, as a tool to tackle inequalities in direct provision (including the leisure cards examined on pages 44–58) (Henry, 1993), and second, as a means to support local groups and events, some explicitly poor, others such as disabled people and ethnic minorities with a high share of poverty.

More narrowly, the Sports Council saw 'two distinct markets' for sport:

> the larger being composed of generally affluent people who are in work, healthy and well-educated, the smaller being people who are less healthy, often unemployed and concentrated in urban and rural areas with a poor economic base.
>
> (Sports Council, 1988: 3)

The Council's strategy went on to say of these markets: 'the former group provides considerable opportunities for the private and voluntary sectors, while the public sector must play a leading role in meeting the needs of the latter.' This begins to hint at the ideas of a two-tier society, of consumer rights for those rewarded with the financial power to exercise them, and of citizen's needs to be met for those who do not.

When John Major replaced Margaret Thatcher as Prime Minister in 1991, his rhetoric was of 'one nation' Conservatism. However, the 1995 White Paper, *Sport: Raising the Game* (Department of National Heritage, 1995), concentrated on a supposed decline in school sport and on overcoming Britain's lack of success in elite/international sporting competition. Introducing the National Lottery initially benefited local sport greatly, but an increasing proportion was directed to excellence after 1997, when no reference was made to encouraging participation from people in disadvantaged groups, other than disabled people. Also, virtually no mention was made of local authorities' role (Collins, 1996). These positions were repeated in the English Sports Council's (ESC) 1997 strategy *England: The sporting nation.* Nonetheless, as we shall see below, by this time half of local authorities had introduced leisure cards providing discounts for several target groups, or even for all residents.

The Blair Government entered office in 1997 with a new rhetoric of social exclusion and of providing a modernised, high-quality local government. The demanding Best Value regime, while removing the 'C' representing compulsion in tendering, required public authorities to demonstrate that they were providing the services all groups of residents and local business wanted, efficiently and to a high quality. After the publication of *Bringing Britain Together* and the eighteen Policy Action Team reports, including one on sport and the arts, the government required all the agencies and Lottery funds it oversaw to have a policy for combating social exclusion. This was all done, however, with a self-imposed spending limit until 1999, and a stress on improving employability as the main way out of deprivation (Levitas' SI Discourse, 1998).

However, the PAT 10 report (DCMS, 1999) hardly mentioned poverty, despite the emphasis on it in background research by Collins et al. (1999). It dealt in text and case studies with at-risk and delinquent youth, and ethnic and disabled minorities, as did Sport England in its Value of Sport documents (SE, 2000a), and the government in its strategy *England: A Sporting Future for*

All (DCMS, 2000). This partly reflected Levitas' moral underclass discourse, harking back to the dual role for sports policy identified by Glyptis (1989).

The ESC had already made one change to its Lottery rules, to encourage applications from deprived communities by designating Priority Areas (defined according to DETR statistics on deprivation) in which local contributions to schemes would be reduced from 35 per cent to 20 per cent. In 2000 Sport England launched Sport Action Zones as priority areas, and within its Active Communities scheme, some forty showcase projects aimed at youth and some excluded groups.

One benefit of Best Value should be that the imbalance between financial and social targets should be able to be addressed, including social inclusion, but the challenge is to address effective outcome measures for 'soft' services. That is why I believe Passports to Leisure are an effective tool – enabling targeting of citizens, distinguished according to deprivation and ability to pay, and using swipe card technology as a means of demonstrating effectiveness for individuals, customer groups and neighbourhoods. Before we examine them, it is useful to review the very limited empirical evidence on prices for sport and leisure and how citizens and customers react.

Sport and poverty, and prices

We have already seen that Townsend saw exclusion as affecting leisure, but also that poverty and exclusion have correlations with crime, suicide, fat- and sugar-rich diets, high rates of smoking and overall poorer health, and feelings of powerlessness over life – 'in Britain overall crime rates are so closely related to measures of deprivation that it is difficult to distinguish between maps of crime and maps of deprivation' (Wilkinson, 1998: 79). There is a strong correlation of income inequality and:

> having control over one's work and domestic circumstances, job security, a regular income, social support, the absence of long-term difficulties and life threatening events, quality of parenting and lack of family conflict early in life,all appear unexpectedly successful in explaining differences in physical disease.
>
> (Wilkinson, 1998: 78)

The Health Education Authority (1999: 6–7) recorded lower physical activity by unskilled manual workers, people with fewer than five GCSE 'O' level qualifications, with disabilities, in ethnic minorities, over 65 years of age, and living in council housing.

Poverty affects access to leisure: apart from a few happy hermits or those who have opted out of mainstream society, there can be virtually no one who is poor and not excluded from leisure and culture, for much of leisure is now commodified and has to be paid for directly, or indirectly though transport, parking fees or food and drink. Dawson, writing from Canada a decade ago, opined that 'to be without access to or opportunity for leisure, is to be poor' (1988: 230).

Based on broad arguments, Polley indicated that, since World War II, choice of sport has been seen as a signifier of lifestyle and indirectly of status, but that:

> what has been notable is the fluidity of this process, linked to disposable income, private transport and the growth of the white-collar work-force. Here, previously restricted sports have become more mixed, and the ownership and control of certain sports has been contested in class terms.
>
> (Polley, 1997: 113–14)

For a minority, sport has also been a ladder to social status, and even more a means of gaining high incomes and professional advancement (Holt, 1990).

It has already been said that there was a tradition of keeping public leisure services as cheap as possible in the UK, and Gratton and Taylor (1994) were convinced that for many in society demand was elastic, i.e. that price increases would be absorbed by users because the value of sport to them was sufficient. As competitive tendering loomed, the Audit Commission (1989) argued for more of the cost of sports facilities be borne by users, because most were from more affluent groups who could afford it, and too much of the burden was falling on poorer groups who made less or no use of them. In the 1980s prices increased steadily above inflation, so that the overall proportion of costs recovered increased from 27 per cent to 44 per cent for sports halls, and from 12 per cent to 36 per cent for swimming pools. In the 1990s, the database was changed to combine the halls and pools data, and by 1998–99 the recovery rate was 30 per cent in England and Wales, but 40 per cent in non-metropolitan districts (Chartered Institute of Public Finance and Accountancy, 1999).

Despite such policy discourse, there was no empirical test of the elasticity of demand and underlying factors until the Scottish Sports Council (Campbell, 1993) commissioned the Centre for Leisure Research (1993) and Gratton and Taylor (1994) to investigate the impact of pricing experiments in four author-ities in Scotland, and subsidised the experiments. These involved:

1   Pricing a new fitness suite in East Kilbride to break even, while increas-ing other prices.
2   Increases in charges for most users of two Edinburgh leisure centres, to be offset by introducing a leisure card for disadvantaged groups.
3   Large increase in prices (between 36 and 100 per cent) from a low base, in rural Biggar's sports centre (Clydesdale).
4   Most radically, abolishing charges for eight months at Port Glasgow's Inverclyde swimming pool, and then re-introducing charges.

Table 4.1 Consumer reactions to four Scottish pricing experiments

	% changes in			Attitude to new price	% constrained by	
	Price	Use	Revenue	% 'too high'	Price	Time
E Kilbride	+10			11	U 11	U 4
New fitness suite	+15	+134	+120	24	P 6	P 16
Old fitness suite	+13	+3	+19	8	N 1	N 23
Edinburgh					U 9	U 3
Leisure centre 1	+70	-37	+11	13	P 6	P 24
Leisure centre 2	+31			12	N 1	N 25
Clydesdale	+71 (+31 to +100 for various groups)	+9	+39	12	U 10 P 1 N 1	U 6 P 15 N 25
Inverclyde pool	−100 (later reinstated)	+15	−54[a]	n/a	U 0 P 1 N 1	U 9 P 11 N 22

Source: Gratton and Taylor, 1994
Note: a Revenue for Inverclyde pool is for other than admission

Table 4.1 shows the changes in price, use and revenue, the reaction of users to the increases, and how far users (U), general sports participants (P) and non-participants (N) in the facility catchments thought price and time were constraints on their sports participation.

As Table 4.1 shows, there was:

- no great resistance to the price increases
- no great reduction in use except at one of the Edinburgh centres; while those who had stopped were mainly young men, at school or unemployed
- free use at Port Glasgow's Inverclyde pool led to 15 per cent more use, mostly because 1 in 3 existing users went more often than because new users were attracted, or diverted from the nearest pool
- price was a constraint on about 1 in 10 users but far fewer residents, in contrast to two or three times as many who saw time as a problem.

Of 1,795 residents, 955 had sports expenditure averaging £3.42 a week, and entry prices comprised only 32 per cent of this. Meanwhile, in an economic impact study for the whole of Scotland, PIEDA (1991) found entry prices to be only 16 per cent of all sports expenditure. So, for the population as a whole, time seemed to be a greater constraint to playing sport than price, as indicated by Kay and Jackson (1991) and Coalter (1991). Gratton and Taylor commented (1994: 4), 'it is likely that the price of time is rising relative to the price of goods.' But these surveys did not differentiate samples of poor people. The day-to-day experience of sports centre managers was often different. They reported that those on limited incomes – youngsters, unemployed people, single parents, many old age pensioners – were 'income inelastic' (Centre for Leisure Research, 1993). Compared with working adults, these groups looked to older, cheaper swimming pools to get as many swims as possible for a given sum, and reduced at least the frequency of their attendance when prices were increased.

In contrast, Glasgow City Council introduced free swimming for young people via two cards – Young Scot Glasgow Card for 16–35s (a Scots version of the Connexions Card in England – see page 210), and the Kidz Card for under-12s. Within months, attendance had increased by 26 per cent (Macdonald, 2001), and the Chief Executive of Young Scot said, 'how young people interact with local council services is crucial to engaging them as active citizens' (see Chapters 2 and 12 for discussion of this concept). Agyll, and Bute and Angus are participating also.

A similar study was the How Much? project in Sheffield, which attempted to attract young people to live theatre through offering substantial discounts on twenty-one drama and music performances. The youngsters, both non-attenders and attenders, said price was not an absolute constraint on attending, rather the uncertainty of getting satisfaction and value for money, though price was the main factor deterring half of non-attenders. The discounts were a major incentive for almost 9 in 10 attenders. The number of participants aged 16–24 grew from 7 per cent of audiences (compared with 16 per cent nationally) to an average of 41 per cent at the How Much? productions. One in three were new customers (Galvin et al., 2000).

In Finland, Puranaho (2000) showed how, even in such a high-income society, the costs of sport training for regular young competitors (equipment, clothing, transport, fees) can be a problem, and most parents wanted costs cut. For example, on average young soccer players spent between £460 a year (when aged 8) and £2,300 (aged 16), while ice hockey players spent £400 and £2,860 respectively at the same ages. More and Stevens (2000: 349) found entrance fee increases over a period of five years for public outdoor recreation areas in Vermont and New Hampshire had lead to 23 per cent of low-income users reducing their use or going elsewhere, compared with 11 per cent of high-income users.

In contrast, McCabe (1993, 1994, 1995) and colleagues attempted to construct a 'modest-but-Adequate' (MBA) family budget for six household types, based on popular leisure goods and services and a free time model based on the Henley Centre's 1991 *Time Budget Survey*. They also set a 'low cost' budget, which included using public transport rather than cars, consuming no alcohol or cigarettes, taking a day trip rather than a holiday, trips to the cinema and stately homes only twice a year, and little or no regular sports participation. Table 4.2 shows that, even accepting the unrealistic assumption about smoking and drinking, for those on the low cost budget, Income Support in 1992

Table 4.2 Modest-but-adequate and low-cost family leisure budgets, 1992 (£s per week)

Family type	MBA[a] leisure budget	MBA total budget	Family type	Low cost leisure budget	Low cost total budget	Income support
Single male, 30 years	16.46	150.34				
Single female, 72 years	12.63	119.30	Lone pensioner/ owner-occupier	4.42	67.06	57.15
2 adults	28.19	210.87	Lone pensioner/ LA[b] tenant	2.81	53.16	57.15
2 adults + 2 children aged 4 and 10	32.24	316.50	2 adults + 2 children aged 4 and 10/ LA tenant	13.97	141.40	105.00
2 adults + 2 children aged 10 and 16	37.19	322.23				
Lone parent + 2 children aged 4 and 10	27.64	296.04	Lone parent/ LA tenant	11.76	110.72	85.60

Source: McCabe, 1993, 1994, 1995 updated for inflation from 1991 in Barclay, 1992

Notes:
a MBA = modest-but-adequate
b LA = local authority

was inadequate to cover the needs of three of the four groups. For the MBA budgets, the leisure figures were less than the medians found in the Family Expenditure Survey for most of the household types.

We now turn to leisure cards as a common form of intervention, but it is notable that compared with general clothing and food retailing, while there are premium brands in expensive tailor-made sports clothing and equipment, and exclusive clubs, especially in golf, sailing and fitness, there is little provision for budget sports brands except in cheap clothing and trainers, and 'back-street' gyms/fitness clubs.

Local authority anti-poverty strategies and leisure cards

The numerous policy initiatives to tackle (urban) deprivation, notably the Urban Programme and Community Development Projects, have been criticised for being adventitious (Alcock and Craig, 1998) or having no strategic pattern because they were based on bidding rather than planning (Oatley, 1998). This lack of central direction or leadership drove authorities, mainly large, urban, and Labour-controlled in the first instance, to review their policies for poor people. Balloch and Jones (1990) looked at the first dozen of these Anti-Poverty Strategies (APSs) for the Association of Metropolitan Authorities. By 1995, Alcock et al. showed 1 in 2 were engaged in some anti-poverty activity, in urban and rural areas and under all forms of political control, including none. Of these forty-five (32 per cent) had a formal strategy. Alcock et al. associated APSs with decentralised delivery of services, reduction or remission of municipal charges, promotion of welfare rights/take-up, debt and money advice and support including credit unions, partnerships with health authorities and other economic and community development activity.

Scottish authorities followed a more strategic framework, but more slowly, Higgins and Ball (1999) discovering that 25 per cent (fourteen) had APSs. Both surveys used case studies but neither indicated the presence or significance of leisure cards. In the mid-1990s the National Local Government Forum Against Poverty was formed, and an Anti-Poverty Unit was set up within the new Local Government Association. An example of a wide-ranging APS in which 'flexcard' concessions play a part in several initiatives was that of the Telford and Wrekin Partnership (1998). The flexcard had 16,300 users, of whom 47 per cent were eligible for concessions.

Anti-poverty strategies have been linked to other work on equal opportunities, for people from ethnic minorities, with disabilities or of female gender. This is often helpful because the work applies often to the same areas and groups, enables officers to reinforce each other's work in solidarity, and prevents equal opportunities (EO) work from being sidelined (Local Government Management Board, 1997). The move from policy concepts of poverty to social exclusion allows a wider view of EO work, as does the advent of Regional and Local Cultural Strategies and a Best Value regime. Fifty-six per cent of authorities had a structure in place by 2001 to deal with exclusion and anti-poverty matters, and half had dedicated staff (LGA, 2001).

As we shall see, having an anti-poverty strategy is a significant factor in developing a leisure card, not least because it brings a corporate approach and awareness of the incidence of poverty and its consequences. In many author-ities with APSs, every major report to elected members has to indicate what impact it will have on race, gender or disability equity matters. This type of 'policy-proofing' for social exclusion has been promised by central govern-ment (SEU, 2001a, 2001b).

Collins and Kennett (1998) described how public leisure services and aware-ness of resurgent poverty grew alongside each other. Initial policy responses were to introduce discounts, first for old age pensioners, then for unemployed people and people with impairments, and then for a wider range of disadvant-ages, making them numerous and very complex for staff and customers alike. Then, when CCT was introduced, the Audit Commission and the government asked local authorities not only to market and manage leisure provision more cost effectively, but also to target subsidies better. Leisure Cards (LCs) or Passports to Leisure were introduced. These were generally cheap to buy, and provide one, two or three levels of discount:

- the highest for deprived/poor people
- the second highest for other groups given some priority, for example students
- all residents (which are being transmuted into municipal Loyalty Cards analogous to those issued by supermarkets and major stores).

Collins and Kennett (1999) undertook a postal survey of British local author-ities in 1997–8 and, from a 52 per cent response, discovered some interesting things about which sorts of authorities held cards, why and how they were introduced, and aspects of operation. Just over half of authorities had cards, more with populations over 100,000, that spent above-average sums on sport and arts, that had higher than average numbers of benefit claimants, and that ranked high on the DETR's index of deprivation. Fifty-five per cent were for concessionary groups only, while 41 per cent had other tiers of charging, for example for all citizens. Perhaps most marked was the correlation with authorities having an anti-poverty strategy: 48 per cent with a card, compared with 14 per cent without.

Cards were introduced overwhelmingly for political or managerial reasons of encouraging low income people into sport (56 per cent), and an ideological commitment to low-income people (24 per cent, see Figure 4.1). Collins and Kennett had hypothesised that economic (such as filling empty off-peak space) or managerial reasons (like simplifying complex discounts) might be signific-ant, but clearly these were of minor importance, though they may have helped

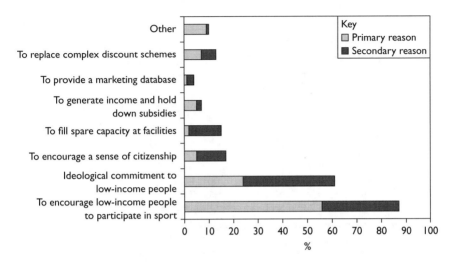

Figure 4.1 Reasons for establishing leisure card schemes

to get the card idea accepted. Market research prior to launching was sketchy, often limited to contacting a sample of operating schemes, leading to much 'copy-cat' management.

The early leisure cards were concentrated in metropolitan authorities, but later they spread to smaller towns and rural areas. From 1999 the Chartered Institute of Public Finance and Accountancy gathered data on cards as part of its annual survey of estimated expenditure on public leisure services (Chartered Institute of Public Finance and Accountancy, 1999). This showed, from an 82 per cent response, that the numbers of cards, including those styled as loyalty cards, had increased to 228, or 76 per cent of all authorities (Table 4.3),

Table 4.3 Local authorities with leisure and loyalty cards, 1999

	No. of leisure/loyalty cards			
	No. (% of groups with cards)	Including sport	Including arts	Including commercial leisure
London	22 (27)	22	8	11
Metropolitan authority	30 (100)	30	13	9
Unitary authority	30 (88)	33	15	15
Non-metropolitan authority	130 (70)	129	39	41
Wales	13 (68)	13	3	1
Total	228 (76)	227	78	77

Source: Chartered Institute of Public Finance and Accountancy, 1999

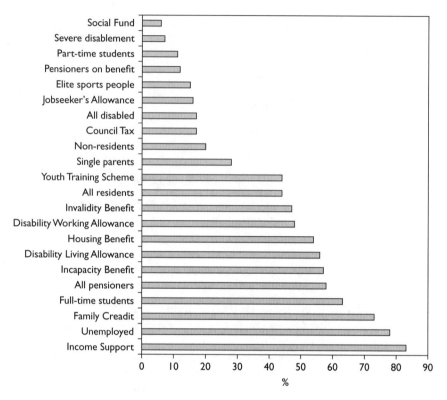

Figure 4.2 Groups targeted by leisure card schemes

very close to what the authorities had told Collins and Kennett four years earlier. All but one of the cards offered sport, but only 37 per cent in England and 20 per cent and Wales offered public arts and only 36 per cent and 23 per cent respectively commercial leisure and retail services. Consultations of the sort required under Best Value with potential customers, residents' groups, or commercial businesses were much less common, by one in four or five authorities.

For ease of operation, card operators selected target groups directly related to categories of welfare benefits: 89 per cent targeting Income Support recipients, 73 per cent Family Credit, 79 per cent Unemployment Benefits, 64 per cent full-time students, and 59 per cent all old age pensioners (see Figure 4.2). Subsequently, Sport England (2000) showed that 79 per cent of English leisure centres had reduced prices for eligible people, 35 per cent had a passport scheme for all citizens, 30 per cent an access card only for low-income groups, and 19 per cent some other membership scheme. The biggest issues over targeting were whether to include part-time and full-time students, all pensioners or only those on benefits, carers for disabled people and the dependants of cardholders.

In terms of services offered, virtually all of the sample discounted municipal sports provision at 30 to 50 per cent, 2 in 5 discounted arts and culture, and less than 1 in 3 discounted private leisure and other commercial operations, at 10 to 15 per cent (notably cinemas and some professional soccer clubs; discounts also applied to taxis, photographers, sports and arts equipment retailers, florists, steam railways, zoos, etc.). The sporting bias would exclude many citizens who were 'not sporty' – almost two in five according to the Allied Dunbar National Fitness Survey – especially women and older people.

In terms of access, many cards could only be purchased at town halls and leisure centres, but Cardiff used post offices, the facility most used by poor people, while Leicester and a few others employed marketing staff who used outreach methods to reach target groups (see page 000 below). More recently, information appears on councils' websites. Marketing was very conventional, through low-impact leaflets, council newsletters, tax mailings and posters on council hoardings and buses, but there was little use of paid advertising or local radio/TV. The more substantial schemes send members a regular magazine advertising new services and special offers, as in Leicester, or a directory of outlets, as for Chester and Windsor, and Maidenhead's advantage card, whose 24-page colour magazine listed 163 outlets. The District Council claimed that 64 per cent of its 90,000 residents had a card.

Two other marketing issues were whether to limit Card use to off-peak hours, and the turnover of eligible customers. Some respondents did so openly, to fill unused space, others because they feared losing peak trade. Others objected on the grounds that disadvantaged people should be able to enjoy their leisure at these times as much as anyone else, and that to limit access thus was a new, more surreptitious form of stigmatisation. As an Oxford manager said, 'it's an appalling assumption that just because people are unemployed, they can only come between 9 and 5.' The Audit Commission cited an authority that excluded concessionary users, mistakenly believing they would crowd out full-price swimmers, when in fact the pool was only 57 per cent full, commenting that 'low income families were being unnecessarily excluded, and potential additional income was being lost' (1999: 27).

While some groups did not change status and eligibility much (like disabled and retired people), others who are unemployed and on low incomes because of low skills get short-term jobs and go on and off benefits (Walker, 1997, Walker and Park, 1997). So, authorities started to offer longer memberships to the former groups and shorter ones to the latter, to reduce administrative costs and 'free riders', respectively. A leisure card is essentially a membership scheme and needs the same care and attention to retention and marketing that commercial fitness chains like David Lloyd and Fitness First give. Neglect means waste: Cardiff did little follow-up in 1995–6 and only four of 1,439 lapsed members renewed! Some authorities had thought that introducing cards under the rules of CCT would be difficult because of the subsidy involved, an issue given some prominence in Sports Council advice (Eady, 1994). But the few problems were solved by either renegotiating clauses in contracts, or by specific payments, and then by incorporation into second round tenders.

In fact, resources and budgets were very limited:

• 29 per cent of authorities had no staff dedicated to managing and marketing their cards and only 18 per cent had two or more
• one in four had *no* budget for operating their cards, and another one in seven under £5,000 a year; the small scale of many operations was demonstrated in that a third received under £500 in revenue. Only one in seven earned more than £40,000. This was partly because prices were kept low: 37 per cent of concession cards were free, and 37 per cent cost £3 a year or less for adults.

With the advent of better information technology, Kennett (2002) suggested that one part-time staff member would be needed for every 5,000 members.

So the lack of money and staff goes some way to explaining but not excusing the low level of promotion. Indeed, only 1 in 3 authorities had set a target for the penetration of its card sales, and 1 in 4 had no target for usage. It also meant that monitoring and review were not uniformly rigorous and systematic, only 2 in 5 conducting an annual review, and despite computerisation of membership records, and of facility ticket sales, many had no one skilled to reduce the mountain of data to useful information.

The success of schemes can be judged by the extent of take-up, the accuracy of targeting, and the degree of use and income to facilities. Apart from the quality of recording technology, there is also an issue of accuracy because many schemes allow applicants to record membership using the most convenient form of evidence rather than the most appropriate, blurring the statistics. Multi-tier schemes aim at much if not all of the population are compared with the deprived segments targeted by concession-only schemes. Thus in Collins and Kennett's sample, 1 in 3 concession schemes had fewer than 1,000 members compared with 1 in 12 multi-tier, whereas 1 in 3 multi-tier schemes had more than 10,000 members compared with only 1 in 7 concessions. Relating this to the populations served: of multi-tier schemes, 7 in 10 reached 10 per cent of citizens or fewer, and only 1 in 20 more than 16 per cent. Meanwhile, of 34 concession schemes giving data, six (18 per cent) reached 1 in 7 or more of the deprived population, and 23 (two-thirds) reached a tenth or less (as shown in Figure 4.3). Of those authorities that provided CIPFA with membership details, take-up averaged 9,750 for ordinary members and 5,580 for concessionary cards. But some had large enrolments, like Nottingham with 79,000 members of whom 29,000 were in low income/benefit categories, to which were expected to be added some 17,000 young people with Connexions cards offering discounts and free gifts as rewards for sustained attendance in post-16 education (Chartered Institute of Public Finance, 2000).

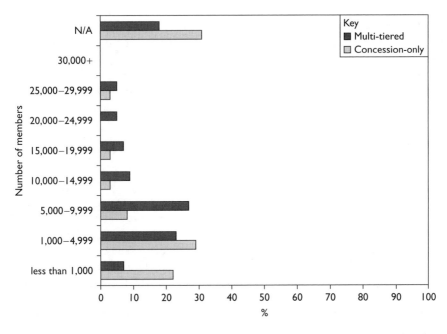

Figure 4.3 Membership as a percentage of the population: concession-only and multi-tiered leisure cards

Regarding targeting, many authorities were only beginning to collaborate with social services departments in the review and re-launch of cards. The Leicester and Oxford case studies below show relatively successful schemes, in terms of numbers and targeting. But like many bicycles bought with good intentions of exercising, many of which remain in sheds and hung on walls, ownership of a card does not equal use. Only with the advent of integrated management information systems and the use of swipe or smart cards can the disparate site data be brought together with the membership data at head-quarters. Thus holders used their cards about six times a year in Leicester, twenty in Cardiff and between twelve and forty in Oxford. Card use can vary greatly by facility according to its catchment – 38 and 68 per cent of total use was at two Coventry sports centres, just under half at the four Oxford facilities.

If 1 in 2 authorities had cards, why had not others taken one up? Collins and Kennett hypothesised that it would be because some thought they had no poverty/deprivation problem and thus no need for a card (which turned out to apply to only 1 in 5), or for lack of a strong core of leisure services (which hardly anyone admitted to), or the costs of administration or subsidy (both identified by 1 in 3, not surprising given the facts about budgets above). In fact the authorities without cards were generally smaller and rural. But this need not prevent them running a card. Tynedale, geographically the largest English district with one of the smallest populations (37,000 people), only two staff in its leisure department and five small facilities, runs a successful card. Brighton and Hove is a large authority (245,000), has people with a major deprivation problem, fairly limited leisure facilities run by three separate contractors, an anti-poverty staff team but no card. Officers considered leisure cards 'a scattergun approach . . . a bureaucratic nightmare . . . ineffective in increasing participation.' There were numerous discounts, but no data measuring their effectiveness.

As time went by, using cards as part of the marketing and image-making of a council became more common, first as resident cards, like that of the Royal Borough of Windsor and Maidenhead, and then as loyalty cards, emulating stores and petrol stations, as in Chester where the directory lists 293 outlets. This move risks burying or diluting the social purpose at their core, but appeals to generic management teams and committees. Thus, when Oxford City launched its Slice Card in 1998 it was intended specifically to generate income across the whole leisure service, to subsidise access for target groups.

In 1998 the Department for Education and Employment latched on to card technology as an incentive for youth training. It introduced a Learning Card for 16- to 18-year-olds, and after the report *Bridging the Gap* (Social Exclusion Unit, 2000a), the government determined to extend this to create a Youth Card, which was introduced in pilot locations. Young people obtain points for attendance and achievement on education and training courses, which accumulate on a smart card, and are recorded on a national database. The young people can then use these points in free or reduced cost travel, in discounts on entrance to leisure facilities, or for 'lifestyle' products (well-known brands of food and soft drinks like MacDonalds and Coca Cola, and discounts for Virgin cinemas and CDs, etc.). They also have access to a major database on learning (Summerson, 2000). The complication with all of this is that this overlaps with local authority card schemes, 3 in 5 of which already targeted full-time students. It remains to be seen what impact this scheme will have on local cards, when it has the power of national commercial partners. Perhaps youngsters will use both.

Case study 1: Leisure cards in Leicester and Oxford

Leicester

Leicester launched its Leisure Pass early, in 1985, with the objectives of: encouraging and making accessible sports participation amongst low-income and disadvantaged groups; increasing use in both peak and off-peak times; minimising income loss by negotiated discounts; and encouraging take-up by a range of attractive concessions (Leicester City Council, 1985). It had been intended as part of an anti-poverty strategy, but the city has not published one. Its clients incorporated previously targeted groups of unemployed, disabled, full-time students aged 16 to 17 and Youth Training Scheme trainees, but added single parents, senior citizens, low-income groups and dependants of all these groups. Carers of disabled people were added in 1991 through the Leisure plus One card.

The cards were free, and offered 50 per cent discounts for municipal sport; soon, other municipal arts services were added and events like the Leicester Show and then private retail, cinema, zoo, steam railway, and other outlets, a total of 95 by 1997. The philosophy was to maximise take-up and this, said the responsible officer, involved offering a range 'from veg to Verdi'. In fact, four of the five most popular services were commercial.

By 1987 membership reached 6,800, but doubled to 14,000 by 1988, as did administrative staff (from one to two); adjacent authorities were invited to buy cards and subsidise them or re-charge eligible citizens. Oadby and Wigston did so in 1988, and currently five districts and five parishes together purchase over 900 passes. A focused campaign on students was the main feature behind the increase to 21,700 members by 1992. This group was recruited by taking photo card laminating machines to colleges during autumn registration, and then to other venues – job centres for the unemployed, clubs for women, disabled people, ethnic groups. In 1996 the composition of Passholders was:

	%
People aged 60+	45
Young people	20
Income Support/low-income recipients	12
Unemployed	9
Disabled	9
Single parents	3
Carers	1

The budget in 1996–7 was £44,500, including £7,000 for marketing; since the only direct income was the sale of cards outside the city (£10,100), the deficit was £34,400, or £1 per Passholder. A significant reduction in budget in 1998 raised the question of whether to charge for the Pass, though officers were reluctant, saying 'it would be met with resistance . . . it would put people off . . . it could be costly.' In a user survey in 1996, 2 in 5 holders said they would continue participating without a free Pass, but only 1 in 5 of low-income holders and 1 in 3 young people would. In contrast, 1 in 3 of the latter groups would give up, confirming the narrow margins and importance of incentivising subsidies for poor people. Leicester has one of the highest concentrations of ethnic minorities in Britain, at 39 per cent of the population. Passholders were almost representative, at 34 per cent of the total (30 per cent of them Asian).

In terms of take-up, therefore, Leicester reached 11 per cent of all its 270,000 citizens. It can be calculated, using Gordon and Forrest's (1995) index and allowing for overlaps that this encompassed 1 in 3 of the eligible target disadvantaged groups in the city (Kennett, 2001: 286), a penetration that any commercial operator in a competitive market like leisure would judge successful.

In 1996, moreover, 84 per cent of holders intended to renew and only 2 per cent to cancel, a measure of value and satisfaction. But membership peaked at 30,071 in 1995. Even after the formation of a unitary authority, whereby Leicester recovered the education and social services functions it lost in 1974, successive cuts had to be made in the leisure budget, and after some years of protection, this meant the loss of dedicated administrative and marketing staff. The Assistant Director said this was 'sad, but not as sad as the alternative of closing facilities . . . we will maintain the scheme as far as we can, but we won't be able to market it in the way we have in the past . . . to a degree it will have to become self-marketing.' No example of self-marketing operations can be found in marketing textbooks, and anyone who discovered one would soon be wealthy!

In fact, since the staff and marketing activity has been reduced by a third, the Leisure Pass has lost 10,000, or one-third, of its members (Figure 4.4). Given the Pass' objectives, it remains to be seen first whether usage will hold up under the decline in Passholders, and second, how this decline will be viewed by Best Value inspectors.

After the financial cuts, the Assistant Director believed the emphasis should be 'on not how many people have a Pass but how many people use their Pass.' The use of leisure centres had doubled in the previous five years, partly as a result of the individual annual average of visits increasing from 5.2 in 1992–3 to 6.5 in 1996–7. Low-income members made most frequent use, with 1 in 5 attending once a week. Swimming was by far the most popular activity for 9 out of 10 Passholders, with weight-lifting/fitness, badminton and aerobics/keep fit a long way behind with 1 in 5. Cultural activities came second to sport:

	%
sports facilities	92 (one swim a week saves £50 a year)
libraries	59
museums	53
Odeon cinema	43 (one showing a week saves £60 a year)
Haymarket theatre	40
De Montfort concert hall	40 (saving £15 a year)
Bonfire night (Abbey Park)	27
Twycross Zoo	23 (saving £1 per adult ticket)
Leicester City FC	12 (saving£125 a year on a season ticket)

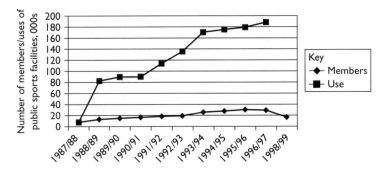

Figure 4.4 Use of Leicester Leisure Pass compared with membership totals

The list also shows the five most popular commercial offerings, and the savings Passholders can make. The facility members would most like to have was a discount at the other cinemas in the city.

Oxford

In 1997–8 Oxford re-launched its Slice Card, to replace a Leisure Card that had attracted only 4,000 people, 3 in 5 being concessionaires and getting it free. It had failed to attract young people aged 15 to 25, retirees and ethnic minorities, and only half the population had heard of it. Nine out of 10 holders used it only for swimming (Oxford City Council, 1998). The city's objectives were: to increase income so as to be able to subsidise targeted groups, as the Client Services Manager said, 'on the Robin Hood principle'; to increase use and income overall; and to target groups without discrimination, especially people with low incomes. This was a mixture of social, economic and marketing factors, and seen as a corporate rather than a departmental initiative, and involved the Chief Executive's and Social Services departments, the latter notably via the anti-poverty officer.

It decided on a swipe card, provided by the largest supplier, and the card's introduction coincided with a new computerised system for all Oxford's leisure centres and pools, which was capable of yielding information in detailed form, greatly improving the capacity for monitoring. Oxford decided to have three commercial and two concessionary tiers:

- *Cool Slice* – unlimited access for ice skating, swimming, sauna, aerobics/ fitness, racket sports, creche
- *Active Slice* – as for Cool Slice but without skating, priced £24 a month for adults, £12 for juniors and seniors
- *Aqua Slice* – unlimited access to swimming and sauna, priced £22 a month

- *Bonus Slice* – concessions of 33–70 per cent for unemployed, disabled, people on Income Support/Housing Benefit/Family Credit/Council Tax rebate, priced £2 for a year
- *Student Slice* – similar discounts for full-time students and those on Youth Training Schemes, £2 a year, but cards issued for 6 months

The marketing was slick, avoiding any sense that the cards were of municipal origin. It was hoped this would increase usage of facilities by 50,000 visits a year (6 per cent), and income by £0.5m (33 per cent). The services were limited to municipal sport, but plans for Phase 2 were to extend to commercial leisure and retail services.

One member of staff was allocated for administration, a post the manager expected 'to pay for itself twice over', while the marketing was handled as a corporate function. The day-to-day operation was managed by the city's contractor, City Leisure. The budget was £28,000, of which £15,000 was for administration, £6,000 for marketing, and £7,000 for card purchases and depreciation of hardware and software.

Membership exceeded expectations, and attracted 14,000 of Oxford's 110,000 residents after only nine months of operation; Cool and Active Slices took 14 per cent, Aqua Slice 29 per cent and Bonus and Student Slices 48 per cent of the total. The Bonus card reached 13 per cent of the 33,800 low-income people in the city. As a sport-only venture, this was a tribute to the skilled marketing. The Audit Commission (1999: 56) cited Oxford as 'a neat example of how one tariff tool can be priced for a range of target groups and segment the market.' A similar postcode analysis of geographic take-up was done as for Leicester, and again at this scale there was no significant correlation with deprivation (Spearman RO $= -0.13$ $(n = 17)$). The distribution of Bonus Slice concessionary holders suggested that more marketing was needed in inner city wards and in the deprived outer estate of Blackbird Leys.

As I have said, take-up does not equal use. In contrast to Leicester, concessionary Bonus Slice holders used their cards less often than the others – once a month compared with 2.6 for Aqua and 3.1 for Active Slice holders. A quarter of all Bonus holders lived in Blackbird Leys, and would be likely to use Temple Cowley pools to swim. After only three months nearly half of all use at Oxford's four facilities were card holders, ranging from 83 per cent at Blackbird Leys leisure centre to only 17 per cent at the ice rink. The computerised system allowed detailed breakdowns of use by demographics of users and activity and time of day/week/month.

Analysis

Having a list of postcodes for Leicester's Passholders allowed Kennett (2001) to relate them to deprivation as measured by the Department of the Environment, Transport and the Regions' (1999, 2000) index, by a laborious analysis

Table 4.4 Postcode Index of Deprivation and number of cardholders: Leicester

Postcode	PDI[a]	No. cardholders	Postcode	PDI	No. cardholders
LE1 2	7,47	159	LE3 9	1,49	866
LE1 5,6,7[b]	6,23	118	LE4 0	0,12	902
LE2 0	6,07	457	LE4 1	−1,57	273
LE2 1	2,56	494	LE4 2	2,99	624
LE2 2	−1,90	178	LE4 5	2,06	683
LE2 3	−3,44	547	LE4 6	3,60	1019
LE2 6	1,93	839	LE4 7	−0,82	848
LE2 7	4,97	184	LE4 9	−1,9	282
LE2 8	−1,15	759	LE5 0	2,98	409
LE2 9	2,44	632	LE5 1	−0,96	646
LE3 0	0,74	440	LE5 2	−0,19	833
LE3 1	4,31	645	LE5 3	3,52	422
LE3 2	−1,54	232	LE5 4	2,05	793
LE3 5	0,68	285	LE5 5	0,57	692
LE3 6	0,08	752	LE5 6	−3,53	923
LE3 8	3,47	31			

Notes:
a Postcode Index of Deprivation
b LE1 5,6,7 were joined due to the overlapping of all three postcodes in one area

using the PC2ED programme to convert 7,000 postcodes into census Enumeration Districts (EDs), entering them into the MIMAS database, calculating from the figures for constituent EDs a Postcode Deprivation Index (PDI), and finally entering over 20,000 Passholders' addresses. The sectoral PDIs and the cardholders allocated are shown in Table 4.4. Spearman's rank order correlation coefficient was used to test the correlation between level of deprivation and the number of cardholders, which was not significant ($r = 0.12$ ($n = 31$)). This may be because of the small number and large size of postcodes and the mix of both affluent and deprived housing areas or because other factors are involved. For example, Beaumont Leys contains EDs with both the lowest and highest indices in the city at −6.02 and 7.81. So, ED level analysis would be more likely to identify pockets of deprivation for marketing and to show relationships. Leeds City Council (Social Exclusion Unit, 2000b) has been developing such a geographic management information system.

Figure 4.5 illustrates the take-up of Leisure Passes by postcode for Leicester (in italics) superimposed on a map of wards showing the 1998 DETR index by shading. Leicester was the 32nd most deprived authority in England. The take-up was higher in the least deprived wards and postcodes LE 2 3 and LE5 6 in the south and east, and in LE2 6, LE2 8, LE3 6, LE3 9, and LE4 7. The most deprived areas were in the centre of the city, the north and the outlying western wards, and here there were lower levels of take-up. But LE4 6 includes

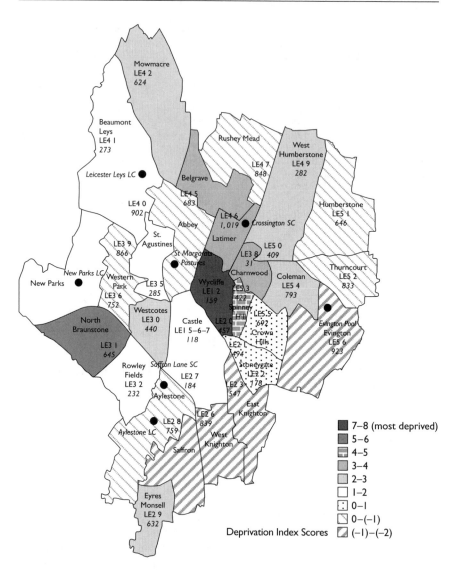

Figure 4.5 Geographic take-up of Leicester's Leisure Pass

Latimer and Belgrave, the areas of greatest Asian ethnic population, yet with the greatest take-up (1,109) despite being one of the most deprived wards. This may have been due to the proximity of two sports centres. From this analysis in Leicester, there was a clear need to increase take-up in the more deprived areas, especially in the city centre and the peripheral estates.

Kennett suggested that the early waves of cards typified by Leicester showed 'Fordist' features, including:

- limited market research and development
- production of homogeneous/mass products
- a conflict between the client's social and the contractor's managerial objectives
- unresponsiveness within hierarchical organisations
- with poor financial and human resourcing, squeezed discounts reduce consumer attraction
- inefficient allocation of resources due to 'free-riding' and
- limited investment in technology and new products.

He concluded that 'the majority of schemes seemed to be like a favourite toy kept into adulthood – fondly and zealously preserved, but out of date' (Kennett, 2001: 278).

In the new generation of cards typified by Oxford, Kennett saw post-Fordist tendencies, notably:

- a blurring of the social and economic/managerial objectives (Mayer, 1994) and subordination of the former to the latter (Jessop, 1992)
- flexible production processes through new machine and human systems
- flatter organisational structures –'unglued' organisations (Peters, 1992)
- increased departmental and sectoral co-operation
- increased demand for new, differentiated goods (Harvey, 1994)
- increased research and development, and investment in technology.

He judged, though, that the movement had not proceeded far as yet, and described the cards as 'Fordist proximity', which were struggling to achieve their potential. The new technology of smart cards is spreading. Southampton is undertaking a three-year experiment with Gothenberg and other continental cities and the card specialist Schlumberger. Perhaps because few public leisure services operate on as broad a base as in Britain, the concept has not been adopted widely elsewhere. The Netherlands would appear to be an exception, with residents' cards in at least thirteen cities. The Rotterdampas (Reitsma, 2000; Rotterdampas, 2000) is an example, with:

- 80–85,000 Passholders (about 11 per cent of the population)
- 75 per cent of Passholders were on low incomes or state benefits, 19 per cent being senior citizens with a pension, paying about £2.90, £7.35 and £36 sterling equivalent respectively
- discounts of a third off educational courses and between 10 and 50 per cent at libraries, theatres, cinemas, and shops, many more of which are seeking to join the scheme
- 56 per cent of holders use their Passes once a month or more often.

What can we conclude about leisure and loyalty cards? They are a flexible mechanism, which can be targeted and marketed in ways that are suitable for and can be designed by local officers and members. With modern swipe card systems any stigma of identification can be removed, and close monitoring of use by facility, time, activity or target group, and place of residence can be undertaken. One could go so far as to say that they are a managerial mechanism that can help implement social-democratic equality and inclusion policies. They can be the trigger or stimulus to a corporate management information system (Eady, 1994).

But in present circumstances they are often poorly designed, managed and monitored, operated as political tokens, often in isolation and under great constraint, and are under-performing both as a social policy action and a management tool. The great majority of politicians and managers want their scheme to be a redistributive policy tool, but cannot demonstrate its unit cost-efficiency or its effectiveness. Coalter (2000) criticised Collins and Kennett (1998) for presenting leisure cards as unproblematic attempts to combat social exclusion, failing to confront the fact of low take-up. I reject this, in the explanations set out above. Adapting Chesterton's wry comment about Christianity, leisure cards have been tried and found difficult, and mostly left as insensitive, under-resourced and tokenistic attempts at anti-poverty and inclusion policies. The few good examples show the potential but also the policy resolve and management skill needed.

Conclusion

With limitations due to the lack of specific data on money and leisure behaviour, I have tried to show in this chapter how poverty limits and excludes people from leisure. There are people excluded by factors of racism, ageism, gender-blindness, disablism, and geographic isolation, as we shall see in Chapters 5 to 10, but the bulk of people thus excluded are also poor. The SID discourse of social insertion in European, French and UK policy would argue that getting an adequate income through work is the most logical and effective action to combat poverty. I agree, *but*:

- this is not possible overnight, so there is a major transition period to come
- to date many of the jobs created have been part time, low skill and low paid, and employment/investment policies have to deal with this supply side; training can improve personal skills but the jobs have to be there
- still there will be people who will not be able to work at all, or for enough hours, or at pay rates which will lift them above the poverty threshold, for whom policies to offer sport and leisure as part of an adequate quality of life will still be needed.

Frisby et al. (1997) described how a mixture of price concessions and sympathetic action enabled groups of Canadian women and children to not only take part in sport, including skating and ice hockey, but also to take partial control of its management. The Leicester and Oxford case study and the Edinburgh pricing study showed that reducing price alone is not enough, even when price is a constraint: one has to have other supportive policies in marketing and outreach, in improving transport, etc. But the Audit Commission (1999) argued that pricing is a strategic tool for moving towards an overall policy of combating exclusion and meeting fiscal targets. While I support the New Labour idea of enabling everyone to work who wishes, there will be those who cannot do so, and and remain on low incomes and need economic help.

The case study above shows that cards can be an extremely effective – flexible, sensitive to local needs and capable of having built-in mechanisms for monitoring take up and use and to indicate outcomes and effectiveness. Once swipe and smart technologies are employed, they also avoid stigmatising groups who are not in paid work. These schemes, however, are not generally being taken seriously by politicians or top managers. Best Value reviews should expose these shortcomings and tokenism more widely and effectively than Collins and Kennett (1998) were able to do, and should challenge authorities to invest, market and manage more effectively, or to face the challenge of giving up the inclusion policy altogether as too difficult. A third option, of creating a more effective mechanism for tackling poverty as the core of exclusion, is not evident on current policy agendas.

Chapter 5

Exclusion, education and young people's sport

Introduction: Children and poverty

This chapter will investigate whether inequality starts where sport starts – in childhood – and flourishes – in youth. According to the Chancellor of the Exchequer, 'child poverty is a scar on the soul of Britain' (Brown, 1999). The Prime Minister, Tony Blair, had said, 'poverty should not be a birthright. Being poor should not be a life sentence. We need to break the cycle of disadvantage' (Blair, 1999), and he pledged to eradicate it in twenty years. Poverty affected 34 per cent of children in 1997–8, compared with 10 per cent in 1979, and was the highest in the European Union. Looking at the dynamics, Hill and Jenkins (2000) found that 14 per cent of pre-school and 8 per cent of primary age children were poor in every year from 1991 to 1996, compared with 6.7 per cent of the whole population. In the poorest fifth of households this meant that there had been no real increase in their spending on toys, children's clothing, shoes and fresh fruit and vegetables over three decades (Gregg et al., 1999).

Analysing the complex of factors in home and childhood is immensely complex; using the data for the March 1958 cohort of the National Child Development Study and hierarchical and stepwise models, Hobcraft (2000) looked at outcomes at ages 23 and 33. He came to some striking conclusions, when we relate them to the facts about poverty above and in Chapter 2, and to the persistence or fragility in sports interests below:

- educational qualifications show a strong relationship with every measure of disadvantage at both 23 and 33, after controlling for all sorts of factors
- the most frequent predictor of negative adult outcomes was childhood poverty
- mother's interest in education was more salient for women, father's for men
- low parental interest in school, frequent absence from school, and low educational test scores were quite influential on subsequent disadvantage

- the father being in Social Classes IV and V was a clear predictor of males growing up in the same class at 23 or 33, net of all other factors.

Bradshaw (2001), taking an even wider review of outcomes of poverty, divided them into four domains:

- *physical* – including mortality, morbidity, accidents, teenage pregnancy, child abuse
- *cognitive* – including educational attainment
- *behavioural* – including school exclusion, youth crime, smoking, alcohol, drugs, suicide, child labour
- *emotional* – including self-image, happiness, subjective well-being.

His analysis sought evidence as to whether these have got worse over the last twenty years, whether worse outcomes are associated with poverty in the UK, and whether poor children have fared worse than those who are not. Table 5.1 gives his answers for factors with definite evidence; for the others it was too mixed or not available.

Some improvements, and some declines, can be attributed to policy intervention, for example:

- infant mortality and child care
- dental health and fluoride in water
- fatal accidents – prevention policies

Table 5.1 Outcomes of child well being in the last 20 years

Outcomes worse	Outcomes improved
Over 20 years for all children	
Low birth weight; infections; homelessness; school exclusion; crime; girls smoking; alcohol; drugs; male suicide	Mortality; dental health; fatal accidents; teenage pregnancy; poor housing; educational achievement
For poor children in UK	
Mortality; most morbidity; fatal accidents; neglect/physical abuse; teenage pregnancy; poor housing; smoking; suicide; educational attainment; self-esteem	Crime; sexual abuse; homelessness; drugs; alcohol; child labour; unhappiness
Poor children worse than others over 20 years	
Child mortality; low birth-weight; accidents; teenage pregnancy; poor housing; educational attainment; suicide	Infant mortality; chronic illness; alcohol; drugs, child labour

Source: Bradshaw, 2001

- less freedom to roam from home in play
- teenage pregnancy and contraception
- poor children in road/home accidents
- low birth survival in ethnic minorities
- homelessness and limited/costly public housing
- growing differentials in school standards.

Bradshaw concluded that policy does matter, but it has to address not just outcomes but also underlying causes, instancing health and education. How can health intervention help low birth-weight, he asked, when a third of pregnant women depend on Income Support which has not increased in real terms over 20 years? He commented, 'the impact of poverty on educational attainment is profound [as numerous studies like Bynner, 1999, show], perhaps too profound to be overcome by investment in schools' (Bradshaw, 2001: 68). None of the studies mentioned so far incorporate leisure or sport, no doubt partly because they were seen as marginal, but also because there is no effective longitudinal data. The National Child Development and British Birth Cohort Studies contained no suitable questions.

The remainder of this chapter looks at children's successive involvements with sport – in play and primary schools, secondary schools, sports clubs and out-of-school clubs, and after dealing with higher levels of performance, a case study on linking schools and clubs. I do not deal here with the use of sport to integrate disaffected youth, or to prevent or treat delinquency, which are covered in Chapter 10.

The early years: Home, play and primary schooling

Children play, and in doing so learn about the environment, themselves, their friends and adults. Many playworkers argue that play is essential to human development and worthwhile in its own right. Because play develops motor and other physical, cognitive and affective abilities, it is delivered against a host of disciplinary theories (Child, 1985) and by professionals and volunteers in a wide variety of settings, including schools, homes, workplaces, and hospitals (Moore, 1986) by public, commercial and voluntary agencies. Local authorities deliver play services through housing, education, social and leisure services. After-school clubs are currently used by only 2 per cent of children but large government inputs mean that perhaps 1 in 4 primary children may have the opportunity after 2002. Many clubs do not promote equality of opportunity in terms of gender, race, or disability (Smith, 2000).

Although there were two short-term attempts at having a central advisory agency similar to Sport England or the Arts Council, both were terminated by government because of management shortcomings; the central vacuum (Collins, 1994) has been filled to an extent by a voluntary Children's Play Council (CPC).

Candler (1999) showed other models of provision and policy across the world, all divided and in his view falling short of giving children's play the status the United Nations wished in its Charter for the Rights of the Child.

Fear of 'stranger danger' and of traffic accidents means that the range and milieux of play has become more limited and home-centred since the 1950s, especially for young children and girls until their mid-teens (MORI, 2000). The classic study of the effects of children's play on development was by Schweinhart and Weikart (1997), who traced people in USA to their early 20s, and argued for better school and work outcomes for those with rich play lives. Drawing partly on this, the CPC (Children's Play Council, 2000: 13) listed the effects on children of a deprived play life as poorer abilities in: motor tasks, physical activities, dealing with trauma or stress, assessing and managing risks, and social skills (relationships, and dealing with conflicts and cultural differences). Several recent studies underline the myth that living in the countryside confers better play opportunities than in towns, Smith and Barker (2001: 175) arguing that they are limited 'owing to geographical isolation from other children, the privatisation of rural land, and fears over children's unsupervised use of public spaces.'

One of the few play schemes that has been evaluated is the Venture Centre for play and library clubs on a very deprived estate in Wrexham, providing for 4,700 under-5s, and 16,000 children a year in total. It also ran sixty trips and events a year. Parents attested to its value: 'the Venture has brought my children up; it's always there.' The evaluation team reckoned that it produced cost-effective family support and a valuable preventive service (Hill-Tout et al., 1995). Some other play interests in north-east Wales would claim that its very success has attracted disproportionate resources, leaving other schemes short.

The Secretary of State for Culture, Media and Sport, Chris Smith, claimed his Department was the *champion of play*, but under the Blair Government there are no less than twelve sources of funding from the DfEE, totalling £202m (Walker, *Guardian* 1 May 01). The main aim has been to free mothers and male single parents to work; so while childminders have declined in number (possibly because of higher standards for facilities and staffing), day nurseries and out-of-school clubs have been growing (Day Care Trust, 2001):

000 places	1997	2000
Childminders	385	320
Day nurseries	193	264
Out of school for 5–7s	79	141
Total	638	725

Allison (1999) expressed concern that there may be too much emphasis on cognitive or social care objectives and that play be judged too narrowly on that basis.

Children move from play to primary school and learn generic running, jumping, throwing and catching skills. Unlike many countries, Britain has never had a tradition of specialist primary physical education teachers; in 1999 only five per cent of schools had a full-time specialist teacher and 14 per cent a part-time one (MORI, 2000). Some question whether this slows down the development of specific sports skills in the two years before transfer to secondary schools. Also, the most common facilities were multi-purpose halls and playgrounds, though 7 per cent and 10 per cent of schools didn't have these and 17 per cent had no outdoor pitch or sports field, a situation Campbell (2000) called 'close to being a crime'. These have been improved by some education authorities providing specialist spaces in joint schemes with district and parish councils, with public use in the evenings and weekends, but only 36 per cent of teachers thought them adequate in 1999, three-quarters having access to a pool but only 1 in 7 to a sports hall. The Space for Sport and Arts programme should improve this situation.

A broad aspiration of the PE profession is to have two hours or more lessons a week for PE and sports, but between 1994 and 1999 there has been a sharp reverse to this aspiration, with a decline from 32 per cent to 11 per cent (MORI, 2001). It led Sue Campbell, Chief Executive of the Youth Sport Trust, to say, 'Primary school PE should be the foundation for life long health and sporting excellence. It is no good pumping millions of pounds into top sport when the base is crumbling away' (Campbell, 2000: 22). In 1994 a new National Curriculum order reduced the number of areas that had to be covered. The Qualifications and Curriculum Authority (1999: 4) commented that three-quarters of schools reported a static or reduced 1998–9 budget, such that many wondered whether they would have enough money for equipment and in-service training, resources having been *directed at numeracy and literacy strategies*.

Table 5.2 gives some of the basic data on sport in and out of school for children in years 2 to 6. It shows:

- a stable situation in terms of range of activity, with a greater focus on individual rather than team activities
- a widening range of out of school activity in the average 6.5 hours a week spent on this, with some increase in extra-curricular and competitive sport
- club membership is dominated by soccer and swimming
- a high level of enjoyment and wish to do well, and
- a gendered difference already appearing, with more girls not seeing themselves as sporty or receiving parental encouragement, and disliking aspects of sport.

Table 5.2 Sport for children of primary age, 1999

Item	Boys	Girls	Change 1994–9
In lessons			
Average no. of sports done at least once a year	7.4	7.6	+0.1
Average no. of sports done 10+ times a year	3.3	3.5	none
Out of school			
Average no. of sports done at least once a year	10.1	9.5	+0.3
Average no. of sports done 10+ times a year	4.7	4.5	+0.2
Place (%)			
Extra-curricular, school	45	38	+9
Sports club, outside school	52	32	+4
Youth club/other organisation	46	51	−2
Competition (%)			
Against other schools	28	25	+4
Between clubs	28	10	+5
At national/international level	3	3	+5
Attitudes (% agree strongly)			
I enjoy PE and games lessons in school	71	64	none
I enjoy sport and games in my leisure time	77	63	+1
I am better at PE/games than most subjects	30	17	+1
I want to be successful at sport	70	47	+1
My family encourage me in sport/exercise	60	50	+4
I am a 'sporty' type of person	56	36	+3
I have sporting heroes	81	52	na
Attitudes (% mind a lot)			
Getting cold and wet	12	21	−2
Getting hot, sweaty, dirty	7	18	+1
Having to change into/out of sports clothes	8	14	none
Going outside in bad weather	14	29	−3

Source: MORI, 2000

What this survey did not measure, however, was the intensity of exercise; moderate or vigorous is necessary to get health and fitness benefits. The Institute of Sport and Recreation Management (2000) summarised a range of evidence for the emergence of a generation of 'couch potatoes':

- children are becoming fatter, with 4 per cent of 4-year-olds and 17 per cent of 15-year-olds obese, more because of less exercise than fattier or sweeter diets
- the proportion of children under 17 walking to school has fallen to 1 in 2 in 1986–96, and only 1 per cent cycle
- 96 per cent of intense activity for 6- to 10-year-olds lasted less than 15 seconds, while a quarter of 11- to 16-year-olds spent more than 4 hours

a day watching TV, and 1 in 10 boys of this age spent more than ten hours a week playing computer games.

In the Nestlé Family Monitor survey of parents (MORI, 2000), 80 per cent agreed sport was a vital part of a child's development, but almost as many felt that contemporary children were less active than they had been as children, despite 3 out of 5 agreeing that opportunities had increased in the last thirty years. More parents from social groups D and E agreed that academic subjects always should take precedence over PE, than parents from groups A and B (74 compared with 59 per cent).

The reduction in the amount of PE in the curriculum alarmed members of Speednet, the consortium of UK PE organisations:

> The indicators are loud and clear that more children may be literate and computer literate, but many more than usual will remain physically illiterate.
>
> (British Association of Advisers and Lecturers in PE)

> We are in danger of changing the old quotation to read 'a healthy mind in an unhealthy body'.
>
> (Pat Smith, National Council for School Sport)

At primary level sport is seen by most children as fun, becoming more serious in secondary school; gender inequity emerges, with a sample of Welsh girls saying that they did not have enough opportunities in clubs, many of their interests being in sports like gymnastics, trampolining and swimming where memberships tend to terminate younger. Too many clubs still expressed interest only in those with marked gifts in sport (Hutson, Thomas and Sutton, 1995). There seems to be no evidence of issues regarding disability, ethnicity and poverty or geographically concentrated deprivation, but Sport England commented (MORI, 2001: foreword), 'the decline in PE curriculum time . . . will affect children from less well off backgrounds the most . . . who will be least likely to be able to take up the opportunities offered by extra-curricular and club sport.'

Developing sports interests: Secondary schools and clubs

Youth is seen often as a transition from school and childhood to work and adulthood, and those who struggle or drop out of work are deviant, or even an 'underclass' according to Charles Murray, who also claimed that they ended there by their own (moral) choice. The numerous contributors on youth and social exclusion to MacDonald (1997) overwhelmingly rejected this view as labelling and demeaning youth's rights of citizenship. They spoke of structural influences on their opportunities; Baldwin, Coles and Mitchell (in MacDonald, 1997) strongly emphasising these for two particularly vulnerable groups – young people in care, and disabled young people.

Rees and Miracle began a recent challenging review of sport and education literature thus:

> Sport in schools has been credited with teaching values of sportsmanship and fair play to participants, increasing athletes' educational aspirations, developing a sense of community and group cohesion amongst students, helping to reduce dropout rates, and giving poor and minority youth access to higher education.
>
> (Rees and Miracle, 2000: 277)

In the American adaptation of the English public school model, Rees and Miracle accepted evidence that sport reinforces academic progress and reduces drop-out at High School level, but that results for career development (whether academic or sporting), and equality of opportunity by race, gender and class are much more ambiguous at college and university. They claimed the research suffered generally from a divorce from broader educational sociology studies.

Sport flowers from physical recreation in childhood and youth, and throughout the world thereafter declines in terms of penetration in the population. In consequence, sport is more often associated in government with youth and education than any other function. Sport has become increasingly entrenched in school curricula in England, Australia, Ireland, Canada, and the USA, with the growth of programmes like the National Junior Sports Programme in England and Aussie Sport in Australia. Meanwhile, PE has not been able to establish a clear role for itself, having not resolved the competing aims of preparation for competitive sport, developing an interest in recreational lifetime activity or in health-related exercise (Houlihan, 1997).

Hardman and Marshall (2000: 66) reviewed the state of PE around the world, and their summary was gloomy: at the very least, in many countries PE has been pushed into a defensive position. It is suffering from:

- decreasing curriculum time allocation
- budgetary controls with inadequate financial, material and personnel resources
- low subject status and esteem, occupying a tenuous place in the school curriculum, and not accepted on a par with seemingly superior academic subjects concerned with developing a child's intellect
- marginalisation and under-valuation by authorities.

So far as inclusion was concerned, 4 out of 5 countries thought it had been achieved for gender but barely half for disability. Ethnicity was not covered.

Table 5.3 Sport for children of secondary age, 1999

Item	Boys	Girls	Change 1994–9
In lessons			
Average no. of sports done at least once a year	9.3	9.4	+0.1
Average no. of sports done 10+ times a year	3.7	4.0	none
Out of school			
Average no. of sports done at least once a year	11.3	10.3	+0.3
Average no. of sports done 10+ times a year	4.8	3.6	+0.2
Place (%)			
Extra-curricular, school	36	41	+9
Sports club, outside school	35	36	+4
Youth club/other organisation	53	50	−2
Competition (%)			
Against other schools	38	29	+4
Between clubs	31	18	+5
At national/international level	19	9	+5
Attitudes (% agree strongly)			
I enjoy PE and games lessons in school	62	42	none
I enjoy sport and games in my leisure time	71	45	+1
I am better at PE/games than most subjects	38	20	+1
I want to be successful at sport	60	37	+1
My family encourage me in sport/exercise	41	29	+4
I am a 'sporty' type of person	52	28	+3
I have sporting heroes	80	64	na
Attitudes (% mind a lot)			
Getting cold and wet	10	20	−2
Getting hot, sweaty, dirty	11	23	+1
Having to change into/out of sports clothes	10	14	none
Going outside in bad weather	17	32	−3

Source; MORI, 2000

Indeed, until 1994 there was no English survey of participation in school sport until the Sports Council commissioned the Office of Population, Censuses and Surveys (Mason, 1995); a similar survey was done in Northern Ireland (Kremer et al., 1997); but neither gave attention to class or material resource differences. The English update survey in 1999 (MORI, 2000) showed that all secondary schools had at least one full-time specialist PE teacher (and usually three or four), only 7 in 10 have access to an indoor sports hall, and 2 in 5 to an indoor pool. The equivalent data for sports participation and attitudes already discussed for primary schools is shown for secondary ages in Table 5.3.

This shows a wider range of sports in secondary school and a similar small increase since 1994. The increases in out of school sport were likewise larger. The gap in attitudes between girls and boys becomes more marked, including the issue of sporting heroes/role models. Flintoff and Scraton (2001: 18) point out that for girls 'many activity contexts, such as mixed PE classes, remain controlled largely by men and boys,' that there is much macho, destructive male behaviour in PE, and that there is a gap between the school programmes and young women's active lifestyles out of school. The Institute of Youth Sport is seeking to address the teaching and management issues for girl-friendly PE, and in successful pilot schools this entailed (Kirk et al., 2000):

- changing traditional teacher–learner interactions
- changing subject matter to support task-oriented rather than competitive/ ego-oriented styles
- tangible support from colleagues and managers
- planning, commitment, flexibility, and effort by teachers.

Subsequently, MacPhail et al. (2001) surveyed the opinions of 600 young people aged 14 to 18 and 2 in 5 wanted a wider range of choice in schools and clubs, at levels appropriate to their skills.

Penney and Evans (1999: 124) were very strong in their judgement on the National Curriculum, as continuing to feature 'disproportionate attention to a narrow range of competitive team games, sex differentiated programmes, and teaching characterised by a limited range of teaching methods and strategies.' Hendry (1992) reinforced this view. In Wales 86 per cent of schools claimed to teach health-related fitness in 1997–8 (up from 70 per cent in 1993–4), but divided between PE, a specific module and Personal and Social Education (Sports Council for Wales, n.d.). Nonetheless, the Sports Council for Wales expressed the same concerns about timetable time, facilities, lack of extra-curricular provision and budgets.

As children get older, interest in sport starts to diverge; casual participation drops off for boys and girls in and out of school; the range of serious participation is sustained for boys but drops more markedly for girls, as the 1999 data shows:

	Boys		Girls	
	Years 7–9	Years 10–11	Years 7–9	Years 10–11
In school				
10 times in last year	3.7	3.8	4.3	3.5
Out of school				
At least once in last year	11.7	10.5	10.7	9.4
10 times in last year	4.6	5.0	3.7	3.3

Sport England's (2001) *Sport Equity Index* showed that by Key Stage 3 girls' participation was down to 90 per cent of boys', while children from ethnic minorities at Key Stages 1, 2, and 3 participate at only 81, 89 and 86 per cent of white boys respectively, though recovering to 96 per cent by Key Stage 4.

Part of this divergence of interest by gender may be due to the growth in popularity of physical education/sports studies as examination subjects – 110,000 sat GCSE exams in 2002 (*Guardian* 22 Aug 02, page 10) (2.8 per cent of all boy candidates and 1.3 per cent of girls). Fifty six per cent achieved A*–C grades, compared with 58 per cent in all subjects. For the AS levels introduced in 2002, 24,000 candidates sat (2.4 per cent of the total), and 27.5 per cent achieved A and B grades, compared to 31.5 per cent in all subjects. Finally at A level, 17,100 sat (3.3 per cent of all male candidates and 1.7 per cent of all female, sustaining the gender difference). Of these, 29.5 per cent gained A and B grades compared to 42.6 per cent of all candidates, a gain of 42 per cent over 2001 (*Guardian* 15 Aug 02, page 10).

Apart from the constraints related to schools already mentioned, young people in Scotland (Centre for Leisure Research, 1999) mentioned first the same lack of time that adults offer – 26 per cent for boys, but 33 per cent for girls, the latter indicating a greater responsibility for housework and child care than boys. Both sexes mentioned homework and part-time jobs, essential to the economy of poorer households, though much of the work was low skill, low paid and even illegal (Mizen et al., 2000). They also mentioned 'nowhere to play near home' (1 in 4), and 'costs too much' (1 in 8).

So far as time devoted to PE in the secondary curriculum is concerned, 61 per cent of year 7 to 9 children had two or more hours, but this dropped to only 34 per cent for years 10 to 11, as the academic demands grew. This was a reduction since 1994 of 5 per cent and 2 per cent respectively. The Health Education Authority's recommendation for physical activity for all primary youngsters was a hour of moderate physical activity a day, starting with half an hour for the sedentary; for secondary children it recommends activities vigorous enough twice a week to enhance and maintain muscle strength, flexibility and bone health. The government has agreed (Social Exclusion Unit, 2001) that every child should have access to two hours of activity a week in total, in and out of school.

Stone et al. (1998) examined eleven secondary school-age studies to look at outcomes, and found some improvement of knowledge and attitudes to physical activity, but mixed results for increased activity. A study in Olso following up 13-year-olds at age 25 found early physical activity levels were predictive of adult behaviour. Nonetheless, Sport England (MORI, 2001: 14) assessed the situation as 'a solid platform for promoting the value of sport and exercise among young people', but attributed the girls' reduced interest to lack of family support, lack of role models, less confidence in their ability, less interest in competition, and the features they disliked, as listed in Tables 5.3 and 5.4.

Does the area of residence or the type of school make a difference? Educationalists in the UK have voiced concerns that an 'open market' in which parents choose which school to enrol children in, and the publication of league tables of exam results, will lead to social polarisation. Two accepted measures of this are the percentage of children obtaining free school meals and the percentage awarded five or more GCSE passes at grade C or above: while the national aggregate figures showed improvements, Gibson and Asthana used local catchment figures for schools to demonstrate that:

> within local markets . . . high status schools are drawing to themselves the most socially advantaged pupils within their catchment areas and that this will in due course, and perhaps already does, mean that they are able to improve their GCSE results faster than their local 'competitors'.
>
> (Gibson and Asthana, 1999: 315)

Again for sport and PE, there is no good data on geographical or social class or cultural differences.

As for investment in schools, while there is evidence that it can improve academic outcomes and popularity with parents, we cannot be sure that this will improve social inclusiveness; Mortimore and Whitty (cited in Sparkes, 1999) suggested:

> If all schools performed as well as the best schools, the stratification of attainment of achievement by social class would be even more stark than it is now. This would happen because socially advantaged children in highly effective schools would achieve even more than they do now in less conducive environments and the gap between them and their less advantaged peers would increase.
>
> (Mortimore and Whitty, cited in Sparkes, 1999: 21)

The UK has one of the lowest levels of educational qualification in Europe, and the government has set a tough target that every pupil should obtain a GCSE. Two schemes have been devised to use the attraction of sport and leisure to encourage participation in education, aimed particularly at those who are under-performing or truanting. 'Playing for Success' set up study support centres for pupils at Key Stages 2 to 3 (10 to 14 years) at professional soccer clubs where in six four-hour sessions a week they can learn literacy, numeracy, and IT, and link soccer to geography, European studies and other topics. The courses are run by a manager and college or university students as assistants. In return, the pupils get to meet professional players. Sharp et al. (1999) monitored seven of the twenty-three clubs operating in the first year, who together took 4,934 pupils from 209 schools, just under a third with special educational needs, and discovered:

- most attended more than four in five of the sessions, and there was no problem with filling the lists
- there was nothing pupils did not enjoy, and their schools would be glad to take part again
- self-confidence, self-esteem and attitudes to learning improved and on average reading score were improved by 6 months for primary and 8 months for secondary pupils.

Getting sponsorship and the involvement of professional players, unless special sessions were arranged, proved problematic. But the scheme reached its target group and achieved its aims.

Consequently, it has been extended to the lower division soccer clubs and professional cricket, rugby union and league, and basketball clubs.

Connexions is a wide-ranging programme to support learning in the 16 to 19 age range, and features individual mentoring. For every course a young person attends, they can accumulate credits that are recorded on a computer database. These credits can then be traded against training or material costs, or via a Connexions smart card for leisure goods or services, for which DfEE have sought national sponsors. In the first year at the time of writing, pilots are being run in eight places, with some 31,000 young people and 350 sponsors. It is not clear how it will interact with local authority discount cards (Chapter 4).

Dropping out or sustaining interest? Sports clubs and out-of-school schemes

When moving into the adult community, young people need information and confidence to access opportunities; they also have lower purchasing power than adults. Thus, in 1997 Sport England (2000) found:

- 76 per cent of authorities had a policy in their management contracts regarding young people, but only 19 per cent had specified targets for throughput
- 73 per cent of sports halls and swimming pools in England offered concessions to full-time students, and 67 per cent to under-16s
- 33 per cent of hall space and only 19 per cent of pool space was programmed for schools and young people under 19 and less than 3 per cent of users were young people holding discount cards.

One of the main concerns of the Wolfenden report (Central Council for Physical Recreation, 1960) that led to the setting up of the Sports Council and introduction of the Sport for All programmes was that provision for youth sport was poorer than in many European states, and that getting further education and training, and getting married and having children, led to drop-out and a 'post-school gap' – *a manifest break* between school and adult participation. Subsequent research showed that the position was more complex than this, but that there were many constraints on the transition to adult sport. Nevertheless, drop-out in adolescence 'is reported from all countries where researchers have studied the phenomenon', recorded de Knop et al. (1996) in a collection of studies from nineteen countries.

The Sports Council provided two experiments in helping to sustain participation and its health and social benefits. First, information, coaching, tournaments and taster sessions for local sports were provided in Streatham and Hastings. Wade (1987) showed that these had an immediate effect, but could not be sustained without new resources. In Active Lifestyles, coaches in Coventry were brought into schools, the curriculum was widened beyond traditional sports to include health-related fitness, and information and support was provided. Follow-up surveys showed that participation in existing sports was substantially sustained as the school leavers hoped, but that far fewer new sports were started than had been intended (Sports Council/Coventry City Council, 1989). Health Education Authority targets for intervention to promote physical activity are aimed at girls aged 12 to 18, youth of low socioeconomic status, and adolescents aged 16 to 18, including those from ethnic minorities, with disabilities, or with clinical conditions like obesity, diabetes or depression (Health Education Authority, 1998: 6).

Undoubtedly, involvement in out of school sport has grown substantially from 1971 (CLR, 1999): in 1971, 30 per cent of boys and 57 per cent of girls did no out of school sport; by 1994 only 18 per cent of boys did sport on less than one day a week in term time, and 26 per cent of girls. Issues about girls' opportunities and the quality of the participation experienced remain, especially in deprived areas. The work of Roberts and Brodie (1992: 81) in six cities clearly showed that 'the number of sports played when young was the best predictor of whether individuals would continue to play into adulthood', i.e., having a portfolio of skills and interests is the best preparation for overcoming the changes and constraints of adulthood, and a broad-based curriculum is the best ensurer of this. This was also the consensus of a Carnegie Corporation conference in the US (Poinsett, 1996: 117). But the Qualifications and Curriculum Authority (1999: 3) reported that in many schemes of school PE 'little attention is given to the needs of the least and most able pupils.'

In Germany, Anders (1982) reported a much larger drop-out from sport among lower social class youth, from 65 per cent at 21 years of age to 25 per cent by 25, compared with 55 to 60 per cent in middle-class groups. Roberts and Fagan (1999) examined youth leisure in three post-Communist East European states, and found that traditional class and gender divisions survived, even with reduced incomes and opportunities, indicating their strength of influence. In Ontario, consultants for the interestingly titled Ministry of Citizenship, Culture and Recreation argued that the service gaps and community concerns centred on 12- to 17-year-olds (SMC Management Services Inc., 1998) and needed new leadership and focused initiatives.

These have been called 'the dangerous years,' and were the focus of the Action Sport projects that launched the sports development sub-profession (Rigg, 1986). Initially they focused on young people, especially those unemployed, and involved three principles

- getting into young people's peer network rather than expecting them to come to publicly provided centres
- working with new partners (not necessarily for sport) linked to youth and later to other target groups and
- using sites and buildings already available in communities.

Later schemes were aimed at women, ethnic minorities, older people, workers, health-at-risk groups, PE teachers and their pupils, and disabled people (McDonald and Tungatt, 1991). Similar Roving Leader programmes were run in Chicago in the 1930s, New York, San Francisco, Los Angeles, Buffalo, and other cities in the 1960s, and San Antonio in the 1990s (Crompton and Witt, 1997).

Schemes in Leicester, Birmingham and Derwentside for young unemployed were evaluated by Glyptis, whose conclusions coincided with Rigg's on Action Sport:

> the idea that sport can contribute substantially to the lives of most unemployed people is unfounded. The idea that leisure in general can contribute is more plausible. . . . From the evidence to date leading a full life demands a source of structure. Leisure cannot provide it. Leisure can, however, fulfil its present role as part of a balanced lifestyle, if a source of structure and purpose exists alongside it. If work in the conventional employment sense cannot survive in sufficient measure for all, then work is the concept to be examined.
>
> (Glyptis, 1989: 159, 161)

Nine years later, from an Australian perspective, Lobo came to similar conclusions:

> many young people live with deprivation, impermanence and temporary relationships in new ways. Emergent lifestyles include intermittent employment, the establishment of middle term careers, welfare claimant 'careers', extended full-time education, pre-marital cohabitational arrangements, and single parenthood.
>
> (Lobo, 1998: 8)

One of the constraints to post-school sport is that until recently many sports clubs were interested only in the few talented young people who found their own way in, or were spotted as a result of high performances in school or junior competitions. Now many governing bodies make a much greater attempt to set up 'youth-friendly' clubs (de Knop et al., 1995). Many Welsh young people stated that they found sports clubs 'intimidating' and 'unwelcoming' places. Few clubs actively recruited junior members, most having been introduced only through parents who were already members, or sport teachers associated with particular clubs. Only 47 per cent of 11- to 16-year-olds belonged to youth organisations, with half that number belonging to sports clubs. The study concluded that:

> this level of membership indicates that where community links do exist, the base for children's involvement appears to be very small and narrow. If continuity of participation is to be achieved when children leave school, then the strengthening of the children's section within clubs will be a necessary condition.
>
> (Sports Council for Wales, n.d.: 28)

In Belgium, although membership was being sustained, de Knop et al. (1995) suggested that there was something of a crisis in clubs from a shortage of volunteers, small numbers of professional staff, and competition from other forms of leisure including commercial sports and fitness providers. Drawing also on Dutch experience, de Knop and de Martelaer (2001) suggested clubs must ensure more varied and quality-assured staff and programmes designed for youth's objectives, and with youth input. Running Sport is Sport England's voluntary and less formal version of this.

But this involvement is easier in Denmark (Thomson, 1998) and Germany (Heinemann and Schwab, 1999), where municipal support is more generous and better guaranteed than in Britain. These much larger clubs (averaging 300 but sometimes reaching 3,000 or more members) mean that youth leaders, coaches and mentors can more easily be found and dedicated to youth work than in Britain's small clubs, which average only forty-three members. Many, such as single-side soccer and most table tennis clubs, are smaller than this. Larger size allows specialisation of roles, but also makes the clubs a more secure place to invest public money in facilities and especially professionals – German clubs in the largest category may have eight to ten paid workers, as managers, coaches, groundsmen and animateurs. In Finland there is a long tradition of involvement of parents in sports clubs, which has a strong influence on children (Seppanen, 1982, and Heinila, 1989).

The Department for Culture, Media and Sport (1999) (2000) has floated the idea that there should be 'hub' and 'satellite' clubs, but imposing this, even with the 'bribery' of grants, would be anathema to Britain's fiercely parochial, independent club system. In some sports an 'elite' group of larger, well-endowed clubs has emerged and is recognised. But governing bodies and their clubs must be persuaded to develop this cluster-type structure of their own will. Likewise, a new interest in large multi-sports clubs has revived, but these, too, are an exception, and have not come about in the same way as on the continent, where they sprang from urban/rural workers' or religious movements in which sport was part of the social contract (Riordan and Kruger, 1996). This has hardly happened in Britain except in a small way, mainly in now-defunct industries – notably coal and the railways. The British workers' movement was preoccupied with hours of work, holidays, pay and occupational health (Jones, 1988). Again, such clubs have to grow organically, and cannot be 'manufactured'.

A range of schemes have been devised to link children with sports clubs or youth groups, many of which are out of school clubs – sometimes at lunchtimes, but more often in the 'latch-key' period between the end of lessons and when working parents come home. By 2000, seven out of 10 English schools provided seven or more out of school activities, involving primary children two hours a week and secondary children three hours a week. These included homework, but also PE/sports which was the most popular choice (by 2 in 5 boys, but less than 3 in 10 girls – Department for Education and Employment, 2000a). These happen in affluent areas through parental interest but in poorer areas and where youth is 'disadvantaged/at risk' it needs deliberate interventions by public or voluntary agencies in partnership.

Witt (2000) examined the effects of three out of school programmes for year 3 to 6 children in Dallas, Texas, compared with pupils who received high and low supervision at home. There were no differences in school grades, but in terms of self-perception and 'protective factors' (like an ability to handle conflicts and deal with others), the programme participants had higher scores at the end of a year than the high supervision children, while scores for the low supervision group declined.

Team Sport Scotland was an attempt under Scottish Sports Council leadership to promote twelve team sports inside and outside schools in 1991–6, prior to the current wave of activity. It achieved (Alstead, 1996):

- 1,200 events involving over 100,000 children
- the introduction of small-sided games in six of the sports, including two specially devised for netball and shinty
- the increase in qualified women coaches from 23 to over 2,000
- the development of a network of sport-specific development officers in nine of the sports
- a stable partnership team which provided a 'lighthouse' to guide decision-making (Allison and Taylor, 1997: 23).

Nonetheless, more female coaches, participants and club activities were needed. Penney and Harris (1997), immediately in the wake of *Sport: Raising the Game*, argued for England and Wales to have a more balanced extra-curricular programme in terms of games and non-competitive activities, and in gender terms, and for better resourcing.

The value of sport in diversion and 'character-building', explored much more in Chapter 10 in relation to delinquency, is evidenced in its role in summer play schemes and, especially in America, in the growing number of after-school clubs demanded as in more household both parents work by choice or necessity. Studies in Texas by Baker and Witt (1996), Witt (1997), Bundrick and Witt (1998), and Witt (1999), show short-term benefits to self-esteem, scholastic endeavour, parental satisfaction, and to a limited extent reduced involvement in minor crime. Hellison (Martinek and Hellison, 1997) has spent a career developing the use of PE and physical activity as a means of building resilience and moral values in young people. The use of individual, team and outdoor adventure sports in work with underprivileged youth has been likewise documented in France (Anstett and Sachs, 1995; Charrier, 1997; Hindermeyer, 1998) and Belgium (Stassen, 1996), including those with alcohol, drug, or other health problems, and with a focus sometimes on migrant communities (de Knop et al., 1997).

The voluntary youth movement and statutory Youth Service has had a strong role in sport traditionally (Stead and Swain, 1987), but suffered an £8m (2 per cent) cut in the mid-1990s (English Sports Council, 1997). There is no link between youth and sport in EU policy, and Becker et al. (2000) recommended that new experiential learning programmes be created in the European Voluntary Service and Youth for Europe exchange programmes. The overwhelming majority of a large number of English schemes submitted to Policy Action Team 10 claimed benefits to youth, but few had any evaluation data on outcomes – those with evidenced outcomes are highlighted in Table 5.4.

To summarise this section, Roberts (1983: 176) believed that it must be accepted that there can be no single form of leisure provision that will voluntarily attract all young people: 'There is no "right" club or centre which, once . . . marketed will capture and retain all the 11–21 year olds, or any other age span.' From research to date, the need for a full understanding of why and how teenagers either resist or co-operate with efforts from the adult world remains incomplete. What has been made clear, however, is that co-ordination between sectors is necessary if youth provision is to be enhanced. White and Rowe (1996) summed up this issue:

> Although there are many imaginative and innovative schemes for promoting youth sport in England, provision is variable and the development of sport for young people has been hampered by a lack of vision and poor co-ordination between different agencies.
>
> (White and Rowe, 1996, cited in de Knop et al., 1996: 124)

Thus whether or not there is a participation gap or just a slide, there is undoubtedly an institutional gap on leaving school. Most children are taught to change a fuse, use a bank, fill in tax returns and attend unemployment

Table 5.4 Some good practices in youth sport

Scheme	Partners	Include private sector	Skilled leaders	Outcomes	Source
Youth Charter for Sport, Mosside/Toxteth	YCS + many others	yes	yes	Sustained participation Community spirit/morale Locally trained leaders Jobs/income generation	YCS, 1998
Charlton Athletic RaceEquality, Charlton, London	Charlton Football Club + many others	yes	yes	Community confidence Locally trained leaders Crime prevention? Changed attitudes	CARE, 1998
Oldham MBC Soccer Scheme, and others for ethnic minorities	NACRO + others	yes	yes	1,200 new participants Changed attitudes 100+ new coaches/leaders – all sustained? Achieved in similar netball scheme proposed?	NACRO, 1998
Waterville children's projects, Meadowell, Newcastle	North Tyneside Borough Council + many others	yes	yes	Sustained participation Trained youth leaders Reduced crime in Meadowell	WCP, 1998 CPC, 1999
Deerness Valley Gym Club	City of Durham	?	yes	Continued international success of 100-member club in mining area	DCC, 1999

Sources: Mosside/Toxteth: Youth Charter for Sport, 1998; Charlton Athletic: Charlton Athletic Race Equality, 1998; Oldham: National Association for the Care and Resettlement of Offenders, 1998; Meadowell: Waterville Children's Project, 1998 and Children's Play Council, 2000; Deerness Valley: Durham County Council, 1999

Table 5.5 Schools' involvement in Sport England initiatives

Scheme	Primary (%)	Secondary (%)	% rated good at improving pupils' sport
TOP Play/TOP Sport	66	27	75
Sportsmark/SportsmarkGold	n/a	42	55
Coaching for teachers	16	36	90
Lottery Sports Fund/School Community Sports Initiative	6	38	61
Champion Coaching	3	27	73
Sporting Ambassadors	43	7	43
Base	77	74	From 7 to 71

offices or job centres, but few are given consumer skills to find their way through the sport and leisure maze, with its gaps and tenuous links. In the next section we look at a scheme intended to bridge the gap between schools and clubs, and to provide a continuing pathway for young sportspeople.

Since introducing its policy for youth sport in 1993, Sport England has introduced and re-branded a whole host of programmes and products, viz

- TOP PLAY – Youth Sport Trust equipment and training for teachers
- Sportsmark/Sportsmark Gold – pound for pound award schemes funded by DCMS to reward and help develop schools' links with communities, clubs and sponsors
- Coaching for teachers – training
- Lottery funding – with higher rates for priority areas and schools open to the community
- Champion Coaching – already described
- Sporting Ambassadors – professional sports people as role models.

Table 5.5 shows to what extent these had been taken up by schools by 1999, and how far PE teachers thought they contributed. They have now, of course, been added to by Specialist Sports Colleges funded by the DfEE (83 at the time of writing, but to become 250 by 2004), Sports Co-ordinators in 1,000 schools by the same date, and the Space for Sports and Arts grants. In November 2000 Kate Hoey (Department for Culture, Media and Sport, 2000) announced the formation of the School Sport Alliance, comprising the DCMS, DfEE, New Opportunities Fund, and the Youth Sport Trust, to set 'a strategic framework'. What Houlihan (1999) called 'a crowded policy space' has become even more crowded! It remains to be seen whether central government, the new Active Sport partnerships or individual schools and communities can co-ordinate this to good effect.

Developing commitments: Sports performance and excellence

Leisure is an important part of youth lifestyle – consuming 14 per cent of household expenditures for under-25s, but unequally – 37 per cent for males and 23 per cent for females (Mathieson and Summerfield, 2000). For sport, Hendry (1992: 71) suggested that 'school sports will be most liked by pupils who are highly skilled competitive and achievement-oriented.' The Performance and Excellence in Nottinghamshire Sport Scheme, and schemes now multiplying under the World Class Start programmes of Sport England with Lottery funding, are about structured talent identification and nurture, not only using a more professional cadre of coaches but also specialised sports scientists (physiologists, psychologists, biomechanists, nutritionists), physiotherapists and medics.

The much-vaunted programmes of the Eastern bloc in the Cold War era was as much attributable to hard training and harder competition as to science, and was not backed up by longitudinal studies (Thomson and Beavis, 1985), but with the Institutes of Sport in Australia, Canada, West Germany and the UK more similarities are evident (Oakley and Green, 2000):

- a clear understanding between the several agencies involved and good formal co-ordination and informal co-operation administrators, coaches and scientists in an athlete-centred model including lifestyle support and preparation for retirement from competition
- effective identification and monitoring of athletes
- well-structured competitive programme with continual international exposure
- accessible and specialised facility provision, and
- adequate funding for people and infrastructure.

As Gratton (1996) remarked, Britain seeks to support excellence in a wide range of sports, as it does in participation. This may underpin its relative decline in Olympic fortunes. In the 1980s and 1990s Australia, Canada, Italy, Spain, and the Netherlands made strategic investments in identifying and preparing athletes. In the UK in the 1990s, after decades of resisting specialist provision in schools for other than drama and music, the Department for Education and Employment supported programmes for specialist sport, arts, and technology colleges, providing money for extra staff (teaching or coaching), and for programmes to extend participation and improve performance. A report on the first twenty-six colleges after two years (Office for Standards in Education, 2000) demonstrated:

- improved links with feeder primary/high schools and sports clubs
- in-service training of teachers and coaches

• improved examination results (a result shared with other forms of specialist college).

In relation to improved links, it has to be pointed out that candidates had to show good links in their business plan to be selected. The target for sports colleges is 150 out of 7,000 secondary schools. One thousand will have sports co-ordinators whose work is meant to extend to a cluster of schools. When students get into full-time further and higher education, they are in a privileged environment, with subsidised or free facilities, and opportunities to self-organise specialist clubs. Loughborough University is possibly the most developed example, with sixty clubs in its Athletic Union. It is not surprising that both sports activity rates, at 76.3 per cent in the last four weeks compared with 62.5 per cent for 16- to 19-year-olds in general (excluding walking) and sports club membership, were the highest in the population in 1996 (the latter at 18.1 per cent compared with 8.1 per cent – Rowe, Moore and Mori, 1999).

Nonetheless, at these ages in the population as a whole, a gap between doing enough moderate or vigorous activity to gain health benefits and actual participation had already appeared (Mathieson and Summerfield, 2000):

	% thinking they were doing enough to keep fit 1998		% undertaking physical activity 5 days a week 1995–97	
Ages	16–19	20–24	16–19	20–24
Males	66	44	53	49
Females	44	37	29	29

Higher education is becoming, as in America, a base for elite sports training with the bulk of the specialist facilities for the UK Institute of Sport, with £120m of investment in facilities. In 1997 Sir Roger Bannister predicted that 1 in 3 elite athletes would come from higher education. But access to higher education is socio-economically biased (Platt, *Guardian* 13 Aug 00):

%	Professional	Skilled	Semi/unskilled
15–19s with 2 A levels	40	12	8
With 2 A levels going to University	82	78	71

This bias is reflected geographically in the affluence of households in an area (Higher Education Funding Council for England, 1997).

In Britain, Searle (1993: 5) reported on 'gaps which leave even gold medallists in debt or dependent on parental or spouse support.' Of the 1992 Olympic squad, 45 per cent were in debt to an average of £5,000 because of sports costs, only 38 per cent had ever obtained prize money or sponsorship, and those that did only averaged £1,000 a year. The Lottery gave British athletes in the late 1990s the sort of 'broken time' payments in lieu of salary and support costs that had been common elsewhere for years. In 2000–1 this World Class Performance Funding (WCPF) was distributed as set out below; the provision for paralympic sport had been boosted by great success in the Sydney Games (UK Sport, 2000).

	No. of athletes	No. of coaches	£m	
17 sports	488	58.5	13.63	over £1m for athletics
11 sports for disabled	166	14	2.87	over £1m for athletics, cycling, rowing, sailing, swimming

With an average subsistence award of £7,000, nine out of ten athletes agreed that WCPF *had made a significant difference to their ability to train and compete*, but nearly half felt it was still insufficient (UK Sport, 2001).

We will see in the Nottinghamshire case study how social area and household differences divided opportunities unevenly for the performance squads (Buller and Collins, 2000). Unless there is a sustained effort of redistribution, the next generation of sports performers will reproduce the current inequalities. Rowley (1992a, b) demonstrated the imbalance of middle class support for his promising young athletes in swimming, tennis, and to a smaller extent gymnastics and soccer. The *Development of Sporting Talent* study (English Sports Council, 1998) showed that 38 per cent of the members of elite squads in twelve sports studied were from professional and managerial groups compared with 19 per cent in the whole population (Figure 5.1). Only rugby league, with 22 per cent AB, came anywhere near the population average, and some like swimming at 83 per cent had four-fifths of their squads from privileged backgrounds.

Interestingly, the proportions were reversed when it came to employment in professional sport, with 25 per cent of C2, D, E compared with 14 per cent of A, B, C1. The English Sports Council concluded that

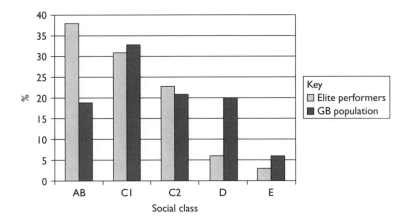

Figure 5.1 Social class of elite performers

the opportunity to realise sporting potential is significantly influenced by an individual's social background. So for example, a precociously talented youngster born in an affluent family with sport-loving parents, one of whom has (probably) achieved high levels of sporting success, and attending an independent/private school, has a 'first-class' ticket to the sporting podium. His or her counterpart, equally talented but born in a less favoured social circumstance has, at best, a third class ticket and at worst no ticket at all. The chances of the former achieving high levels of sporting success are very good while the chances of the latter are minimal. The differences in opportunity clearly affect the country's ability to compete and win in international competition.

(English Sports Council, 1998: 13)

Lord Killanin, honorary life president of the International Olympic Committee, said it should be possible for everyone, in spite of very different beginnings, to have an equal chance to obtain the standards of high level international competitions (quoted in Kennett, 1997). Kay (2000: 166) showed just how much time, moral support, transport and money, and sacrifice by parents and/or siblings was involved in having an elite athlete as a member of a family, concluding the absence of such support may exclude children from realising their own talent. This is very much a first world: third world problem, but as we have seen still bedevils developed societies like Britain.

Case study 2: Sport for secondary schoolchildren – Go for Gold and Champion Coaching in Nottinghamshire

White and Rowe (in de Knop et al., 1996) argued that there was a gap in communication and integrated functioning between the school PE and sports system and adult sports clubs such that:

There is no unified network or programme which provides opportunities for young people to participate in sport and develop their sporting potential. Provision is uneven and fragmented and much depends on the locality in which young people live, their family circumstances, their gender and their ability level.

(de Knop et al., 1996: 115)

Many attempts have been made to encourage more youngsters to continue with sport for its physical, mental and social benefits. In Britain the 1980s saw a growing awareness of the importance of more technically proficient and ethically aware amateur coaching in the wake of the National Coaching Foundation being established. It launched the Champion Coaching (CC) scheme in 1991 with the sole target of developing an after-school sports programme, with an original mission to 'promote quality assured youth sport coaching for performance motivated children within a co-ordinated community structure' (National Coaching Foundation, 1996: 3). In the first two years it developed twenty-four pilot schemes across England. Each CC scheme was co-ordinated by a part-time or volunteer Youth Sports Manager. By 1996, 105 local authorities were CC partners, and Geoff Cooke, NCF's third Chief Executive, could claim:

Champion Coaching is the success story of the decade. In the last five years it has provided challenging sports programmes and quality coaching for more than 25,000 young people. It has also proved an excellent vehicle for recruiting and developing over 2,000 coaches. . . . I believe that many of the young people involved in Champion Coaching today will be tomorrow's sporting heroes.

(National Coaching Foundation, 1996: 1)

Nottinghamshire, unusually in England, had a county leisure service and co-operation across its districts in seeking to encourage youth sport. Nottinghamshire had a generally buoyant mixed economy in the south, but successive waves of pit closures in the 1980s and 1990s virtually removed its coal industry and led to high unemployment in the towns and villages in the north of the county.

In November 1989, Nottinghamshire's Leisure Services Committee established the Nottinghamshire Sports Training Scheme (NSTS) with the help of a £200,000 grant from the Sports Council East Midlands Region. Its purpose was: 'to increase the number of young people participating in sport, to identify and develop it towards integration into County programmes.' This rather broad aim was elaborated into four guiding principles, to:

• be organised to meet the needs of participants at all levels of ability
• be phased and achievable

- represent a long-term commitment in the county to sports development, and
- recognise that the support and co-operation of a large number of organisations, associations and authorities are essential to its success.

The last principle was perhaps the key to the success experienced by NSTS. This used the club and governing body system to work in association with PE teachers and schools in a range of sports, using education, municipal, and voluntary club facilities in all district councils, irrespective of political control. The original Scheme set three levels through which children could progress: Taster→ Improver→ Advanced. Selection for 'taster' courses was on a strictly first-come-first-served basis, primarily referred through schools. Children could only progress to the 'improver' and 'advanced' courses by invitation from one of over 200 registered coaches. Prices were set at a matter of pence per session in order to prevent cost being a barrier.

In October 1991 with another Sports Council grant, the Performance and Excellence in Nottinghamshire Sport Scheme (PENS) was added as a stage subsequent to Champion Coaching, allowing children identified as having talent to progress into top level clubs or into county, regional and, potentially, national squads (Nottinghamshire County Council, 1993). The County Council organised a pre-Champion Coaching programme called Go for Gold (GfG) for 9- to 17-year-olds which:

- could be completed by all levels of ability
- was shorter by two weeks than CC, so easier to fit into school terms
- was easier to market by offering a cheaper rate if paid in advance, and
- allowed youngsters to move directly on to another GfG course.

The initial success of NSTS was striking, with some 2,600 children in 1990, 60 per cent in taster courses. But the numbers dwindled by more than 1,000 over the next three years, and taster entrants fell to 48 per cent. Another problem became evident in the early years: it was initially intended that participants who did not progress to improver or advanced courses would be directed to existing voluntary clubs with junior sections, or where they were not available to a junior club set up by NSTS. However, constraints made this impractical, even though a guide to 'youth friendly' clubs was published for two or three years. In the hope of meeting these problems, NSTS was re-launched in 1993 when CC, GfG and PENS were incorporated into a 'new' Training Scheme, illustrated in Figure 5.2. It now had five objectives, to:

- effectively cover the levels of the Sports Development Continuum (introduction to sport, participation, performance and excellence) throughout the county

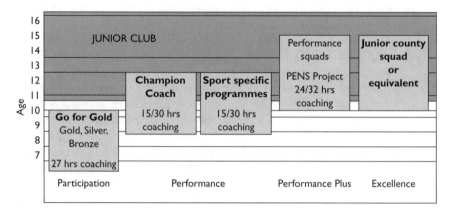

Figure 5.2 The 'new' Nottinghamshire Sports Training Scheme
Source: Nottinghamshire County Council, 1994

- provide a clear and accessible performance pathway for talented young-sters
- increase the number of junior clubs
- maximise the effectiveness of the coaches employed, and
- complement work going on in schools.

In the period from 1994 to 1998 (prompted by national initiatives including the establishment of the Youth Sport Trust), the NSTS underwent further changes. Local government reorganisation meant that the city council started its own sports development programmes from 1995. The 'PENS' perform-ance squad work was revamped as Performance Resources (PR), in order to support the county Governing Bodies of Sport and School Sports Associa-tions. This presaged a Nottinghamshire Active Sports partnership in 2000, which tied them in joint development plans with the two education author-ities and the districts under a manager appointed with Sport England's exchequer money.

As a result of its innovation, scale and coherent management, NSTS set the pace for pioneering youth sport development work throughout England, but while monitoring of registration of players and coaches was set in train, The *Champion Coaching Guide* (National Coaching Foundation, 1996) dealt only briefly with evaluation. This case study sought to remedy that deficiency.

Details of methods are set out in Collins and Buller (2000), and Buller and Collins (2001). Given the range of sports and geographical spread, the returns of 39 per cent for CC (352 children and 310 parents), 38 per cent (549 children) for PR, and 31 per cent for GfG gave robust and reliable data. In-depth inter-views were held with chief coaches and secretaries of clubs popular with the youngsters. The sample of children ranged in age from 10 to 18; in CC boys and girls were 49:51, in GfG 40:60. We shall look at four outcomes:

1   How satisfied were the children and their parents with CC and GfG?
2   What sport did children do after NSTS?
3   What was the take-up of Performance Resources?
4   Did NSTSA demonstrate social inclusion or exclusion?

Outcome 1: Children's and parents' satisfactions with NSTS courses

Initially the children were asked whether they had enjoyed their CC course. Very encouragingly for Nottinghamshire County Council, 96 per cent of CC and 95 per cent of GfG did so. Of the fifteen respondents who did not, five found it *too basic*, three claimed it was *monotonous* or *boring*, and only three mentioned unfriendliness of the group or the coach. The aspects they particularly enjoyed highlighted, perhaps unsurprisingly, that they enjoyed the games most, followed by being coached:

%	Champion Coaching	Go for Gold
Playing the games	27	31
Coaching	21	23
Learning new skills	23	18
Making friends	12	16

Interestingly, the girls found the games and meeting new friends more appealing than boys (26 per cent compared with 16 per cent in CC, and 15 per cent compared with 7 per cent in GfG). Boys enjoyed competition more than girls (14 per cent compared with 9 per cent of girls). This supported Hendry et al.'s (1993) and Mason's (1995) characterisations of male sports as more competitive, and the social benefits as of greater significance for females.

Forty-four different venues were used by the CC respondents in the nine sports, suggesting good access for many young people in Nottinghamshire. Eighteen CC youngsters, mostly girls, encountered access problems, of distance, poor transport, and parents not free to provide lifts. The participants were asked about satisfaction with the coaching staff in four respects: friendliness, helpfulness, quality of organisation and punctuality. The first three responses showed very high levels of satisfaction – from 89 to 96 per cent for both schemes – and the fourth was a little lower at 80 and 83 per cent.

The children were asked whether they received information about local clubs or other opportunities to continue playing when they finished their course (in

Table 5.6 Children's sports activity after attending the Nottinghamshire Sports Training Scheme

Type of participation	Go for Gold (%)	Champion Coaching (%)
Give up	–	12
Recreational	52	46
Club	31	25
County	11	17
Regional	5	–
National	1	–

CC jargon 'exit routes'). Only 60 per cent for CC and 56 per cent for GfG said yes. Even allowing for forgetfulness, this figure was too low to be satisfactory, given that providing such information effectively would meet a key objective of the NSTS – to allow participants to progress or to widen their range. It seemed that (in these nine sports at least), this objective was not being fully achieved. This was particularly worrying because the percentage had decreased every year from 1994. This issue will be further considered below.

Outcome 2: Children's sports participation after NSTS

The answers to whether sports participation continues are illustrated in Table 5.6, showing that the largest group, around half, carried on with their chosen sport as recreation, compared with only 1 in 3 or 4 who joined a local club, perhaps reflecting the lack of information given or received. Once again, there were aspects for concern. One in 8 CC children gave the sport up entirely, giving three main reasons – lack of time, inadequate opportunities or facilities, and not enjoying it.

Providers could only do something about the second reason. More detailed analysis demonstrated that team sports players were more likely to continue than those involved in individual sports (85 compared with 77 per cent). In GfG boys were more likely to continue than girls (62 in contrast to 45 per cent). But individual sports players seemed more likely to progress to higher levels – 10 per cent joined a county squad, compared with only 4 per cent in team sports.

The children were also asked whether they currently belonged to a sports club (at times from one to four years after the course). Three out of 5 CC respondents were members of at least one club, covering 21 sports in 97 separate clubs, while 136 GfG children joined 68 clubs in 15 sports. Six out of 7 CC children felt that the junior sections were strong, that they were offered coaching, and were kept busy. More encouraging was the result that CC children who joined clubs found them rewarding (24 per cent in team sports, and 44 per cent in individual sports). Ninety-seven per cent stated their club was friendly, while 9 or more out of 10 said they had the opportunity to compete, improve their skills, were encouraged or made new friends. Figures for GfG were very similar (Table 5.6).

Two-thirds of volunteered comments were positive, such as:

"CC helped me progress and carry on in the sport."

(Hockey, anon., 17)

"CC has a very friendly atmosphere between coach and trainee."

(Squash, boy aged 14)

"CC was enjoyable and made me think about my skills, so therefore I can play netball a lot better than I used to."

(Netball, anon.)

Parents of CC children were asked to rate their satisfaction with five aspects on a scale of 1 to 5, and the averages of 310 answers were:

Standard of coaching	4.22
Organisation of sessions	4.03
Parental contacts by coaches	3.03
Administration from centre	3.59
Enjoyment of child(ren)	4.38

Three-fifths of parents rated enjoyment as 'excellent', but amount of contact received the most criticism, and a lack of information was volunteered as a problem; for example:

"More information and suggestions for when course ends. Didn't really have a chance to talk to coach about further courses/clubs – no follow-up so child lost interest. Coaching was first class!! Well worth the small cost."

(Parent)

That this situation was class-linked was confirmed by the Nestlé Family Monitor (MORI, 2000) where parents from social classes A and B said they used all forms of information more than those in classes D and E, except word of mouth from friends and family, and especially from teachers (26 compared with 17 per cent) and from clubs (27 compared with 13 per cent).

As a form of triangulation, the clubs' views of NSTS and the young players they received were checked out in interviews. Coaches and secretaries confirmed the importance of NSTS to recruitment, as just two examples showed:

"Without the NSTS running central organised activities to send the kids to, our membership would be considerably depleted."

(D. Dreycote, Keyworth Table Tennis club,
9 August 1998, 40 juniors)

"integral to the success of the club . . . we need all the assistance we can get!"

(Secretary, Trent Bridge Squash Club, 25 juniors)

Trent Bridge Squash Club took a proactive approach by having a 'junior friendly' membership fee and an 'adopt a junior' scheme where adult members were encouraged to pay the junior players' membership fees. The importance of youth friendly sports clubs was stressed in *Running Sport: Starting a Junior Section* (Sports Council, 1995).

Thus nothing appeared to be wrong with the clubs that acted as exit routes. It can be concluded that Nottinghamshire has a large number and wide range of clubs for its young people, and most provide a service to their junior members which is much praised and appreciated.

Outcome 3: Take-up of Performance Resources

As with CC and GfG, the Performance Resources (PR) children gave high satisfaction scores for enjoyment, the quality of the sessions, facilities and coaches (from 7.4 to 8.4 out of 10). When asked about the highest level of participation they had reached prior to attending PR, 2 out of 3 had entered from GfG or CC, and nearly 1 in 2 was involved in county or higher level competition. Suggestions for improvements to PR included having smaller squads to allow more individual attention, and changing the time of the sessions to avoid evening rush hour traffic. The coaches were pleased, but had suggestions for improvement (see Buller, 1998). Thus, Performance Squads were well received by everyone involved, suggesting the pathways provided were appropriate and successful.

Outcome 4: Social inclusion or exclusion in NSTS?

CC was organised by the governing bodies in partnership with the county, and aimed to be available to all youngsters, but not to take specific affirmative actions amongst poor children. The local authority managers of GfG hoped that their local knowledge would make it more sensitive to social need. To examine NSTS' effectiveness in outreach, the addresses of children registered were related to the deprivation rating of 200 zones in the county's study of *Social Need in Nottinghamshire* (Nottinghamshire County Council, 1994: 4).

Across the county, almost a third of the population in 1991 lived in areas defined as having some social need. Table 5.7 provides definitive evidence that a disproportionate share of children from non-deprived areas took part in these schemes than in more needy places. Put another way, only 8 per cent of GfG and PR participants and 13 per cent of CC came from areas of moderate, serious or extreme social need, compared with 29 per cent of the population.

Table 5.7 Residents and performance participants living in areas of social need in Nottinghamshire (per cent)

Level of social need	Go for Gold registrants (%)	Champion Coaching registrants (%)	Performance Resources registrants (%)	Nottinghamshire residents (%)
Below average	92	87	92	71.3
Moderate	5	4	4	11.1
Serious	2	7	4	10.2
Extreme	1	2	0.3	7.3
Base	951 in basketball, cricket, netball, orienteering 1994–8	751 in 9 sports 1994–8	315 in cricket, table tennis, squash 1995–9	994,000

Thus, participants were not representative of the population as a whole. Put most starkly, as in Figure 5.3:

•   For GfG, in four major sports over five years, only 8 per cent of children registered from only 19 areas of social need. Thus 56 areas of need registered no one, though Nottingham City took only a small part in this scheme.
•   In CC 13 per cent came from 25 areas of need, leaving 42 from which no one registered; only two children came from the six most deprived areas, all in the city.
•   For PR, 8 per cent came from 25 different areas of need, leaving 50 areas of social need where there had been no participants since its introduction in 1995.

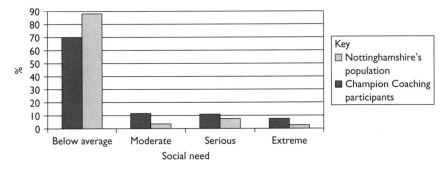

Figure 5.3 Distribution of population and Champion Coaching participants in Nottinghamshire

It is clear that there is a social gradient in take-up, related to income/social class, but also to physical opportunity. Rushcliffe, in southern

Table 5.8 Likelihood of young people getting involved in Champion Coaching according to social need

District	(Population aged 5 to 17)	Social need				
		(1) Extreme	(2) Serious	(3) Moderate	(4) Below average	% in 1 to 3
Ashfield	(17,100)	n/a	0	1 in 455	1 in 379	18
Bassetlaw	(16,500)	0	n/a	0	1 in 2668	19
Broxtowe	(16,200)	n/a	n/a	n/a	1 in 376	0
Gedling	(17,400)	n/a	n/a	1 in 186	1 in 91	3
Mansfield	(16,700)	1 in 1250	1 in 483	1 in 250	1 in 133	55
Newark	(16,800)	n/a	1 in 364	1 in 408	1 in 164	16
Rushcliffe	(15,400)	n/a	n/a	n/a	1 in 350	0
Nottingham City	(41,100)	1 in 839	1 in 261	1 in 789	1 in 187	70

Nottinghamshire, is one of the most affluent districts in the country. It had eight NSTS venues, no zones in social need, and registered 240 (1 in 4) of PR registrants compared with its share of the population. This issue is clearly serious, especially given the aim of the NSTS to *be organised to meet the needs of* all *participants at all level of ability.*

Using the Nottinghamshire County Council 1994 document and the 1991 census data for all 5- to 17-year-olds, one can calculate a 'likelihood ratio' for a child becoming involved in NSTS schemes for each district. Although there are some minor problems with the method used to calculate these figures, they provide a valuable profile of probability. The full results for CC are shown in Table 5.8.

Table 5.8 clearly illustrates the low chances of children in Bassetlaw and Mansfield. A geographic analysis of facilities (Buller, 1998) showed the vast majority of Nottinghamshire's population lived within 3 km of a CC venue. There was an obvious and strong relationship between the location of venues and the areas from which large numbers of CC participants came. For example, forty-four and forty-nine CC participants resided in just two enumeration districts, in Bingham and Retford, with six venues. In contrast, both the Worksop area and the north-east of the county were poorly provided, where Bassetlaw District with a youth population of 16,533 had only two venues and five CC participants (though it should be noted there was no sports development structure in place at the time of study).

This analysis of the four outcomes shows that children in well-off areas had a much higher chance of becoming NSTS participants than those from places with some or great social need. This situation was true of every district, and particularly of Mansfield and Nottingham with the largest needy populations.

This study is of only one county and eight districts. But Nottinghamshire is a fairly typical English county; the politics of its districts are varied; the scheme was well worked out, and while modestly staffed, it was run by experienced staff with substantial continuity. This suggests that the social inequalities are structural rather than circumstantial. A replication of the study in authorities which implemented Champion Coaching in different ways, and in others running their own youth sports programmes, would confirm this.

The results suggest that more venues are needed in or accessible from deprived areas, but also that more direct promotion has to be done with parents in deprived households and with PE teachers in schools in deprived areas. While the rhetoric surrounding the Sports Lottery Fund and Active Sports/ Schools/Communities implies social inclusion, nothing seems to be written in to the guidance specifically on the deprivation issue. If it is as structural an issue as this case study suggests, then any programme which ignores this is doomed to reproduce the limitations found in this case study.

One can understand that some parents in deprived areas cannot manage or afford to get their children to a venue (though once there, the low average cost of 50p a session can be waived on application), or they may just not see CC as 'for them'. But why were referral rates so low; what were the PE teachers in these areas doing? This requires a closer analysis of referral routes, possibly through focus group research, and follow-up with those parents and children who have overcome the barriers and succeeded in developing both participation and performance, as Roberts and Brodie (1992) suggested some did, to see what factors can be reproduced. Collins and Buller (2000) suggested that needed improvements were:

- better information to everyone, for example by re-introducing the junior club directory
- direct outreach with primary teachers in schools in deprived areas, and meetings with parents
- drawing in more facilities and sports development officers in such areas
- drawing in more youth-friendly clubs, and
- undertaking qualitative research with successful participants from deprived areas to discover what to do in direct outreach.

While I have recorded criticisms of NSTS, the overriding picture from the participants, their parents, and the coaches, together with a selection of club secretaries, was that the Nottingham Sports Training Scheme had been a resounding success. As two young participants said:

> "I felt it has made me a better player and it has made me aware of the other organisations that I can join."
>
> (Squash, girl aged 13)

"I really enjoyed taking part in the course and it improved my skills dramatically. I really hope that my younger sister and her friends can take part in a few years."

(Hockey, anon.)

Conclusions

Even though sport has been synonymous with school-age children in English history, there is remarkably little cross-sectional and no longitudinal data on participation, and little on its physical, psychological or social effects. The balance of opinion is that, besides intrinsic enjoyment, sport helps academic performance, though Lindner (1999, quoted by Centre for Leisure Research (1999)) believed the evidence is more ambiguous. It seems to work as an instrumental aid to learning when linked to the glamour of professional sport. The best data is the retrospective reconstruction of Roberts and Brodie (pages 220–1), which shows a long-term growth of involvement.

Although we have studies of what children like and what they do not, we do not have typologies of youth lifestyles for educational or sporting policy purposes. In a not dissimilar society, slightly less affluent, and with more concentrated poverty, but with a similar range of sports, would we replicate the typology discovered in a factor/cluster analysis of 4,000 young people aged 13 to 21 in Germany? Brettschneider (1990) identified five types:

1   *No sports* (5 per cent) – slightly overweight, good family relations, but interested in computers, music, or other leisure.
2   *Activity/motion* (4 per cent) – interested in body image, using sport and exercise; relations more with friends/peers than adults; no clear future plans.
3   *Negative body concept* (17 per cent) – would like to be more active, but delicate health/physical discomfort.
4   *Stylistic hedonism* (13 per cent) – absorbed in promoting a personal style (in sport, slim/fitness, fashion, music) – not close to parents or concerned about the future.
5   *Balanced lifestyle* (61 per cent) – *a surprisingly large group of inconspicuous adolescents* – looking for both fun and achievement in sport, satisfied with their body images, on good terms with parents and peers and with a positive outlook on life.

From the limited survey data and the international research literature, it is clear that there is a social and income gradient in youth sports participation, that girls' choices are not as wide as boys, and that, despite high levels of enjoyment, there are several points at which dropping out can occur, when:

- PE becomes optional and/or children become involved in intensive study for career-forming exams (in England, GCSEs)
- getting involved in vocational study or full-time work
- getting married/cohabiting, and having children, especially the first
- moving house or job and breaking up social networks.

Piachaud and Sutherland (2000) asked *How effective is the British government's attempt to reduce child poverty?* They attempted to model the impacts of different programmes announced to January 2000, and concluded:

- the Minimum Wage and tax benefits would increase income for 1 in 9 poor households with children, but reduce them for the other tenth (benefiting 840,000 people)
- New Deal and return to work policies, because of interactions with benefit limitations for lone parents, would make a modest difference – probably benefiting 160,000 people.

They pointed out this will only be achieved if job creation is kept up or unemployment is kept down. This reduction of about a million represents about a third, but Piachaud and Sutherland reckoned that policies would have to be accelerated for Blair and Brown to reach their target of eradication in 20 years. In April 2001 the government launched a bond scheme for £500 for each poor child, to be topped up by £100 at ages 5, 11 and 16, to mature at age 18, and a matched £ for £ savings scheme (Wintour, *Guardian* 26 April 01). Hill and Jenkins (2000) modelled a flat rate payment of £5 targeted at currently poor households with under 11s, and pointed out that this would reduce chronic poverty by a third.

Poor households have little money for leisure (Chapter 4), but their children do need money to be able participate in sport alongside their more fortunate peers. The potential for Sport for All can be epitomised amongst higher education students who mostly have local cheap or free facilities, fairly flexible timetables and the highest participation rates in the country; but few poor and deprived children make it into higher education.

The Chairman of Sport England, introducing the 1999 (MORI) survey, wrote:

the costs to individuals and society of this declining commitment to primary school PE may not be felt now. They will, however, be measured in the years to come in terms of heart disease and increasing obesity, osteoporosis and stroke . . . in addition . . . we must not forget the potential waste of sporting talent and missed medal opportunities.

Public sector sports planners can do more in looking to make facilities more physically accessible, and managers could be more welcoming and open, but for young people it needs the understanding and encouragement of parents, teachers and coaches, and then the reinforcement of peers, and then the support of youth-friendly clubs where parents are active. While factors of class, gender, geography and to a lesser extent race all have an impact, it would seem that what may be needed is what in vocational training Rudd and Edwards (1998) called *structured individualisation*, that is, tailoring provision to individual needs. We shall see that this can make a considerable difference in counselling schemes for young delinquents, and to the extent that it was possible, so it did in NSTS. The Connexions service is based on making mentoring available. Such services are not cheap, but neither are area initiatives if a high proportion of the benefit is devoured by active, informed, mobile, and more affluent residents.

Roberts and Parsell (1994) argued that social class divisions in leisure were becoming more blurred, but confirmed Hendry's findings that participation in sport was likely to be higher in middle than working class settings. By 1996, Roberts, reviewing Mason's and two other studies of youth sport, opined dryly:

> Sport and leisure are fields in which the wills of policy makers are rarely decisive. Shakespeare and religion have not soared as popular leisure pastimes through their promotion in schools. Competitive team sports are likely to fare similarly whatever governments pronounce and schools promote if young people prefer other activities. Leisure effects in education are often unintentional. Breaking down class divisions in leisure was not among the principal reasons why the 11-plus was abandoned in Britain, or why post-compulsory education was expanded. The 1988 Education Reform Act seems to have persuaded schools to upgrade their sports facilities and publicise these provisions not via the National PE Curriculum but by extending parental choice. Sport and leisure policies are always most likely to succeed when they flow with and harness broader tides.
>
> (Roberts, 1996: 56)

Coalter came to similar conclusions:

> there has been a relative decline in more 'traditional' team and partner sports, accompanied by increased participation in a more diversified range of activities . . . one conclusion might be that the key policy issue is to encourage current, committed participants to increase their frequency of participation rather than commit resources in an attempt to expand the base of (possibly reluctant) participants.
>
> (Coalter, 1999: 36)

But sustaining the broader choice at school is likely to support life-long participation.

Chapter 6

Gender, sport and social exclusion

Tess Kay

Introduction: Sport and the gendered experience of social exclusion

In this chapter we focus on the reciprocal relationships between sport, gender and social exclusion. Although the relationships between gender and poverty have now been well studied, as have those between gender and sport, the connections between these two pairings have not. There has been little reason for analysts of women's experience of social exclusion to address sport: sport is generally less prominent in women's lives than in men's, and particularly so among women most likely to be affected by poverty. In gendered analyses of sport, more attention has been paid to the general underrepresentation of women in sport, than to the situations of the most disadvantaged women. In this chapter we therefore have the opportunity to forge stronger links between women's experiences of sport and of social exclusion, and to consider the relationship between them.

The common bond between women's experience of sport and women's experience of social exclusion is that in both institutions women experience strong discrimination stemming from a pervasive gender ideology. This concern with ideology may imply a rather theoretical level of analysis, but in fact this is not what is offered here. Instead, the point is to examine how women are disadvantaged in welfare provision and in sport, and to examine the linkages between them. Women's treatment under the British welfare system stems from an underlying gender ideology which first positions women primarily as mothers and carers, and second (and critically) values and rewards these roles less than that of paid work. The same gender ideology is evident in sport, where expectations of sex-appropriate behaviour remain strongly influential.

Sport is uniquely positioned to reinforce the key elements of the basic ideology – that women are less powerful and are 'inferior' to men, and that these differences are natural (i.e. biological) phenomenon, rather than the products of social processes. This, however, also makes sport a prime site for challenging gender ideology, and it is therefore a particularly valuable area for encouraging involvement by the most disempowered women. The contribution that sport can make to combating women's social exclusion is also discussed here, while some practical ways are identified in which sport can be made accessible to women. The chapter concludes by taking stock of the potential and limitations of sport to contribute to overcoming women's social exclusion.

Throughout the chapter no specific attempt is made to define 'socially excluded' women. It is not just that the measures are too imprecise and the group too diverse, but also that women's lives are too dynamic. At present, for example, one-fifth of women in Britain are lone parents and thus carry one of the highest risks of being in poverty (see Table 2.3, page 13) – but many others have experienced lone parenthood in the past and still more are likely to in future. Similarly, many women who have never experienced poverty during their adult lives may well encounter it in an acute form when they enter old age, especially if they join the growing number of very old women who spend many years dependent on a State pension. This chapter, therefore, is primarily about the experiences that are common to many women who for different reasons may at times be classed as socially excluded. These experiences are likely to be heightened for women who also experience other dimensions of disadvantage dealt with elsewhere in the book, including older women (see also Chapter 7), women from racial minorities (see also Chapter 8), and disabled women (see also Chapter 9).

Women's experience of poverty and social exclusion

The majority of poor people today are women – as they were two hundred years ago. Across centuries rich with social, economic, political and industrial transformations, women's greater vulnerability to poverty is a constant. The creation of modern systems of welfare have done little to reverse the trend: far from protecting women from poverty, modern welfare practices have seen the number experiencing poverty significantly increase. Twenty-four per cent of adult women were poor in 1998 compared with 20 per cent of men (Department of Social Security, 1998).

In Britain today the key to the 'feminisation' of poverty lies in the assumptions that underpin contemporary welfare provision. The founding assumption of the 'modern' UK welfare state was that 'women's place and security lay in the family' (Pascall, 1997: Preface). Aspects of this have clearly changed: women have become increasingly visible in places other than the family, and are less able to assume that their family will provide a continuous source of security. Few women today live out their adult years in the full economic dependency of an unpaid wife and mother, and an increasing proportion encounter household changes that include periods of family breakdown and, for many, reconstitution. All of these developments run counter to the traditional views that provided the basis for women's initial incorporation in the welfare state and institutionalised both their subordination and their dependency. But policies based on traditional family patterns and women's roles have changed much more slowly than families and women themselves, and current policies perpetuate many aspects of the inequitable treatment of women that were embedded in the post-war welfare settlement (Kay, 2000). They continue to give primacy to the public sphere over the private, and so elevate the rewards associated with paid work over those of domestic labour.

Unfavourable treatment by the welfare system is a key factor that puts women at greater risk of experiencing poverty than men. This results from the centrality of paid employment as a basis for welfare entitlement, which disadvantages women and other groups under-represented in the labour market. Despite their increasing educational and professional qualifications, women are more likely to be in low-paid employment than men, more likely to work in insecure jobs, more likely to reduce or cease their labour market participation during parenting years, and much more likely to take part-time employment. Domestic caring responsibilities play a significant part in influencing this pattern: the 1994–5 Family and Working Lives Survey (in Land, 1999: 27) showed that the working arrangements of 2 in 3 mothers were affected by having children, compared with those of only 1 in 6 men. Women's employment histories, therefore, are more complex and less consistent than men's, giving them limited entitlement to a wide range of insurance-based welfare support, including unemployment benefit and pensions. By performing the family-related responsibilities implicit in the 'breadwinner' model of welfare provision, women are more likely to damage their personal entitlement to welfare support than enhance it. At a time when rising levels of separation, divorce and lone parenthood have made more women dependent on precisely these resources, this has profound consequences for women's exposure to poverty.

Until the late 1990s generic data on poverty was not usually disaggregated by sex, thus concealing the gender imbalance. This omission was an important part of processes that not only kept women's experiences of poverty relatively invisible, but also materially affected their experiences. During the 1980s, for example, data from the International Labour Office showed that several hundred thousand women were missing from the official unemployment count in Britain. The financial circumstances of these 'missing' women were usually *worse* than those of unemployed men, because the criteria that excluded women from the official count were the same that denied them entitlement to full unemployment benefit. Today it is easier to show that in Britain more women than men experience poverty. Although women share with men the risks of experiencing poverty as either a pensioner couple (24 per cent at risk) or a couple with children (22 per cent), they comprise the great majority of higher risk groups – single-parent households (60 per cent) and single pensioners living alone (32 per cent) (Oppenheim, 1998). Women were therefore disproportionately affected by the rise in poverty from the late 1970s to the mid-1990s.

The growth in women's poverty during this period was greatly affected by changes taking place primarily (but not exclusively) in families, and by the particularly inadequate social policy responses that accompanied these developments. In Britain marriage rates fell, divorce rates rose to the highest (by far) in the European Union, and the numbers of cohabitant, lone parent and reconstituted family households increased. All social classes were affected by these trends, but episodes of family breakdown were more likely to occur in lower income families than in higher ones. Family employment situations also changed, leading to polarisation between those who benefited from labour market restructuring (dual-earner families), and those who lost out (no-earner families). The combined effect of these changes was to increase women's vulnerability to poverty.

Changes in families affect both sexes: after divorce, for example, both partners are likely to be significantly worse off financially than when they shared a household. However, the financial consequences are usually particularly acute and long-lasting for women. In the first place, separation and/or divorce are likely to remove women from their household's main source of income (i.e. the male partner's), and to make them dependent on the limited state support already discussed. In addition, many more mothers than fathers become primary carers for children following family breakdown, and bear the associated costs; and while fathers make maintenance payments, these may not take effect immediately and in some cases may never be forthcoming. Finally, women are often less well-positioned than their former partners to support themselves adequately through employment: they are less likely to work full-time or at all, may have a background in low-paid jobs, and may be heavily constrained by childcare responsibilities. In short, in Britain today being a woman increases the likelihood of becoming dependent on social assistance, and automatically increases the risk of poverty, given British benefit levels (as discussed in Chapter 2).

Being in poverty compromises traditional male and female roles in the household in a way that can be devastating to both sexes. However, there are some differences in men's and women's experiences that we should note. For men, the inability to provide sufficient finance to support a household signifies a failure to live up to a tradition of man as the provider that stretches back through time to the world of the hunter-gatherer. For women, inability to produce a sufficient standard of living out of insufficient finance and resources represents a failure in caring. In everyday terms, women may confront the practical difficulties of this situation more directly and continually than men, because of their greater responsibility for the functioning of the household. On a day-to-day basis, cash shortages are more likely to be encountered as immediate problems by women because generally it is they who supply meals, launder clothes, and provide an adequately warm and comfortable home. It is well-documented that, faced with this situation, many women sacrifice their own needs to those of the rest of the household. Self-sacrifice is not a uniquely female strategy: for example, when food is short, both parents are more likely to feed their children than themselves. However, wives are also likely to put their husband's needs before their own. There is also some evidence that some women are more conscious of 'failing' in their domestic role in a household in which there is a male partner: left alone as a single parent poses many challenges, but for some there is a little comfort in 'the freedom to do without'.

The fact that women's experiences of poverty differ qualitatively and quant-itatively from men's suggests that women will only benefit from policies that are sensitive to these gender differences. In the next section we begin to exam-ine the implications of this for the inclusion of sport in policy interventions to address social exclusion.

Women, sport and social exclusion

Having shown that the inequities of the gender order are evident in the sexes' different experiences of welfare, we argue that sport contributes to these unequal social relations, by elevating male experience over female in a particularly powerful and visible way. Sport, therefore, is a site where the unequal social relations that underpin women's experience of social exclu-sion are very persuasively reproduced.

Taking part in sport on a regular basis is a minority activity for British women. The most recent data shows that in 1996, only 38 per cent of women aged 16 or over had participated in sport on at least one occasion in the four weeks prior to interview. The comparable figure for men was 54 per cent (Office for National Statistics, 1998). As women grow older, their sports par-ticipation declines quicker than men's; also, sport also appears more likely to retain men as participants to a later age. Women's sports participation is far more affected by the growth of family responsibilities than is men's, with particularly strong constraints on women's sports participation when their household contained a child under the age of 5.

The patterns of gender inequality in sport vary between sub-groups of women and these variations correlate strongly with variations in women's exposure to poverty and social exclusion. There is a strong social class effect on women's participation – stronger than on men's. The gap between male and female participation rates widens going down the socio-economic scale; in group V (unskilled manual), women's participation rate is only two-thirds of men's (Table 6.1). In other words, women's sports participation appears more vulnerable to the impact of other social structural constraints. It is only women who are relatively favourably positioned within the social structure who come close to closing the sports participation gap with men.

However, while sport plays a smaller part in women's lives than men's, trends over time suggest that it is nonetheless a growing part of contemporary women's lives. Levels of female sports participation have been rising since the 1970s, especially in health and fitness activities. There has also been some broadening of the range of sports in which women participate, with more now taking part in sports formerly considered a male preserve, such as rugby,

Table 6.1 Sports participation rates by sex and occupational group, 1996 (percentage participating in four weeks before interview)

	Men aged 16+ (%)	Women aged 16+ (%)
Professional	78	85[a]
Employers and managerial	72	62
Intermediate and junior non-manual	78	63
Skilled manual	66	53
Semi-skilled manual	66	48
Unskilled manual	54	42

Source: Office for National Statistics, 1998, Table 13.13

Note: a This data is an unexplained anomaly. It exceeded the forecast by nearly 20 per cent

football and cricket. Yet by many measures, women's sports participation remains low in absolute as well as relative terms. Despite the relative popularity of health and fitness activities, for example, few women lead active lifestyles and most have physical activity levels below the threshold required for maximum health benefits. Women and girls appear particularly distant from the commodified sports product of the contemporary global economy – the high-profile, competitive, commercial and professional world of sport that dominates media. And within this general picture, it is the least powerful women in society who are most distanced from sport.

The marked differences between men's and women's relationship with sport mirror the broader pattern of social relations within which sport is situated. The predominant pattern of female participation in sport is very much in line with the model of the less powerful female, and stems from a female socialisation process that perpetuates the ideology of women as nurturers and carers that is entrenched in welfare policy. Sport provides evidence that these traditional and supposedly outdated views retain strong currency. While women's participation in sport is both increasing and diversifying, the areas of greatest involvement and growth are those that conform with conventional notions of femininity.

The gender socialisation process that underpins this begins early, instilling different sports-related experiences and attitudes from the very start of life. Child development research has shown that even as babies, girls are encouraged to be less independent and adventurous, and this sex typing becomes more explicit as children grow older (Greendorfer, 1983). By the time children reach school age, a link has been made between sport and masculinity, and a distance established between sport and 'feminine' behaviour. Later, during adolescence, many girls turn away decisively from sport: there is an 'almost catastrophic decline' in the proportion of girls who enjoy PE in school, which drops from 74 per cent at primary school age, to less than a third (29 per cent) by school leaving age (Rowe, 1995). Girls' participation rates remain high, but they are artificially inflated by compulsory school sport. As pointed out in Chapter 5, girls are much less likely to take part in sport outside school than boys, are less likely than boys to be frequent participants in sport, and more likely to be non-participants. At the end of their school careers, young women's post-school participation declines more than young men's.

Some of the blame for this has been laid at the door of secondary school experiences of PE, but there are other influences on adolescents outside the school environment. Many girls do not associate sport and physical activity with femininity, and sport is more likely to be seen by as typical of the 'un-feminine' girl. There is a mismatch between girls' growing concern with their bodies' appearance, and the use of the body as active and functional in sport. Some girls may also be discouraged by the supposed association of sport with lesbianism at a time when they are particularly concerned with establishing their (heterosexual) identity (Griffin, 1989, and see Chapter 12). In short, sport sits uneasily with the experiences and aspirations of teenage girls. In any case, girls' school sport experiences often seem irrelevant to adult female life: the activities traditionally offered to schoolgirls do not enjoy either the mass participation or elite status of boys' football, cricket and rugby. Sport is seen as something more likely to be left behind than continued as part of the transition to female adulthood, especially when establishing heterosexual partnerships. This encourages women to adopt 'appropriate' feminine behaviour, and to express their sexuality through attractive appearance, with the female body presented as decorative rather than active. Once again, to many women, most forms of sport appear irrelevant to these priorities. The growth in fitness and exercise activities confirms the over-riding importance given to their physical appearance.

Of course, there has been some loosening of such restrictive views of femininity, that have long proved an obstacle to female sports participation. Views of gender and sexuality have been changing: by the 1990s 'well-honed athletic female bodies' were becoming acceptable as sexually attractive according to heterosexual criteria (Hargreaves, 1994). More diverse role models became available to young women from a stream of female popular artists whose images drew on quasi-'sporty' dimensions such as energetic dance routines and 'fitness chic' clothing. The incorporation of sport was highly selective, however, and used to heighten rather than replace the performers' conventional feminine sexualised glamour.

Other changes that appeared to challenge traditional gender expectations had similar limitations. The increase in women's labour market participation, and especially in those who continued working while bringing up young children, suggests a move to more equal, less differentiated adult roles. However, women in employment continue to bear by far the main responsibility for domestic and child care tasks, and traditional ideologies are proving resistant to change. Changes in labour market roles are not transforming domestic ones – and in any case, are concentrated amongst better-qualified, more affluent women. More women lie outside this relatively privileged sector than within it. Being a wife-mother remains the central role for most women, but is particularly prominent for women in lower socio-economic groups, many ethnic minority women, and for the growing number of women heading a household alone (Kay, 1996a). Women in these groups have low levels of labour market attachment and invest greater proportions of their time in domestic and caring responsibilities. To this extent key areas of their lives continue to be in accord very much with traditional gender expectations.

Societal constraints on women's involvement in sport are reinforced in sport itself. Institutionalised sport is strongly masculine in its culture and organisation; compared with their male counterparts, women hold fewer positions of power in sport, and they hold positions of less power (Fasting, 1993). Rather perversely, at a time of supposedly increasing gender equity, male dominance of sport structures has been increasing rather than declining as sport has become more professionalised. Media coverage of sport reinforces its masculine image and is highly influential in promoting a view of sport that limits its appeal to women. This is not confined to sports-specific reportage. Media products targeted at general markets portray sport as a very central component of men's lifestyles, but very peripheral to women's. Kay's (1999) study of sport in women's magazines found most emphasis being given to body-shaping activities, with some articles going so far as to offer women 'sport-substitute' activities, to allow them the benefits of sport without actually having to take part in it. The over-riding message was that, even in the late 1990s, 'real' sport was still not something for 'real' women.

Increasingly sophisticated efforts have been made to combat gender inequity in sport. In Britain, early policies that concentrated on increasing female participation (for example, through appropriate programming and facility design) came under criticism as being superficial responses to problems more deeply embedded in the sports structure. In the early 1990s the first comprehensive national 'women and sport' policy (Sports Council, 1993 and the *Brighton Declaration*, Sports Council, 1994, from an international conference) explicitly recognised female under-representation in sports organisations as a fundamental barrier to gender equity, and advocated greater women's involvement in all aspects and all levels of sports participation, provision and management. However, in sport as elsewhere, formal policies do not guarantee effective action, as McKay's (1997) in-depth analysis of resistance to 'affirmative action' initiatives in sports organisations in Australia, Canada and New Zealand showed. To date, policies to promote gender equity have too often foundered in the face of organisational and societal cultures where gender differentiation was entrenched.

Obstacles to women's involvement in sport, therefore, continue to have wide currency. They also continue to be potentially most significant for women amongst whom traditional female roles remain most influential, many of whom are also vulnerable to social exclusion. It is questionable as yet how much tangible benefit such women have obtained from the overarching gender policies instigated in sport. In the next section we examine how they have fared in policies more specifically targeted at them.

Sport, gender and social exclusion: Issues and initiatives

We have argued that sport is far more peripheral to women's experiences than men's: collectively, women identify with sport far less than men do. Sport also seems to be least valued among women most vulnerable to social exclusion, including those from lower social class groups, those from non-white populations, and disabled and elderly women. So, while sport may seem to be one of the most obvious ways for reaching out to men who may have become distanced from other social institutions, it appears particularly ill-matched as a vehicle for women's integration. Why then should we concern ourselves with the notion of sports-based interventions for women who experience poverty and social exclusion?

The simple answer is that women individually can derive as significant benefits from participating in sport as can men. Rather than detracting from their personal development, sports participation appears to offer women substantial gains (Duquin, 1982; Hargeaves, 1994; Talbot, 1989). Women who are involved in sport report positive changes in self-esteem and sense of 'self', and increased physical power and well-being, just like men. For women experiencing social exclusion, the everyday practicalities of taking part may also have a special value – for example, by providing opportunities to get out of the house, engage in physical exercise, have some social contact, and participate in personally meaningful, enjoyable and relaxing activity.

These benefits in themselves provide sufficient rationale for encouraging women's involvement in sport. They suggest that sport is not 'unsuitable' for women, and that their absence from it results primarily from obstacles to their participation. More to the point, if sport offers significant benefits to women experiencing hardship in their lives, then to deny them these experiences amounts to an additional dimension of their broader social exclusion. There are persuasive individualistic reasons for bridging the sporting gap for these women.

However, it has been argued also that encouraging women's involvement in sport has a more fundamental contribution to make to their lives. Contemporary sport is a highly visible social institution, global in its reach, which offers a shared experience that crosses national and cultural boundaries. But a shared experience is not necessarily an inclusive one, and there are many ways in which sport is not unifying but divisive. As we have seen in relation to gender, sport is a powerful mechanism for delivering a *non*-inclusive version of society – one that promotes white above black, male above female, physical prowess above alternative qualities, and certain body types above others. Sport therefore carries a social significance that reaches far beyond its own sphere, yet para-doxically does so while appearing to be outside 'real life'.

Consequently, theorists have argued that, because of its significance in con-structing gender relations that expose women to greater hardship than men, sport has a very direct and fundamental relevance to combating women's social exclusion. Far from being separate from real social relations, sport can strongly influence them. This is particularly true in relation to the gender debate: the physical nature of sport reinforces widely held assumptions that relationships of power between the sexes are based on 'natural' or biological factors (Birrell and Theberge, 1994). 'An ideological view comes to be deposited in our culture as a commonsense assumption – of course women are different and inferior' (Willis, 1982: 130).

If sporting practices reinforce hegemony in the rest of society, then challeng-ing them amounts to challenging gender inequity in social relations. This is an ambitious project, but one with some empirical support. Researches into women's experiences of sport have shown that the gains obtained can contribute to a more general feeling of empowerment (Deem, 1986). Women report devel-oping a stronger sense of identity and self-direction – what Talbot (1989) has described as 'being herself through sport' Thus sport may have implications for women's lives beyond the boundaries of sport itself. Duquin (1982) suggested that, by giving women the chance to discover their physical potential, test their ambitions and 'realise their ability to create their own destiny', sport might lead women to restructure the cultural and personal boundaries shaping their lives.

If sports experiences have the potential to equip women to challenge their subordination in a patriarchical society, they are potentially of greater value to those women most disadvantaged. But how in practice do women at risk of poverty and social exclusion respond to sports-based interventions? We already know that their overall response to sport is limited, as evidenced by the low participation rates of the sub-groups within this population – for example, women in lower socio-economic groups, women from non-white communit-ies, and older women. However, one of the purposes of this book has been to go beyond the aggregate picture to examine what happens when more special-ist initiatives are set up to 'use' sport with socially excluded groups. Making a robust assessment of how this has worked for women is particularly difficult; the range of initiatives has not been matched by a corresponding volume of research and monitoring, and so much of what has been learned and experi-enced is undocumented. More fundamentally, the issue of providing sport for disadvantaged women to a great extent has been overshadowed by other emphases in the movement for gender equity in sport. Both participation policies and broader gender equity policies have been concerned more with overcoming barriers to sport for all women than tackling those specifically handicapping disadvantaged women.

Very varying emphases have been given to gender issues in sports projects to tackle social exclusion. Many national sports initiatives have indeed provided for women, insofar as they have not overtly discriminated between the sexes.

This approach would be termed 'gender neutral' by some, 'gender blind' by others. Questions certainly arise about how, with their very different relationship to sport from men, women might respond to provision that purports to provide for both sexes. Is sport in this form likely to be as accessible and attractive to females as to males? Rather paradoxically, the potential for gender discrimination has sometimes been *more* acute in sport policies that ostensibly address inclusion.

Gender bias in sports provision addressing social exclusion has been most evident in initiatives targeted at specific aspects, such as unemployment or crime. In social policy as a whole, both these issues and policy responses to them have been regarded as primarily 'male', i.e. numerically and culturally dominated by men, and this has been paralleled in sports policy. The experiences of Street Sport in Stoke and Sports Counselling in Hampshire reflect this (in Chapter 10). The tendency to link sport with 'male' issues has been a tradition first fully articulated in modern times in the 1960 Wolfenden Report, and made flesh in linking sport and recreation with urban policy in the 1970s and 1980s. In the latter, it was noticeable that although diverse groups were identified as sufferers of urban disadvantage, sport was more vigorously promoted to those believed to pose a threat of social disorder. It was on this basis that programmes like Football in the Community emerged, offering much to young men, but little of obvious relevance to other deprived urban dwellers such as older people or housebound young mothers. The contribution that sport could make to individual well-being for *all* groups of citizens thus took second place to its potential value in offsetting the threat of (male) urban unrest.

In Britain in the late 1970s and early 1980s, when the first national sports development projects were emerging, 'gender' had yet to achieve real profile in sports policy. In these circumstances it was down to key individuals attuned to these issues to tackle the problems. The efforts of one particular partnership, the (male) directorate of the West Midlands' inner city Action Sport project, showed how deeply gender discrimination could be embedded in even determinedly pioneering projects. To develop how they worked with women and girls, the project directorate commissioned investigative research among its own staff (Glyptis, Kay and Murray, 1985).

The research soon cast a harsh light on just how invisible women could be. As one of the male area team co-ordinators admitted, initially he and others had simply dismissed women as completely irrelevant:

> I will admit now that I never even considered women ... it was well into the project – 6 to 8 months – before we really decided to think seriously of women as participants ... It all started at the co-ordinators' meetings. I suddenly realised that women did exist.
>
> (Glyptis, Kay and Murray, 1985: 2)

A female sports leader pinpointed how the project staff's low expectations about women's involvement led to much poorer provision for females – whilst arguing that women's lower involvement in sport should make them a greater rather than a lesser priority than men:

> I find that all male Action Sport leaders believe they involve both males and females in activities – but in reality only a few do. Others tend to believe it is totally the objective of female sports leaders like myself. When females make up half the population it is ironic that most activities are directly related to men – all leaders motivate men and work with them. It should be vice versa.
>
> (Glyptis, Kay and Murray, 1985: 16)

Some extreme views were in evidence when sports leaders explained what they thought constrained women's involvement in Action Sport:

> Many are just too lazy to come and see what is happening.
> Women can find excuses for doing nothing ... They should not be allowed to look for ways out, e.g. children, too fat, no money, not interested.
>
> (Glyptis, Kay and Murray, 1985: 14)

Some felt that women bore the responsibility for making their own participation a positive experience. In strong contrast to more recent emphases on recognising and responding to women's different needs, some sports leaders showed a marked reluctance to reach out to this target group:

> They do not feel part of the session.
> The girls do not feel at home because they have not got the energy to keep up with the boys.
>
> (Glyptis, Kay and Murray, 1985: 14)

However inadvertently it has arisen, a significant proportion of sport initiatives that have addressed social exclusion have had a stronger focus on disadvantaged men than disadvantaged women. What is unfortunate is that the neglect of disadvantaged women has not been counterbalanced in gender equity drives in sport, where the over-arching concern with the overall under-representation of women continues to dominate. The move to a broadly scoped policy that incorporates provision issues may in fact exacerbate this, if it diverts attention from drives to introduce women to sport in the most obvious way – as participants. In the long term, greater female influence in the production of sport is necessary to make sport more accessible to women at all levels of performance and in all roles. In the short term, however, management and leadership roles are unlikely to be entry points for many women who are outside sport, and may be particularly irrelevant to those diminished by experiences of poverty and social exclusion.

However, alongside these early examples of discriminatory provision, there were nonetheless indications that women's capacity for sport went far beyond the commonly assumed range of 'suitable' activities. The West Midlands Action Sport research also recorded sports leaders, of both sexes, suggesting that this was the case:

> Women are far more adventurous and capable of doing any sport.
> (Glyptis, Kay and Murray 1985: 14)

> Most of my work is ladies' keep fit to music sessions, which are becoming increasingly popular; however, the ladies I deal with are prepared to have a go at anything from rock-climbing and assault courses to rounders and netball.
> (1985: 4)

> There are *no* activities that are not popular with women.
> (1985: 5)

Mixed-sex provisions like some Action Sport sessions revealed some very positive indications of women's affinity for sport. However, the strongest statements of this originated elsewhere, from women-centred provisions. From the 1980s projects focused specifically on females emerged as striking examples of good practice. They tended to be locally based, with some emerging from the larger local authorities, some from municipal partnerships with other local organisations, and two through the Sports Council's National Demonstration Projects.

Where outcomes of these projects were documented, they were generally highly favourable. Of the National Demonstration Projects, the two that focused on women's participation 'arguably [had] the greatest impact' (McDonald and Tungatt, 1990: 1) – a women's sports promoter in Norwich and sports activities in Women's Institute branches in Cambridgeshire. Extensive success was reported in attracting women to participate and to continue to do so. Similar outcomes were reported elsewhere. In Coventry, a series of annual Women's Activity Weeks run by the local Women in Sport Group was used to raise the profile of sports continuously available to women and girls at local facilities (Coventry Women in Sport Group, 1991). Women participating generally found it *very worthwhile and enjoyable* while the facilities involved recorded a very positive impact on the numbers of female users. In North Tyneside, the first nine months of the council's Women's Sports Development Project saw more than 5,000 women attending fifty-nine different activities (North Tyneside Council, 1990).

More recently, there have been projects aimed specifically at disadvantaged groups like the Wild Outdoor Women (WOW) and Getaway Girls projects in Leeds and Bradford/Huddersfield aimed initially at involving inner city ethnic minority, disabled and poor girls and women in adventurous outdoor activities, and then at encouraging them to train and act as leaders (Collins, 1996).

There is evidence, therefore, not only that sport offers benefits that may have a special value to those women at risk of social exclusion, but also that women respond to appropriate provision. That provision *is* 'appropriate' appears to be crucial. In North Tyneside they concluded that 'the most encouraging and important point to emerge during the first year was that there is an overwhelming demand for sport of all kinds, for women of all kinds, *given the right conditions*' (North Tyneside Council, 1990; current author's emphasis). We now go on to consider what are these 'right conditions'.

Feminising sports provision

An extensive debate surrounds promoting gender equity in sport. Many writers have argued that only through making fundamental changes in sport to lessen its 'maleness' and give women power within it, will women have true access to sport (e.g. Deem, 1986; Fasting, 1993; Hargreaves, 1994; Kay, 1996b; McKay, 1997). Often such analysts rather dismiss strategies that try to incorporate women into sport in its unchanged form, typically through providing 'appropriate' activities. They argue that it is not enough to address issues of women's participation alone; more fundamental shifts are required in sports structures and above all in the sports culture.

However, while involving women in managing and providing sports activities is a more fundamental way of addressing gender discrimination, it is also a difficult one, and projects which try to do this have often met with limited success. In the late 1980s the Norwich women's promoter project found that even women highly enthusiastic about their sports activities found it hard to take on the level of continuous responsibility required to assume some form of leadership role (Research Unit, North West, 1986). This is very much in line with experience in other initiatives that have attempted to promote grassroots sports leadership (by either sex) in local communities. This does not imply that such initiatives are not worthwhile, but that they are particularly tough to establish and sustain in deprived communities, and are unlikely to be the major platform for a successful policy thrust with socially excluded women.

So, the significance of 'only' raising women's sports participation levels should not be underplayed: it is a fundamental component of any broader strategy to increase women's presence and influence in sport, and is in itself a substantial challenge. Initiatives to increase participation also have been important for identifying a wealth of achievable, often low- or no-cost tactics that can be taken to modify sports provision to reduce practical obstacles to women's involvement. During the 1980s, Sports Council suggestions for making sports provision operationally better oriented to women included making more local provision, running suitable activity programmes, timing sessions to accommodate women's child care responsibilities, and providing child care at sports facilities.

Taylorson and Halfpenny's (1991) analysis of facility management identified the importance of: staff training on gender issues, monitoring target groups' participation rates, developing activities targeted at women, improving publicity and marketing aimed at women, and investing in facility design so as to reflect women's needs. They and other writers also emphasised the need to seek the views of women themselves, taking full account of the diversity in female population and including the views of female non-participants in such research.

Recently these and other ideas were brought together in a Sport England Factfile (Campbell, 1999) on *Women-friendly Sports Facilities*. Grouped under the headings of Confidence, Comfort, Choice, Convenience and Consultation, the factfile identified practical actions providers and policy makers could take to counter intervening constraints (Chapter 3) on women's participation. These addressed women's confidence about participating in sport; their concerns about safety when travelling to facilities and privacy in them; direct constraints on participation such as time and money; and the variations between women, and in individual women's circumstances at different stages in the family lifecycle. Recommendations were made for steps that could be taken at three stages of sports facility provision – in land use and sports planning; in facility design; and in facility management. Only a few of these points were highlighted as being particularly relevant to encouraging less advantaged women; most were regarded as relevant and important for all potential female users.

It provided little detail on the importance of promotional materials in portraying sport as accessible to women, but other researchers have given greater prominence to this, drawing attention to the fact that women respond best to personalised forms of information, that they require full details about participating and using facilities, and that images used can be influential in encouraging/discouraging them. Personal contact and word-of-mouth information appears particularly significant for bridging the gap of women's unfamiliarity with sport – especially for non-participants. The image of sport conveyed by promotional material is central: 'Advertising should not exclusively depict slim, fit, beautiful young and experienced white women. Quite obviously the health, fitness, fun and social benefits are valid for a much wider market' (Southern Council for Sports and Recreation, 1989: 8). Language and illustrations should also be chosen to make the activity seem as accessible as possible, for example by using 'Recreation' and 'Leisure' rather than 'Sport'. Publicity aimed at women should also be displayed in a wide range of locations that reflect women's use of local amenities – for example, playgroups, schools, hairdressers, libraries, shopping centres and corner shops, health centres, doctors' surgeries, community centres, tenants' associations, employment centres, social services departments, residential homes and day centres. Once launched, promotion and publicity should be a continuous process: 'It is crucial to keep up the momentum' (West Midlands Council for Sport and Recreation, 1988: 11).

In general, guidelines for improving women's access to sport through management practices have not been specifically aimed at women who may be socially excluded. This does not compromise their relevance to such women. To a considerable extent the differences in women's situations are matters of degree – but an extreme degree. Compared with men, typically women have fewer financial resources, greater time constraints, more responsibility for child care and other domestic functions, and less personal freedom. Among women who are disadvantaged, these constraints operate to an extent that can be crippling. If anything, the steps that can be taken to counter some of these issues through sports management practices may make more difference to disadvantaged women than to the female population as a whole. Whether they *can* make *enough* is a different question.

Conclusion

This chapter has shown that sport not only reflects but also contributes to women's social exclusion in sport and wider society. This positions sport as a site where the exclusionary effects of gender disadvantage can be meaningfully confronted. Sufficient experience has been gleaned from more than twenty years of sports development work to allow this battle to be joined: there is extensive evidence of how positively women respond to sport, how much they benefit from getting involved, and what steps are required to facilitate their involvement. It is also apparent, however, that socially excluded women are not automatically equal beneficiaries of either sports initiatives that tackle social exclusion, or even of those that tackle gender inequity in sport. Realising the full potential that sport has to offer these women is likely to require a more explicit focus on this multiply disadvantaged group.

Chapter 7

Exclusion and older people in sport

Freysinger (1999: 254) commented on the lack of longitudinal studies of ageing and the scarcity of studies of the leisure of those 'on the margins of society – persons with disabilities, persons of colour, persons with sexual orientation other than heterosexual, the poor, and until recently women.'

Introduction: Age and social exclusion

Exclusion among older people comes from poor health, poverty and disability, all of which may be compounded by isolation and poor mobility. That is why maintaining physical activity with its impact on coping and mobility pays off most in this age group, shown in numerous studies, including the Allied Dunbar National Fitness Survey (Sports Council/Health Education Authority, 1992).

Because some people over retirement age never had the opportunity to develop an occupational pension, more of them depend on State pension and benefits. In the UK the Conservative Government broke the link between State pensions and average earnings in 1981, as a result the UK pension is about a fifth of average earnings, compared with about half in many other European countries. The Tory solution was to promote second, private pensions that can be exchanged for an annuity on retirement. Of course, being based on stock market investments, there is a risk factor which means not everyone will share the general growth of 6.25 per cent annually on European stock over the past 30 years (Denny, *Guardian* 20 Oct 99). The Blair Government (Department of Social Security, 1999: 113) declared its key priorities as:

- ensuring that more of tomorrow's pensioners can retire on a decent income
- tackling the problems of low income and social exclusion among today's pensioners; and
- improving opportunities for older people to live secure, fulfilling and active lives.

Pensioners have experienced the same inequalities as workers as a whole; the top fifth of single pensioners had increases in income of 76 per cent from 1979 to 1997, the bottom fifth of only 28 per cent (equivalent figures for married couples were 80 per cent and 34 per cent). The latter were dependent on benefits because only 5p in the £ of their income arose from savings compared with over 20p for the former. This was correlated with poor housing, poor health, lack of transport and fear of going out, limiting social life. Only 1 in 3 of Clarke's (1993) north London sample claimed that they were able to do what they liked, and the two most mentioned constraints by far were 'cost too much', and 'not liking to go out at night' (47 and 52 per cent respectively). Elderly women are more likely to be poor than elderly men.

The Blair Government also has endorsed the private pensions approach (for 3 out of 5 employees to have a non-State pension by 1996–7, Department of Social Security, nd), though in 2000 it introduced a minimum income guarantee for the poorest of £92.15, and £140.55 for couples. This will produce an unprecedented 8 per cent increase in these households' income in 2001 (Atkinson, *Guardian* 10 Nov 00), but the Age Concern lobby group pointed out that in 1999 they were still lagging £30 a week behind the figures adjusted for inflation (*Guardian* 9 Nov 00). Consequently the UK government does not face the same 'pensions time bomb' as its European neighbours, but it means that a sizeable proportion of retired people will need welfare benefits to top up income for the foreseeable future. The recession in stock market prices, however, has taken the steam out of 'stakeholder' pensions: in 1990 a pension 'pot' of £100,000 purchased an annuity of £11,000 but by 2001 this had declined to £6,000 (Fakenham and Rake, *Guardian* 16 Apr 01).

The DSS (Department of Social Security, 2000) projected:

- A 48 per cent increase in people of pensionable age from 10.5m in 1998 to 15.5m in 2040, assuming women retire aged 65 like men by 2020. This is partly because of growing life expectancy, and partly because the baby boom generation born after World War II will retire between 2005 and 2010.
- Over 30 years:
    i)   A real increase in retirement pension of 1.7 per cent annually
    ii) Via the Minimum Income Guarantee, a real increase in Income Support for older people by 3.4 per cent a year
    iii) A real increase in public spending on older people (excluding disability).

The government said the short-term increase was affordable, depending on the numbers of people aged between 50 and retirement needing sickness or disability benefit.

As people get older, more become dependent on domiciliary health and welfare services (like meals on wheels, home helps, and mobile libraries); in

1996–7 one in 12 households received intensive care (six or more visits in a week – Department of Social Security, n.d). With further frailty, they then need residential care; but the rising costs of the latter has reduced both. Those over 80 will increase from 50 million in 1991 to 137 millian in 2025, with a rising share in developing countries. The extent of leisure provision for institutionalised folk varies, but has barely been studied, like similar setting for children and youth in care. Scase and Scales (2000) predicted two tiers in retirement, one healthy, affluent, mobile, and with an active leisure life and wide social network, and the other with low incomes, poor health, tied to home or locality and with narrow social and leisure horizons, a problem particularly for men.

Regarding the 'old old', in a sample of 1,317 over-80 readers of *Yours* magazine, 3 out of 5 lived on less than £160 a week and 1 in 5 were below the poverty level of less than £80 a week. This figure included a quarter of women but only 4 per cent of men (*Guardian* 5 Oct 99). The concerns of this group were:

•   lack of money
•   declining health
•   loneliness
•   inability to get out
•   'lack of things to do'.

McPherson (1999: 5) stressed that while there is a decline in physical capacity with ageing, 'successful ageing and adaptation in later life is as much a social as a biological process'. Nor, he argued, is it closely linked to chronological age. 'The elderly', so often lumped together, comprise several cohorts, and now cover a 30 to 40 year span. Also, in later years they are dominated by women, many living alone by choice, divorce or widowhood, and often not as close to their children as in previous generations. Gant (1997) emphasised the prevalence of disabilities, and therefore the importance of public transport and of the macro (location) and micro design (entrances, lifts, signs, etc.) of facilities in town and country.

Ageing, leisure and sport

The literature on leisure for older people is remarkably sparse, given the ageing of European populations. McGuire (2000) criticised the lack of attention by leisure researchers, and their reliance on mainstream gerontology for many concepts, such as the idea of 'disengagement,' selective optimisation of activity while compensating for falling incomes and failing faculties. In the UK, Bernard and Midwinter have been the greatest students and advocates of active leisure lifestyles for older people, the latter being concerned about the growth of aimlessness after retirement. Armstrong, Midwinter and Wynne-Harley (1987) looked at four schemes (the University of the Third

Age, [the lack of] provision in residential homes, CB radio, and the Niccol Arts Centre in Cirencester). Bernard (1988) catalogued a wide range of local and adventurous activity schemes.

But Long and Wimbush showed as long ago as 1979 that for men retirement *per se* meant more continuity of past activities than disengagement or taking up a host of new interests. Freysinger (1999: 257) confirmed 'while previous participation in an activity does not guarantee continued participation, it makes it much more likely.' They did not have the resources to study older women's retirement, which is often said to depend on socialising both away from, but especially at home. Only recently have Scraton, Bramham and Watson (2000) looked at the leisure of older women in Leeds, including ethnic minorities – which is substantially home-based, and often constrained by continuing obligations of housework and grandchildren (Seigenthaler and Vaughan, 1998). Age Concern's latest study on older people from ethnic minorities concentrated wholly on social and cultural activities but argued:

> becoming involved in leisure and educational activities, and meeting other older people, often enables people to find out about and benefit from other services, and entitlements.
>
> (Age Concern/Commission for Racial Equality, 1998: 7)

Stanley, Freysinger, and Horn (1996 unpublished, cited in Freysinger, 1999) followed a cohort of American over-50s for sixteen years, and examined the effect of age, gender, and health on nine activities:

- six declined (playing sports, hobbies, civic and fraternal organisations, social and spectator activities, and travelling)
- two stayed much the same (church-going and watching TV/listening to the radio), and
- one, reading, increased.

In similar vein, the Department of Social Security report (2000) mentioned only using libraries and watching TV as leisure activities for this group.

Even in women's sport, men may be in control, as Boyle and Mackay (1995) showed with reference to lawn bowls. And even in health-conscious Canada, many older women were unaware of their doctors' views on exercise, and those most active had been so from childhood, and had a strong support network (O'Brien Cousins, 1995). O'Brien Cousins (1999) spoke of the need to restore an active tradition in North American societies dominated by inactivity, and both she and Hawkins (1999) stressed the ethnic/cultural variations in sport and recreation patterns, found also in England by Verma, and Rowe and Champion, quoted in Chapter 8 (pages 127–31). Low levels of activity are found amongst working class women and those of Asian origin. Amongst the latter, deprivation and poor health is concentrated – 47 per cent of Bangladeshi and Pakistani pensioners experience three or more types of disadvantage compared with 42 per cent of Caribbeans, and 19 per cent of whites. Three-fifths of them struggled in the bottom fifth of the income range compared with half of Indians, a third of Caribbeans, and just over a fifth of whites (Carvel, *Guardian* 13 Sept 00).

Learning is a form of leisure that also has socialising benefits. But the most recent (1999) survey by the National Institute of Adult and Continuing Education showed that, while 2 out of 5 of all adults had taken part in the last three years, amongst older people there had been a fall of up to 20 per cent (*Guardian Education* 18 May 99). Finch's (1997) in-depth interviews for the Health Education Authority of people aged 50 to 85 living at home and in care showed 1 in 4 were active, over 1 in 3 inactive, and 1 in 5 rejecting activity. Barriers they identified included the young, fit image of sportspeople, embarrassment and lack of confidence, lack of interest, fears of overdoing it and possible dangers to health 'at our age' and a lack of time both real and as a cover to other factors (Finch, 1997: 51).

For Clarke's (1993) sample of 129 older north Londoners, leisure was mostly passive and sociable, though the majority claimed not to do much at home or away:

	% involved monthly	% never
Visiting friends	16	40
Entertaining friends	21	59
Out for a drink	7	81
Dancing	8	71
Going for a meal	23	65
Going for tea/coffee	13	70
Cinema		87
Museums/galleries		82
Leisure centres		87
Theatres		80
Bingo		69

Regarding sport, 1 in 5 did some, half going swimming and 1 in 10 saying they were members of a sports club, about the same as attended a day centre or luncheon club. Clarke commented that familiarity was an important feature which bred 'content, comfort and security' (1993: 7). Maybe the low rates of participation explain why Kelly and Ross (1989) found that the idea of leisure being an identity former for retired people was not strong, though most common in sport, culture and travel. Such activities require input of effort and money and provided the highest social and personal benefits.

McPherson (1991) believed that for older people social support is very important in their leisure, but so is having a good deal of autonomy to plan and run their own programmes. Stead et al. (1997), from focus group research, suggested that older Scots emphasised the psychological and social aspects of activity, while exercise and health professionals tend to emphasise the physiological and health benefits, and perhaps should reflect on this difference in future health promotional work. Finland is reckoned to sustain one of the most active lifestyles in the developed world, with about two-thirds of older people walking for fitness, one-third doing callisthenics at home, and a small minority doing other forms of exercise. Hirvensalo et al. (1998) followed up a sample of senior citizens after eight years and found three-quarters of their 65- to 84-year-olds walked for fitness and half did callisthenics at home. But even here, with an 'Evergreen' promotional campaign, 2 out of 5 did nothing but chores, the majority not exercising, saying that it was because of their poor health.

Retirement populations are also unevenly spread; many of those who can afford to move from cities to congenial locations do so, to the 'costa geriatrica' of England's entire south coast and Cornwall and Devon's north coast to Minehead, the North Wales and Lancashire coasts, Yorkshire around Whitby and Scarborough, and parts of Norfolk and Suffolk, but also inland to the Welsh Borders and southern Lake District (Law and Warnes, 1976; Gant, 1997). Having a large elderly population puts a larger demand on health and welfare services, but also a different view on physical activity. After ten years of growth, only now is the fitness industry in Britain thinking about recruiting more older people as fitness instructors, and developing centres that focus on older customers.

There has been what Midwinter (1992) called a 'research gulf', despite the ageing of society, and the English Sports Council has, for nearly a decade, accorded it no priority or advice, despite the fact the its *50+ and all to play for* pack has been reprinted more than once since the 1980s and widely used. If the data on older people's leisure is sparse, so is that on sports participation. The Allied Dunbar National Fitness Survey showed the decline of vigorous and moderate exercise with age, to a degree where a majority of men over 65 and almost all women had significant arm and leg weaknesses. These were to an extent which would limit their mobility (in getting up and down stairs, bus platforms and armchairs) and the radius of their walking capability; five years later only 14 per cent were active enough to bring health benefits (Health Education Authority, 1999: 6).

In terms of sport, the General Household Survey showed a steady increase in participation from 1987 to 1993 but a decline in the recession to 1996 – no doubt a factor linked to a decline among the D and E social groups which are a disproportionate part of the older population (Chapter 4), and a small decline in women taking walks longer than two miles. This is shown in Table 7.1. This decline was in both sports activities, especially keep fit, but also walking. Swimming, however, kept on growing. In contrast to a strong commitment to

Table 7.1 Sports participation amongst people aged over 45 in Great Britain, 1987–96 (percentage participating in four weeks before interview; percentage of population average given in brackets)

		Aged 45 to 59 (%)	Aged 60 to 69 (%)	Aged 70+ (%)
At least one activity	1987	56 (92)	47 (77)	26 (43)
	1990	63 (97)	54 (83)	31 (48)
	1993	64 (100)	51 (80)	32 (52)
	1996	63 (98)	55 (86)	31 (48)
At least one activity, excluding walking	1987	35 (75)	23 (51)	10 (22)
	1990	42 (88)	28 (58)	12 (25)
	1993	43 (91)	27 (60)	16 (34)
	1996	40 (87)	30 (65)	13 (28)
Bases		4,140 to 3,686	2,654 to 2,024	2,541 to 2,305

socialising in clubs, sports club membership drops substantially with age (Rowe, Moore and Mori, 1999: 10):

	% of adults who were club members in the previous 4 weeks, 1996			
	total	45–59 years	60–69 years	over 70 years
social club	2.8	2.2	2.7	1.7
sports club	8.2	7.7	6.0	2.9

A 1997–8 survey of the management and use of sports halls and pools (SE, 2000) showed clear under-representation of people over 45 in both halls and pools – 26 per cent and 31 per cent compared with 44 per cent of the population as a whole. But they only had 3 per cent of the programme time in sports halls and 1 per cent in swimming. By far the most popular activities in sports halls were badminton and keep fit/aerobics/yoga, as for users overall, but the third was short mat/carpet bowls. Almost 9 out of 10 facilities offered concessions for people aged over 60, and 72 per cent claimed specific policies for over-50s, but only 18 per cent had specific targets. Only 4 per cent of hall users were senior citizens with discount cards, and 6.7 per cent of swimmers (that was 1 in 7 and 1 in 4 respectively of all card holders). Comparing surveys in the last four decades demonstrated a steady growth in sports hall users aged over 45, accelerating in the 1990s, perhaps because of the interest in fitness:

Table 7.2 Sports participation by age in three European countries (per cent)

Age groups	Finland		UK		Italy	
	Groups 1 and 2[a] (%)	Groups 6 and 7 (%)	Groups 1 and 2 (%)	Groups 6 and 7 (%)	Groups 1 and 2 (%)	Groups 6 and 7 (%)
50 to 54	38	22	20	60	3	88
55 to 59	41	24	118	67	3	90
60 to 64	46	28	14	69	3	93
65+	–	–	10	82	1	97

Note: a Groups 1 and 2 were involved in sport on 120-plus occasions a year; Groups 6 and 7 were involved in sport on none or fewer than 12 occasions a year

4 per cent in the 1960s; 9 per cent in the 1970s; 6 per cent in the 1980s; 24 per cent in the 1990s.

Participation in active recreation and sport in all countries shows a general fall with the ageing process. Using data from five countries in Europe, Rodgers (1977) argued that this was accentuated because many people over 50 at that time had had a very limited experience of sport in childhood; they had never learned the skills or ethos of sport; they were 'sports illiterate.' Harahousou (1999) showed how a new affluent sports-literate group in Greece is moving into retirement, but that they are a minority. Nevertheless the wider school sport curricula of the 1960s onwards will have equipped future generations better for exercising choice. The seven-nation Compass Survey (UK Sport/Sport England/CONI, 1999) demonstrated that participation fell swiftly during people's third decade in all the countries, even though the overall levels were much higher in Scandinavia than southern Europe, with western Europe somewhere between. But there were significant differences for those over 50 (Table 7.2):

- Intensive participation remained much higher in Scandinavia and very low in Italy and Spain, even increasing after 60 in Finland and 65 in Sweden.
- The converse of this was a much lower rate of non- or low participation in Scandinavia than in the UK.

The reasons cannot be conclusively adduced, and cannot just be attributed to commuting on skis (which only a minority do), but socialising around an active club culture remarkable for young people attending with their parents is probably a factor (Seppanen, 1982; Heinila, 1989), together with a widespread adoption of a healthy lifestyle in which exercise is accompanied by a 'good' diet and little smoking.

Povlsen and Larsen (1999) outlined the situation in Denmark, where sports participation of the over 60s rose from 12 per cent in 1975 to 27 per cent in 1993. What is perhaps salutary for Britain where the situation is reversed, is that the participation of older women was higher than of men, rising from 15 per cent to 27 per cent (for men from 9 per cent to 26 per cent, so the gender gap is being slowly closed). The most popular activities were the same as in Britain (swimming, exercises, walking and rambling, cycling and badminton), but more were competing and more were sports club members (10.3 per cent). Denmark has achieved this in a small country of 5 million people, with 22,000 clubs but no sport ministry – policy being shared by those for Culture, Health and Social Services. Also, as in Britain, a minority are intensively involved in extreme and strenuous sports with associated injury risks. Govaerts (1993: 24) commented that generally in Europe there had been a growth in participation since 1980 but judged that it was 'insufficient . . . in the light of demographic and economic changes', and called for a move from experiments and model programmes to full scale policies to encourage participation.

While in consumer markets 'grey power' has been identified in the USA, the same age group is less vocal and less powerful in the UK. These are people with time to commit to volunteering and they play vital roles in many welfare organisations; in sport the dominance of older people on British national governing bodies has been derided as being out of touch – notably in the ruling bodies of cricket and rugby union, branded as 'old farts' (a derogatory comment, originally made by England captain Will Carling of the Rugloy Football Union), a very different view of the experience of age, venerated in many Eastern and Southern cultures.

Conclusions

While 'veteran's' sport has increased greatly in popularity, in competitive terms this mainly means people in their 40s, except in bowls and running. Most older people's sport is for fun and socialising. But it can be a great boon to health. Whereas the costs of injuries outweigh benefits for younger people, for every year after the mid-30s the balance of benefits over costs grows, through maintaining independence and improved body functions (Nicholl, Copeman and Williams, 1993). Given the expected growth of the population over the age of 60, it is surprising how virtually no attention is now paid by Sport England to encouraging participation. Having been told to leave Sport for All to other agencies, notably local authorities, it has abandoned *50+ and all to play for*, one of its cheapest and most successful promotions, and no participation targets for older adults are included in its 1997 strategy (Collins, 2002). The English Sports Council's 'hands-off' commentary was that the reduced spending by local authorities on parks was likely to reduce opportunities for walking, cycling and bowls, and that:

Table 7.3 Projected population aged over 65 years, 1990–2025 (millions)

Region	1990	2005	2025
World	328	475	822
Less developed regions	183	289	566
North America	35	39	67
Europe	68	82	105

Unless the remaining subsidy for sport can be more accurately targeted towards the less wealthy, they will become increasingly disadvantaged. The divergence in incomes of the retired will be reflected in a divergence of sports participation.

(English Sports Council, 1997: 9)

As if it was not already thus. Only ten of over 1,500 local Sports Development officers were devoted to working with older people, eight in the Eastern region, the only region to make this group a priority.

Many local authorities have maintained programmes, sometimes jointly with health authorities. Sixty per cent of GP referral programmes prescribing exercise were hosted in their leisure facilities. But much has been left to the Health Education Authority, with its programmes emphasising walking, stair climbing, dancing, swimming and cycling. That sort of casual activity, however, will not close the gap in sports participation between Britain and Scandinavia, which must be seen as the site of good practice, in binding generations into a sports club network.

The global growth in numbers of people aged over 65 (Table 7.3) will be very great (McPherson, 1999: 7), and that will magnify the importance of social life and leisure for a longer part of the life span, even if the retirement age is raised. Japan's retirement population has doubled to 14 per cent of the total in only 26 years, compared with 115 years for France, and this is likely to be the mode for the developing world. Harada (1999) berated Japan's government for failing to set up preventive health and activity programmes on a scale to match this change. He also foresaw, in a work-dominated society, the need for programmes of adult education to 're-socialise' people into leisure. Some might argue likewise for Britain! As more people gain decent pensions, they will expect fulfilling leisure; the patterns of the past may be little guide to what is needed (Hawkins, 1999; O'Brien Cousins, 1999).

Chapter 8

Social exclusion and sport in a multicultural society

Introduction: From race to ethnicity

The issue of race in sport comes to Britain from the United States where the discourse has focused until recently around African Americans and skin colour; more recently studies have included Hispanic groups. In Britain from the late 1970s serious study has developed from the issue of skin colour to that of culture, though studies of South Asian, Chinese, and even more, white cultural minorities in sport (Irish, Polish, Ukrainian), are progressively rarer. In the US, issues have been:

- why black people are well- or over-represented in some professional sports (notably athletics, American football, basketball and baseball) but not much or at all in others (such as tennis, golf or swimming). In Britain these same contrasts are made between athletics, soccer and cricket and other sports; but in 1999 the Football Association held a major conference into the lack of Asian players
- the idea of 'stacking' – the placing of ethnic minority professional players in certain positions within a team
- the use of professional sport as a route 'out of the ghetto', and
- more recently, the unequal chances of participation by minorities in sport as recreation.

These same issues have been raised in Britain, though with less emphasis on stacking (though Maguire 1988, 1991 and Melnick, 1988 have studied it in soccer and the former also in rugby). Collins contrasted the involvement of black professional players and coaches in Rugby League with their slow and late emergence in soccer and Rugby Union. He commented on the stacking of black players in non-decision making positions, shared with the other team games, and the lack of black supporters (Collins, 1998: 152). He attributed this to 'an ideology ostensibly based on meritocracy' but within a wider setting, 'shaped by business exigency and the underlying racist assumptions of British society.' Later he concluded, 'Rugby League is . . . a deeply contradictory phenomenon. A long history of achievement by black players and coaches coexists with deep-rooted racial stereotyping and estrangement from local communities' (Collins, 1998: 166).

Horne, Tomlinson and Whannel (1999) dealt with the issue as a matter of black identity. Cashmore (1982, 1989, 1996) has looked at the emergence of black professional, elite athletes and discrimination against them. Here we shall focus more on discrimination than the other aspects. Although the political and academic discourse is about multiculturalism, in the pub and the popular media it is about race (Polley, 1998: Chapter 6).

The previous studies have to be viewed against the backdrop of society's reaction to the waves of immigration from Africa and the Caribbean, East Africa, India, Pakistan and Bangladesh, Cyprus and Turkey, with the steadier trickles from Hong Kong and many other places. Although black people had been coming to Britain from the eighteenth century, it was the immigration from the West Indies in the 1950s and 1960s that brought concerns about competition for jobs and housing opportunities, epitomised in Enoch Powell's 'rivers of blood' speech, at a time when only 3 per cent of the population were not white/Caucasian. In the popular version of his study for Political and Economic Planning (1968), Daniel demonstrated in housing, employment and public services 'racial discrimination . . . varying from the massive to the substantial'. Political action led to Acts of Parliament in 1965, 1968, and 1976 to outlaw such attitudes and actions and to promote equality of opportunity, led by a Commission for Racial Equality. When polled in 2001 about the most important problems facing Britain and Europe respectively, respondents put race relations and immigration fourth out of ten in both cases (Bramen, *Guardian* 22 Jun 01).

By the millennial year, ethnic minorities comprised 7.1 per cent of the population but 11.5 per cent of schoolchildren; 84 per cent lived in the four conurbations of Greater London, the West Midlands, Manchester and West Yorkshire, 7 out of 10 in the eighty-eight most deprived local authorities (Cabinet Office, 2001).

In sport, the first move was probably the British Boxing Board of Control's decision in 1948 to allow anyone 'normally resident' and having lived in the UK for 10 years to hold British titles. The anti-apartheid movement's opposition to South African 'rebel' cricket and rugby tours and the maintenance of segregation kept the issue alive through the 1970s, as did the Government's stance on the same issue. Herman Ouseley, chairman of the Commission for Racial Equality (CRE), commented about discrimination in 1995, 'some people think it's all over . . . but it hasn't gone away' (1995: 1). The Sports Council said:

> In sport individuals and organisations deliberately discriminate against black and ethnic minority people. There are others who unintentionally discriminate, mainly because they fail to acknowledge how racial inequality, cultural variance, and their own organisational behaviour restrict

equal opportunities. Because many people in sport have understood racism to consist only of overt and deliberate forms of discrimination, more subtle and unintentional racism is not even detected.

(Sports Council, 1994: 17)

Carrington and McDonald (2001: 12) agreed: 'sport, like many other cultural areas, is a site of contestation, resistance and struggle, whereby dominant ideologies are both maintained and challenged . . . this applies as much to "race" and ethnicity as it does to gender, sexuality or class'. In 1993 the CRE joined the Professional Footballers Association in a campaign, 'Let's kick racism out of football'. In 1999 the Football Association promoted a conference and campaign to get more Asian players into the amateur and professional game.

Thus stereotyping and discrimination have not gone away despite the growing numbers of ethnic minority players visible in professional sport, and of both mixed culture and culturally representative teams in amateur sport. There still are views that 'black people are not suited to managing teams or clubs', or 'black people aren't suited physiologically to swim or play hockey', 'Asians cannot play contact sports and can only play hockey' (see also Sleap, 1998: 111). Academic research has, thankfully, revealed that race 'is essentially a social construction and not a natural division' (Hudson and Williams, 1995: 117).

There are also stereotypes about low skill and low income amongst ethnic minorities; Platt and Noble (1999) looked in detail at Birmingham, where 22 per cent of the population are from minorities. Their analysis of Housing Benefit or Council Tax relief covering 270,000 people showed:

- an over-representation of Pakistani and Bangladeshi groups
- notable concentrations of couples with children in Bangladeshi households (55 per cent), and lone parents amongst Afro-Caribbeans (45 per cent)
- 94 per cent of Pakistani and Bangladeshi lone parents received Income Support, whereas 24 per cent of black Afro-Caribbeans were working in jobs above that threshold
- Pakistanis are more likely to be buying their own homes, while there are more Bangladeshis in public and housing association accommodation, like the white population.

Means-tested benefits did not always help as much as they might, and schemes like the New Deal were not relevant to older lone parents with few employment skills and experiences. The work of the Policy Action Teams of the Social Exclusion Unit stimulated data collection; its overview concluded:

People from minority ethnic communities are at disproportionate risk of social exclusion . . . are more likely than others to live in deprived

Table 8.1 Features of ethnic disadvantage

- 56 per cent lived in the 44 most deprived local authority areas.
- 34 per cent of Chinese people lived in households with below half average income, 40 per cent of Afro-Caribbean and Indian, and over 80 per cent of Pakistani and Bangladeshi (compared with 28 per cent of the total population).
- From 1994–5 to 1997–8 Afro-Caribbean pupils were 4 to 6 times more likely to be excluded from school, though no more likely to truant than others.
- Ethnic minorities were 2 to 3 times more likely than white people to be unemployed.
- One in 7 lived in overcrowded housing compared with 2 in 100 white households.
- In 1995 there were an estimated 382,000 racial incidents, of which only 3 per cent were reported to the police.
- Black people were 6 times more likely to be stopped and searched and 4.3 times more likely to be arrested than whites.
- 32 per cent of Indian/Pakistani/Bangladeshi children attained 5 or more GCSEs at grade A* to C compared with 50 per cent of whites.

Source: Cabinet Office, 2000, 2001

areas and in unpopular and overcrowded housing. They are more likely to be poor and to be unemployed, regardless of their age, sex, qualifications and place of residence. Minority ethnic communities experience a double disadvantage. They are disproportionately concentrated in deprived areas and experience all the problems that affect other people in these areas. But . . . also suffer the consequences of racial discrimination: services that fail to reach them or meet their needs; and language and cultural barriers in gaining access to information and services.

(Cabinet Office, 2000: 7–8)

Table 8.1 illustrates some of the features of this disadvantage.

The Cabinet Office (2001: 37), examining and extrapolating from past trends in employment, housing, welfare housing and crime, concluded that 'the most likely pattern for the future appears to be widening differences for most ethnic minority groups and most dimensions of inequality', and that there was no apparent coherent policy for tackling these issues. PAT 10 on sports and arts recommended that these activities should be part of reviving communities in deprived neighbourhoods, and specific equal opportunities action should be taken in local authority cultural strategies, Lottery, New Deal and other programmes, and their evaluation.

Riots in Bradford, Oldham and Burnley in April and June 2001 led to separate inquiries and an overview – the Cantle report (Home Office, 2001). This said that white and minority communities lived 'parallel lives' with little communication. It condemned weak community leadership and discrimination by private sector employers. It also said a 'meaningful concept of citizenship' needs to be established and championed (Home Office, 2001: 22).

Multicultural participation in sport

The General Household Survey (GHS) in 1996 included for the first time identification of ethnic origin, and it became clear that participation in sport by black people is closest to white patterns overall. Bangladeshis participated much less and Indians substantially less, but interestingly the other groups participated more. Black and South Asian people walked considerably less than white people. These patterns may be related to the Households Below Average Income statistics displayed in Chapter 2. It was not possible to look at specific sports because of the small sample sizes. But Sport England undertook a separate survey (Rowe and Champion, 2000) with a sample size of 3,084 adults (Table 8.2).

Black 'other' groups (not African or Caribbean) participate more than average, notably because of their high male rate of participation; indeed the gender gap was more marked (21 to 35 percentage points) for this group than in the population as a whole (15 percentage points). Walking regularly and briskly is an important contributor to a healthy lifestyle; none of the groups reached the population average of 44 per cent for walking two miles or more, only 1 in 5 of the Bangladeshis doing so.

Ethnic minority groups did not take part in activities popular amongst the white majority – bowls, fishing, table tennis, squash and horse riding. Table 8.3 shows those they did take part in, featuring

- keepfit/aerobics as the second most popular
- snooker, slightly more so than generally
- swimming, lower than its second place for England as a whole.

It also shows the variegated patterns of activity by group and in the more detailed data by gender, none so strong as to sustain stereotypes like 'black people can't swim.'

Table 8.2 Participation in sport 1999–2000 by ethnic group (percentage aged over 16 undertaking one or more sports/activities in last four weeks, excluding walking)

Ethnic group	Total (%)	Male (%)	Female (%)
GHS 1996 All	46	54	39
Any ethnic minority	41		
Black Caribbean	39	45	34
Black African	44	60	34
Black other	60	80	45
Indian	39	45	31
Pakistani	31	42	21
Bangladeshi	30	46	19
Chinese	45	54	39
Other	46	51	41

Source: Rowe and Champion, 2000

Table 8.3 The five most popular sports undertaken by ethnic minorities 1999–2000 (percentage in last four weeks)

	Black Caribbean (%)	Black African (%)	Black Other (%)	Indian (%)	Pakistani (%)	Bangladeshi (%)	Chinese (%)	Other (%)	GHS[a] 1996 (%)
Walking	34	37	36	31	24	19	28	42	44
Keep fit	19	17	24	13	9	7	16	15	15
Snooker	9	8	16	10	6	10		10	11
Swimming				11	8	8	8	15	15
Soccer	8	11	14	7	9	8		6	5
Cycling	8		14				8	6	11
Running		13						6	4
Badminton							10		2
Table tennis					6				2
Weight training	9								6

Source: Sport England, 2000

Notes:
a GHS = General Household Survey
b Some responses are too small to be calculated

Indeed, variety is also shown in answers to a question about what sports they would like to take up that they did not currently do, the top three answers for each group by gender being shown in Table 8.4. From 51 per cent of Bangladeshis to 81 per cent of the black 'other', all communities mentioned something. Taking up swimming was a popular idea amongst men and, especially, women from all groups; women also wanted to do keep fit, self-defence, badminton and yoga. Men wanted to try soccer, tennis and motor sport.

When asked what factors had prevented them taking part in sport in the last year, the answers were very similar to those given in surveys of mainly white users:

• home and family responsibilities ranked first, for over 2 in 5 women in all minority communities and both men and women from Indian and Bangladeshi communities
• lack of or unsuitable facilities was quoted by 48 per cent of Bangladeshis and 45 per cent of black others.
• Lack of money was cited by more black Caribbean and black other groups (25 per cent).

Finally, only 6 per cent said they had had a negative experience in sport due to their ethnicity, though the figure for black others was 17 per cent. When asked about whether they had enjoyed sport in school, only 3 per cent said

Table 8.4 The top three sports in which ethnic groups would most like to participate (percentage of each group; figures for males on the left and females on the right)

	Black Caribbean (%)	Black African (%)	Black Other (%)	Indian (%)	Pakistani (%)	Bangladeshi (%)	Chinese (%)	Other (%)
Swimming	10 12	15 31	17	10 22	14 16	9 21	13 18	13 21
Keep fit/yoga	22	26	10 25	19	13			17
Soccer			13	8	8	18		
Badminton				12	10	17 10	13 13	11
Self-defence/ martial arts	10 12		17			11		
Netball		11	18					
Tennis		15	10				15 10	
Motor sports			18				13	11
Golf								11

Source: Sport England, 2000

something had deterred them from taking part, and two-thirds said they had enjoyed it, ranging from 74 per cent amongst black Caribbeans and Bangladeshis to 60 per cent amongst Pakistanis and 54 per cent amongst Chinese.

Rowe and Champion commented (2000: 37): 'the results . . . challenge stereo-typical views that suggest that low levels of participation in sport (and in certain sports in particular) by certain groups are more a reflection of culture and choice rather than other constraints such as provision, affordability and access.' Given that the second and third generation schoolchildren in these households are taking part more and more in the National Curriculum and are becoming more acculturated, it will be interesting to watch these participation patterns evolve.

In Manchester, Verma and Darby (1994) interviewed 721 people from five Asian, African, Caribbean, and East African Asian groups, and a white group of 190, about their leisure, and social and religious life. Their sports participation is shown in Table 8.5, which uses a less stringent and more inclusive measure of casual participation than the GHS. With a substantially larger female than male response, participation rates would have been lower than the national average, but the rates for the white city dwellers were also lower.

The Table also shows how the pattern of use of facilities of different providers varied – the most recently arrived groups from Bangladesh and East Africa depending more on their own community's provision; the availability to the various sub-groups was not catalogued. The number of those who felt unable to use local authority facilities but wished to was small, but noticeable, including sizeable proportions of white and Pakistani women.

Table 8.5 Participation and use/non-use of sports facilities by ethnic group in Manchester

	Bangladeshi (%)	African (%)	Caribbean (%)	Chinese (%)	East African Asian (%)	Indian (%)	Pakistani (%)	White (%)	Other (%)	Total (%)
Sports										
Male	32.7	23.2	32.4	33.0	42.9	39.1	35.4	33.1	–	34.1
Female	9.9	29.0	25.9	25.1	28.1	23.5	10.9	24.1	–	21.9
Places used										
Local authority facility	34	17	45	25	27	35	23	46	–	35
Sports club	8	6	7	14	39	19	18	10	–	14
Own community centre	28	1	1	6	15	7	1	0.4	–	7
Youth club	3	3	16	2	6	2	7	0.4	–	4
Education	6	6	8	31	–	7	19	7	–	12
Company	6	21	10	9	3	16	17	20	–	14
Wish but unable to use local authority facilities										
Male	16	24	14	9	6	16	4	6	–	12 (52)
Female	18	24	26	9	50	16	19	26	–	21 (99)
Base Male	*55*	*19*	*38*	*80*	*9*	*53*	*62*	*71*	*7*	*313*
Female	*49*	*26*	*80*	*53*	*12*	*98*	*81*	*129*	*9*	*408*

Those sports chosen by significant numbers were:

	Men (%)			Women (%)	
	White	Ethnic minorities		White	Ethnic minorities
Soccer	37	47	Badminton	22	28
Snooker	25	28	Swimming	57	23
Swimming	47	20	Keep fit	25	15
Badminton	17	14	Aerobics	22	10
Pool	18	24	Dancing	17	11

More recently in 1997, Sport England (2000) discovered that ethnic minorities were fairly represented in a sample of English sports halls (5.3 per cent compared with their share of the population, 5.2 per cent), but were substantially under-represented in using swimming pools, at 2.8 per cent. In contrast, Ravenscroft and Markwell (2000), sampling visitors to eight large, medium and small Reading parks, discovered a consistently greater share of black and Asian visitors than in the neighbourhood populations, whereas earlier surveys had found under-representation at other public leisure facilities. Also, they found a greater segregation of groups at the neighbourhood parks, and a lower level of satisfaction with the equipment and facilities by black compared with white and Asian youths.

In Amsterdam and Tilburg, Elling, de Knop and Knoppers (2001) found the lowest level of female participation in sport to be amongst Turkish girls (18 per cent), compared with Surinamese or Moroccans (around 40 per cent), while Indonesian girls participated as much as the majority group, at around 68 per cent; boys always participated more than girls. Turkish, Moroccan and Surinamese children were about twice as likely to attend an ethnically mixed sports club as the others, but sports clubs had been the main place to make friends for only about 1 in 10 children.

So far as elite sport is concerned, there are again inequalities in representation. In eleven sports in 1997, 2 per cent were black Caribbeans (twice the proportion in the population), and only 1 per cent were from Asian backgrounds, compared with three times as many in the population (English Sports Council, 1998).

Arguments about race and ethnicity in sport, therefore, fall into three groups:

- unequal treatment relates to and cannot be separated from the *social deprivation* of many ethnic groups
- ethnic minority groups make different leisure choices from the ethnic majority population, reflecting different meanings and values, and

- sport is a site of discrimination as much as other areas of life, emanating in poorer access to resources, expertise and power.

Sport, ethnicity and exclusion

The popular press has promulgated stories of, in particular, footballers, cricketers and boxers who have 'climbed out of the ghetto' through sport, and yet also of lack of equal opportunities and racism in sport. In Canada, Stodolska and Jackson (1998) found little discrimination against a Polish minority, though this may be due partly to effectively 'closed' clubs. In Britain, the Sports Council and governing bodies have sought to promote non-discriminatory attitudes to combat racism, and to open up organisations to equal opportunities. Brownill and Thomas (1998) argued that while some resources were successfully targeted at ethnic groups and projects under the Urban Programme, more recent initiatives – City Challenge and Urban Development Corporations – have been 'racially blind', less involved with local representative processes, and have failed to involve minorities in 'associational democracy'.

Some argue that problems of stereotyping and lack of equal treatment begin at school. Fleming (1991), in studying a comprehensive school, suggested that for Asian male school children a self-fulfilling situation occurred where they were not expected to do well in sport, and lived up, or down, to this view (valuing sport less and having few role models). De Knop et al. (1996) recorded how copying of Muslim countries in introducing physical education for boys but not always for girls took place among Muslims in Western Europe. Meantime, Asian girls in the UK and Western Europe lived under a strong cultural pressure about revealing their body, and finding less satisfaction in British rather than Asian forms of dance. Leaman and Carrington (1985), in contrast, found sport to be a means of self-expression and recognition for Afro-Caribbean pupils that they did not always get in 'academic' subjects. Carroll and Hollinshead (1993) argued that in mixed culture situations, teachers have a dilemma of acknowledging cultural minority authenticity, without having the curriculum being driven by their needs. Bayliss (1989: 1) argued that superficial responses like separate showering and activities for Asian girls do not respond adequately, and schools should ask four questions:

1   *Entitlement*: Are the school's aims rooted in individual needs?
2   *PE*: Does the department have multicultural aims that relate to cross-curricular themes?
3   *Delivery*: Do teaching styles, grouping, attitudes and expertise reconcile the needs of all groups?
4   *Monitoring*: Is there regular evaluation to see how ethnic issues are addressed?

In sport, Verma and Darby (1994) have given the most detailed overview of ethnic minority sport in England. Their survey, carried out in Manchester (see Table 8.5), confirmed the same interest in sport among ethnic minority children as their white counterparts, but also the more limited opportunities of women and girls. The latter was exacerbated in the case of Islamic females, by restrictions on body exposure and participation in mixed groups. While sport was ranked first amongst leisure pursuits for six of the eight male Muslim groups and a close second for the other two, it was third behind passive entertainments and socialising for the women's groups.

Scott Porter (2001) undertook qualitative research in Scotland. There, people of Asian origin were heavily influenced by the role of parents and 'significant others', by the problem of training during the Ramadan fast, and the girls also by the issue of modesty. Scott Porter divided their sample into: the *security seekers*, who were least likely to play sport and only then in safe, segregated settings; the *harmony seekers*, who sought to reconcile their sport with cultural and religious expectations; and *independents*, who saw themselves first as Scots citizens, and wanted to share the culture of their neighbours. There were few community-specific barriers, by far the largest being 'an experience or fear of racial discrimination [which] is not just about physical or verbal abuse but also institutional racism' (Scott Porter, 2001: 32), which most had undergone. The authors provided examples of current practice across the UK.

De Knop et al. (1994) had similar findings in Belgium. Provision of segregated transport and sport sessions have been successful in supporting participation in the short term – for example Asian women's swimming, fitness and sport schemes for Asian girls and women, such as Sitara Fitness and Health in Batley, Blackburn, Leeds, Birmingham and other places. Jones (1998) stressed their fears of harassment and assault, but also their frustrations at a home-centred lifestyle.

In South Africa, apartheid had maintained the most strict form of segregation ever seen, while sustaining a rhetoric about sporting contact 'building bridges' where, as Merrett (1996) pointed out, both ends were white; the anti-apartheid movement provided a means of protest which contributed to the downfall of the system. After the establishment of the 'Rainbow society', there was much to be done. While a wide range of activities were undertaken in black townships, participation was severely restricted by the poor infra-structure, and participation and leadership very much related to educational attainments (Wilson and Hattingh, 1992). Even given the universally pressing local needs in South Africa, Burnett and Hollander demonstrated that the national government has been lead to concentrate resources on elite facilities and players rather than Sport for All, opining that:

> impoverished communities need the government and national stake-holders of sport and recreation to introduce economic incentives to alleviate poverty, create employment, alleviate the social ills such as

alcohol abuse, early school drop-out, criminality and violence (between gangs, in the public and private sphere). The scarcity of resources complicates the recruitment of volunteers to afford the delivery of sport to impoverished communities as they do not have access to resources or find it impossible to carry a double workload.

(Burnett and Hollander, 1999: 13)

The Sports Council's demonstration project in Scunthorpe suggested that linking leisure to health and education as a stronger part of lifestyle was a helpful precursor to promoting particular sports programmes (MacDonald and Tungatt, 1991). In Germany, Polish migrants to the Ruhr in the early twentieth century used football to reproduce cultural identity and have been assimilated, but the postwar 'guestworkers' (*gastarbeiter*) cannot have citizenship unless one of their parents is German, and in particular the 28 per cent (1.92 million) from Turkey have by law and discrimination remained a separate group in sport, with virtually no professional footballers emerging. There is a network of separate Turkish sports clubs, virtually all male, with little participation by girls in PE and almost none in sport (Merkel, 1999).

As we shall see in Chapter 11, inner city youth schemes, both in general and targeting at risk or delinquent youth, involve them as participants and as coaches and leaders (for example, Football and the Community schemes). For the small minority of ethnic minority elders, the Commission for Racial Equality and Age Concern (1998a) spoke of 'double discrimination' in isolation as well as poverty or poor health; all their good practice case studies in leisure (Commission for Racial Equality/Age Concern, 1998b) came from library services.

In the USA, studies on physical exercise amongst ethnic minorities (for example Taylor et al., 1998) often found weight loss in a large group of African American women sustained six months after exercise classes for 45 per cent of their sample, and by 55 per cent of another similar group three months after aerobics classes; and increased walking in a mixed ethnic group 30 months after an exercise programme. They pointed out that interventions had been aimed at Afro-Caribbean and Mexican populations, and more work was needed amongst Latinos, native Indians, and Asian immigrants.

In countryside recreation, lower participation shown in national surveys has been attributed, with limited evidence, to a combination of lower average incomes and car ownership, concentrations in inner cities at some distances from the countryside, and a lack of tradition in countryside day trips in ethnic cultures. This has been little explored in Britain; in the USA, Floyd, Gramman and Saenz (1993) found less use by Mexican and Spanish speaking citizens, and Johnson et al. (1998) markedly lower use of the countryside by poor blacks. Baas, Ewert and Chavez (1993) found that in the Mecca hills of the Mojave Desert, Mexican and US-born Hispanics desired equipped sites (toilets, picnic areas, garbage disposal, marked trails) and favoured group sports and picnicking, while Anglo visitors preferred informal sites, trails, walking and backpacking. No studies were found of schemes to promote participation in the countryside specifically by ethnic minorities, though the Getaway Girls scheme in Leeds and the Wild Outdoor Women project in Kirklees aimed to encourage outdoor sports participation by inner city women, including white, ethnic minority, and disabled (Glyptis, Collins, and Randolph, 1995).

Thompson (1999: 215), relating the work of the Youth Charter for Sport on Merseyside and in Manchester, stated the best aspirations for sport in this group in the YCS' Charter: 'sport is education, the truest form of education, that of character. Sport is culture because it enhances life and, most importantly, does so for those who most importantly, have the least opportunity to feast on it.'

Interventions

Ethnic minorities have been a target of national sports policy since 1982, leading to the Scunthorpe national demonstration project, and to the installation of managers and sports development officers from and to work with ethnic groups, especially in inner cities. When the marketing device of targeting fell out of favour on the (undemonstrated) grounds that it was stigmatising, a new racial equality policy was introduced: 'to work towards the elimination of racial disadvantage and discrimination in order to achieve better quality sport for black and ethnic minority people' (Sports Council, 1994: 7).

Case studies of good practice in promoting sports, especially cricket, and awareness training and courses for ethnic minority members to become coaches, officials and administrators were included in two Sports Council documents (Sports Council NW, 1991 and Sports Council Y&H, 1995). The English Sports Council (1997) gave examples of good practice for local authorities in:

- policy planning for multiculturalism (Leicester City)
- the use of race relations advisers and customer care (Birmingham)
- employment schemes (Watford and Southwark)
- recognition of the issue in Compulsory Competitive Tendering (Newham)
- inclusion in sports development programmes (Oldham and Watford), and leadership training (Kirklees).

The Scunthorpe project demonstrated ways of linking sport with other actions, like:

- more publicity and information in minority languages, needed just as much for housing, social services, and citizens' advice
- involving and empowering local minority groups (as seen in CARE, page 139)
- better awareness training for staff and volunteers

- linking sport to cultural/religious festivals like Diwali, the Festival of Lights, as in Leicester
- linking with health promotion and anti-poverty work.

Racial abuse by spectators at professional football matches has become widespread; Perkins at the Sir Norman Chester Research Centre at Leicester found 36 per cent of spectators at Rangers matches and 38 per cent at Everton reported hearing such abuse, compared with 11 per cent at Wimbledon and 12 per cent at Charlton (Brown and Chaudhury, *Guardian* 7 Jan 00). The problem even involves amateur and junior soccer, leading the Football Association to launch the 'Let's kick racism out of football' campaign. In West Riding soccer, with 2,300 clubs, no member of any county committee was African, Caribbean or Asian, only 2.4 per cent of referees, and in half the leagues three-quarters or more of teams had no black players. The Centre for Leisure and Sport Research (2001: 8) recorded that all the black players 'had experienced racism in physical and verbal forms as well as what they interpreted as institutional forms (e.g. differential treatment by officialdom).'

Cricket has followed suit with 'Hit racism for six'. Long and Hylton (2000) recorded 46 per cent of Rugby League spectators having heard racial abuse directed at players. Long (2000: 2), examining the issue in rugby league and amateur West Yorkshire cricket, demonstrated Riggins' 'discourse of othering,' causing 'whiteness to be "inside," "included," "powerful," the "we," the "us," the "answer" as opposed to the problem, and most of all unspoken.' He recorded examples of denial of prejudice, of defensiveness about practices ('we don't get good enough black players', 'look at the (few) black stars'), concluding 'because of the privileges bestowed by whiteness, moving in and out of identities is in fact easier for whites than it is for blacks.' Only a third of the League clubs had an equal opportunities policy. Having examined both professional and amateur cricket, Carrington and McDonald (2000: 67) judged that, if reform was implemented, it 'has the potential to be used as a model for a modern, democratic and multicultural society rather than being seen as the last cultural vestige of a pre-modern, imperial cultural formation.'

More recently, Sport England and the Commission for Racial Equality (1999) have set up an organisation called Sporting Equals to promote equality, offering Millennium Festival grants from £500 to £5,000 under the Lottery Awards for All scheme. They instanced schemes for a Black and Ethnic Minority Sports forum (BEMSPORT) in Yorkshire and Sportworks employment placement service in Sheffield, a Bangladeshi sports association for Chicksands Estate in London, an Asian community centre in Accrington, and a multicultural netball club in Bolton. Sporting Equals has produced *Achieving Racial Equality: A Standard for Sport* (ISRM, 2001) as a guide for national governing bodies, showing ways of recording the realities of anti-racist actions.

While training for staff is now widespread, and is starting amongst volunteers, through the Running Sport programme, it is clear that locally many sports clubs do not yet take action to broaden their cultural base (Collins, Jackson and Buller, 1999). The advent in 2000 of local broad-based Cultural Strategies will bring together interests in ethnic minority arts and sport much more closely.

Policies and practices for cultural inclusion, therefore, have to address matters of deprivation, stereotyping and discrimination, but also allow the choice of authentic separate development of clubs and teams. One can outlaw discrimination but not historic and cultural reality, as the Australian Soccer Association had been discovering regarding Italian, Croatian and other teams: enforced assimilation as opposed to gradual acculturation by choice will be resisted (Deane and Westerbeek, 1999).

MacGowan (1997) described the belated but extensive promotion of sport for Aboriginal people in Australia; Taylor and Toohey (1996) pointed out that women from *any* ethnic minority were invisible in Australian sport – as much because of expected gender and family roles as discrimination. But evaluation of outcomes is absent. The Hillary Commission recently implemented an extended Maori sports programme involving extensive grass roots development actions (Hillary Commission, 1998).

Immigrants bring cultures which often include sports. The imposition of the British Empire and its educational and cultural values as well as military and administrative systems brought British forms of sport and its values. So soccer, rugby, cricket, badminton, hockey, and squash in particular became part of the sports scene in Africa, South Asia and Australasia, and helped the acculturation of immigrant sport which has been extended through two generations who have gone through British schooling. But it has only been in the last ten years that national games like kabbadi, carramboard and gulli danda have been accepted and established in cities with major ethnic population concentration – notably in Birmingham with the Birmingham Pakistan Sports Forum (Chisti, 1991). Johal corrected the view that Asians don't play much sport, arguing that:

> there is an almost Machiavellian tautology that operates whereby South Asians are forced into creating their own mono-ethnic football teams in order to protect themselves from racial abuse and still partake of the sport ... the growing professionalisation of kabbadi and the separate burgeoning of South Asian football have engendered two distinct sporting events.
>
> (Johal, 2001: 165)

Arnaud (1996) undertook a political science analysis of sport and recreation interventions with deprived ethnic minority neighbourhoods in two post-industrial 'second cities', Lyons and Birmingham. In Birmingham, *all* city council policies were scrutinised for impacts on ethnic minorities, a target of 20 per cent for employing them was set, and after the Handsworth riots in 1985, several affirmative actions were taken including a forum of seven umbrella/community groups, and later the Pakistani Sports Forum mentioned above was set up. Lyons reflected the French national policy, which focused on urban and economic problems at the expense of recognising ethnic issues.

Both cities developed substantial sports development policies and programmes, but Henry identified differences. In Birmingham, it was operated as a market that needed development and targeted response: an officer said 'they are a market and we cannot ignore this' (cited by Arnaud, 1996), and it was based on consulting community groups and encouraging independent action, sometimes with grant aid. In Lyons it was seen as part of the city's and region's joint attack on poor housing, jobs and environments through the Développement Social Urbain network and programmes for *sports du quartier* (neighbourhood sports), projects grant aided but under very strict rules and supervision from the regional office of the Ministry of Youth and Sports. There are signs of hopeful development in both cities but major outcomes build slowly – as shown in the Youth Charter for Sport Culture and the Arts work in Merseyside and Manchester (see page 78).

Conclusions

As newcomers, immigrant minorities spend much of their first generation finding a workplace and a home; leisure and sport concerns gradually become more important; there is a balance between maintaining authentic 'home' culture and adopting host culture. This is more starkly seen in the arts than in sport, where the influence of empire has already introduced several European sports to colonies and trading partners. There is a theoretical debate as to how far sport and culture for ethnic communities are structured by race and discrimination, by poverty/income, or by subcultures (Taylor, 1992). In Britain at the beginning of the twenty-first century, all of these are influences: racism, sexism and ageism all affect ethnic minorities and need combating; concentrations of poverty coincide with minority communities and need the same complex of policies as for the majority population.

Interventions to overcome exclusion have to encompass

- sensitive provision in PE classes, drawing on the wish of children to participate because sport is fun, and in youth work, especially as a safe site for Muslim girls (de Knop et al., 1996)
- working to persuade parents of the benefits of sport and physical activity, even where there might be cultural resistance, as in some Islamic households
- training all leisure services workers in race awareness, and operating mentoring schemes to overcome the shortage of black leisure managers (Hylton, 1999), a shortage reflected in the law, police, civil service and parliament (Travis and Rowan, 1997)

- providing dedicated youth, community and sports development workers, discount schemes, targeted programmes and separate transport and coaching/participation sessions, at least for a prolonged transitional period
- not forcing public or club providers to integrate for its own stake, especially when they have genuine local community roots, and freely express ethnicity (Floyd, 1998).

There are several reports outlining good practice schemes (English Sports Council, 1997b; Sports Council NW, 1991; Sports Council Y&H, 1995). The PAT 10 report (DCMS, 1999: 100–2) gave extensive coverage to a multi-agency, 'bottom up' scheme: the Charlton Athletic Race Equality partnership (CARE).

CARE was instigated by the London Borough of Greenwich, using Single Regeneration Budget funds. But it was implemented by a partnership including the Charlton Athletic Football Club and its Supporters' Club, relocated at the new Valley ground in 1992 and needing to revitalise its community roots; the local university and higher education college; the Metropolitan Police; and local multi-faith, victim support, and ethnic minority cultural and social groups. It employs three full-time workers and produces a newsletter, the *Equaliser*.

Its many initiatives included

- tickets at less than half price for games at the Valley for CARE members
- 'Show Racism the Red Card' and 'Roots of Racism' library/education packs
- Face Value project in school for young people aged 10 to 16, exploring exclusion, peer pressure, prejudice, racist violence and mixed race relationships; Cuban carnival costumes and music for primary school children; PATH theatre and playschemes summer project for 16- to 21-year-olds.
- mini-soccer for primary girls; Plumstead Common sports festival
- a study centre for 10- to 14-year-olds to help with homework, literacy, numeracy and using computers.

But while all the frameworks and outputs connected with CARE and other schemes seem to offer all the right signs for positive outcomes, no baseline studies were done before their establishment, and no systems for evaluation have been set up. Although the PAT 10 report concentrated on illustrations from ethnic groups, the European social exclusion rhetoric has not recognised the multicultural reality of many major Western states – not only the UK but also Germany (where many thousands of former Yugoslavians have joined Turkish immigrants), the Netherlands (again Turkish, but even more Indonesian and West Indian groups), France and Spain (Moroccans, Algerians and Tunisians) and Greece (Albanians).

Gramann and Allison (1999) speculate about the ethnic future of the USA, where immigration and high birth rates mean that larger areas will have non-white majorities. Reflection on the deaths in two world wars and lower-than-replacement birth rates means that much of Western Europe will be importing large numbers of workers from the former USSR, Turkey and North Africa. For third and fourth generation citizens of black and Asian extraction acculturation processes will pull in one direction, and the deliberate attempt to rediscover or re-invent authentic culture and personal identity will pull in another, in sport as much as in other social spheres. Difference will continue to attract attention, whether admiring or abusive; what matters is how society and individual citizens deal with it.

Chapter 9

Sport and disability

Introduction: Attitudes, policies and structures

In 1999 the Disability Rights Task Force reported:

> there is a common misconception that disabled people are only those
> with mobility difficulties or sensory impairments, such as deafness or
> blindness. In reality, people with a very wide range of impairments and
> chronic or recurring health conditions can be disabled. For example
> people with mental health problems, asthma, diabetes or epilepsy might
> be disabled. The failure to appreciate the diversity of disabled people
> means that not all of them benefit from new policies.
>
> (Disability Rights Task Force on Civil Rights for
> Disabled People, 1999: 6)

The Task Force recommended extending the definition to include people
with HIV and serious cancer. In history, disability has been misunderstood
and vilified; in biblical times it was seen as the result of a person's wrong-
doing, or that of their parents. Nixon said disabled people have been accus-
tomed to being:

> treated as members of a deviant minority group. Deviant status has
> meant that disabled persons have been relegated to a position outside the
> mainstream. Minority status has meant that disabled persons as a stere-
> otyped and stigmatised category or group have been accorded degraded
> status, little power, and few opportunities for economic advancement or
> success.
>
> (Nixon, 2000: 423)

As Dattilo and Williams (1999: 452) commented, a person's disability is
not the origin of a stigma or deviancy. Rather, society assigns stigma and
deviant labels to people with 'undesirable' differences.

For centuries, societies preferred disabled members of the community to be kept 'out of sight, and out of mind', many in closed institutions. Then as medicine grew, doctors became interested in the most extreme and chronic conditions, and recorded personal experiences of disability. This led to the 'medical model' that saw disability as a pathology happening to passive victims, needing treatment and rehabilitation, and required disabled people to do their best to adapt their behaviour in a predominantly non-disabled world. As Oliver (1996a: 30) wrote, 'the assumption is, in health terms, that disability is a pathology and, in welfare terms, that disability is a social problem'.

Education and social science, however, have come to see things differently, following the 'social model' in the way they consider the issue; in this model, many disabled people are in situations partly determined by social structures, policies and 'disabling attitudes' (West, 1984). Poverty adds to the restrictions on mobility and social, voluntary and political involvement that disability brings in its train (Beresford, 1996). This was pithily encapsulated in the title of the former Radio 4 programme, *Does he take sugar?*, implying that many people ignore disabled people and speak to their families and carers as if they were absent or incapable of speaking for themselves, and not independent persons. Even when in 'mainstream' school situations, disabled students are often under strong surveillance, made to sit together in class and at lunch, and often cannot share leisure settings like fast-food restaurants with their non-disabled peers because they don't feel they could ask their friends to push their wheelchairs all the time. Then there is bullying: 'we all get picked on' (Watson et al., 2000).

The social model takes into account a wide range of factors – family circumstances and finances, education, employment, environment, housing, and transport (Barnes et al., 1999: 11–37). But it also includes issues of empowerment, and increasingly disabled people have begun to organise themselves in provision as citizens and as participants, coaches, administrators and volunteers in sport, and campaigning and lobbying by pressure groups have become significant activities (Beresford, 1996). Wheelchair users have been in the vanguard of these movements, as have people with acquired rather than congenital disabilities, using their prior knowledge of how networks of influence work. Paterson and Hughes (2000: 30, 35) went farther and argued disability has 'been transformed from an individual or medical problem into a civil rights issue . . . conceptualised . . . not as an outcome of physical impairment but as an effect of social exclusion and discrimination'.

The Department of Social Security suggests that 9.4m. adults and 0.6m. children are affected by disabilities or serious limiting, chronic illness (ETC, 2000, cited in Smith, 2001), half of them over 65 and including 72 per cent of women over 60. In 1995–96, only 2 in 5 were economically active compared with more than 4 in 5 of the population, and 21.2 per cent were unemployed compared with 7.6 per cent amongst the non-disabled population (Sly, 1996). Often the work that disabled people get to do is poorly paid, low-skilled and part-time (as Walker, 1982, called it – 'underemployment'). But one of the ironic side-effects of introducing a National Minimum Wage of £3.60 an hour was to lead employers to dismiss an estimated 1,000 people with severe learning difficulties because they could not afford to keep them on with low productivity (Brindle, *Guardian* 4 Feb 00).

Disability often incurs extra living, travel and care costs, and consequently, many disabled people and their families are dependent on welfare benefits; Martin and White (1988) estimated this to be as high as 3 in 4; disabled Income Support recipients rose from 8.5 per cent in 1991 to 14 per cent in 1996 (Department of Social Security, 1997). Thus many are poor – almost half of severely impaired women compared with 1 in 5 of the non-disabled (Townsend, 1979: 733–4). In 1999–2000 the Blair Government, believing that paid work is the core means of preventing poverty, sought to introduce a bill to means-test disability benefits previously given as of right. Many opponents claimed this would make disabled people even poorer and more dependent, especially if rewarding work could not be found. The BCODP (British Council of Disabled People) criticised Ministers for thus sticking to the 'individual tragedy' rather than the social model (*Guardian Society Extra* 3 Nov 99).

Healey (1998: 62) stressed the importance of local leisure provision and transport as part of the local social worlds, 'particularly for those with limited mobility and access to work and leisure opportunities'. In its latest planning guide, Sport England (1999: 12) sought to persuade local planning authorities to include policies in their development plans that take account of the sporting needs of disabled people and enhance access to built facilities and natural resources for sport.

Barnes et al. (1999: 210) said that 'historically, images of disability have been generated by non-disabled people, and have been more about the prejudices and decisions of mainstream society than the reality of the disabled experience'. The media can work in conflicting ways in representing disabled people – by under-representing them in popular features like soaps, and picturing them as victims, not attractive and not powerful, which is oppressive. The British Social Attitudes Survey 1998 showed that 3 in 4 Britons thought there was prejudice against disabled people. Some of the most powerful people in disabled sports organisations have not been disabled, a situation shared with other voluntary organisations (Drake, 1994).

Alternatively, the media can show them as active free agents. For sport, the TV coverage of the Paralympics and of wheelchair sports people in famous marathons has made disabled sport an accepted element of sport overall; but even this can glorify the trained athletic body over the average one engaged in physical activity for recreation. The Health Education Authority (1999) identified the lack of prominent role models for disabled people; Tanni Gray's success in wheelchair marathons in Britain is a first move in improving this situation.

The International Year of Disabled People in 1970 coincided with the Chronically Sick and Disabled Persons Act, which required public buildings to be made accessible 'so far as reasonably practicable' for disabled people. Though much has been done, the continuing deficit in this area, combined with the realisation brought to light by research and lobbying of continuing neglect and discrimination about paid work opportunities as an aspect of social exclusion, led to the Disability Discrimination Act 1995 (Institute for Leisure and Amenity Management, 1997; Wetherby, 1998).

This Act enshrined new rights to access to goods, services and facilities, in buying or renting premises and in employment, to which suppliers and employers were required to respond by 2000. There is now no shortage of advisory guides on design for disability in sports venues (for example, Thomson, 1984; Sports Council, 1994; BSAD, 1994) and activist access groups are organised under the aegis of the Centre for Accessible Environments.

Criticisms of shortcomings in this law led the Blair Government to set up a Disability Rights Task Force (DRTF), and in response to its interim report, they created by law a Disability Rights Commission in 2000. Amongst many other recommendations, the DRTF wanted to remove voluntary organisations (including sports clubs) from an exemption under the Disability Discrimination Act, so as to bring their premises and operating practices under scrutiny for fairness of access.

The concept of segregated physical activity or competition was started by the British Deaf Sport Council in 1930, but was brought to public notice by the neurosurgeon Ludwig Guttman, who organised the first International Wheelchair Games at Stoke Mandeville Hospital in Aylesbury in 1948 to coincide with the London Olympics. Although a 'single-minded autocrat and maverick' (B. Atha, quoted by Thomas and Houlihan, 2000), he inspired the disabled sports movement in Britain. A national organisation for paraplegic people was set up in 1948, for blind sportspeople in 1960, amputees in 1978, and mentally handicapped and Cerebral Palsy sufferers in 1981. An umbrella body was formed in 1961 (the British Sports Association for the Disabled, or BSAD), which developed a regional network. The first Paralympics was held in Rome in 1960 and has become a huge event. The medical and functional classifications are complex, leading to 700 events compared with 350 in the Olympics, and to increasing disputes over the officials' fairness as TV coverage has brought fame with medals, especially in the successful millennial event in Sydney.

There is no data on participation in sport by disabled people as a whole; in 1997 Sport England commissioned a survey of usage of a large sample of 155 sports centres and swimming pools in England. This showed low use by disabled people – only 7 per cent in sports halls and 11 per cent in swimming pools of people with a long-term illness or disability which limits daily activities compared with 22 per cent of the population (Sport England, 2000).

Barnes et al. (1999: 180) said that the burgeoning of disability groups and organisations can be theorised as 'a new social movement or as a liberation struggle'. Oliver (1996b: 117–18) cast these organisations into four types:

1   *Partnership/patronage*: operating *for* disabled people in providing ser-
    vices or consultation/advice, for example, Royal National Institute for
    the Blind, SCOPE.
2   *Economic/parliamentarian*: operating *for* disabled people – single-issue
    researching/campaigning groups, for example Disability Income Group,
    Disability Alliance.
3   *Consumerist/self-help*: organisations *of* disabled the people, sometimes
    campaigning nationally or locally, for example the Spinal Injuries Asso-
    ciation, British Blind Sport.
4   *Populist/activist*: organisations *of* disabled people, undertaking personal/
    political action, consciousness raising; may be less keen on partnership
    actions. For example, British Deaf Association, Union of the Physically
    Impaired against Segregation.

Most sports organisations are of the third type, though some have
altruistic/welfare aims to benefit others, for example Riding for the Disabled. Even though the Paralympics are held in the same city and venues as
the Olympic Games, the International Olympic Committee and the International Paralympic Committee remain separate organisations, highlighting
the abled–disabled segregation. The US Olympic Committee has been declared the umbrella body for Paralympic sports, and it remains to be seen if
this gap can be bridged (Hums, Moorman and Wolff, 2000). As interest in
sport by disabled people has grown, the Sports Council (later ESC and SE)
has seen support for them as a priority in every period since 1982. The
current arrangements in England are:

*   English Federation of Disability Sport (EFDS) – a charitable company,
    with a council comprising seven representatives of the National Disabil-
    ity Sports Organisations listed below and four representatives from the
    regional union.
*   Ten national disability organisations – including British Amputee
    and Les Autres Sports Association, British Blind Sports, British Deaf
    Sports, British Wheelchair Sports Association, Disability Sport Eng-
    land, Cerebral Palsy Sport, English Sports Association for People with
    a Learning Disability.
*   Ten regional federations – mirroring the national, served by an EFDS
    manager, who works with local authorities, education authorities and
    groups.

While this body links the former BSAD regional network and the 'vertical'
lines of management of disability-specific bodies, and gives them one voice
and a sizeable budget, only time will tell if it can influence the over-300 sport-
specific governing bodies, many of which have given little attention, let alone
priority, to provision for disabled people (Thomas and Houlihan, 2000).

But, as the governing bodies develop their disability awareness, so competition with adapted rules and equipment and specialised coaching evolve: currently thirty-two sports have disability committees or associations: not just angling, archery, basketball, bowls, swimming and riding, which may have become familiar, but also athletics, badminton, canoeing, cricket, cycling, fencing, dance and fitness, football, hockey, judo, martial arts, motor sports, golf, paragliding, rowing, rugby, sailing, scuba diving, shooting, skiing, tennis, triathlon, volleyball, waterskiing and yoga. The English Federation of Disability Sports (2001) has twelve priority sports – athletics, basketball, boccia, cricket, football, goalball, hockey, netball, rugby union, swimming, table tennis, and tennis.

Numerous local initiatives are now proceeding, though it is too early to judge outcomes maturely; there are disability officers appointed, for example in Birmingham, Leeds (Sports Council Y&H, 1995), and Leicester (see Case Study 3, pages 151–6). Play schemes integrating disabled and non-disabled children are more common (as in Kirklees – Sports Council Y&H, 1995 – and Oldham – Thomas and Green, 1992), and governing bodies regionally and locally are opening up new participation opportunities (Sports Council Y&H, 1995). Local sports development units are active: Kent's Disability Sports Development Officer facilitated Gravesham's Sportslink project, which increased attendances by disabled people at the district's two leisure centres, Cascades and Cgynet, from 5 to 300 a week (Kent Sports Development Unit, 1999).

Sport and disability, mental illness and learning difficulties

Mowl and Edwards (1995: 1) opined that 'the proliferating numbers of studies on leisure inequality have generally omitted an explicit discussion of disability'. Those concerning physiology show that many people with disabilities are sedentary and obese. Kitchin (1998) argued that disability is socio-spatially constructed; 'disablist' attitudes have traditionally disadvantaged and segregated people with disabilities and learning difficulties in schools, in workplaces (as 'unproductive'), on public transport, and in public buildings. Proactive policies need to go further than the changes to buildings and spaces achieved since the 1970 Act.

Modell (1997) showed that 7 in 10 leisure activities of a group of American children with learning difficulties were family-based; only 1 in 5 included disabled members in their leisure activities. After adjusting for age, he showed that those in more integrated settings participated significantly more in inclusive activities than those in segregated educational settings. Anderson et al. (1982) compared the activities of 119 disabled and 33 non-disabled teenagers. They discovered that the former spent more time in passive, solitary pastimes like watching TV and listening to music: they were less likely to see their school mates after school hours. They rated 2 in 5 of the disabled youngsters as having a 'severely restricted' social life compared with 3 per cent of the others. Indeed, the reality of disability was and is 'hard for friends to confront' (Morris, 1989: 105). Barnes et al. (2000) showed how disabled children in both special and mainstream schools spent a great deal of time under adult surveillance and much less time than children in general with other children, circumscribing the scope and style of playing.

Most studies in this area are practical, looking at how to serve these groups; de Pauw and Gavron (1995: 11) described the barriers as similar to those for women – lack of organised programmes and informal early experiences, role models, and access, and exacerbated by economic, physiological and social factors. They also said (1995: 223), 'the original therapeutic purpose through sport has given way to sport for sport's sake, and competition for competition's sake'. Cavet (1995: 60) said 'there is now an increasing focus upon community involvement and learning in community settings rather than training for leisure prior to introduction to the real leisure environment'. This obviously involves greater public understanding and volunteer support. Reviewing twenty-eight schemes in six European countries, Cavet (1995: 61) identified three (not exclusive) philosophical emphases, on:

- social role valorisation, normalisation, an ordinary lifestyle and integration
- education and the development potential of people with learning difficulty
- leisure, relaxation and enjoyment as valid ends in their own right.

Scott Porter (2001) did qualitative research in Scotland, and classified their sample into: *dependents*, with the lowest sports participation, who needed others to help with transport, changing, companionship and emotional support; *independents*, who were happy to try anything their non-disabled neighbours played, and in unsegregated settings; and *unconfidents*, who needed some support and were likely to seek, initially at least, segregated settings. The authors provided seventeen Scottish and twenty-four other UK examples of current practice.

The (English) Sports Council has supported the development of national bodies for disability sport and the appointment of specialised regional and local development officers. With the advent of Sport England, funding is focusing on the English Federation of Disability Sports framework and on targets for activity, for example in the Active Sports programme and the county-based Millennium Youth Games. This network has only just begun to work, and so studies generally describe good practice in improving social involve-ment, and participation in sport for recreation and competition (for example Collins et al., 1994; McConkey and McGinley, 1990). The Everybody Active demonstration project in Tyne and Wearside is also often cited (Tungatt, 1990; Williams, 1988). The latter clearly pointed out the need with these groups for:

- generating confidence and trust in a lifelong counselling context; such programmes cannot be 'hit and run'
- undertaking positive, long-term, committed outreach
- involving and encouraging ownership by the client groups, and 'mainstreaming' disability.

Messent et al. (1996) and Borrett et al. (1996) reminded readers that many people with disabilities and learning difficulties are obese and relatively sedentary, but showed that they enjoy, benefit from and achieve as much as any other citizens in a hierarchy of sports competitions leading to the Paralympics. They see as vital providing appropriate activity, help with transport and support to gain confidence, since an increasing number of disabled people are looked after by elderly carers.

The author agrees with Cavet's (1995: 25) conclusion that 'research studies into the results of making changes in the environment of people with profound and multiple disabilities often appear too short term and not sufficiently fine grained in their estimation', presumably because of resource constraints. She asserted that any new research should also address racial issues. Doll-Tepper et al. (1994) identified a huge research agenda for the International Paralympic Committee, including identifying barriers to participation, inclusion, equity issues, youth sport and issues of motivation and adherence common with able-bodied sport. In the East Midlands, the Centre for Leisure Research (1995: 22) identified that paradoxically there were often more systematic opportunities for disabled children to play and compete in special schools, whereas those in mainstream schools, 'were largely marginalised from the opportunities', a situation confirmed nationally by Sport England. Adult disabled sportspeople also feared that an effect of mainstreaming would be that their scope for competing would be restricted.

The Sports Council (Sports Council Y&H, 1995) showed good practice in governing body schemes in table tennis, canoeing and gymnastics and in programmes and training provided by local authorities in Leeds, Kirklees and the then-Humberside county; Collins, Randolph and Sellars (1994) highlighted schemes enabled by the East Midlands Initiative Trust in netball and powerlifting. The Open Country project in Harrogate brought the resources of the borough and county councils, the Yorkshire Health Authority, the Fieldfare Trust, the Countryside Commission, Powergen and the Yorkshire Field Studies Trust together in a partnership to provide countryside visits for those with disabilities in that area (numbering some 29 to 30,000 – Glyptis et al., 1995). Kent Sportslink (Kent Sports Development Unit, 1999) promotes disabled use of leisure centres very effectively – the Cascades centre received only 70 users in the year before the project; by 1996–7 about 7,800 had attended, with another 3,900 at the Cygnet centre. The Kent report also quotes David Phillips' statement (1999: 2) that 'the creation of accessible facilities can attract new business'.

After a review of accessibility for informal recreation in the countryside, the Countryside Agency (2000) recommended greater attention to design of routes and especially to gates and alternatives to stiles, and much better information for intending disabled visitors, especially to National Trails. Two of the workshop participants made telling comments:

"Disabled people should be able to decide what is an acceptable risk."

"Disabled people have become used to being excluded, therefore they need to know it is for them."

Three factors were major constraints mentioned in the Making Connections survey (Stoneham, 2001): physical barriers (by more than half), lack of information, and insufficient toilets (by 2 in 5).

Relatively few studies have examined the therapeutic benefits of exercise and sport in helping people with mental illness. Dishman's (1995) review concluded that

- small to moderate decreases in self-rated anxiety and depression accompany acute and chronic exercise, according to numerous studies with small, non-clinical samples
- the few population studies show stronger relationships
- increased aerobic fitness does not appear necessary to achieve these reductions
- various psychological, biochemical, and physiological mechanisms have been suggested but not researched.

Taylor, Baronowski and Rohm Young (1998) criticised exercise studies for focusing on people with cystic fibrosis, chronic low back pain, osteoarthritis and pulmonary disease, and neglecting para- and quadriplegia, poliomyelitis, and visual/hearing/learning disabilities.

Levitt (1991) came to similar conclusions, focusing on outdoor recreation, and stressing the socialising benefits. Hogg and Cavet (1995) sought to make concrete proposals for programmes for people with multiple and profound learning difficulties. Greenfield and Senecal (1995) demonstrated how recreation-based family groups at a day centre had involved unwilling parents in helping their children suffering from attention deficit disorder with hyperactivity, reducing family conflict and improving the adults' parenting skills. Newman (1988) showed the psychological benefits of countryside recreation. Denyer (1997) showed how guided walks in the Peak District organised by a partnership of the park and local health authorities helped both low-income families and those recovering from mental illness. 'Getting away from it' in a beautiful landscape was one feature, but so was socialising. With these groups, however, the transition to independent leisure practice is slow; withdrawal of organising, support staff and free transport would lead to a loss of benefits

Table 9.1 Sports participation among disabled children and all 6- to 16-year-olds (per cent unless stated)

	Disabled children, 2000	All children, 1999
Not playing frequently in school (10+ times a year)	26	6
Number of frequently played sports	2	4
Less than 3 hours a week of secondary PE	20	53
Time playing in summer holidays		
15 hours a week or more	10	29
1 hour or none	32	10
Popular sports for disabled		
swimming	37	30
horse riding	6	1
Members of clubs outside school	12	46

Source: Sport England 2001

and a major feature of these people's social lives, so continuing subsidy, painfully gathered, is essential.

Sport England has commissioned surveys of sport among disabled children and adults; at the time of writing only the former was published. It surveyed 2,293 children aged 6 to 16 and showed much lower participation than among youngsters – in school, in clubs and in the community (Table 9.1).

The constraints on their taking part that the children mentioned were:

		%
1	Cost (probably including transport)	37
2	Health issues	37
3	Unsuitable local facilities	37
4	Unwelcoming staff and clubs	32
5	Discrimination/children's own inhibitions	32
6	Lack of others' time to accompany them	32
7	Clubs do not provide for my disability	32

Thus numbers 1, 3 and 4 imply a large gap between policy aims and delivery.

The preliminary hints from the adult survey (Rowe, 2001) demonstrate the additive effects of gender and class on disabled people's participation compared with males aged 16+ as the benchmark:

	%
Males with a disability	−47
Females with a disability	−59
Classes AB with a disability	−39
Classes DE with a disability	−65

The practical outcomes of sports programmes for disabled people have been little studied; in the next section, I look at the efforts of a not untypical English city, Leicester, as it attempts to meet the requirements of the Acts, and the needs and wishes of its disabled citizens.

Case study 3: Disability and sport and leisure in Leicester

The Arts and Leisure Department (ALD) of Leicester City Council (LCC) has spent two decades investing in improvements to its buildings, signage, and staff training, and trying to support community organisations with information and grants. It wished to: establish the current and desired use of its facilities and services; establish what barriers disabled citizens faced, review provision and recommend any ways of improving customers' satisfaction.

So, Collins et al. (1999) asked 639 disabled Leisure Pass holders (see Case study 1, pages 50–7) about their use and problems, audited seventeen ALD sites and interviewed eighteen city and voluntary managers. Where possible, comparisons were drawn with Community Consultants' (1989) survey of 489 Leicester residents.

Leicester City Council's policies and activity regarding disability and leisure

The English Sports Council's (1998) guide to good practice in race relations is a useful analogue for disability, under seven headings.

*   *Policy*
    There must be a vision of what could be, and for Leicester this was stated as:

    > Leisure is essential to everyone's health and feeling of well being. Our purpose is to make Leicester a city unparalleled for leisure activities and experiences. . . . We will do this by ensuring equality of access for all cultures, with particular regard to groups and individuals experiencing social or economic exclusion.
    >
    > (Frith, 1999)

*   *Dedicated staff*
    Unfortunately, budget cuts had reduced the departmental complement from three posts for race, gender and disability to one.
*   *Training of staff*
    Staff awareness of disability issues and customer care was believed to vary greatly (as will be shown later).

- *Employment of disabled people*
  Several disabled people were employed in ALD.
- *Information and communications*
  Means such as minicoms, language leaflets, video/audio tapes, and special signage were common but not yet universal; only eight sites had minicoms.
- *Physical adaptations*
  The city had made many adaptations, for example ramps/lifts, doors, toilets, and parking. Nonetheless, of the fifty-two facilities listed in ALD's *Access Guide*, there were nine that did not have any parking, and fourteen with no Orange Badge (disabled person) spaces.
- *Voluntary organisations*
  Over thirty disability-specific groups operated in Leicester (Voluntary Action Leicester, 1998). Grants regularly supported nearly forty schemes covering children's play, arts, outdoor activities, a city farm, ethnic groups, and community centres.

Additionally, the city, county and Rutland education authorities were committed to a joint *Sport Through Education* Strategy, and with the East Midlands Initiative Trust had audited schools and special schools provisions for disability (Leicester City Council, 1999). This audit found:

- Most special schools and specialist units wished to see further development of specialist INSET training for PE teachers, curriculum support through links with clubs, and competitions between schools at Key Stages 3 and 4.
- Day centres highlighted the need to support their sports sessions with coach education, better information on up-coming events, and links with clubs.
- Disability clubs needed to strengthen their competitions, coach development, and sports development know-how, for example on equity training, Lottery Awards for All.
- All schools, centres and clubs wanted to develop particular priority sports, viz:

Special schools	*Day centres*	*Disability sport clubs*
Swimming	Bowls (including ten-pin,	Swimming
Football	short mat)	Athletics
Athletics	Boccia	Football
Basketball	Unihoc	Boccia
Gymnastics	Snooker	Bowling (indoor)
Multi-sport	Pool	Equestrian
	Table games	Fishing
	Multi-sport	

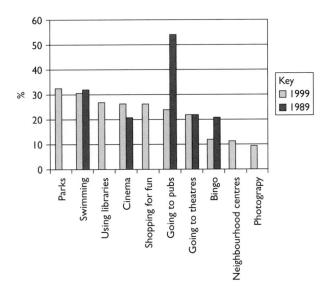

Figure 9.1 Top ten activities for people with disabilities in Leicester in 1999, compared with 1989

Current leisure participation, aspirations and barriers

The sample took part in ninety-eight leisure and twenty-nine sports activities. Figure 9.1 shows that most frequent were visiting parks, swimming, using libraries and cinemas, and shopping for fun. In comparison with 1989, it is obvious that disabled people's participation had almost doubled, with 84 per cent undertaking their favourite activity weekly in 1999. While 2 in 5 said they would like to go out more in 1989, in 1999 a quarter said there were activities they would like to do – notably swimming, health and fitness and more day centre activities.

Five major issues were identified in the Leicester interviews and discussions – transport, physical barriers, staff training, information and communications. As Leishman (1996) pointed out, improvements for disabled people benefit many other groups, especially pregnant mothers, those with small children, and older people.

Transport problems

Mobility and independent travel are major everyday issues for disabled people (Heiser, 1995). Sharkey (1996: 18) said 'getting to a building can often be more of a problem for handicapped people than actually using it'. All fifty-two ALD facilities were on at least one bus route, but that says nothing about frequency of service outside the peak hours. The three most frequent barriers to using public transport were said to be cost, infrequency (especially in the evenings and at weekends) and lack of information about services, notably for people with physical and multiple disabilities, and learning difficulties. Staff awareness was often poor, for example bus drivers failing to stop, driving off, and giving disabled people inadequate attention.

> "I don't like buses much as they tend to drive off before you sit down. They also get ruffled because it takes me so long to get off. I tend to use taxis but can't afford that many."
>
> (physically disabled respondent)

When the Leisure Pass was set up, for some technical legal reason it was said not to be possible to include transport discounts.

Physical and human barriers to access

Four in 5 respondents found no problem with LCC sport and leisure facilities. Apart from ramps and lifts, signs were difficult for both visually impaired and learning difficulty groups; when having to ask what was written because signs were too small or unclear, as one visually disabled person said, 'Why am I forced to let everybody know I am disabled?' (David, n.d.). Swipe cards for Leisure Card schemes, of course, conceal such differences from other customers and onlookers. Regarding staff, 7 in 10 said the staff at their most frequented facility were helpful, but there were numerous mentions of problems, especially by people with learning difficulties.

Programming

Three-quarters of respondents were happy with the scope of their activities, but there was concern about the lack of leisure opportunities for disabled children, and lack of follow-up to taster programmes. The provision of new services was complicated by the fact that equal numbers of people wished to go on their own, with a helper, in groups with the same or other disability, or in integrated sessions. Leicester has a Leisure Plus One card giving accompanying helpers discounted access.

Information

The main ways disabled people found out about leisure events/opportunities are shown in Figure 9.2. Although the daily *Leicester Mercury* was most popular, the fact that word of mouth came second means that people rely on friends and relatives to discover what's on. Half would like mailshots, compared with the 1 in 7 who said they received them. Leisure Pass holders received regular news of events and offers; in 1989 a total of 42 per cent of

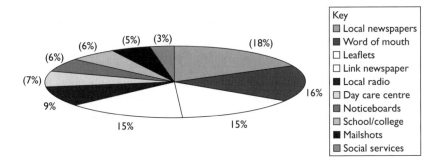

Figure 9.2 How disabled respondents found out about leisure events/opportunities

respondents said they had a Pass and 34 per cent used it; while in 1999 a total of 84 per cent said they had one.

Implications

Leicester City Council had tried hard to improve the quality of leisure for its disabled citizens; but there was clearly room for improvement in each issue.

Transport

Frequency and late-night running are part of a general policy issue of improving public transport. Issues of bus and bus stop design (for example talking bus stops) are in part to be dealt with in the new PSV Regulations introduced for large vehicles from December 2000 and for all other new vehicles by 2005 (Department of Environment, Transport and the Regions, 2000). The most common issue for all disabled groups was lack of understanding and empathy in bus crews.

Physical access

Observation audits and reports did not highlight major problems with ramps, doors, lifts, etc. although convenient parking was a problem. One of the most common complaints that could be dealt with at reasonable cost is the difficulty of reading crowded, wordy and ill-designed signs.

Access: Human resources

Although ALD was generally perceived as helpful, it was also seen by client groups as lacking awareness, especially for people with visual, hearing and learning difficulties. Awareness training should be provided for existing staff who have not had it, and become part of induction for new staff. This is vital for leisure centre and library assistants where there is significant turnover.

Programming

As discovered in Sheffield, taster days and special events were good ways of opening up new activities, but clients perceived a lack of follow-up. They could, and some would like to, be involved as volunteers in running such events. They also thought that better links between schools, LCC facilities, clubs and day care centres would extend options. They believed more tailor-made sessions for particular groups would be popular – arguing that not every session has to be integrated. Choice in this is crucial, to encompass the needs of the confident and reticent, the slightly and severely impaired.

Information and consultation

No method of communication is infallible, and as in Sheffield, this was a concern for all client groups. Their preferred method was mail-shots, but these can be costly, and usually engender a low response. It was suggested that disabled people be encouraged to obtain a Leisure Pass, and that a regular newsletter for marketing regular and special services be produced, with a section targeted at additional disabled groups. Copies should go to the day centres, and the Leicester Centres for the Deaf and Visually Impaired to target current non-Pass holders, including braille, large print or tape versions. Other media avenues could be implemented – returnable audiotapes, PC disks and e-mail versions of the Leisure Card News could be developed, along with features in the *Leicester Mercury* and on *Radio Leicester*.

Clients commented on the very short time often allowed for consultations by the City Council, allowing for the fact that it is less easy for those groups to meet to co-ordinate their views, and that their ideas seemed not to be acted on. The authors felt that a new Disability Network might aid this process; in fact one was set up for the city, county and Rutland linked to the main Sports Forum.

Monitoring and review

Continuous monitoring is crucial, but it must be done with the citizen and clients groups and partners involved. The proposed network could do this. Another follow-up study should be done in five rather than ten years. Data from the computerised tills being installed should provide local data on usage, and a more detailed marketing database.

In conclusion, the overall level of satisfaction amongst Leicester's disabled users was found to be fairly high, and activity choices seemed to have been extended over the past ten years. Therefore as far as the Arts and Leisure

Department is concerned, the challenge is not huge, nor, except for adapting the buses, is it costly. Perhaps the most urgent, as part of the process of social inclusion, was the training of ALD and bus staff to ensure that disabled people do not perceive themselves as different to or separate from other customers and users.

But regarding the City Council as a corporate whole, a larger challenge must be met. In a multicultural city, disability has a cross-departmental dimension. Issues of concern include transport and communication. Transport is possibly the major current factor in limiting many disabled people's leisure activity participation, as discovered also in Coventry by French and Hainsworth (2001: 146) to the extent of 'an extensive mismatch between policy development and the experience of disabled people'. Partnership with the increasingly strong local groups is also essential. Thus, despite policy commitment, continuous (if constrained) investment, and dedicated staff, Leicester City Council still faced substantial challenges, but attending to them will undoubtedly help it in pursuing its Best Value objectives.

Conclusions

Internationally, Riordan and Kruger (1999: 185) judged that biographies and case studies, rather than research literature, are stressing inclusion and contributing to more enlightened and tolerant attitudes about disability in sport. Sport for disabled people is a high-profile area for Sport England, which is assisting the field materially by supporting organisational change, ensuring the inclusion of disability issues in National Governing Body strategic planning, coach development, and youth sport programmes. But the creation of the English Federation of Disability Sports (EFDS) may be a convenient mechanism for Sport England in dealing with a touchy, increasingly high-profile issue (Thomas and Houlihan, 2000).

Yet many barriers still exist in public and even more especially in private provision, in employment discrimination and limited welfare support. Some of the most intractable barriers are, as Sandra Pew, East Midland Initiative Trust (Pew, n.d.) said, 'barriers of feeling' – barriers which keep out disabled people who are too unsure to enter new environments unaccompanied. What seems not to have been accepted generally is that 'not only are inclusive leisure services efficient, all participants can benefit from such services' (Dattilo and Williams, 1999: 452). Thomas (2001) judged that 'disabled people's participation in sport is an attempt to emulate non-disabled values and an example of disabled people's struggle for acceptance in a predominantly able-bodied world'.

Despite this, more research and evaluation of the effectiveness of present provision is necessary to ensure future investment is appropriate and productive, as advocated by Barnes et al. (1999). The debate current at the time of writing about disability benefits highlights the particular extremes of isolation and cost which poor disabled people bear. But this has not been adequately reflected in social exclusion literature, where much of the discourse seems to have focused on social insertion through employment – the SID discourse – and for many disabled people, this is not a real option. Nor, despite the formation of the EFDS, is there yet a coherent policy of provision for disabled people's sport.

Chapter 10

Sport and youth delinquency

So long as there is neither school nor work, mischief fills the empty hours.
(Burt, 1925: 29)

In the first section, we examine the recent background to youth justice and offending, then at reviews of the links between sport and prevention or rehabilitation of young offenders, terminating in a new synthesis by McCormack (2000); after reviewing recent evaluations of schemes in Britain and elsewhere, there is a case study of primary and tertiary interventions.

Introduction: Youth and crime – the facts

Rebellion of youth has been a problem to every older generation; even when it grew to be a social problem and to incur significant communal costs, it was often excused by Burt's or some other version of the old adage 'the devil makes work for idle hands'. 'Rational recreations' were devised by the middle classes to prevent the urban mass workforces getting into debauchery (Bailey, 1987). After the inner city riots of the late 1970s, the same idea was basic to the Scarman report (1982) into their causes. Part of society with 'time on its hands' is unemployed people, especially youngsters. Glyptis (1989) conclusively showed that constructive recreational activity programmes could not replace the role of work in filling time, providing a framework of structure to life, or produce income and offer equivalent achievements. If delinquency is linked to factors other than simply boredom, such as a need to achieve status, this may question the validity of sport and recreation provision in preventing it.

The proportion of young people in Britain's population has declined over the last 150 years, and by 1991 only 6 per cent of people were aged 10 to 14. The 15 to 19 age group had undergone a reduction by a quarter in the 1980s, though non-white minorities had much higher proportions of young people, making youth overall more culturally diverse than ever before. This has consequences for lifestyles and culture during adolescence, that Hendry et al. (1993: 1) described as 'a time set aside for waiting, developing and maturing and for accomplishing the rites of passage between childhood and adult status'. Hendry suggested that contemporary adolescence has grown to a longer stage in the lifecycle, with young people entering from puberty earlier, being exposed much more through media to society's consumption, problems and dilemmas, and leaving it later for adult status that involved gaining employment, financial independence and leaving home.

Coleman (1979) characterised the adolescent as a succession of foci, to which Hendry (1993) related leisure, suggesting that at age 13 young people are more interested in groups, clubs and organised activities. By 15 they are more likely to be involved in casual leisure activities such as 'hanging around'. By 17, they are more strongly influenced by commercial leisure activities, a pattern supported by his research with 10,000 young people in Scotland. Observation suggests that if anything these changes have moved even earlier. Hendry (1993: 53) implied that the 'hanging around' of the mid-teens may be extended later for youngsters at risk of offending, since unemployment or low income may prevent them progressing to the commercially focused stage of adolescent leisure.

In an Audit Commission report (1996), young offenders acknowledged the importance of leisure, 13 per cent saying that sports participation and 11 per cent that leisure activities would prevent others offending. This could support the idea of better-structured leisure education, to add to skills learned in the citizenship part of the curriculum, as argued by Bacon (1981) and Roberts:

> Are today's young people being better prepared for their futures? . . . we have still not developed effective means of delivering recreational interests to all young people, especially girls, and male and female early school leavers, mainly from working-class homes.
>
> (Roberts, 1983: 58)

Roberts (1996) suggested that young people generally had a better grounding in sport in schools, better facilities and more money and hence were participating more than their predecessors. We shall see how far this is true of those at risk of or having offended.

At the turn of the third millennium there were concerns about the levels of truancies and exclusions from school (Office of National Statistics, 2000), of unemployment (up from 13 per cent in 1981 to 16 per cent in 1991 for 16 to 17 year olds and to 22 per cent in 1999, but much higher amongst unqualified young people and often twice as high amongst ethnic minorities – *Social Trends*, 2000. Hence, Tony Blair introduced the New Deal package of training options with subsidies for short-term job creation for employers, a policy criticised as a stop-gap. Rising rents and purchase prices for property make it increasingly difficult for young people to find independence, often leading to frustration, sometimes alleviated by theft.

Further, more young Britons are unlikely to experience a stable nuclear family background, Smith (1992: 10) estimating that 1 in 5 children would experience parental divorce by the age of 16. The number of single parent families also doubled between 1971 and 1987 to 14 per cent (Central Statistical Office, 1991: 38).

The home setting for youngsters most at risk has also deteriorated, from 1979 when 18 per cent of children were living close to or in poverty to 1987 when this had increased to 30 per cent (Smith, 1992: 13). *Social Trends* (Office for National Statistics, 2000) reported that almost half of children living with non-working single parents and other benefit groups were in the bottom fifth of families by disposable income in 1997–8. Substantial numbers of young people also spend their youth in local authority care, often involving regular moves, reducing the opportunities for them to develop stable relationships and lifestyles.

Increased media coverage can be seen as one trigger of growing public concern about the risks and extent of crime, though it exaggerates them and the likelihood of violence. However, some areas, often inner city housing estates, have become crime 'black spots'. Young people aged 16 to 29, people earning less than £10,000, and from ethnic minorities, fear crimes of theft, burglary, mugging or rape more than other groups (Mirlees-Black and Maung, 1994). This public concern about crime led to a common belief that the more lenient sentencing policy advocated during the 1980s was misled.

An amended Criminal Justice Act in 1994 increased the powers of courts to incarcerate young offenders and controversially provided the means for this through the construction of new secure units. What are the facts? Over half the crimes solved in 1987 were traced to an offender younger than 21. Criminal statistics suggested that recorded crime rose by 900 per cent from 1950 to 1991, from about 1,100 to just over 10,000 per 100,000. Meanwhile the number of convictions fell from 555,000 in 1980 to 509,000 in 1990 (Home Office, *Criminal Statistics*, 1992). In *Misspent Youth*, the Audit Commission (1996: 12) suggested that 'A disproportionate amount of crime is committed by young people, especially young males. In 1994, two out of every five known offenders were under the age of 21, and a quarter were under 18.'

It also showed that youngsters reported handling stolen goods as the most common offence, followed by fighting, and then burglary and theft for boys and shoplifting and vandalism for girls, but only a handful got involved in serious crimes against the person. In contrast, car crime was a strongly male preserve, according to Cooper (1989). Table 10.1 shows the patterns of crime self-reported by youth.

Since the proportion of offenders who were juveniles in 1990 was 46 per cent, albeit having declined by 8 per cent from ten years earlier, it is a considerable social problem. There is a second more serious trend already mentioned: although 4 out of 5 young offenders will not commit another offence after the first, a minority are responsible for large numbers of reported crimes: 'six per cent of known offenders are responsible for seventy per cent of known crime' (Faulkner, 1987: 9). This group has become a target for policing and prevention activity.

Table 10.1 Youth participation in offending (self-reported involvement)

Offence	Male (%)	Female (%)
Handling stolen goods	11	9
Fighting	9	5
Burglary	5	0.5
Other theft	4	2
Hurt with weapon	3	1
Vandalism	3	4
Bike/motorbike theft	3	0.5
Shoplifting	3	5
Theft from school	2.5	2
Arson	2.5	2
Theft from and of cars	2	1.5
Used stolen cheques	1	–

The point in development before which a child cannot be held responsible for its actions is commonly recognised by legal systems as the age of criminal responsibility (in Britain age 10). This concept is difficult to define, since children develop at different rates. Crimes committed by people under 17 years, therefore, are treated differently from adult crimes, in juvenile courts, and are given some consideration for being committed short of 'adult' status (West, 1967: 1). The profile of young offenders in Britain can be summarised as follows:

- *Age*
  If rebellious youth is a phase, then crimes will peak and many will not be repeated. In 1991 in England and Wales, young people sentenced for indictable offences numbered 192,000 aged 14 to 16 and 920,000 aged 17 to 20 (Home Office *Statistical Bulletin* 1993). Webb and Laycock's (1992) study in Manchester and North East England clearly revealed that initial participation in car crime began at 13 to 15 years, while other types of juvenile offence were committed by younger people, Cooper (1989) demonstrating that shoplifting peaked at age 13.
- *Gender*
  Cooper (1989) identified rates of conviction for boys at 7 to 10 times higher than for girls, confirmed by the Home Office for 1997 when only 12.3 per cent of convictions for juveniles aged 14 to 17 were of girls. But Graham and Bowling's (1995: 1) study for the same department suggested girls at this age were as likely to offend as boys; perhaps they are better at avoiding identification!
- *Ethnic background*
  The same Home Office research on self-reported crime among young people concluded that 'young Asians are less likely to commit offences and/or use drugs than whites and Afro-Caribbeans' (Graham and Bowling, 1995: 1).

In terms of juvenile crime management, approaches to treating young offenders have swung between the two concepts of punishment/retribution and reformation. The Ingleby Committee in 1956 on the working of juvenile courts suggested a connection between class, crime and justice, and that 'delinquency might be an indicator of social deprivation' (Pitts, 1988: 1). This connection led to the creation of family advice centres and the first broad concept of treatment rather than punishment, after which the advocacy of the Longford Report in 1964 led to the idea of therapeutic centres. Pitts (1988) argued that Labour policy under Harold Wilson sought the depoliticisation and decriminalisation of social issues, in the White Papers *The Child, The Family and The Young Offender* in 1965 and in *Children in Trouble*, in 1968 and then the Children and Young Persons Act 1969.

But a change of government in 1970 meant proposals to raise the age of criminal responsibility to 14 and to prevent courts from giving sentences for custody in borstals were not enacted. Immediately another Act combined social work and the junior penal system to form a new juvenile criminal justice system. From 1973 to 1977 the number of juveniles imprisoned rose dramatically and the number referred to social work declined. The penal system appeared to have gained control in a 'backlash' against what it saw as ineffectual social workers, though Thorpe et al. (1980: 3) explained the increase as the outcome of 'collusion and cock-up' between policemen, social workers, probation officers, magistrates and social services administrators, leading to a failure to implement any reforms following the 1969 Act.

In a process of re-politicisation, conservative Home Secretary William Whitelaw introduced the 'short sharp shock' for young offenders, with a new regime in two young offenders institutions based on deterrence and punishment through enforcing a physically and mentally demanding environment imitating American 'boot camps'. The 1982 Criminal Justice Act sought to strengthen the law relating to juveniles, and to limit imprisonment through introducing Youth Custody Sentences, Community Service Orders, Secure Care Orders for under-16s (in local authority homes), and Night Restrictions (curfews to prevent youngsters from committing offences).

Juvenile court procedures had become complex, tortuous and costly – 'identifying a young offender costs the police around £1,200. It costs a further £2,500 to prosecute an offender successfully' (Audit Commission, 1996: 44). Young offender institutions were criticised as poorly staffed, under-funded, and places for breeding hardened criminals. But they were costly – £1,730 per month in a closed institution and £2,071 in open ones (Cook, 1997: 97). In 1997, per-month Community Service Orders cost £140, Probation Orders £190 and Supervision Orders £180. Coopers and Lybrand (1994) estimated every criminal event prevented would save the nation £2,300, half public and half private money.

At a time of government concerns for controlling public expenditure, the case for non-custodial sentencing for less dangerous first-time offenders seems strong. It is weakened, however, by public perceptions that the punishment should fit the crime. Many non-custodial sentences do not deliver a 'pound of flesh' in the public's eyes. Punishment should also act as a suitable deterrent for reducing recidivism and preventing first-time offending.

The 1990s were dominated by the Criminal Justice Act of 1991, which introduced for young offenders:

- Probation Orders for 16-year-olds (applied to 6 per cent of youth disposals in 1995)
- Curfew Orders for offenders from 16 years
- Supervision Orders for offenders up to 18 years (12 per cent in 1995)
- allowing them to appear in youth courts until age 18
- financial penalties and the binding over of parents of offenders aged 18 and 16 respectively (Jason-Lloyd, 1993).

Nine per cent received Attendance Orders, and 7 per cent Probation or Community Service Orders (Crown Prosecution Service statistics, 1996).

A new Labour government launched another major change in law and order policy in the Crime and Disorder Act 1998, based on Home Secretary Jack Straw's belief that:

> Today's young offenders can too easily become tomorrow's hardened criminals,. For too long we have assumed that they will grow out of their offending behaviour if left to themselves . . . an excuse culture has developed within the youth justice system. Parents are not confronted with their responsibilities. Victims have no role and the public is excluded.
>
> (cited in Muncie, 1999: 148)

Its main outcome was to create a Youth Justice Board to oversee the process and promote good practice through establishing local inter-agency Youth Offending Teams to handle prevention and to manage young offenders through Youth Inclusion Programmes operating as primary interventions. For persistent and serious offenders, the Act introduced a fast-track sentencing programme and a new system for allocating suitable places in secure custody.

Jack Straw, adopted as hard a line on offending as his Tory predecessor, building more prisons for adults and juveniles, not just to ease overcrowding. But Home Office research concluded:

> Custody is the most expensive disposal, and is no more successful at preventing offenders obtaining further convictions than other disposals. But it protects the public from the risk of further harm . . . while the imprisonment lasts, and satisfies the public's need for retribution. . . . In 1994 it was estimated that a 25 per cent increase in the prison population was needed to achieve a one per cent reduction in crime.
>
> (Home Office, 1998)

The concerns over the effectiveness of non-custodial sentences may be a reason behind the greater number of juveniles receiving custodial sentences in Britain (95.3 per 100,000) than in Germany (87.9) and France (84). Twenty-three per cent of its prison population is aged under 21, or roughly double the proportions in the other two countries, a gap that would be widened by any policy of increased custodial sentencing.

Causes and triggers of youth delinquency, and forms of intervention

McCormack (2000) scoured the sociological (for example, Giddens, 1997), psychological (for example, Bynum, 1996), and leisure studies literatures (for example, Purdy and Richard, 1983) for factors identified in the genesis of or triggers to delinquent acts. There is no space here even to summarise these numerous studies, but in her synthesis McCormack differentiated between structural factors in society, and internal factors related to young persons, their values and attitudes, as below, with major examples of sources:

External	Poverty and urban deprivation (Audit Commission, 1996)
Structural factors	Social residential setting (Mays, 1954)
	Breakdown in public morality
	Lack of early parental guidance and control (Farrington, 1996)
	Attempt to conform to negative social labelling (Cohen, 1980; Muncie, 1984)
	↑
	Peer pressure and group dynamics (Cohen, 1955; Audit Commission, 1996)
	↓
Internal	Expression of boredom or frustration (Scarman, 1982; Clarke and Critcher, 1985; Marshall, 1994)
Agency factors	Search for status and recognition (Downes, 1966; Cooper, 1989)
	Search for entertainment and challenge (Webb and Laycock, 1992)
	Phase of rebellion against society (Mays, 1972).

This shows a range of factors, from structural ones to personal agency factors (Giddens, 1982). At one end of this range, West (1967) suggested that the welfare state had removed the need for considering poverty, but juvenile poverty in the terms discussed in Chapter 4 had risen from 16 per cent in 1961 to 33 per cent in 1992. By this time consumerism was placing huge pressures on young people to achieve status through obtaining material goods. Such pressures may lead young people living in poverty to resort to crime to support their consumer needs, as Roberts explained:

> there is a contradiction between the 'good life' of cars, motor cycles, audio equipment and fashionable clothing, and the predicaments of young people who cannot afford the bus fares to claim their social security. Should we be surprised if some of these young people use the meagre resources at their disposal to construct contra-cultures within which to preserve some dignity and self respect?
>
> (Roberts, 1983: 144)

For some young people, this may be restricted to deviance from social norms short of law breaking, but for others will result in delinquent behaviour. But most 'come to a reasonable resolution of their problems in relation to identity and the development of self-esteem' (Hendry, 1993: 19). Thus it is even more important to heed the warnings of the societal reaction theory, and to avoid labelling young people which may make it more difficult for them to move on from this phase.

The Audit Commission (1996: 57) summarised the contemporary 'risk factors' for delinquency as 'inadequate parental supervision, aggressive or hyperactive behaviour in early childhood, truancy and exclusion from school, peer pressure to offend, unstable living conditions, lack of training and employment, and drug and alcohol abuse.'

Witt and Crompton (1997), having surveyed schemes in over thirty places in the USA, provided a wider range of risk factors, as listed in Table 10.2.

A framework is needed to relate these interventions, and the one widely used was offered by Brantingham and Faust:

Table 10.2 The relationship between risk factors, risk behaviour and health/life compromising outcomes

(A) Risk factors	(B) Risk behaviours	(C) Health/life compromising outcomes
Poverty	Illicit drug use	School failure
Illegitimate opportunity	Drunk driving	Legal trouble
Models for deviant behaviour	Tobacco use	Low work skills
Low perceived life chance	Delinquency	Unemployability
Low self-esteem	Truancy	Disease/illness
Risk-taking propensity	Unprotected sex	Early childbearing
Poor school work		Social isolation
Latch key situations		Depression/suicide
		Amotivation

Source: Witt and Crompton, 1997: 4

Primary prevention – the modification of criminogenic conditions in the physical and social environment at large.

Secondary prevention – early identification and intervention in the lives of individuals and groups in criminogenic circumstances.

Tertiary prevention – prevention of recidivism.

(Brantingham and Faust, 1976: 284–96)

Different objectives may be sought at each of the three levels:

Primary   to improve youth welfare
Secondary to promote socialisation (Witt and Crompton, 1997)
                    to provide diversion (for example summer schemes – Crime Concern, 1992)
                    to deter youth from offending (Lundman, 1993)
Tertiary   to allow society to exact retribution
                    to give offenders chance to atone
                    to divert youth from re-offending

For individuals, crime prevention can be focused at pre-offending and offending individuals through secondary and tertiary interventions. Primary prevention, on the other hand, is directed not at individuals, but at physical environments and social structures which encourage crime and delinquency. They can include holiday schemes like Splash (Crime Concern, 1992), youth clubs and community centre projects. Delimiting the influences and effects of such schemes is difficult, and few have been evaluated. Bolton has been developing 'Recreation Zones' in an area of high crime needing regeneration (Morgan, 1998a, b). The case study of a primary intervention on pages 174–91 is of Street Sport in Stoke-on-Trent.

At secondary level, intervention is based on theories of prevention before offending occurs, for example, directed at socialisation (affecting positive attitude development), diversion and deterrence, as demonstrated in a wide range of schemes, for example, by Witt and Crompton (1997). Tertiary responses have been most commonly evaluated, since they deal with serious and repeat offenders who incur large social costs; they seek to alter ingrained behaviour, aid self-development and offer a setting for other therapeutic work. These interventions are based most commonly on retribution or punishment, the concept that society should have its pound of flesh for offences through detaining offenders (Muncie, 1984). However, detention whether in secure units, borstals, or prisons does not seem to create better attitudes or behaviour upon release, since over 70 per cent commit further offences; indeed, the young people involved frequently develop a serious history of crime. The aims of non-custodial measures is (apart from seeking lower cost measures) to give opportunities to atone, to avoid opportunities to offend, to establish better physical and social situations, to learn constructive attitudes and behaviours, and in some cases to make reparation for vandalism or theft. Interventions may include community homes, attendance centres, supervision orders, Intermediate Treatment, which in the philosophy of the 1969 White Paper *Children in Trouble* seeks to bring 'the young person into contact with some constructive activity' (Muncie, 1984: 56). Comparison between custodial and community routes of correction is therefore not straightforward. The case study of a tertiary intervention on pages 174–91 is of Hampshire Sports Counselling.

Interventions can be grouped into four types: three are found in North America and widely across the world – wilderness adventure/challenge programmes, sports, and community based multiple interventions involving a range of 'constructive leisure' MacKay (1993: 27). To these may be added one which has developed in Britain to the epidemic of 'twocking' – taking away a motor car without the owner's consent – that of motor car schemes (Martin and Webster, 1994).

In his literature review, Coalter (1996) raised the issue that almost universally the causal links between delinquency, recreation as an intervention and outcomes were unclear. McCormack (2001) also criticised schemes for having either no clear aims, or too many vague and overlapping ones, more than they could realistically claim or demonstrate. Having codified origins of delinquency, the modes of sporting and recreational interventions and the objectives of each level of intervention, it was possible for her to provide a new analytic framework that allowed each scheme to be interrogated for its aims and outcomes (Figure 10.1). This she tested by investigating six very different projects, all of

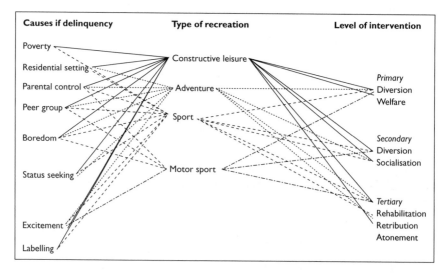

Figure 10.1 A framework to link the causes of delinquency, the benefits of recreation and philosophies of intervention

which could be accommodated in her schema without problems, showing it to be robust. Two form our case studies.

The growing interest in sport as an intervention in youth delinquency

During the birth and writing of this book, the coverage of sport and recreation as an intervention has grown five or six fold. This has been mostly in the form of reviews of literature or surveys of schemes for central, provincial or local governments, in Canada (Parks and Recreation Federation of Ontario, 1997; Duck, 1998), the USA (Mackay, 1993; Witt and Crompton, 1997), Australia (Potas et al., 1990), New Zealand (Sullivan, 1998), France (Anstett and Sachs, 1995; Duret and Augustini, 1993) Belgium (de Knop et al., 1997) and the UK (Coalter, 1989, 1996; Coalter, Allison and Taylor, 2000; Robins, 1990; Utting, 1997; Long and Dart, n.d.; Long and Sanderson, 2001).

The consensus from these studies of both outdoor recreation projects and community-based schemes, is:

- Sport, and perhaps outdoor activity, increases self-esteem, mood and perception of competence or mastery, especially through outdoor re-creation (Sullivan, 1998; Potas et al., 1990; Badenoch, 1998; Barrett and Greenaway, 1995).
- They reduce self-destructive behaviour (smoking, drug use, substance abuse, suicidal tendencies).
- Schemes lead to improved socialisation both with peer groups and adults.
- In most cases where this was investigated, participants enjoy improved scholastic attendance and performance (Baker and Witt, 1996; Bundrick and Witt, 1998; Witt, 1999, 2000, Sharp et al., 1999).

But Utting (1997) made the point that there has been insufficient information on which programmes, settings and activities work best, though the small group counselling scheme in Hampshire (Tungatt, 1991, see below) and the one-to-one scheme in West Yorkshire modelled on it (Taylor and Nicholls, 1996) would suggest that it is the support and counselling that are as import-ant in bringing benefit as than the activities, if not more so. Some schemes involved teaching self-restraint in the very activities that one might think would professionalise the deviancy – motor projects for those who had stolen cars or their contents (Martin and Webster, 1994) and martial arts (Twemlow and Sacco, 1998), but most assessments were positive on most of the points above.

Two studies stand out in contrast as presenting mainly negative findings. Trulson (1986) found that offenders doing a martial arts programme were more aggressive afterwards. Begg et al. (1996) recorded self-reported delinquent acts after a course amongst 800 male and 900 female youths at ages 15 and 18 in New Zealand. They showed that males with high and females with moderate to high sporting activity were more likely to be delinquent than those with low levels.

The Home Office yardsticks for such interventions seem to be completion of the programme, and re-offending or recidivism. Attendance at such schemes, whether voluntary or mandated, is often sporadic, with youths experiencing lack of motivation, lack of daily time structure (Glyptis, 1989), and other distractions, including 'signing on'. Whether schemes reduce re-offending for youths given community sentences is less clear, partly because of the difficulty and cost in establishing the true re-offending rate amongst a very mobile population, even when costly access is given to the national computerised crime records (Taylor and Nicholls, 1996). Mackay (1993), from just a few American studies, suggested that there was a benefit of reduced recidivism for two to five years after offending, but that thereafter the two rates coalesced, though offences by attenders remained less serious. Tsuchiya (1996), looking at one to two year recidivism rates in four British schemes, suggested that they were very good value for money compared with custody, with its high costs and 79 per cent re-offending rate after two years.

The major problem with all such studies are, first, that the lower levels of delinquency may arise because the young people who come onto schemes are self-selecting and more likely to offend less. North American studies with experimental and control groups reporting reduced recidivism, but only three had adequate internal quality controls coming anywhere near Kelly and Baer's (1968) seminal study of 60 offenders and a matched control group. Likewise, thirteen out of fourteen reported positive changes in self-concept, but most were similarly flawed. Nichols and Taylor (1996) attempted to project the likelihood of offending for West Yorkshire attenders and suggested that the outcome was lower than expected re-offending. Second, such schemes rarely run beyond three months and some last a matter of days. A sail training week or a mountain expedition may be a life-changing experience in psychological terms, but if the youth returns to the same physical and social complex or deprivation, the pressures, values and conditioning of many years are likely to quickly re-assert themselves.

The constant cry is for longer schemes and prolonged follow-up support, but this happens in only a handful of cases, mainly because of the lack of core public sector support. A claim that some youngsters might become dependent if programmes last too long has never been able to be tested in Britain (Taylor et al., 1999). Hampshire Sports Counselling, praised by the Home Office as a model for probation services to follow (Sports Council, 1989), was successively reduced from twelve to eight to four weeks' duration, and then subsumed into a New Deal scheme for unemployed people with little sports content (see below). West Yorkshire Sports Counselling, modelled on Hampshire but delivered one-to-one with serious offenders, was put out to tender and the new private contractor provided only half the contact time. The experienced and specially trained and recruited team became disenchanted and dispersed (Nichols and

Taylor, 1997). Taylor et al. (1999), evaluating fifty-four UK probation schemes including sport and adventure, reinforced earlier conclusions and warned against seeking to emphasise numbers in throughput before cost-effectiveness.

Thus, Coalter (1989: 59) agreed with American writers Segrave and Hastad (1984) that 'the efficacy of sport . . . as an antidote to delinquency is by no means settled', though seven years later he tempered that view and wrote, 'although sport is rarely the solution, in many circumstances and used diagnostically, it can be part of the solution' (Coalter, 1996: 17). Proof of avoiding offending is a form of negative evidence that is very difficult to obtain. The Home Office gave up predictive modelling of offending in the 1980s because of its low reliability, in favour of reducing the opportunities to offend (through better design of housing, better locks on cars, community use and surveillance of public spaces, etc.).

Case study 4: Intervening to make a difference? Street Sport, Stoke, as a primary intervention and Hampshire Sports Counselling as a tertiary one

McCormack's fieldwork for these studies comprised documentary analysis, interviews with clients, managers and staff, and in Stoke with local residents, police, school and college staff. In Hampshire questionnaires and interviews were done with participants on entry in 1996–7 and some were followed up in 1998, including the completion of twenty-one detailed life history profiles. With the younger children in the Street Sport observation, simple questionnaires, interviews and group discussions were done throughout 1999. With its contextual study, this approximated to Nichols' (2001) call for using a social realist approach.

Background to Street Sport and Hampshire Sports Counselling

In 1994 the City of Stoke on Trent made a successful application for three years' funding to the West Midlands Sports Council to build on existing detached youth work in Hanley, which had grown from a single worker in 1971 to a team of sixteen in 1986 involving 'a programme of activities including play schemes, play training, community events, establishing residents' associations and formal community' (Manager of Community Recreation, 15 July 1997).

It then became part of the Leisure Services programme, and had to find accommodation with work based in parks, open spaces and play schemes. A major issue was identified, that 'we have become increasingly aware of the ever widening gap between adults and young people' (Leisure and Recreation Committee, 14 September 1993).

Street Sport (SS) developed as a 'participation' level intervention, described as:

Intended to provide an insight into the effectiveness of recreation outreach work on young people in terms of deflecting negative behaviour into constructive activity.

... A pilot project directed towards exploring ways of using play as a gateway to introducing sport to infants and juniors so that they may develop an appetite for it through their lives.

... A project directed towards exploring methods of using recreational activities with young people as an approach to promoting harmony in communities.

... Intended to offer a valuable indication as to how we can have a significant effect on improving relationships between communities and adolescents in our further recreational strategies.

(Leisure and Recreation Committee, 14 February 1995)

This attracted a further Sports Council contribution of £40,000 annually for 1993 to 1996, and the next strategy paper described it thus:

The approach recognises that the greatest chance of achieving success in the development of sporting activity with young people comes from being part of what they do. The activities have to fit in with what already exists using street venues and meeting places.

The City Council believes that investment in sport and recreation activities for young people will produce a reduction in damage to property, reduced crime and reported incidents of nuisance and so makes social and economic sense.

(Stoke on Trent City Council, 1994: 24)

In 1997 the scheme was extended to the whole city. Sessions operated on a drop-in basis, Monday to Friday evenings, with additional daytime sessions throughout school holidays. Portable equipment was carried in a converted transit van equipped with gas powered telescopic spotlights. Although Street Sport did not provide regular head counts, diary entries and observations suggested that average attendance was twelve participants, or an annual total of 4,200 attendees. There was 'no upper age limit or cut off point so long as [children] are not detracting from the effectiveness of the session for other players' (Ian, Outreach Worker, February 1999).

Street Sport was not actively marketed, and did not aim to bring more young people out on the street, but rather to identify and provide for the recreational needs of young people already there. In this way it directly addressed a significant cause of community concern in young people 'hanging about'. Such young people are often seen as the cause of friction and crime, but they are also vulnerable to becoming victims of crime.

The Community Services Department was also responsible for parks and playgrounds, leading to the idea of Sports Courts, multi-purpose hard areas marked out for sports including football and basketball, with fixed goals, basketball posts and timed lighting for evening use, and a seating area, not dissimilar to provision planned in Bolton.

Hampshire Sports Counselling (HCS), set up with the aid of a Methodist minister in 1983, was the brainchild of a committed local businessman and magistrate, convinced that many of the young people referred to him through the courts needed support for constructive leisure and an opportunity to burn up energy through physical activity. It could be seen as political protest against the growing contemporary lobby for harsher penalties for young offenders. It gained the support of the Manpower Services Commission (MSC), which funded one staff post, and operated initially from a judo hall in Southampton, where young people could drop in or attend activity sessions such as unihoc and archery. With evidence from monitoring attendance and some assessment from the county probation service, it achieved three years' security in 1985 as a Sports Council National Demonstration Project, and expanded, with two teams of MSC-funded workers in Southampton and Portsmouth. It began functioning through a more formal relationship with the probation service, via outreach work and leisure facility visits. The distinctive features were a full introductory interview to establish recreation interests, the assignment to a mentor who both introduced attendees to small groups and participated with them one-to-one.

Funding was extended in 1987; clients became formally referred by the probation service. An evaluation was undertaken by the Sports Council through an action research project involving a longitudinal study of individual participants, which concluded that

> We believe the Solent Sports Counselling project has done the ground work for the Probation Service to play a significant role in sports development, particularly amongst young unemployed people, and for sport to play a major role in the mainstream work of the Probation Service.
>
> (Tungatt, 1991: 87)

By 1989 the project was 'mainstreamed' into probation delivery, and promoted as good practice through a national conference. It was frequently a victim of its own success, as shown by comments by two key funders cited by Tungatt (1991):

> "If it's so successful why don't the Home Office do it, why do we need to be involved?"
>
> (Sports Council Southern Regional Director)

> "We shouldn't be leading this – let's recommend that the probation service takes it on board now."
>
> (Sports Council National Director)

By 1990 the latter's wishes were achieved, and Hampshire's probation service took responsibility for the project, which remained almost intact for four years. But by April 1992 the management bowed to budget cuts, calls for higher productivity, and concerns about clients' dependence on sports counsellors, and the number of sessions per participant were reduced from twelve to eight.

The manager, Keith Waldman, identified the broad aims of HCS as:

> The Sports Counselling Scheme aims to encourage and enable offenders aged 14 and upwards to make constructive use of their leisure time: in particular to participate in sporting and leisure activities with the emphasis on developing links with other participants within the local community.
>
> (Base Camp, 1994: 109)

From 1995 to 1998 the probation service gradually reduced the funding allocated to HCS, and in 1995 the sessions were further reduced to four weeks, and the building in Southampton was lost. Its administration was moved to probation offices in Winchester, and then, in 1997, again to Southampton. In late 1997, facing more severe funding cuts which threatened redundancy for probation officers, the probation service decided to incorporate the objective of constructive leisure into a streamlined youth referral process. The Manager explained these changes thus:

> It is sad to see such a successful and well known scheme disappear, but the financial climate which is creating redundancy in the probation service, combined with the new political climate for young unemployed people created by the New Deal, meant that a complete rethink was needed. There is still potential for leisure counselling within the community links referral and there is less chance of young people missing out since this is an automatic process.
>
> (Keith Waldman, Manager, February 1998)

By February 1998 the sport counsellors had been retrained in basic literacy counselling, and in March 1998 the Sports Counselling Scheme was effectively stopped, sinking any attention to leisure patterns into a compulsory multistrand assessment consisting of three sessions with the Community Links officers.

The funding for these two schemes was modest; for the first three years of each it was:

£000	HCS		Street Sport
Sports Council grant	67.5	Sports Council grant	120
Hampshire Probation	309.5	City of Stoke	120

Table 10.3 Attendance patterns for Hampshire Sports Counselling

	1987/8	1988/9	1991/2	1992/3	1995/6	1996/7
Referral	380	380	483	505	636	773
Starts	380	380	323	354	476	581
Completed 4+ sessions (% in parentheses)	n/a	n/a	107 (33)	160 (45)	209 (44)	290 (50)
Completed 8+ Sessions (% in parentheses)			153 (47)	103 (29)	n/a	n/a

Sources: Final Evaluation, 1990; Hampshire Probation Service, 1993, 1997

The staffing was: for Street Sport in November 1999, two full-time and ten casual/part-time workers; and for HSC in March 1997, five full-time, four on work placement, one administrator, and a manager. When money was tight, the autonomy of Street Sport enabled its manager to search for alternative sources, but when Hants Probation had to cut its budget, as a subsidiary service HCS had to take its share.

HSC's attendances, including for the key period of evaluation in 1995/6 and 1996/7 are shown in Table 10.3. At its peak the throughput and completion rates were both substantial, as such schemes go.

Street Sport and HCS as interventions

Using the framework established above (Figure 10.1), it is possible to set out the objectives of these two schemes, as shown in Figures 10.2 and 10.3.

Street Sport sessions had several intended outcomes for both young people and their communities. Firstly, Street Sport and Sports Courts were designed to divert young people from street corners into positive activity. This process would remove them from peer pressure and other delinquent influences. It would offer them a new perspective on opportunities, and provided fun and entertainment. For communities, this process reduced the perceived threat posed by young people, and reduced community friction. The sessions offered outcomes in terms of education and skills development through an interested adult mentor. The specific outcomes for young people from this process might be improved confidence, communication skills and changed views of their community and citizenship.

The HSC mentoring process and individually designed programmes aimed to alter leisure behaviour, through several distinct outcomes:

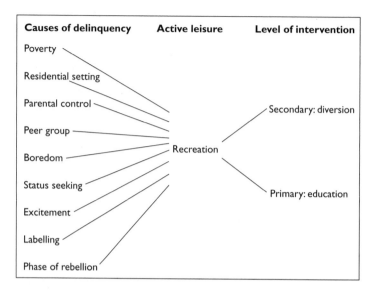

Figure 10.2 Theoretical framework for Street Sport, Stoke on Trent

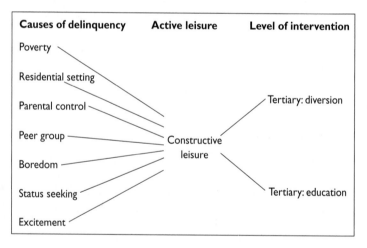

Figure 10.3 Theoretical framework for the Sports Counselling project, Hampshire Probation Service

- improved self-confidence
- greater knowledge of leisure opportunity
- improved awareness of health and lifestyle choices.

The relationships between these two interventions and the causes of delinquency are as shown in Table 10.4.

Table 10.4 Relationships with causes of delinquency in Street Sport and Hampshire Sports Counselling

Cause	Street Sport Stoke on Trent	Hampshire Sports Counselling
Poverty	Free/low-cost ongoing activities	Low cost, selected activity profile
Setting	Local sessions, sports courts	Improved knowledge/access to local facilities
Parents	Community development	Mentors
Peer group	Group sessions	Integration into new groups
Boredom	Activities to target 'hanging around'	New activities
Status	Involvement in community consultation	Client-centred targets for completion
Excitement	No 'buzz', emphasis on fun	Recreation, some adventure
Labelling	Not 'hanging around'	–
Rebellion	Inclusion in community	General counselling

Counsellors generally saw outcomes in terms of constructive use of leisure time, improved self-esteem, improved knowledge of local facilities, relaxation and getting fit, reflecting the most easily quantifiable outcomes. The sports counsellors found other objectives difficult to quantify or measure – for example, improved self-esteem or relationships with authority figures.

Street Sport had less formalised criteria and, despite quarterly reports, could demonstrate little consistency in its evaluation process: the play, daytime and holiday Street Sport sessions concentrated on the numbers and demographics of attendees, while the evening sessions were recorded retrospectively in staff diaries in variable detail. Staff measured the success of sessions according to the numbers attending regularly, how far youngsters saw the sessions as fun, whether new faces joined in, and if no friction occurred. The positive outcomes identified were: personal development, improved leisure patterns, pride in their community, and self-confidence.

In both case studies the evidence provided was related to participant outcomes. HSC produced limited recidivism data during the Sports Council's evaluation, which showed that 'Almost half the clients have maintained a trouble free record since being involved with the project and a further half dozen clients appear to have reduced their previous rates of offending' (Tungatt, 1991: 61).

Once HSC was reduced to only four sessions, re-offending patterns could be seen as linked only tenuously to the intervention. Street Sport produced occasional anecdotal evidence related to a general reduction in juvenile crime rates in the targeted areas. These claims were explored with police and community members. Generally Stoke police valued any diversion that reduced 'calls related to disturbance and vandalism' (Sergeant Taylor, Burslem LPU, September

1999), but could not identify direct links with more serious crimes such as burglary, assault and car crime.

The young clients, their leisure and the impact of the schemes

When built in the 1950s, Bentilee in Stoke on Trent was the largest council housing estate in Europe. Large and sprawling, it consists of a number of 'villages' in which recent initiatives had sought to engender a stronger sense of community spirit. It suffered from high unemployment, which most of the young people had experienced personally or in their families. Also, it had a large proportion of young single parents, which may partly explain the lack of young women at the Street Sport sessions (they suggested that their free time for leisure was almost non-existent due to child care). In recent years the housing associations that dominated the estate management had invested to improve the quality of housing and address problems of drugs and burglary so prevalent that some areas were considered 'no go' for most families.

A number of play schemes and youth clubs addressed the needs of younger children, but as they grew out of these activities, there was no acceptable alternative. Hendry (1993: 56) showed the transition from structured leisure activity for his Scottish sample of young people at 13 or 14 presented similar problems: 'This seems like the classic no win situation . . . A number of respondants claim that the rules at leisure clubs, youth clubs and sports clubs were too strict. On the other hand lack of supervision was clearly not appreciated.' This resulted in young people hanging around areas such as the shops, causing disturbances for other residents. A similar situation in the multi-cultural estate of Cobridge was further strengthened by negative media coverage of young people, as 'young criminals . . . making life a misery for families on the Grange estate' (*The Sentinel*, 7 Sept 99). There, youths from ethnic minorities were seen to be breaking away from the strict family control traditional in their communities (youth worker, Cobridge Community Centre, interviewed May 1999) and were now 'involved in petty crime and drug dealing, as well as some cross-cultural conflict'.

In the Stanfields estate in north Burslem, Stoke on Trent, 59 per cent of residents were aged under 30, but many youngsters faced unemployment (11 per cent) and generally low-paid work. Also, here was the poorest level of leisure provision of the Stoke area, and consequently it received two Street Sport sessions each week, the extra one achieved through external funding. A large area of open space next to Port Vale Football Club was used during the summer, as was a red gra pitch at the high school in winter, which had the advantage of having basketball posts and a hard surface suitable for roller blades.

The twenty-seven young people McCormack (2000) interviewed comprised nineteen males and eight females, four participants, four spectators, and seven non-participants involved in a NACRO Moves project for Year 7 children excluded from school. Twenty were in Street Sport's target age range of 14 to

18 years. Over half claimed to attend most or every Street Sport session, and to have done so for six months or more. Unsurprisingly, drugs and crime were the concerns most commonly identified by them and by adults, who felt better leisure provision would help to prevent them offending. The Audit Commission's (1996) sample gave a similar response.

Of HSC participants, forty were monitored by McCormack using questionnaires and entry interviews in 1996–7, while a group of twenty-one was followed for eighteen months to May 1998, using detailed life history profiles and follow-up records. As was to be expected among offenders on probation, they were generally older than in Street Sport, 72 per cent older than 21. Of all HCS clients referred, 43 per cent did not attend a session, but of those who did, half completed four sessions and 17 per cent ten or more. While the offending history of this group could not be revealed by the probation service, the pattern of those McCormack questioned was like that discovered earlier by Tungatt (1991), with assault and theft or burglary most common.

The constraints on the leisure patterns of these two samples of pre- and post-offending young people had much in common (Table 10.5). Accessibility was defined by Torkildsen (1992) as combining four distinct aspects: physical, social, perceptual and financial. Physical accessibility was cited as a constraint by 35 per cent of the young people interviewed in Stoke; and cost by 70 per cent. An important constraint for young women was their physical safety at night, mentioned in Bentilee and Stanfields. Finally, the perceived accessibility of recreation opportunities was critical. These constraints were demonstrated again in the post-offending case histories from HSC. The age difference between the two samples may explain why transport presented greater problems to the Stoke sample, who generally depended on adults for transport.

Table 10.5 Constraints on the young people's participation in the two case studies

Constraint	Hampshire[a] (%)	Stoke on Trent[b] (%)
Cost	46	35
Transport	8	35
Information	25	6
Fear of crime		100 (female)
Confidence	21	16
Peer pressure	8	
Company	38	10
Lack of skills		19
Health problems	8 (physical)	13 (physical)
	38 (mental)	
Family/work commitments	4	10
Lack of facilities	4	48

Notes: a $n = 21$
      b $n = 27$

The picture shows that after offending, young people became isolated, and lack of information about opportunities and of companions became significant factors influencing their leisure behaviour. Although rates of physical health problems severe enough to preclude participation remained constant, after offending mental health problems, especially depression, became noticeable. These young people were usually unemployed, with few qualifications, and had failed to make 'the transition to adulthood, trapped in a limbo between youth clubs they had out-grown and "adult" provisions that were too expensive' (Hendry, 1993: 53).

The detailed follow-up of some HSC clients allowed the completion of life history profiles, mapping the pattern of leisure activities before, during and after the counselling project, and recorded life events and offending, extending the model developed by Hedges (1986) and used by Brodie, Roberts and Lamb (n.d.). These life histories showed common patterns, of:

- low levels of support for childhood leisure, and frequent moves, breaking up continuity of attachment to places, people or activities
- alcohol and/or drug abuse (over 50 per cent)
- spells of mental ill health (40 per cent)
- sporadic or frequent entry and release from institutional care (60 per cent) and custody (23 per cent).

A typical case is that of Martyn, aged 22 (Figure 10.4), who had a long history of petty offences and care (and perhaps abuse); he had been involved in football and swimming coaching before that, and played some badminton while in care. He lived with an older partner in a bedsitter in a deprived area of Southampton, both claiming disability benefit. His counsellor believed he might have learning difficulties, and was certainly not easy to communicate with. He started swimming and cycling at HSC, and continued with these and badminton afterwards with a volunteer from the scheme. His bedsitter became clean and tidy. After six months contact was lost, but HSC had provided consistent support for his lifestyle choices.

This demonstrated the need for formal leisure education/counselling. The common middle-class assumption that positive leisure patterns and support just evolved, is not the case for young people with chaotic upbringings. The general picture of leisure patterns for young people at risk of offending demonstrates very impoverished leisure experiences which had only previously been guessed at. From both samples there was evidence that these young people lacked the knowledge, skills and confidence to effectively access public sector leisure opportunities. The young people lacked role models from whom to develop positive leisure patterns. They had experienced little support in developing and sustaining sports activity.

If the benefit of reduced boredom was to result in lower levels of re-offending, sustained changes to leisure patterns were required. Attendances at Street

Sport sessions (all for football) in Stanfields and Bentilee demonstrated that many young males aged 14 to 20 were diverted from hanging about on the streets, and 69 per cent rated the football as the most important feature of the project. Open-ended support produced examples of educational activity to meet changing needs and abilities. The workers facilitated setting up and equipping a junior league soccer team. One player, with adolescent problems of drug abuse, unemployment and crime attended open sessions regularly for over four years, and appreciated the acceptance of any standard of play, and lack of pressure. This gentle approach to counselling and youth work helped him to survive difficult years.

The diversion from the prevalent 'hanging about' was important to the youngsters, as well as older residents:

"I found out about Street Sport through my friends when we were just hanging around. . . . I don't hang around on the streets as much any more, in summer I prefer to play sport in the parks, in winter I only go out now if my friends are there."

(Lindsey, aged 16, Stanfields, September 1999)

Participants made greater use of parks, and took part in a variety of activities – including football, tennis, snooker, golf, rounders, cinema, pubs and play schemes. They wanted to participate in recreation primarily to socialise and for enjoyment. Competition and exercise were secondary motivations.

For post-offenders it was a matter of changing the established habits of a (short) lifetime. In HSC, diversion was a long-term objective, combined with that of leisure education. Seventy per cent of the sample had joined HSC as a conscious decision to improve their health and fitness, which would often need longer than the standard four sessions ('completers' of the programme averaged eight sessions).

There was little evidence of constructive leisure for the young people before starting HSC, demonstrated in that prior to referral 46 per cent of them had never visited a leisure centre, and only 8 per cent had joined clubs, many of which were for snooker or gambling. For example, Stuart, aged 25, had a complicated history of serious offending, and suffered from depression, but after ten sessions he reported sustained changes to his leisure, continuing to attend a bridge club, play bowls and mix outside the pub. Nine out of ten who completed the scheme reported in their exit interviews an intention to continue participating. Seventy-nine per cent intended to continue to use leisure centres after the project ended, though some sustained a view that 'they are too expensive, really only there for people with jobs and money who play well' (Stuart, Portsmouth, 1997).

The success of HCS in changing leisure behaviour was assessed by reviewing patterns over the year after completing the scheme, as shown in Table 10.6. Ninety per cent who completed four sessions had tried at least two activities,

	Age	10	11	12	13	14	15	16	17	18	19	20	21	22	23	24	25

Life event

Life event	10	11	12	13	14	15	16	17	18	19	20	21	22	23	24	25
Probation												X	X			
Alcohol																
Care	X	X		X	X											
Custody										X						
Employed							X									
Excluded		X	X													
Psychiatric hospital												X				
Move		X		X		X		X		X						
Relationship													X			
School	X			X												
Sports counselling													X			
Training																
Truant		X														
Unemployed							X	X	X	X	X	X	X			
Age now													X			

Leisure

Leisure	10	11	12	13	14	15	16	17	18	19	20	21	22	23	24	25
Cinema																
Pubs/bars						▬	▬	▬	▬	▬	▬	▬	▬			
Gambling																
TV/video	▬	▬	▬	▬	▬	▬	▬	▬	▬	▬	▬	▬	▬			
Live music																
Gardening																
DIY																
Night clubs							▬	▬	▬	▬	▬	▬	▬			
Pub quiz																
Shopping																
Computer games																
Car repairs							▬	▬	▬	▬	▬	▬	▬			
Other																

Figure 10.4 Leisure Life History Chart, Martyn

Sport Recreation

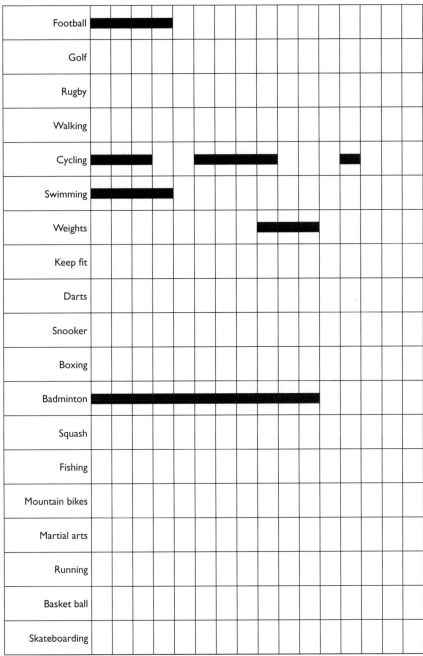

Figure 10.4 Cont'd

Table 10.6 Hampshire Sports Counselling: Patterns of continued participation

Past leisure patterns[a]	Intended to continue at exit stage (%)	Playing after 6 months (%)	Playing after 12 months (%)
Previous leisure centre use	100	67	58
Non-participant	75	67	33
Total	88	67	46

Note: *n* = 21

and after six months two-thirds were still participating in activities introduced by HSC. Drop-out at twelve months was often related to new work commitments, what could be considered successful outcomes in themselves.

Public services failed to support their leisure education; in the care system many reported little continuity of support for their leisure, and those remaining in school reported a sports delivery system that encouraged only those showing ability. This process had left many of these young people lacking a sense of direction in their free time, mainly hanging around on the streets, to be supplemented later by visiting pubs and clubs. This shows that young people at risk of offending lack the support mechanisms to allow a smooth transition through adolescence (Hendry, 1993), but while pathways are stressed for the keen and talented (Chapter 5), leisure transitions for the deprived are forgotten in public sector responses to this problem.

Perceptions of the two schemes

The young Street Sport participants saw it primarily as a means of playing football, informally in Bentilee and for the team in Stanfields, and secondly of making friends:

> "Street Sport is great. . . . I don't get to play a game anywhere else . . . the rest of the week it's just kick around with mates."
>
> (Male aged 18, Bentilee, July 1999)

> "I play for the team now and train more seriously with them but I still like to come here to meet my mates and have a bit of fun."
>
> (Male aged 17, Stanfields, July 1999)

Overall the young people's perceptions of leisure and Street Sport can be summarised thus:

- unemployment was a prime concern for all respondents
- they needed places to meet where there was no conflict with older residents and the police

- they were concerned about crime levels in their communities, many feeling threatened by the violence they witnessed
- the weekends in particular, and school holidays, were identified as key times when they needed something to do
- much free time was spent hanging around with peers, a situation they thought increased risks of juvenile crime, drug and alcohol abuse
- generally they needed adult support to create effective sports and leisure opportunities
- the level of sports participation was low and the range of sports very limited, skateboarding and BMX being the most common alternatives to football
- knowledge of the Recreation Key discount scheme was low
- even in childhood, parents had little input into leisure patterns, siblings and peers being the most common mentors
- many activities on offer were team- or course-based, aiming at performance level sport, but many young people wanted to play sport simply for fun and relaxation
- they liked Street Sport because it was informal, friendly, regular, free and close to home
- they would like more frequent Street Sport sessions, as once a week leaves a lot of empty time.

How was it seen by non-participants and the community? At a high school drop-in centre in Bentilee, its young people had not heard about Street Sport. At Willfield Community Centre in Bentilee one 17-year-old young woman regarded it as a weekly football session for young men, and a youth worker regarded it as another 'limited quick-fix solution to a complex problem' (Youth Worker, Willfield CEC, May 1999).

Street Sport was generally supported by local schools; the head teacher at Haywood High School felt it had reduced vandalism in the school grounds. The police believed it had played an important role in reducing community tension, yet felt it should run during the holidays alongside play schemes, a time of increased crime risk. Community workers in Stanfields regarded it positively, but only as a short-term diversion for young men, since it did not address young girls' needs. In Cobridge a new community centre with sports facilities was open only to adults, and so Street Sport was viewed as a valued and popular, if sporadic, contribution to young people's leisure.

Perceptions of the Hampshire Sports Counselling (HSC) scheme varied between those young people who failed to complete it and those who completed four or more sessions, who, not surprisingly, were more positive. For example, Dean, who at 22 already had numerous convictions, including a period in custody for firearms offences, and had spent ten sessions with his counsellor, thought that no changes were needed, and 'I loved it.' Jason had enjoyed four sessions, but was no longer involved in sport after twelve months, citing cost, a lack of equipment and companions: 'I would love to join a football team but how to go about it, I haven't got a clue.' Colin cited conflict with his job at MacDonalds, involving uncertain shift patterns. In fact HSC could not cope with the needs of employed or full-time student clients; after Phase 1 eight of McCormack's sample had left early. Others with mental health problems, like David, saw the scheme as another hurdle rather than a help: 'I'm having enough problems keeping the basics together, I am not ready for this sort of scheme.' Matt returned to playing badminton regularly which helped to rebuild his self-esteem, and after twelve months had added regular football and fencing. He reported: 'I found the benefits to be immense [including] increased health and fitness, also an increase in self-esteem and self-confidence.' Inevitably, some said that they were not interested in the activities available, including eight who failed to complete their programme.

The relationship with the sports counsellor was reported to be of primary importance in all twenty-one individual cases: 'my sports counselling officer was very good and he did everything possible to help me' (Client P7, spring 1997). Among those who completed the scheme, the only criticism was that counsellors were too busy to offer sufficient time.

Ending the programme was an issue for HSC, although more than half the Phase 2 sample were offered more sessions, when counsellors' analysis justified continued support on special grounds, such as depression. So, staff had to plan from the first interview for 'exit routes' that would allow continued participation. This was approached in a number of different ways: integration into clubs, increasing participant confidence in accessing leisure, selecting volunteer support and integration into drop-in sessions.

The participant's perceptions of the Hampshire Sports Counselling scheme can be summarised as:

- participants generally liked and valued HSC
- its most important aspect for participants was the support of the sports counsellor, more important than the actual activities offered for three-quarters of them
- most participants wanted more sessions, even if they needed no more to satisfy the requirements of the sports counselling process
- after six months, 2 out of 3 were still participating in activities introduced by the scheme
- after six months, 2 out of 3 participants reported improvements in general health and well-being
- perceived benefits of the scheme were improved knowledge of leisure facilities and confidence to use them, improved self-esteem and some reduction in boredom
- their perception of leisure opportunities was significantly improved through participation and this had a reported benefit for other members of their families.

Table 10.7 Changes in personal factors among Hampshire Sports Counselling follow-up sample

	Much better (%)	Better (%)	No change (%)	Worse (%)	Much worse (%)
Self-image	14	64	21	–	–
Relationship with authority figures	57	–	43	–	–
Knowledge of local leisure facilities	14	57	29	–	–
Attitude to health and fitness	21	50	29	–	–

Changes in personal factors among the Sports Counselling follow-up sample are shown in Table 10.7. The results show that the schemes had positive impacts on boredom and a lack of adult role models. They were successful in medium-term diversion by creating positive leisure opportunities. The fixed length contact in the Sports Counselling scheme and the single session per week in Street Sport were both perceived by young people as significant limitations. Nonetheless, the majority of clients felt that there had been an improvement in one or more of their self-image, relationship with authority figures, knowledge of local leisure opportunities, and/or their attitudes to matters of health and fitness.

Managing such interventions

Street Sport and HSC shared six important features:

1   Dedicated, consistent managers (Robins, 1990: 91), with clear vision and strong leadership to give projects the direction and backing to survive after initial funding stopped.
2   Start-up funding committed for three years, subject to monitoring.
3   Staff members with good interpersonal skills and empathy with young people, whether in group work as in Street Sport, or one-to-one as in HSC.
4   Striving to provide local, affordable and popular recreation activities.
5   Participants who were volunteers and consulted on activity provision.
6   Attempts to evaluate and produce evidence of performance related to aims and outcomes.

Both schemes, however, had limited attraction for girls and young women, not through lack of female leaders, but through the activities on offer. The female worker appointed to HSC commented, 'it's all weights and football, there's no mention of aerobics or netball, women see that and decide it's not for them' (Counsellor C, April 1997).

Three key differences were:

1   Group sessions were suitable in the primary intervention for reaching influential peer groups to try to prevent offending. However, individual sessions were needed for many alienated and 'labelled' individuals after they had offended.
2   Evaluation was easier to design for fixed length programmes for individuals, while outreach services provided a greater challenges to producing detailed, standardised evidence.
3   Although portrayed as a negative management feature by Robins (1990), Street Sport showed that managers who stick to their ideology and explore new avenues of funding may survive longer than those who tailor projects to the prescription of the main funding.

Kevin Sauntry in Stoke fought for and pursued over many years a 'style of community recreation I believe communities want and value' (interview, June 1997), but relied on a team of skilled managers and workers to deliver it. Keith Waldman in Hampshire led HSC from its birth in 1984 to its demise in 1998, and had a team with much less hierarchy and direct 'hands on' delivery, but increasingly had to work within the structures and priorities of the probation service, which may have affected HCS's image in the eyes of some potential participants.

The evidence supports Street Sport as an example of primary intervention, which achieved both community development and diversion for mainly male youngsters at risk of offending. At tertiary level, Hampshire Sports Counselling showed that community integration was more difficult to achieve, since many community groups resist the integration of known offenders, who can be unsure of or impatient about getting involved in groups or organisations. This suggests that primary intervention more effectively integrates young people into their communities and addresses issues of labelling, status and a need to belong.

Impacts on the causes of delinquency

With reference to Figures 10.2 and 10.3, these case study schemes demonstrated the following effects on particular causes of delinquency.

Poverty
Both schemes operated with low charges, and in Southampton and Portsmouth HSC clients could use discount Leisure Cards (see Chapter 4) to combat the significant financial barrier. However, removing cost alone as a constraint was not sufficient to establish participation.

Residential setting
Street Sport helped communities to create sports courts in local areas, using waste ground and other open spaces, and this improved the setting, but also

residents' perceptions of it and of the scheme. By concentrating on local leisure, HSC altered the young persons' perceptions of opportunities close to home (64 per cent saying their opinions had improved), and reduced the power of negative influences by introducing legitimate activities.

Parental support

Seventy-five per cent of Street Sport participants felt the contribution of the sports counsellors was an important aspect of the scheme. As one said, 'the sports leaders were great, they never pushed an issue or passed judgement but were there every week for us' (Cobridge former participant aged 21, September 1999). Even the short-tem work of HSC's counsellors provided the personal support and advice lacking in most of its clients' lives. At the time of conviction, 21-year-old Scott's view of leisure was a hedonistic search for excitement prompted by extreme boredom and frustration. Over ten sessions his mature sport counsellor was able to provide a positive role model missing in his earlier life, and Scott reported sustained participation in weight training and swimming. He did not offend in the year after attending HSC.

Peer group

Street Sport worked with the peer group as a whole: 'the Street Sport team helped us to form a football team, we have now played for two seasons and are a strong team on and off the field . . . we needed their help to get motivated' (Male footballer, aged 17, Stanfields, July 1999). The HSC introduced participants to new leisure activities, but not necessarily to new peers or friends.

Boredom

It was in this area that the most obvious results were seen. They were less significant for Street Sport, where 92 per cent of the participants aged under 17 reported extreme boredom outside the weekly sessions and in school holidays. Of the HSC Phase 2 sample, 7 out of 8 felt it had reduced their levels of boredom, a view they sustained during the twelve-month follow up.

There was no evidence to suggest that either scheme offered a sustained impact on status-seeking behaviour or a search for excitement. However, the follow-up analysis of individual HSC participants reported sustained improvement in their improved self-image (74 per cent), relationship with authority figures (57 per cent), and attitudes to health and fitness (71 per cent), all of which contributed to greater self-confidence and reduced their need to achieve status.

Although some previous studies contained individual participants' profiles and a general analysis of their offending backgrounds (Tungatt, 1991; Taylor and Nichols, 1996) there has been no attempt to analyse the existing leisure patterns of young people joining schemes, or to examine how these patterns emerged and might be modified. The results showed Street Sport as an example of primary level intervention that achieved both community development and diversion for young people (mainly male) at risk of offending, and reached influential peer groups. In contrast, at tertiary level, HSC showed that community integration was more difficult to achieve, since many community groups resist assimilating known offenders. This would suggest that primary intervention may more effectively integrate young people into their communities and address the issues of labelling, status and a need to belong, whereas individual sessions are needed for many alienated and labelled individuals in post-offending schemes.

In summary, there are six points that can be made.

Research and evaluation methods

The framework developed in Figure 10.1 proved robust across six schemes, including the two investigated in-depth, and it would be good to see it more widely tested. For the offenders, the life history charts proved a very useful tool as a framework for the periodic interviews, as a way of relating changing activity profiles across the life span, and a help to counsellors in devising a personal activity plan for the clients involved. Lord Warner, Chairman of the Youth Justice Board, announced in November 1999 a strategy to provide such on-going support for leisure interests developed in custody, when youngsters are released.

Cost and efficacy

The reported average cost of tertiary interventions in 1998/9 was £379 per place, which (allowing for drop-out and non-attendance) leads to a cost per completion of £730 (Taylor et al., 1999). This would provide an average of eleven sessions of four hours' duration. The cost of one person attending Street Sport for two hours a week for a year in 1997 (100 hours) was approximately £290. Although this calculation depends on sessions operating at an average take-up of eighteen people for fifty weeks a year, it demonstrates in this single case study the potential cost advantage of primary intervention.

Support from schools and adults

It is clear that the National Curriculum provides a poor social education framework to develop the skills and confidence to access local leisure resources and the life history profiles serve to demonstrate the almost complete lack of adult support and mentors in the development of constructive leisure. In or out of school, adult support and encouragement were almost non-existent for at-risk and post-offenders, compared with the levels for children with average participation rates as shown in Chapter 5.

Benefits from appropriate activity or counselling

A common them in intervention schemes is that the activities at some point must give the same 'buzz' as offending, for example in abseiling, tall ship racing or go-karting. McCormack's findings, however, suggest this is less important in terms of sustained diversion than the process of skills development in order to access what the local community has to offer. Activities were not rejected for lack of 'buzz', but because of barriers of cost, and physical, social and managerial access. HSC clients had particularly impoverished leisure lifestyles, and so the offers were beneficial for most who stuck with the course. Thus there may be a link between the lack of positive leisure patterns and the development of delinquent behaviour. But, if pushed to judgement, both McCormack (2000) and this author would say on balance that it is the availability of a mentor who listens without judging, who can be a role model and playing companion, that was probably the more significant factor in tertiary schemes. This was less marked for the briefer contact through group work in Stoke.

Timing and durability
The timing of the intervention is clearly crucial, since many other factors in young people's lives alter at different stages of intervention. The results demonstrate that primary provision can effectively address groups, which reduces the cost per participant significantly, and so ongoing support can be afforded. Sustained participation and skills development should be possible within such schemes, since youngsters do not need to develop independent exit routes. Tertiary provision was shown to require significant one-to-one counselling, thus increasing the cost per participant and reducing the potential for ongoing support.

Young people value consistent and reliable/durable interventions, which they have often lacked. With very mobile populations like offenders, establishing exit routes or follow-up may be difficult: HSC offered the Southampton drop-in centre, but some of those in Fareham, Aldershot, Farnborough and Basingstoke, where such sessions were not available, felt deserted, 'back to square one.'

Involving the youngsters and the community
The important act of community integration was more easily achieved in primary intervention. By the time young offenders justified tertiary intervention official criminal labels or records made integration difficult, and sports clubs generally resisted membership of known offenders, although pub football teams and running clubs were more welcoming. Even more important is involving the young in designing the programmes: Street Sport used extensive outreach work to establish their needs, while the HSC initial interview involved each participant in planning his/her own programme. McCormack (2001: 21) commented that Street Sport 'dedicated considerable resources to community liaison and consultations' with significant effects on staff workload and costs, but had experienced friction in approaching other forms of youth work.

Giddens (1982) suggested that both structure and agency have equal importance in dictating individual actions. The reported outcomes from both schemes concentrated on personal (agency) factors, although the positive role models provided by each scheme and the improved perceptions of young people of leisure opportunities in their residential settings may address some of the external causes. This supports the findings of Coalter (1996) that active leisure interventions may be part of, but unlikely to provide all of, the solution to juvenile delinquency.

Conclusions

It is easy to agree with CLR (2001) that 'there are strong theoretical arguments for a potentially positive contribution which sport can make to the propensity to commit crime', from psychology, sociology, criminology, education and leisure studies. The fact is that schemes have often lacked focus in objectives and outcomes. Providers have also not been concerned to measure these until recently. Nor has there been any real baseline data about the sport and leisure behaviour of youngsters beyond a national sample in which at-risk or offending youth are an indistinguishable minority. The HCS case study showed in a new and striking way that amongst the generally poor childhood of young offenders (and by implication from the Stoke evidence, among many youngsters at risk also), leisure education was non-existent. Frequent moves of house, care or schools, and limited or non-existent parenting resulted in really impoverished leisure, with little or no adult support. It produced what McCormack (2000) rightly called 'a leisure underclass'.

It can truly be said that many large-scale diversionary projects have 'vague rationales, overly-ambitious objectives and a relatively unsophisticated understanding of the variety and complexity of the causes of criminality and an absence of robust intermediate or final outcomes' (CLR, 2001: 27). The Street Sport case study shows how difficult it is to get such data even with much effort, but that the young people, the sports leaders, and the community all recognise tangible outcomes, which researchers must try to tease out from multi-sponsor, multi-strand schemes. Recreation Zones in Bolton is one which is commendably trying to get baseline data, as is the Sport England/Youth Justice Board project Positive Futures, working with young drug users, albeit by adapting a model developed from criminological research.

Because regular offenders incur such large costs, both of their crimes and their treatment, interventions with offenders have received relatively larger attention but with little measurement. In part this is because of lack of longitudinal data, and of control groups, but also of a lack of medical-style, 'double-blind' treatments, with which few actors in the British juvenile justice system are likely to agree.

Few interventions have been costed; Tsuchiya (1996) suggested that community schemes were almost certainly less costly than any form of incarceration.

These young lives of impoverished leisure and vandalism or crime do not develop overnight, yet schemes of a few weeks' duration are expected to reverse these supertanker tendencies. Media and political scepticism, and budget pressures, have either reduced the length of interventions as in HSC or transferred management, as also in HSC and in West Yorks Sports Counselling, to a commercial contractor (Nichols and Taylor, 1996). The commitment shown in Street Sport and in HSC is not common.

Monitoring needs to promote clearer identification of objectives, and better tracking and measurements, which will only happen if the schemes themselves are given higher priority, longer timescales and bigger budgets.

CLR usefully summarised such issues:

> Evidence suggests that outreach approaches, credible leadership, 'bottom-up' approaches and non-traditional, local provision appear to have the best chance of success with the most marginal at-risk groups. A needs-based youth work approach may be more appropriate than a product-led sports development approach. Sport appears to be most effective when combined with programmes that seek to address wider personal and social development . . . diversion must be complemented by development.
>
> (CLR, 2001: 27–8)

Chapter 11

Rural and urban perspectives on exclusion and sport

In this chapter I explore the particular manifestations of exclusions in town and country, beginning with the more neglected topic of exclusion in rural areas and countryside recreation.

Rural England: Idyll or exclusion?

Some rural areas within commuting distance of urban markets in southern England are amongst the fastest growing in economy and population. Other remote and upland areas continue to lose people, especially of working age, and severe competition in food markets from cheaper overseas sources and cuts in government and EU subsidies mean that supporting services to and in villages has become increasingly difficult. Consequently it can be said that 'The myth of a rural idyll leads to misconceptions about the countryside, with many people finding it difficult to believe that social exclusion exists in green and pleasant surroundings' (Rural Media Company, 2000: 5). Nothing could be farther from the truth. Rural populations suffer from spatial disadvantage through dispersion over wide areas, leading to higher threshold costs for services including sport and leisure, and higher transport costs. But they may find severe social polarisation occurring in settlements growing through 'counter urbanisation', because of the greater purchasing power of incoming retirees, urban commuters, or 'telecottagers'. In rural Scotland, cost of living prices were 3 per cent higher in 1994 than in Aberdeen and as high as in Edinburgh, where incomes were higher. Transport costs were 13 per cent higher than in Aberdeen and 17 per cent above those in Edinburgh (Scottish Poverty Information Unit, 2000).

As well as being hidden from view for lack of research, Milbourne (1994) argued that many rural dwellers will not own to their own or their neighbours' poverty. Cloke et al. (1994) were perhaps the first to extensively explode the myth, with studies in twelve areas of England and Wales making clear the extent of poverty, shortage of affordable housing, low incomes and limited job opportunities, poor access to cars (especially for women), scanty public transport services, shops and pubs, and the appeal of close-knit communities co-existing with crushing isolation.

Deprivation studies have until recently focused on urban areas, and the indicators used have items of little relevance, such as ethnic minorities and the proportion of people living in flats. White and Higgs (1997) examined eleven indices at ward level but felt that none identified rural deprivation adequately. The Rural Development Commission therefore instigated two studies: one suggested that a more robust measure would be to gather eight bundles of indices (three on employment, two on housing, one each on income, access to services, and physical isolation), though even the 'access to services' bundle did not include a leisure variable (Dunn et al., 1998a).

Testing these indicators in three areas (Durham, Lincolnshire and Suffolk) suggested that there were few differences in deprivation between urban and rural populations, confirming Cloke et al.'s (1994) work in twelve areas of England and Wales which suggested that on average the figure was about 24 per cent. In terms of the processes behind rural disadvantage, neither were there differences in changes in deprivation over time, nor in the numbers of people moving off low income. Unsurprisingly, those least likely to move off were single parent families, families with no earner, and single pensioners; those most likely to do so had good educational qualifications (Dunn et al., 1998b). Many, however, do not climb far out of measured poverty. Chapman et al. (1998), reporting on the Joseph Rowntree Foundation-funded Action in Rural Areas research programme, showed that 1 in 3 people in settlements of less than 3,000 residents had a spell of poverty during 1991–6. The Rural Media Company (2000) reported in graphic personal terms what poverty and exclusion from most of the good things of life, including access to affordable leisure, meant to five households. Lack of leisure and entertainment was emphasized in the work on rural youth in Scotland by Cartmel and Furlong (2000) and Pavis et al. (2000), with the latter pointing out that some of these and other disadvantages suffered by excluded youth is disguised by living in parental homes, usually at subsidised costs.

The New Policy Institute (2000) divided English districts into remote rural (66, with 5.6m people), accessible rural (104, with 10.8m), and urban (the remainder, with 33.1m). Its findings, adding to those above, are summarised in Table 11.1. Clearly, the urban areas have more concentrated deprivation than the rural ones, but there are more people in the lowest 10 per cent of income in the latter, and the remote areas are more deprived than the accessible. Similar patterns are found for heads of households receiving means-tested benefits, children in low-income households, unemployed people wanting paid work, and those with no educational qualifications. More older people die in winter in rural areas, and more are helped by social services to remain in their homes.

Brown (1999) undertook a review of provision of care in eight counties, and reported:

Table 11.1 Some indicators of poverty and exclusion in English rural areas

	Remote rural		Accessible rural		Urban	
	(%)	*(millions)*	*(%)*	*(millions)*	*(%)*	*(millions)*
Households below 50% of average income	22	1.24	19	2.03	27	8.76
Children in low-income households	29	0.35	24	0.55	39	2.90
Receiving means-tested benefits	10		8		14	
Adults with no qualifications						
men	15		12		16	
women	19		17		21	
Unemployed adults wanting work	10		8		12	
Excess winter deaths						
men	20		21		20	
women	25		25		23	
Reliant on State pension/ Income Support						
couples	23		17		19	
men	42		29		34	
women	52		49		50	
Over-65s helped to live at home by social services	59		63		81	

Source: New Policy Institute, 2000

- lack of choice, leading to people refusing services
- some rural care services being less accessible than in towns
- using inappropriate services because they are local/convenient
- relying on historic provision even when it does not reflect known needs.

Brown also recorded that some local social services departments did not acknowledge the extra costs, especially of information services and of travel, with private or voluntary contractors painfully absorbing them in order to retain block grant work. The National Council of Voluntary Organisations (1994) added two other factors:

- higher unit costs of provision to small and scattered populations
- lack of funding to small rural voluntary organisations.

Such challenges are exacerbated by a paucity of a wide range of community services and amenities (Spilsbury and Lloyd, 1998). In 1998 these lacks were recorded as in Table 11.2. The only improvement has been in nursery and playgroup provision, with increased public investment in the hope of enabling higher female employment, much of which is in tourism and services which are often seasonal or low-paid.

Table 11.2 Lack of services in rural areas 1991, 1994 and 1997 (per cent)

	1991 (%)	1994 (%)	1997 (%)
General store	41	42	42
Post office	42	43	43
Village hall/community centre	30	29	28
Public house	n/a	30	29
Daily bus	72	71	75
Minibus/social car scheme	89	91	92
Private child nursery	93	90	86
Library (permanent or mobile)	12	16[a]	12
Sports field	52	n/a	50
Women's Institute branch	39	n/a	41
Youth club	67	n/a	68

Note: [a] Regarded as a rogue/unreliable figure

Children in rural areas often had little space of their own for play, especially in areas of arable farming, and feared threats from bullies and gangs of older children as much as those in cities. They also had surprisingly constrained limits to the distance they could roam from home unsupervised. In rural Northamptonshire there were widespread complaints from youth older than 13 about 'nothing to do' and lack of involvement in deciding priorities for local amenities (Matthews et al., 2000). For older children the issues are 'just somewhere to go in the evenings, like a new café or something, just where we could all be', improved local facilities (including school swimming pools open to the public, more flexible opening hours generally), and more accessible and affordable transport (Hedges, 1999: 7, 49).

A report on social exclusion and transport pointed out that on average people travel five times as far in a year as they did around 1950 when the welfare state was developed, and that while 'transport poverty' in towns affects particularly youth under driving age, women at night, and disabled and older people, in rural areas a much wider range of people are affected 'because access to most facilities is almost impossible in some areas without a car, they are socially excluded . . . since they cannot fully participate, i.e. behave as the vast majority of society behaves'. Having studied fifteen New Deal for Communities areas and four rural areas, the same report concluded 'there appear to be clear connections between transport and social exclusion' (Department of Environment, Transport and the Regions, 2000). Sixty-four per cent of rural dwellers felt that public transport was bad in 1997–9 compared with 17 per cent in suburbia, and 9 per cent in towns (Todorovic and Wellington, 2000: 8).

Although 22 per cent of rural households do not have a car, the poorest tenth of the population are twice as likely to own a car as their metropolitan cousins. By whatever means, the country households with the lowest fifth of incomes travel about 25 miles a week to shop, compared with twelve miles for the equivalent urban households; rural old age pensioners spend 75 per cent more on petrol a week than their urban counterparts, and the gap is even greater between the two groups of unemployed people (Boardman, 1998). However, both rural old age pensioners and unemployed are spending £16 a week for the convenience of having a car available and only £10 or £5 respectively on petrol to travel.

The powerful convenience of the motor car is shown by the fact that the numerous weekend and summer bus and train schemes to provide access to the countryside nearly all need subsidy; but some extend regular scheduled services, such as the Kirklees Wildbus (Glyptis, Collins and Randolph, 1995). While limited diversions of passengers from cars may be possible for journeys to work, school, or shop, the marginal cost and convenience of carrying children, picnics, pets, toys, and sports equipment makes it more difficult to persuade pleasure seekers to transfer. The 'car culture' (Linadio, 1996) is very strong.

One of the problems is that some of those elderly or low-paid who are poor nevertheless feel that they have non-monetary benefits from living in the country, and a high proportion do not claim welfare payments to which they are entitled (Cloke et al., 1994). One of the issues all gave high priority was choice of employment and amenity for young people.

When it comes to recreation, data on countryside recreation day visits in 1998 and tourist trips to the country including villages, both show a gradient by social class, as in Table 11.3.

In terms of the four societal systems distinguished by Commins (1993) – democratic and legal, labour market, welfare state, and family and community (see Chapter 4) – Shucksmith and Chapman (1998) identified in Scotland failures in the first three:

- a sense of powerlessness and distance from policy makers
- very limited opportunities in housing and labour markets, as already mentioned above, with almost non-existent openings for graduates to be retained locally and little or no housing for rent, especially in the public sector

Table 11.3 Countryside trips for recreation and tourism, by social class

	Day visits for recreation, 1998 (%)	Tourist trips to countryside, including villages, 1999 (%)	GB population 1998 (%)
AB	23	32	17
C1	30	33	26
C2	21	20	25
DE	26	15	32
Total		20	100

Sources: Slee, Curry and Joseph, 2001; Countryside Agency, 2001

- low benefits take-up, a lothness to seek official help, difficulties in getting information
- isolation of older people whose younger kin have left the area to seek work.

All of these lead to family and community exclusion. In 1997–9, forty-six per cent of rural residents felt that leisure facilities were bad compared with 36 per cent in suburbia and 36 per cent in towns (Todorovic and Wellington, 2000). Slee, Curry and Joseph (2001) concluded that some people with genuine choice (such as young affluent adults) may choose not to go to the countryside for sport and recreation, but, as Harrison (1991) suggested, some are denied 'by socially constructed exclusion', notably people from ethnic minorities and those who are disabled. I would add to this poor people, and those with no cars.

Three sources give details of schemes to combat exclusion, lead by municipalities and voluntary organisations. Streich (1999) was commissioned by the Countryside and National Youth Agencies to review *Alternatives to the bus shelter* for young people. She identified a range of projects, mostly modest in scale and funding:

Skateboard parks	West Haddon Parish Council, Misterton PC
Places for youth	Improved youth club, Sileby Parish Council and Leicester Training and Education Council
Mobile provision	Pegasus bus and equipment in Daventry area
Information stall	Daventry – at Christmas fetes with Citizens' Advice Bureau
Drug education	Castle Donington, with young peer educators
Youth Council	Whetstone, organising babysitting, disco, theatre group
Participation/lobbying	Vale Hopper bus campaign in Vale of Belvoir
Transport	Wheels2Work – leasing mopeds and subsidised driving lessons in Hereford/Worcester

In similar vein, the Local Government Association (1998) stressed the important co-ordinating and leading role local authorities play in combating exclusion, starting with anti-poverty strategies (see page 43) exemplified by the counties of Suffolk, Northants, Flintshire and Powys, and the districts of Penwith, Tandridge, and Cherwell. Schemes used by the Association to illustrate the range of its' members' activities were:

Sphere	Selected places and activity	Sponsors
Child care	Chipping Norton centre for creches, family support computer training, after-school club and base for many community groups	County/Rural Development Commission (RDC)/Health Authority/ voluntary groups

Elderly	Meals on wheels, Suffolk	Age Concern
Jobs/training	Foyers for housing in seven Suffolk market towns Earby IT centre	Housing Associations Pendle District Council/ RDC/Training and Enterprise Council (TEC)
Ethnic groups	Rural race equality advice for Devon and Cornwall	RDCV/National Association of Citizen's Advice Bureaux (CABx)
Travellers	Hertfordshire scheme for health services to gypsy community	County
Housing	Norfolk Youth Build Partnership: 51 houses, jobs, community facilities	County/two districts/TEC
Advice	Cherwell support for CABx/independent services	District Council
Discounts	Disc card for leisure, library/adult education	Suffolk County
Finance	Wales co-op centre sets up credit unions	Powys County/ European Union/TEC/ Trades union
Agenda 21	Devon Food Links encourage local organic production	County/Districts/ Ministry of Agriculture, Fisheries and Food/ Soil Association/RDC
Transport Youth	Lilbourne community bus, Lutterworth Postbus, North Nottinghamshire youth disaffection partnership – drugs, crime, school exclusion – £6m Single Regeneration Budget money	Leicestershire/ Northamptonshire County/Districts/Police/ Health Authority/TEC

Slee, Curry and Joseph (2001) examined twelve cases that they believed showed elements of promoting social inclusion:

Scheme	Main thrust
1 Fairbridge, Edinburgh	Social integration of at-risk youth, using outdoor activities
2 The Big Issue club	Outdoor activities for unemployed people

3	Vogie Country Park, Midlothian	Access for disabled people
4	Promoting Access in Croydon	To open space for everyone (disabled, ethnic minorities)
5	National Trust Inner City project	Sport and recreation for young and older people
6	Brixworth Country Park, Northants	Access for youth, disabled, ethnic groups, young families
7	Bestwood Country Park, Nottingham	Access for inner city youth, residents including ethnic
8	ARCHES, Ranaldstown, Antrim	Tree planting and cycleways for both communities
9	Black Environment Network	Access for ethnic groups, disabled to historic gardens in Wales
10	Mendip Hills Farm Partnership	Educational trips to Alvis Brothers' Farms
11	Glodwick Community Outreach	Walks for elderly Asian women in Oldham
12	Youth Route 70, Motherwell	Social and recreational trips for youth.

The authors identified seven key drivers of common inclusionary aspects of the projects, that they were:

- *community driven,* giving a sense of ownership, and more likely to be sustained than schemes imposed on the community
- *empowering beneficiaries,* and improving self esteem, not just providing diversionary recreation
- *making social cohesion an objective,* while respecting cultural diversity
- *driven more by partnerships* than a single organisation, sharing expertise
- *developed by specialist outreach staff,* in conjunction with countryside rangers
- *measured qualitatively,* and not just by numbers of attenders
- *effectively marketed.*

The projects were limited by available finance, and in some cases by people becoming dependent on the provision; the latter is very difficult to avoid with clients suffering from long-term ailments like mental illness (as in the Peak Park walks). One thing the authors did not remark on was that the sustainable nature of these projects (only two ran for less than three years, and the Mendip project ran for twenty) was thanks to having a lead agency to maintain commitment and continuity, variously by district, metropolitan or county councils, or private bodies like the National Trust, Fairbridge or the Alvis Brothers farmers.

Chapman et al. (1998) and Dunn et al. (1998b) have just begun to investigate the dynamics of rural as opposed to urban social exclusion. Scott (1994) has argued that the policies of the European Commission on growth, competitiveness and unemployment, in encouraging capital accumulation, are likely to generate greater inequities for some. But the Poverty III programme was focused on the integration of the least privileged. Certainly the Blair Government strongly believes that capital accumulation and social cohesion can co-exist. Its vision (Department of Transport and the Regions, 2000b) in the White Paper *Our Countryside: The future: A fair deal for rural England* was fourfold:

- A living countryside, with thriving communities and access to high quality public services.
- A working countryside, with a prosperous and diverse economy, giving high and stable levels of employment.
- A protected countryside, in which the environment was sustained, and which all can enjoy.
- A vibrant countryside which can shape its own future and whose voice is heard by government at all levels.

The preceding consultation document had said a fair and inclusive society in the countryside will seek to reduce social exclusion, recognise the diversity of rural areas, and incorporate the rural dimension into national policy. The White Paper made little mention of exclusion, but the implementation plan had a more specific programme (see Table 11.4).

The latest review of the contribution of sport to wider social issues (CLR, 2001) said nothing specifically about the rural context, but Francis and Henderson (1994: 3–5) reiterated the particular features of rural society that give strong challenges to effective policy delivery of community development programmes:

- striking diversity and contrasts even in close proximity
- 'glossy' images of the countryside hide many forms of deprivation
- there is a pervading conservative, individualistic culture which slows change and mutual forms of aid
- acceptance of community work is patchy
- many organisations are involved in rural development, but many of them focus on physical infrastructure rather than community work
- the problem of achieving critical mass for services brings in its train higher costs and longer timescales.

As Table 11.4 makes clear, the government certainly intends action across all four domains of exclusion, but it remains to be seen whether all this rapid governmental action can been 'joined up', and whether the benefits reach the excluded or are made use of by the better-off majority.

Table 11.4 Implementing the 2000 Rural White Paper

Selected items	Cost (£m)	Target date	Lead department/agency
Improving village services			
50% rate relief for village shops/pubs/garages		2001	DETR
Community Service Fund to support shops	15	2001	Co Ag
Post offices as one-stop government/shops/banks		2001/03	DTI, PO
Extend community use of schools network	80	2003	DfEE/CEDC
Increase child care and nursery places		2001/04	DfEE
5,000 new local primary care projects	100	2004	DoH
Tackling social exclusion			
7 Sure Start pilots for early education		2001	Sure Start Unit
Extend Connexions incentive for 16- to 19-year-old learning		2001	DfEE
Neighbourhood Renewal Fund for poorest areas	25	2001	Co Ag
70–100 Spaces for Sport/Arts projects		2002	DCMS/ACE/SpE
Housing			
Extend rural Housing Corporation fund from 800 to 1,600 units pa		2001	HC
Transport			
Increased Rural Bus Subsidy/Challenge	192	2001	DETR/BT
New Parish Trust Fund for social car schemes, plus fuel rebate	51	2001	Co Ag
Regeneration			
Extend funding for 100 market towns programme	37	2001	RDAs/Co Ag
Action Plan for Farming	300	2001	MAFF
EU leader development programme	50	2001–06	MAFF
ICT programme	30	2001	MAFF
Eng. Rural Development agri-environment programmes	1600	2001–08	RDAs MAFF
Conserving/enjoying the countryside			
New biodiversity strategy		2002	DETR/EngN/CoAg
New ambient noise strategy re. tranquillity		2001–04	DETR/EA
Right to Roam on 4m acres plus mapping		2001–04	DETR/CoAg
Extend afforestation/forestry grants		2001	For Comm
Local power			
New role for parish/town councils			DETR/LGA/NALC
1000 parish plans		2001	Co Ag
New Cabinet Rural Affairs Committee		2001	Cabinet Office

Source: Department of Transport and the Regions 2001a

Key

ACE	Arts Council of England
BT	British Telecom
Cab Off	Cabinet Office
CEDC	Community Education Development Centre

Co Ag	Countryside Agency
DETR	Department of the Environment, Transport and the Regions
DfEE	Department for Education and Employment
DoH	Department of Health
DTI	Department of Trade and Industry
EA	Environment Agency
Eng N	English Nature
For Comm	Forestry Commission
Ho Corp	Housing Corporation
LGA	Local Government Association
MAFF	Ministry of Agriculture, Fisheries and Food
NALC	National Association of Local Councils (parishes)
PO	Post Office
RDAs	Regional Development Associations
Sp E	Sport England
SS	Surestart units

Sport and exclusion in urban England

The UK, with France and the Netherlands, has explicit urban policy (Atkinson, 2000). Two types of urban area are commonly labelled 'deprived.' The first are the inner suburbs with mixed uses, including factory industries that have in many ways been overtaken by cheap labour manufacture from the developing world, or moved out to more efficient urban fringe/small town single-storey sites. In the inner suburbs poor housing, unemployment and low pay is mixed with ethnic friction, and some areas of high value which have been 'gentrified.' The second deprived areas are the overwhelmingly public housing built in large estates on the outskirts, both high and low rise, with limited employment, shops, services and leisure and entertainment provision (like the three estates in Stoke on Trent in the Street Sport case study in Chapter 10). This has been recognised by the EU (1994). Despite the facts presented in the previous section, comparisons of income show that the urban poor are poorer than their rural counterparts (Countryside Agency, 2001):

	Income per week (£)	
	Urban	Rural
Poor	94	103
Middle income	217	225
Better off	471	474

Robson et al. (2001) remarked on the growing rather than narrowing north–south divide in economic performance between London and the South East, and the cities of the north. He made a contrast with the relatively even gross domestic product (GDP) of French provincial cities relative to Paris, where the lowest are Toulouse, Nantes, and Bordeaux at 61 per cent of GDP, compared with Leeds and Liverpool at 51 and 50 per cent of London's. They wrote also of a pressing need to link the prosperity of city centres to the surrounding areas of impoverished households.

There is a vague presumption that richer areas have better sports and leisure provision, or have access to them by virtue of high car ownership. Amazingly this has not been proven beyond doubt, because of the difficulty of identifying and mapping small-scale public, private and voluntary operations; even the Sports Council's Facilities Planning Model ignores most of this. A small-scale attempt was made to map physical and human provision and residents' responses in two adjacent estates in Stockton on Tees (Boothby et al., 1982). This did show fewer clubs and facilities in Hardwick (the deprived area) than in Fairfield (owner-occupied private housing), but a smaller gap in sports participation. Computerised databases like those developing in Leeds (Hewson, 2000) should enable this to be tested.

From their studies in public, private and voluntary sports facilities in six cities, Brodie et al. (n.d.: 66–67), a sample of 1,254 users showed modest differences in participation between middle and working class groups in 1986–7 and in the follow-up in 1988. Middle class people were more likely to play four or more sports (25 per cent compared with 16 per cent), and more likely to increase the sports they played (38 per cent compared with 33 per cent). Slightly more working class players were likely to give over eight hours a week to their sport (31 per cent compared with 26 per cent), but more had not changed their participation in 1987–8 (40 per cent compared with 36 per cent). Roberts and Brodie (1992: 58) commented that larger gaps were found amongst the two groups of women than men (as all surveys show, and as Kay points out in Chapter 6 (page 101), and that 'working class males who survived in sport into adulthood in our survey areas were thereafter just as active as middle class players.'

What is remarkable in the burgeoning geographical, planning, economic and sociological literature on regeneration and urban management is how little it mentions sports, arts or leisure (e.g. Bailey et al., 1995; Healey et al., 1995); that is a separate literature of its own.

Concern about recreation in the inner cities first welled up around the riots of 1977, and the concerns for particular groups (then described as deprived of opportunity rather than excluded) listed in a report commissioned by Denis Howell were: disadvantaged youth, the elderly, disabled and handicapped people, women, and immigrants (Department of the Environment, 1977: 31). At this time the needs of black British citizens was not identified, nor was poverty an issue. The issues did not go away, the Greater London and South East Council for Sport and Recreation describing them in 1993 as special areas requiring special measures. At this time, and for a few years, government put more money directly into urban sport and recreation through the Urban Programme (in 1982–93 a total of £9.5m on sport and £8.5m on leisure and recreation) than the Sports Council did for the whole country (with £10m – Greater London and South East Council for Sport and Recreation, 1983: 28–32, 38–9).

Yet again, the remedies suggested in 1989 by a group convened by Minister for Sport, Colin Moynihan, were not radically different though more detailed and thorough (DOE, 1989), except that they advocated a package of demonstration projects that would be attractive to the private sector. Those recommendations which were not actioned were:

- schools devoting 10 per cent of curriculum time to PE and sport (if anything, the hoped-for two hours a week has receded)
- priority to training primary teachers (taken up in small part by the Youth Sports Trust's TOPs programme in the late 1990s)
- a new timetable of schemes for community use of schools (never widely taken up under the Lottery Schools Community Sport Initiative; may be boosted by the School Space Initiative for primary schools in 2001 onwards)
- tax incentives for sports buildings open to the community
- private sector funding (developed not as a result of the partnership suggested but as a result of commercial managing agents investing in the second round of CCT contracts, and a few Public Finance Initiatives in the late 1990s)
- incentive funding schemes (an idea overtaken when all the urban central grants were rolled together into the Single Regeneration Budget)
- schemes for older people, developed with non-sporting agents like Age Concern (after the mid-1990s this group ceased to have any priority for Sport England)
- local authorities to establish sport and recreation strategies after consultation (only a third did so under compulsory competitive tendering and most will not, until they produce it as part of a wider local cultural strategy and consultations integral to Best Value service plans after 2000).

One feature of urban leisure provision in the 1990s is that 'leisure boxes', ice rinks, multi-screen cinemas, food courts and interactive amusement halls have been built, a few in regeneration schemes in major city centres but many more in what Evans (1998) has called the 'pleasure periphery' of cities, accessible only by car, and not to most inner city residents. It remains to be seen whether a recent *volte face* in planning policy, requiring urban developments to pass sequential tests for location in the centre, on its fringe, and only in the suburbs or on greenfield sites if it cannot be accommodated anywhere else (DETR, 2000, in Planning Policy Guidance Note 6 revised), is effective in encouraging redevelopment in the centres of smaller cities and towns, or whether the policies of the last twenty years have sucked most of the commercial energy and spending power out of town already.

From the mid-1980s the concern shifted from remedying social ills to generating jobs and income: the value of major events like Euro 96 (Gratton et al., 1998) and associated facilities were extolled, in the most exaggerated form, by 'civic boosterism' in the USA. Yet even after the initial embarrassments of underestimated costs and overestimated sponsorship for the World Student Games, the subsequent benefits the City of Sheffield has gained from the continuing stream of major events should not be disguised (Price, 1999), but even small events in smaller places bring benefits when well chosen and planned (Collins and Jackson, 1998). UK sport has produced an analysis of the benefits brought by both spectator/media driven and competitor driven events, to help bidding cities more accurately estimate the benefits (UK Sport, 1999).

The City Challenge regeneration programme produced evaluation reports, such as that for the West End of Newcastle (Robinson, n.d.), where £37.5m. was invested in housing, new shops and employment, education, a credit union, a health resource centre, and crime prevention. The sport and leisure elements were improvements to open spaces, a community (Asian) festival, and programmes for all ages under the aegis of West End Participation in Leisure (WEPIL). Remarking that in urban schemes, young people rarely had a say in decision-making, even when they were meant to be the beneficiaries, Fitzpatrick et al. (2000: 506–7) commented, 'effective . . . involvement is undermined by both the disadvantaged material position of many young people, and the nature of intergenerational relationships whereby young people are systematically subordinated to adults'.

The DETR devised the Index of Local Conditions which combines eleven measures of deprivation; but this was criticised for not being able to clearly distinguish deprived rural areas, and even more strongly, that by using housing measures which had high proportions of council housing and flats it overemphasised London, and concentrations of white people, because smaller proportions of ethnic minorities occupy social housing (Lee and Murie, 1998). The new edition of the Index, called Local Deprivation (Department of Environment, Transport and the Regions, 1998), uses twelve indicators at the district scale (two each on unemployment, education and housing, three on low income, one each on health, crime and environment), and recalculated earlier ward and enumeration district data. The eighty-eight most deprived districts (Social Exclusion Unit, 2001a) were shown to be:

- fourteen in the Northern region, including Tyne and Wear and Teesside
- twenty-one in the North West including two in Cumbria
- eight in West and South Yorkshire, and Hull
- five in the West Midlands conurbation and Coventry and Stoke
- Nottingham and three other district in the north of the county, and Derby and Leicester
- nineteen London Boroughs
- Great Yarmouth and Luton in the East

- Southampton, Portsmouth, Hastings and Brighton and Hove in the South East
- Bristol, Plymouth, Kerrier in the South West

Change since 1991 had been small, with forty-six of the worst fifty districts remaining in the index. Areas that improved relatively included Leeds, Salford and some other northern metropolitan districts, but also coalfield communities. Bennett et al. (2000: 81) emphasised the difficulty of replacing the higher income coal jobs in a service-based economy, and the importance of local community development projects which help people feel 'included, needed and valuable in places that they feel they are no longer of use'. On the privatisation of the pits, the English Sports Council lobbied successfully for money to enable the Coal Industry Welfare organisation support schemes to retain and develop Miners' Welfare social and recreation centres. A DCMS study demonstrated that these communities obtained fewer and smaller Lottery grants than other towns and:

> Despite traditions of social solidarity and self help, geographical variations in population, voluntary infrastructure, local authority support and variations in Lottery Distribution bodies in eligibility, matching funding and procedures are common across Great Britain, but are suffered harder by coalfields resorts and retirement communities, while they have a lower capability to respond.
>
> (Gore et al., 1999, 2000)

Lottery distribution bodies were asked to give them greater priority and to support local organisations.

Other deprived area were scattered across the south; areas in decline included outer Greater London, Liverpool, and peripheral areas of West Cumbria, East Kent, East Norfolk, West Cornwall. At the smaller scale pockets of deprivation in less deprived districts show up, for example North Paddington in Westminster, and Kesteven in Lincolnshire.

Once the Cabinet Office's new Social Exclusion Unit produced *Bringing Britain Together* in 1998, there was an agenda for eighteen Policy Action Teams (PATs) to work on. The one for Sport and the Arts (PAT 10) determined that it would be the first to report, and it was. Its remit was to report on

- best practice in using sport, arts and leisure to engage people in poor neighbourhoods, particularly those who may feel most excluded, such as disaffected young people and people from ethnic minorities
- how to maximise the impact on poor neighbourhoods of government spending and policies on sport, arts and leisure.

(Department for Culture, Media and Sport, 1999: 5)

It received a great deal of evidence, made visits, and broke into four sub-groups to look at best practice, funding, partnership and links. It commissioned research reviews from Collins et al. (1999) on sports and Shaw (1999) on the arts. With case studies, it looked at the sector's contributions to health, crime, employment, education, economic development, and stronger communities, and put an emphasis on people not buildings. It identified two reasons as to why past initiatives have not 'set in motion a virtuous circle of regeneration' as:

- a tendency to parachute solutions in from outside, rather than engaging local communities
- too much emphasis on physical renewal instead of better opportunities for local people.

(Department for Culture, Media and Sport, 1999: 28)

The PAT also identified seven barriers to wider contributions to neighbourhood renewal (Department for Culture, Media and Sport, 1999: 34):

1 There has been too much focus on the requirements of funders (inputs and outputs) at the expense of the needs of recipients (outcomes).
2 Funding has too often been short-term rather than a longer period of 'mainstream' funding sufficient for sustainable benefits.
3 Arts and sports bodies tend to regard community development work as an 'add-on', a secondary activity.
4 Other bodies in regeneration regard sport and arts as peripheral, and regeneration neglects 'self-help' capacity building in communities.
5 There has been a lack of evaluation of outcomes of projects and of sources of funding for community groups and those at risk of exclusion.
6 Schools could play a fuller role in developing habits of participation.
7 Links between sports and arts bodies, and major organisations involved in regeneration, are often poor.

Collins et al. (1999) had put stress on poverty as the single largest cause of exclusion, which exacerbated factors of gender, age, ethnicity, and disability, but PAT 10 decided without explanation on the two latter. It set out nine principles to guide the involvement of sports and arts in regeneration (Department for Culture, Media and Sport, 1999: 40–7):

1 valuing diversity (stressed in relation to ethnicity and disability)
2 embedding local control
3 supporting local commitment
4 promoting partnerships where all have equal stakes
5 defining common objectives in relation to citizens' needs
6 working flexibly as situations change

7   securing sustainability, 'for services not projects'
8   pursuing quality, from recreation to the highest professional performances
9   connecting with the mainstream of arts and sports activities.

The PAT made forty-seven recommendations that DCMS followed up in its social inclusion action plan under seven lines of activity

1   leading/co-ordinating/informing the social inclusion activity of arts and sport providers
2   monitoring activity (1)
3   extending cultural activities for people at risk of exclusion
4   maximising culture's role in government
5   encouraging and working with organisations expressing the needs of excluded groups and areas
6   implementing research into the impact of culture on exclusion, and devising evaluations as standard elements of social inclusion work
7   supporting best practice guidelines for community development work.

These eighteen action plans generated 569 recommendations, some major and involving many agencies. When the government, as it promised, audited progress nineteen months after PAT 10 reported, it had accepted 86 per cent of them, partly accepted or was still considering 12 per cent and had only rejected 2 per cent; the figures for sport and arts were 40, 7 and nil respectively (Department for Culture, Media and Sport, 2001). Pursuing its concept of accountability, the Social Exclusion Unit (2001) produced a detailed report on what actions had happened in response to the aspects of PAT 10's suggestions. This demonstrates the fairly fine grain and short term to which central policy was now working, albeit with inputs from consultee or advisory groups. It also shows the pace of change expected of government and its partners, a point I shall return to in the final chapter. Kate Hoey, then Minister for Sport, stressed that 'the social inclusion agenda is firmly embedded in DCMS policies' (Social Exclusion Unit, 2001: 130–1) for all the culture sectors, all the agencies it oversees, and all the Lottery fund distributors.

    PAT 10 sought to draw its recommendations to the attention of the seventeen other PATs, in particular those on jobs (1), antisocial behaviour (8), community self-help (9), schools-plus (11), young people (12), learning lessons (16), joining it up locally (17), and better information (18). Nothing specific was picked up in the recommendations of PATs 1, 8, 9, 16, 17, or 18. PAT 11 picked up no references to Connexions or the Children's Fund, but mentioned leisure needs in extended school hours (recommendation 3); Proposed extending the Playing for Success scheme, using links to professional football clubs and other sports to encourage numeracy and literacy, including the Premier League and lower divisions, rugby union and league, cricket and basketball (recommendation

5); and promised to adapt capital programmes to accommodate community projects (recommendation 14). PAT 12 picked up the PE and Spaces for Sport programme in primary schools (recommendation 20). PAT 13 on shops (SEU, 1999) had comments relating to exclusion and leisure in pointing up the withdrawal of retailing choice, of banks, and telephones. This was reinforced by Speak and Graham (2000) and Forrest and Kearns (1999: 36), who commented that such trends 'meant that these neighbourhoods were no longer self-sufficient for many of the functions people sought from them'.

A background report to the Urban White Paper paralleling the rural one, *The State of England's Cities* (Robson et al., 2001: 16, 20–23), identified three sets of important trends:

- a continued strong *urban exodus*, the eight UK conurbations gaining 364,000 people in 1991–7 through net births, and 370,000 through migration from overseas, but losing 543,000 through moving out
- *dangerous mosaics* of social inequality, only fifteen of fifty poverty indicators improving during 1994–9, long-term ill people rising from 3 to 3.6m. during 1991–8; districts with 10 per cent above average mortality growing from 28 per cent to 39 per cent in the same period; and poor children becoming more concentrated in particular schools, preventing them from meeting improvement targets; few authorities moving out of the most deprived list 1991–8–2000
- the particular impact of deprivation on children, with 208 wards where more than 50 per cent of children live in households dependent on means-tested benefits; and larger numbers of children under-performing at school in cities, with the problem growing with age, from 6 to 10 to 15.

The authors (Robson, et al., 2001: 1) cited three strands of new thinking about urban policy:

1   recognising that social and economic life and therefore policies are interconnected (rather than dealing with economic issues in isolation)
2   rediscovering 'an older understanding' that 'space'/accessibility and 'place' (the milieu of locally available connections) matter in the economy and society
3   interest in developmental process to meet 'the storm of change' by urban capacities to be agile (rather than cities being seen as 'the heroic, if ageing, victims of externally driven economic change').

The first theme had already been stressed by Alcock et al. (1998) in their report on local authority strategies for tackling social and economic disadvantage. Blowers and Young (2000) criticise town planning for mainly reinforcing market trends, and neglecting social and environmental matters.

Table 11.5 Government policy actions for urban sport, 2000

Decisions prior to the Urban White Paper
- scrapping entrance charges to English national museums and galleries for children and pensioners
- I million visitors to artistic experience under Arts Council of England's New Audiences programme
- strategic municipal planning via preparing Local Cultural Strategies
- starting a competition for UK Capital of Culture 2008

New measures 2000
- £130m for Space for Sports and Arts scheme for primary schools in selected LEAs
- national standards for public libraries regarding location, access, opening hours
- DCMS Culture online website
- extending access to national museums and galleries, free for benefit recipients and disabled, and £1 for all other visitors

Improving access in deprived areas
- new Creative Partnerships for access for every school pupil, £40m over two years
- commitment by ACE grant holders to extending community impact
- new Sport Action Zones where basic provision falls below 'acceptable standards'
- reallocation of half Sport England's Community Lottery funds to areas of 'greatest need'

Source: DETR, 2000

In 2000 the Government produced its Urban White Paper, *Our Towns and Cities: The Future – Delivering an Urban Renaissance* (DETR, 2000). Its provisions affecting sport are set out in Table 11.5. Paragraph 6.29 said:

A healthy, vibrant cultural, leisure and sporting life enhances cities in a positive way. It helps to create places where people want to be, are proud of and can achieve their potential. It contributes to a city's uniqueness and diversity.

In a leaflet accompanying the White Paper of the same title the government claimed to be making £33bn. available for major services, of which £200m. (0.6 per cent) was for leisure, culture and sport. Action 5 and identified five Public Service Agreement targets:

- raise significantly, year on year, the average time spent on sport and physical activity by those aged 5 to 16
- introduce at least twelve Creative Partnerships by 2004 targeted on deprived areas
- increase by 500,000 the number of people experiencing the arts
- ensure all public libraries have internet access by the end of 2002
- increase numbers of children attending museums and galleries by a third by 2004.

These clearly reflected some of the personal concerns of Secretary of State, Chris Smith. It is notable that, despite sports minister Kate Hoey's claim to close relationships and working with education minister Estelle Morris (Hoey, 2000: 16), the first target did not confront the continuing decline in curriculum time for PE identified in Chapter 5 (pages 67, 68 and 70).

Understanding if area deprivation can affect individuals is an important issue in deciding whether area-level initiatives are worthwhile. McCulloch used British Household Panel Survey data for 9,964 adults to model ward-level effects of deprivation on employment, family finances, social status and likes/dislikes about the neighbourhood, and discovered:

- a marked gradient for all but one factor for men and two for women and a particularly steep differential as regards dislikes of poor areas
- past life-experiences significantly predicted poor outcomes at subsequent interviews
- living in social housing clearly raised the chances of an adverse life outcome (i.e. poor areas do compound the disadvantages of poor people), but were stronger for men than women in poor areas; the reverse was true in affluent areas.

But at ward level the influences of area on individual outcomes were weak, so that 'it was not clear whether policies should be aimed at improving neighbourhoods, helping people to move out, or . . . at improving job opportunities' (McCulloch, 2001: 682). Commentators on this paper could not agree on the significance of his data or the soundness of his methods. Kennett (2002) had a similar result at ward level with his analysis of leisure card holders.

As we saw in Chapter 4, the government consulted on progress on the 1998 Neighbourhood Renewal Strategy and produced an update at the beginning of 2001 (Social Exclusion Unit, 2001b). This focused on the five key areas of jobs, crime, education, health, and environment and housing, and their associated Public Service Agreement (PSA) targets. Culture, sport and art got a brief mention under improving skills – itemising the targets agreed with DCMS agencies, and programmes for priority areas like Sport Action Zones; the £750m for facilities from the New Opportunities Fund and space for sport and arts in primary schools, and the twelve Creative Partnerships (Social Exclusion Unit, 2001b: 39). These were four of the 105 commitments government made to renewal. The poor social outcomes in deprived areas suggest that services may be worse at meeting residents' needs. Duffy (2000) attempted to test whether this was a reflection of greater needs, or a lower starting position and fewer resources. Using a MORI People's Panel survey, he identified two long lists of services used in both deprived and non-deprived areas (Table 11.6).

In all this, it is difficult not to see a continuing marginal position for culture, leisure and sport. Perhaps that could be said to be in balance with the priority

Table 11.6 Urban leisure-related services used at least once a month (as a percentage of sample)

	Deprived areas[a] (%)	Other areas[b] (%)
Used more frequently in deprived areas		
Local buses	85	75
Public parks	59	53
Youth and community centres	15	9
GP	51	33
NHS hospital	14	8
Dept of Social Security	19	9
Used less frequently in deprived areas		
High Street banks/building societies	76	92
Libraries	35	42
Leisure centres	26	33

Source: Duffy, 2000
Notes: a *n = 380*
     b *n = 3,796*

given to sport and leisure opportunities as very important to the quality of life, ranking 15th and 16th at 21.4 per cent and 23.8 per cent in a list headed by violent crime and local health care at 71.7 per cent and 70.3 per cent (Rogerson, 1997 cited in Todorovic and Wellington, 2000). Coalter et al. (2000) argued for benefits of sport in the regeneration process to health, crime, youth and education, ethnic minority life, jobs and regeneration, community development and environment, which they elaborate in the Local Government Association report (2001). On the last point, they emphasise the importance of open space and making use of existing facilities, even when they are not purpose built for sports.

But in multi-strand regeneration the role of leisure is difficult to unravel; the share of total spending is too small to appear in overall financial analyses; so that one cannot extrapolate Bramley's (1998) finding that other environmental services (which includes leisure) was relatively flat across deprived and non-deprived areas; but the Sheffield Centre for Regional Economic and Social Research concluded that the Single Regeneration Budget programme had allowed some authorities to draw anti-poverty elements into bids and schemes. Accordingly, Alcock et al. (1998) recommended that DETR should consider:

- allocating resources according to need and not by bidding, an approach that Oatley (1998) persuasively argued always and systematically disadvantages poor and deprived people because good bids require professional preparation, matching funding and advocacy skills with agencies and funders, and time and persistence
- supporting research linking social and economic regeneration and poverty profiling and audits.

The first problem of getting resources to the most needy is one that has bedevilled welfare payments, allocation of public housing, and other services.

David Byrne (1998), reviewing Geddes' (1997) study of regeneration in North Shields and Wallsend (*Partnership against poverty and exclusion? Local regeneration strategies and excluded communities in the UK*) points out that 'community involvement, especially in the more deprived communities, is often very fragile and that "the community" is often far from being an equal partner in most local partnerships,' and suggests that powerful agencies can use community development to camouflage urban land development deals.

Bianchini (1998: 8), reflecting on European attempts to build cultural industries and job markets, suggested that two developments could be envisaged:

- a transnational network of minority cultural producers (for example, Turkish or Arabic films, videos and music)
- cultural production in deprived neighbourhoods 'often insufficiently recognised or even marginalised by strategies prioritising city centres . . . a universe of locally controlled and innovative spaces in which new, open-minded and pluralistic traditions of cultural production are invented'.

Hall (1998), crystal ball gazing in the same publication, asked whether the creative city of the future is doomed to comprise 'islands of affluence surrounded by seas of poverty and resentment', or whether new technologies can harness creativity in children who under-perform in conventional academic areas. The experiences of young people becoming rapidly expert and confident in animation, video, film, computing, music, electronic publishing, fashion, and their interfaces (recorded in Whyatt, n.d. and Kelly and Wojdat, 1997) suggest this is possible, but it is not clear on what scale. Hall (2000) emphasised the scale of the creative industries (quoting DCMS' (1998) mapping exercise that showed 1 million jobs and £57 billion output. With a look to the new media-related industries in California, he pondered whether new forms may develop in Britain in a similar way. Despite technology, these artistic activities, like sport, cannot be done virtually, they require the face-to-face contact which is the basis of social capital and of city life. Stewart et al. (1999: 70) suggested that the wider availability of electronic media may provide a means of communication for groups that have been invisible or excluded, including ethnic minorities.

There can be little doubt of the honest desire for change represented in all the Blair Government's documents, to work with local groups, to join up government actions centrally and locally more effectively and less bureaucratically, and the release of money which in part, but only in part, restores some of the cuts of the previous twenty years. Launching the strategy, the Prime Minister said, 'Our vision is that within 10 to 20 years, no one should lose out because of where they live. We want to see people living in our poorest neighbourhoods enjoying the same opportunities to build a decent life which

Chapter 12

Policy implementation

Stronger citizenship and social capital through sport?

In earlier drafts this chapter formed parts of the conclusions, but I was encouraged to consider it as a separate chapter. It has to be taken as a very preliminary look at lines and principles of policy, for it is far too early to make any mature and sensible judgements about impacts, let alone outcomes. Yet politicians want to be judged by results, however premature, and DCMS, unwisely in my view, in 2001 commissioned research on good practice in inclusive policy for sport; not surprisingly, since outcome measures had not been agreed and baseline studies not undertaken, its consultants have struggled to make a satisfactory narrative. In the first section, I look at five aspects of policies that have to be thought through and well-constructed if policy is to have any chance of biting and making a difference. Then picking up threads from pages 21–3, I look at the New Labour concepts of the 'Third Way' and the crucial role that the voluntary sports club system has to play as a communal form of social capital, if that idea is to have any validity, and at structural and attitudinal issues which manifest both strengths and weaknesses in the British system, certainly when compared with others in Europe.

Implementing inclusion policies and programmes

In this section, I wish to deal with a number of aspects:

- the policy lifespan
- outputs, outcomes and their measurement
- 'place' and 'people' policies
- sustaining programmes
- sport cannot 'go it alone': the importance of partnerships.

The policy lifespan

Every new minister or agency chief executive comes in with an overblown expectation about the scale and volume of change they can bring about and the speed they can bring to it. Moreover, there is pressure to modify and re-badge programmes to give them more appeal and currency; one of the most successful affecting leisure was the series of programmes that started with the Manpower Services Commission for training and work experience for unemployed youth in the 1980s, which underwent three major transformations before being replaced. PAT 10 (Department for Culture, Media and Sport, 1999) and Collins et al. (1999) commented on the problem of both the government and Sport England producing too many programmes – what *Bringing Britain Together* (Social Exclusion Unit, 1998) had called 'initiative-itis' – and of removing resources and priority from existing to new programmes too quickly.

One of the respondents to a study by Church et al. argued that

> ... sports development is continually inundated by initiatives. One after the other, after the other and often these initiatives are a means to actually secure funding. They're not necessarily the rationale for involvement in these initiatives which is based on what you've identified as a result of a local community audit consultation. In other words, you run with an initiative because it offers money, then your priorities get screwed, and suddenly you're actually doing something which doesn't meet the priority needs of your local community ...
>
> (Church et al., 2002: 18)

There is also a tendency to build new organisations and structures which take time to set up and bed in.

This second tendency had three effects – the cost and hard effort of the design and promotion work does not pay back its full benefit, if it is a national initiative it never reaches the areas where partners are slower to respond, and existing partners, especially local authorities, become exasperated or confused by shifting priorities. One of the exceptions to this was the '50+ and All to Play For' campaign for sport for older people, which was low cost, but its documentation proved so useful that it was printed three times and is still manifest in some local programmes long after Sport England has lost interest in that age group (see Chapter 7).

Programmes intended to produce attitude and behaviour changes cannot come to fruition quickly or easily. In the author's thirty-three years of experience of running and evaluating projects, a typical pattern has been:

Year 1

Pilot/demonstration projects set up, with three-year grant relationships established, market research done, programmes launched; there may be a 'honeymoon' effect of early take-up.

Year 2

Programmes may be extended or new partners may be brought in, usage settles to a pattern; if pleased, sponsors publicise by anecdote or description, and other bodies start to copy (Action Sport for urban youth was a typical example).

Year 3

Staff see the end of the project visible, and leave as soon as they can get another job, reducing the capacity to deliver; evaluation, if any, starts but by now copy-cat schemes are numerous. Agencies slow to adopt the programme cease to receive staff attention.

Year 4

In some cases local sponsors 'mainstream' the scheme, but often with reduced resources and with adapted, often reduced, aims and methods to accommodate it in host departments or programmes; any evaluation is published, with caveats as well as strong points, mostly about outputs and value for money. It is not widely disseminated and readers tend to play down the caveats, because they wish to start their own similar programmes, or move on to new initiatives in pursuit of grants.

Any outcomes of the initial programme will post-date its official operation, and those of its imitators or adopters will only happen in year seven onwards. On such a timescale, even when evaluation is commissioned, the councillors/ministers and civil servants/staff who receive the outcome research are different from those who commissioned it, and the context for receiving and applying lessons has changed, as have political and professional priorities. This is a wasteful model. The Community Projects Foundation, involved in such work since before World War II, will only share resources if they are able to be committed for five to seven years. In any case, sustained interests in participation, major changes in athletic performance, or generation of jobs, take seven to ten years to establish.

Collins et al. (1999) pointed out that most grant aid schemes lasted for only three years, and that research councils will often reject applications for outcome research because they believe government sponsors should have committed the resources for evaluation up-front.

PAT 10 did recommend that timescales should be extended to at least five years, which gives more of them a fighting chance of achieving outcomes. Robinson (n.d.: 69–70), in his evaluation of five years of the £37m City Challenge programme in south Newcastle, said, 'Time is needed for partnerships [in delivery] to develop and enable participation . . . long term commitment and action are needed to tackle deep rooted and complex problems – the regeneration effort has to be sustained'.

On the third issue of new organisation, two comments can be made. First, much of the first year of any programmes is taken up with setting up structures and appointing people; this is clear from reports on the Active Sports partnerships and the Sport Action Zones, where two of the twelve had not been able to find a suitable director. Where possible, time is saved and local people encouraged. After four years of lobbying from Sport England and the Coal

Industry Welfare Organisation, the Tory Government eventually found a small sum of money to help some welfare clubs survive and adapt as community organisations with an active human resource, after their pits closed (Collins and Reeves, 1995). Often their facilities were the best in the area. But many trustees had long since lost heart and closed the facilities, leaving a need for new investment in buildings and organisations.

The Blair Government, in its eagerness to be seen to be doing new things, still produces far too many separate new schemes, belying its slogan of joined-up government, as the issue of special zones indicates, but on the second issue it is gratifying to see some programmes being evaluated over this time span, like Sport England's Active Sports and Lottery programmes, and like that of the New Opportunity Fund for open space and children's play, announced as this book goes to press.

Outputs, outcomes and their measurement

It has been said many times in recent years that focus has been too much concentrated on outputs – the number of projects or partners, the volume of use (not even the number of individual customers or frequency of use), or the number of clients completing a course, rather than the outcomes of personal or social change which are often embodied in policy aims by politicians or senior managers, and expected by the media and the public. Coalter (2000: 48) distinguishes *intermediate* outcomes (physiological or mental health, identity and self-esteem, well-being and social learning) from *strategic* ones (such as reduced antisocial behaviour, positive social relationships or involvements in building civic structures, or better educational performances). His basis for this distinction is not clear: it would seem to be a personal versus social one; he asked elsewhere whether participation must precede inclusion, and it may be connected with this. It is a good question; but it is evident that this link can work both ways. Many sports volunteers start helping in a small way with fund-raising and making tea while their children play; but others brought along as companions, or helpers may become participants.

It is quite clear that there is little outcome measurement in any rigorous or reliable fashion (Coalter et al., 2000). This is partly because of the length of the policy span just discussed, and partly because of the low priority and minute funding that has been available from sponsors. So Collins et al. (1999) found only a dozen programmes of 180 where there was any form of outcome measurement, and only one – the 1986–7 Americas Cup in Fremantle (Selwood and Jones, 1993) – where there had been a standardised before-and-after study. Coalter et al. (2000) and, for youth schemes in the USA, Witt and Crompton (1996) made the same point.

One study that I believe shows a long-term outcome is that of the inner cities study of Brodie and Roberts (1992; Brodie, Roberts and Lamb, n.d.). This sought to look at patterns of sport and exercise of a sample of people using public, voluntary and commercial sports provision in six inner cities in

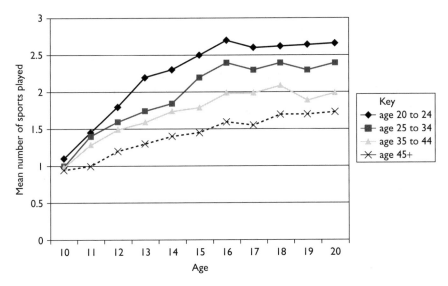

Figure 12.1 Average number of sports played when aged 10 to 20 by male cohorts

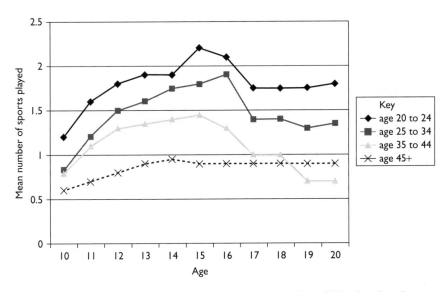

Figure 12.2 Average number of sports played when aged 10 to 20 by female cohorts

the UK, using interviews, life history charts, and fitness tests to measure changes over a short, 12 to 18 month span. In fact the life history analysis, I believe, gave the best evidence of the long-term policy effects of Sport for All that minister Ian Sproat told Parliament in 1995 was not available.

Figures 12.1 and 12.2 show the average number of sports undertaken between the ages of 10 and 20 by three age cohorts of men and women. It can be clearly seen that the average number of sports has increased in successive cohorts for both sexes. Brodie and Roberts commented:

> Such an increase is the delayed, but according to our evidence, reliable by-product of introducing higher proportions of successive cohorts of young people to a wide range of sports. If provisions continue to increase in the future . . . we are confident that the adult participation rate will continue its upward course. This vindicates the liberalisation of the physical education curriculum in schools.
>
> (Brodie and Roberts, 1992: 80–1)

I would add, however, that while the liberal curriculum might be the genesis, it could only continue because of the growth of an ever-wider range of public, voluntary club and commercial sport provision in the community over the same period.

There are difficulties in measurement, as in many social policy areas (Rossi et al., 1999) – the outcomes are long-term, broad, qualitative and affected by many other influences than sport, many groups have been self-selecting and evidence self-reported, control groups and longitudinal studies are difficult and costly to organise, and qualitative data has been scattered and under-rated by policy makers. Also, as Coalter (2001) said, there has been a lack of theorisation of the mechanisms by which sport may bring benefits – to whom under what circumstances, as Patrickkson (1995: 128) advised the Council of Europe. But one cannot expect the levels of proof that laboratory research produces in medical and physical science. Having examined the social impact of library services, Matarasso (1998: 5) wrote, 'the decision-making processes of public administration . . . depend on the balance of probability rather than the elimination of reasonable doubt.'

Sport England (2001c) produced a guide for local authorities which distinguished sporting from process outcomes and these from service and process outputs as well as service inputs, as shown in Figure 12.3. Only the first of these was regarded as a sporting impact.

'Place' and 'people' policies

As said earlier, government has worked through place and people policies. The former used to be operated through a planning process, but under the Thatcher and Major governments became part of a bidding culture, that can be shown to be: profligate in the wasted effort of rejected bids; unfair in systematically disadvantaging poor areas where the social capital of professional help is scarce (as shown in the coalfields study – Gore et al., 1999, 2000); and often misguided in that the majority of deprived people are found outside designated areas (Oatley, 1998). Nether is there evidence of economic 'trickle-down' effects from rich to poor, or from poor peripheral to core areas (Smith, 1985).

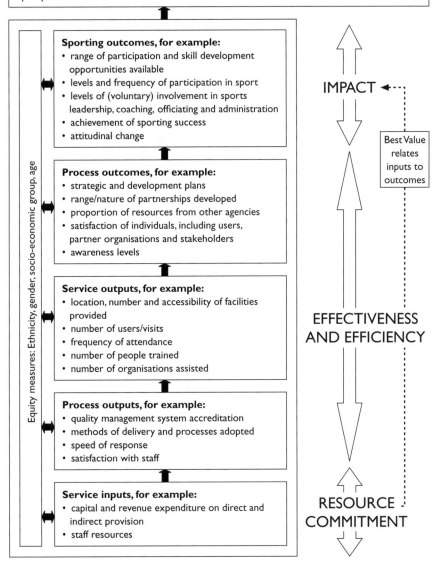

Figure 12.3 Sport England's evaluation framework for sport

Powell et al. (2001: 253) said that 'attempts to secure greater levels of territorial justice or spatial equity in welfare provision have formed a consistent – if not always coherent – part of government policy for the last 50 years.' The SEU (1998) argued that public spending redistribution has focused more on the results than the causes of poverty, and more on regenerating the physical environment than the prospects of residents. Powell and colleagues said 'this means tackling poor schools, adequate adult skills, lack of job opportunities and childcare, improving health, and providing affordable local leisure activities for children and teenagers' (2001: 251). These, to be fair, are the components of the Neighbourhood Renewal programme, but is it joined-up policy?

Nonetheless, the Major Government having amalgamated a dozen programmes from several departments under the Single Regeneration Budget, the successor Blair Government has spawned policy-specific Action Zones for Health and Education, on top of which there are local partnerships for crime reduction, community safety, and Beacon and Pathfinder councils to be models of delivery.

To this mixture Sport England has added twelve Sport Action Zones (SAZs) and forty-five mainly county-based Active Sports Partnerships (SPs) (Sport England, 2001a, b). Currently there are twelve and eventually there will be thirty. These are meant to focus existing resources and only £2m. has specifically been set aside for SAZs, though each SAZ and SP has an – Exchequer funded manager. The present twelve SAZs range enormously in size, from an area of 1,100 people in south Leicester, through 88,000 in wards in Lambeth and Southwark, to 48,200 in Cornwall and the Isles of Scilly and 852,000 in three Metropolitan boroughs in South Yorkshire.

It must be doubted that coordination can be equally exercised and resources adequately targeted over huge areas of places and people. All the efforts in benefits policy has been to draw rules to ensure that money and help get to those for whom they were intended, without including free riders and too many illegal claims; some are still means-tested or have tests of eligibility, as in medical examinations and reviews of disability. Area policies are useful political tools in terms of rewarding councils and MPs who support a particular government, or areas that make a good case for special needs, like areas of concentrated economic restructuring in steel, coal, textile and armaments industries. The latter is the basis of the EU's structural funds like RESIDER, RECHAR and programmes for shipbuilding and textiles. Powell et al. (2001) could find no correlation between income per capita and Standard Spending Assessments between 1981 and 1995 at county level; they suggest that domain-specific measures might be needed, but equally it may be that smaller areas are needed to discover any relationships. The Priority Areas Initiative allows a finer allocation to areas that cover 29 per cent of the population (14.4m. people); it remains to be seen if it can be more than 'a limited, if fairly blunt, instrument for challenging social exclusion' (Henry, 1999: 268).

Sustaining programmes

Apart from the too frequent cycling of programmes for political novelty, there is the issue of trying to ensure that each is a good investment in terms of the work continuing after the experimental/demonstration project/grant aid period. For example, the Sports Council's demonstration project, the Active Lifestyles project in Coventry schools, had a long follow-up and demonstration effect, whereas that for women's sports promoters inside Cambridgeshire's Women's Institutes (WI), despite great success, could not be 'mainstreamed' because the WI saw no way of becoming an employer of a paid promoter for every county.

It seems likely that sustained inclusion is more likely when:

- local people 'own' the work and take active leadership roles – that is, it is driven 'bottom-up' and not 'top-down'
- local ownership is clear to citizens and local agencies, giving them personal and civic confidence to go on
- a main sponsor, public, voluntary or commercial, makes a commitment which provides core funding for others to match or manages to 'lever' contributions; in Slee, Curry and Joseph's (2001) case studies of good practice in countryside recreation all those that had survived more than a few years had such a sponsor – a district or county council, the National Trust, etc.

It may be very important to develop outreach methods, not only by Sport Development Officers but also other professionals (McDonald and Tungatt, 1991; Coalter, 2001) and this may mean more training in the skills of community development (Bryant, 2001). Houlihan (2001: 110) averred that 'there is considerable potential for sport and recreation professionals to support and facilitate the construction of citizenship as a bottom-up process'.

One associated issue is that effective programmes almost universally have strong, dedicated leadership/entrepreneurial skills, at least in their start-up and consolidation stages (Collins et al., 1999). This need was recognised more than a decade ago by the Minister for Sport's Review Group (DoE, 1989).

Sport cannot 'go it alone': The importance of partnerships

Pierre and Peters claimed that the state is:

> restructuring in order to be able to remain a viable vehicle in an era of economic globalisation and increasing sub-national institutional dynamics . . . the Blair government is to some extent 'decentring-down', arguing for mobilising stake-holders and partners, diversifying delivery forms, seeking participation. But the pattern is still with desire for central control by finance and regulation; it is only a limited move from 'power over' to 'power to', from 'rowing' to 'steering.'
>
> (Pierre and Peters, 2001: 196)

Table 12.1 From government to governance?

Changes in the 1990s	Lessons of the 1990s
• from government to governance	• fragmentation limits the centre's command
• more control over less	• regulation substitutes for control
• the hollowing out of the state from above (EU) and below (cities)	• external dependence further erodes the executive's ability to act
• the weakness of the core executive	• fragmentation undermines the centre's ability to co-ordinate
• unintended consequences (e.g. in marketisation)	• knowledge/policy learning has a juggernaut quality, changing problems as policies seek to solve them
• the loss of trust (e.g. between clients and contractors in tendering)	• marketisation corrodes trust, co-operation and shared professional values, undermining the networks it only partly replaces
• it's the mix that matters	• markets, bureaucracies and networks all fail, so, 'if it ain't broke don't fix it'
• diplomacy and 'hands-off' management	• steering networks needs diplomacy, so hands-off management is the only effective model
• from de-concentration to devolution	• decentralisation is a key mechanism for developing holistic government

Source: Rhodes, 2000

Rhodes (2000), reviewing changes in government in the 1990s, took a stronger line on the extent to which the state had been 'hollowed out' and weakened, using nine aphorisms (Table 12.1). He also drew nine parallel lessons regarding its ability to work through dispersed networks, and felt the biggest problem was for politicians and senior civil servants to learn to let go. Taylor (1997) provided one illustration, describing the Department of National Heritage/ Department for Culture, Media and Sport as a body functioning at 'arms-length but hands-on'; officers like David Pickup, Director of the English Sports Council in the late 1980s and early 1990s, would agree very much with the second part but would doubt the first.

The best sports scheme will not have a widespread or long-lasting effect if it is just promoted in isolation by sports interests. Another 'buzz-word' of New Labour is that of partnerships, as Atkinson (2000: 1051) called them, 'a holy grail'. The literature in Britain is now considerable (for example, Department of Environment, Transport and the Regions, 1998; Carley et al. 2000), and it grows in Europe (for example, Geddes, 1997; Conway, 1999). In most current Lottery and agency grant aid schemes, making partnerships is a condition of awards.

The greater the number of partners, the more complex the resolving of resource allocation and of managers satisfying the expectations of all stakeholders, when priorities, timescales, styles of operation may differ. Carley et al. (2000:

25) commented, 'partnerships can lose direction or fall apart upon public squabbling between partners who fail to agree a common agenda'. Also, partners bring differing power and resources to the table. Henry, discussing urban regimes of municipal government and business that seek to use (usually professional) sport and its arenas as a means of income generation that it may neglect the matter of social production and may have 'significant negative implications for less powerful groups in society' (Henry, 1999: 18). Taylor (2001) graphically showed how recreational swimming and teaching declined in Sheffield with the closure of local pools after the building of the Ponds Forge 50m pool, though the city attracted a growing number of national and international events. Byrne (2001: 157) argued for developing 'local coalitions against exclusion, popular fronts based on all social forces which are prepared to act on solidarity as the key social goal'.

The advent of the cross-cutting issues of community safety, health, environment, and inclusion make partnership inevitable but complex. The partnerships in the Sport England showcase projects are illustrated in Table 12.2. Here it is clear that these echo PAT 10 in their geographical focus, in a high proportion dealing with ethnic minorities, disabled people and youth at risk, but several have wide concerns.

In Chapter 2 we looked at the views of citizenship that had evolved since Marshall's 1950 formulation; more recently he wrote of collective goods and services providing:

> A general enrichment of the concrete substance of civilised life, a general reduction of risk and insecurity [and] an equalisation between the more and less fortunate . . . between the healthy and the sick, the employed and the unemployed, the old and the active.
>
> (Marshall, 1992: 33)

These benefits would be conferred by the state on relatively passive citizens. This, for many, would be far too rosy and cosy a view of the likely future. Giddens (1994) foresaw a more active but individualised citizenry, a world of 'clever people' capable of constructing their own biographies, challenging 'expert systems' and choosing their own solidarities, in sport and leisure amongst many other spheres. One can see the business and intellectual elites already doing exactly that in politics as well as in sport. Accordingly, Ellison concluded:

> 'Citizenship' no longer conveys a universalist sense of inclusion or participation in a stable political community . . . instead we are left with a restless desire for social engagement, citizenship becoming a form of social and political practice born of the need to establish new solidarities across a range of putative 'communities' as a form of defence against social changes which continually threaten to frustrate such ambitions.
>
> (Ellison, 1997: 14)

Table 12.2 Sport England showcase projects

	Target groups[a]			Partners[b]		Objectives[c]
	Excluded youth	Ethnic youth	Other	Lead	Others	
West Ham Asians in Football	5–11	yes		West Ham FC	3 LBs	Create coaches/refs; involve more girls and community
Southmead Youth, Sport, Bristol	11–25 D, O, L	yes	girls	Bristol City Council	Avon Health	Prevent drug dependency; quality of life; train leaders; exit routes
Pathway 2000, Bolton	8–24, D	yes		Bolton Metropolitan District Council	Single Regeneration Budget fund	Prevent drug dependency; grow self-esteem; training
Reaching for Success, Teesside	5–16 O			Tees Valley Leisure	4 MBs Teesside Health;	Prevent drug dependency; reducing crime–using basketball
Include, East Norfolk	14–18 O			Norfolk LEA	DCs, Police, YOTs,	Reduce school exclusions; health education
Peabody Programme	? M	yes	senior citizens	Peabody Trust	2 LBs	Capacity building for tenants, community; exit routes
East Oxford	? O	yes		Oxford City Council	YOT	Reduce offending; sports networks
Heart of Portsmouth	?			Portsmouth City Council	?	Club network on multi-games area

Project				Lead	Partners	Aims
Kent Rural Disability Sportslink	yes	yes	all disabled	Kent County Council	Health, Las; vols	cf. Gravesham project, using outdoor/adventure activities
Joining it up Actively, Kings Norton, Birmingham	yes	yes	adults	Birmingham City Council	Voluntary services; New Deal	Capacity building; promoting health; sustainable sport network; create amateurs
Greet Green Explorer	yes	yes		Sandwell Metropolitan Borough Council	New Deal, Health Authority	Capacity building; lifelong learning/health
Race Equality	yes	yes	?	Leicester City Council?	?	Remove barriers
Activ8, Hull	16–24 U, O, L	yes		Raleigh International	Humberside Careers; VSO; Sail Train Association	Training; self-esteem and confidence; transfer to formal education
Oasis (Offering Arts & Sport in Society), Grimsby	0–25 O, D	yes		North Lincolnshire District Council	Grimsby Football Club; Police and 38 others!	Grow self-esteem; reduce crime; quality of life
No Limits, Hull	? C			Kingston on Hull Council		Half-term and holiday programmes to grow self-esteem, reduce crime

Notes:

a Targets: D = drug dependent; O = offenders or at-risk; L = lone parents; M = young mothers; C = in care; U = unemployed

b Partners: YOT = Youth Offending Teams; VSO = Voluntary Service Overseas

c In addition to increasing participation, creating partnerships and monitoring

Within this situation there would be winners and losers in this reflexive practice, while some may adapt to exclusion by choosing to disengage completely as citizens in any public space, 'getting on instead with seeking their own satisfactions' (Jordan, 1996: 107), as those who live in squats, or do not register to vote or pay council tax or join any club, do at present.

Thus if Bourdieu's concept of individual social capital and Putnam's of communal social capital are brought together, people may choose to gather capital in both forms as skills and contributions, as consumers and clients and active members, though the pressure of choice and many obligations may make them more catholic and sporadic in their commitments. So we go on to consider the strengths and weaknesses of British sports clubs as a form of communal social capital.

The Third Way and communal social capital in sport clubs

The Third Way

Giddens has been influential on the Blair Government's view of society. In 1998 he produced *The Third Way*, arguing that globalisation, especially of commerce, the growth of individualism in social life, and the growth of ecological threats and concerns required a new framework for social policy in an inevitably capitalist society. This involved active citizens in *a radical centre*, albeit centre-left (Giddens, 1998: 45, 64). The values of this Third Way encompassed

1 equality
2 protection of the vulnerable
3 freedom as autonomy
4 no rights without responsibilities
5 no authority without responsibility
6 a pluralist, cosmopolitan approach to world and scientific issues
7 a philosophic conservatist approach to the natural world.

It required a synergy between the commercial, state and self-help sectors in all areas, including combating exclusion that is 'not about gradations of inequality, but about mechanisms that act to detach groups of people from the social mainstream' (Giddens, 1998: 104). It required sustaining welfare spending, response to the greater equality of men and women in income, sexuality and new family structures, acting to halt the desertion of public spaces by the middle/upper classes (leading to what Putnam in America tersely called 'private affluence amid public squalor'), and a focus on the social investment state rather than a focus on human capital, or economic maintenance, with education and employment initiatives aimed at the bottom of the social scale. Lister (1998) and Levitas (1998) have criticised Giddens for equating inclusion with equality, and inclusion based on paid work, implying that paid work equals equality of opportunity. Social investment involved a greater role for the third sector through local distribution systems.

Closely allied to the idea of social capital is that of *social cohesion*, said to comprise: elements of common values and a civic culture, social order and control, solidarity and reduced financial disparities, social networks, and territorial belonging and identity (Kearns and Forrest, 2000: 996). Major cultural and sporting facilities may engender place identity, especially through professional soccer teams. Social networks may be strong, and were believed to be strengthened even more by kinship in traditional working class suburbs and villages, though how far this was objectively so is not beyond dispute. Middle class and affluent people develop many more, wider and weaker friendship and interest networks, including for sport, aided by car ownership. Fukuyama (1999) argued that such weak ties may become more important in post-modern society. Baubock (2000: 115) suggested, 'the most important demand of citizenship is to learn to cope with the plurality that is continuously generated by civil society'.

Capacity building involves skilled workers initially helping local groups to work at their own pace (Taylor, 1992; Chanan, 1999) which may be slower than managers and politicians (like many in sport) are used to when driving programmes. It must be done locally and 'bottom-up' (Coalter, Allison and Taylor, 2000; Hambleton et al., 2000; European Commission, 2000; Coalter 2001) and may not look particularly outwardly like the Action Sport and the STARS schemes for unemployed people in the 1980s (Rigg, 1986; Glyptis, 1992). A source of expertise that has been dispersed were the Community Development Officers who worked in the new towns in the 1960s and 1970s. As debated in Chapter 10 and on page 234, in deprived areas human sports infrastructure in terms of clubs may be weaker than in more blessed areas.

Sport England has launched four programmes that are aimed at helping this process:

1   The Priority Areas Initiative, using Lottery money for mainly capital grants, with a requirement for only 20 per cent matching from local sources. The eligible areas are the worst one-fifth of wards according to the Local Deprivation Index. Though these include 29 per cent of the population, or 14.4m people, schemes could be local and closely targeted.
2   The Active Community Development Fund, using revenue grants from the Lottery for schemes aimed especially at helping women, and people who are poor, disabled or from ethnic minorities; £2.5m. will be available in 2001–2, and £7.5m. a year from 2003–4 onwards.
3   Small grants of up to £5000 from the Awards for All lottery fund on a 'fast track' procedure.
4   Sport Action Zones mentioned above.

It is not clear how these relate to each other, rather than as reactions to particular criticisms or policy prods from the government, for example over the Lottery allocation strategy.

Leisure, including sport and the arts, is delivered in all three sectors, though data is much more difficult to get from commercial and voluntary organisations, because they are mainly smaller and more fragmented than public organisations, and only owe accountability to the public when partnerships are formed and grants given. The commercial sector in leisure has grown, and more of leisure has been 'commodified'. Martin and Mason (1998: 33) found that between 1971 and 1996 free time grew by only 5 per cent on average, but money spent on free time activities grew by 101 and 91 per cent per head respectively. Allison (1991) pointed out that this commodification made it all the more difficult for marginalised groups to access facilities and services.

Sports clubs as communal social capital

Sport is delivered through a wide range of voluntary bodies, but often as part of a spectrum of activities for leisure, education or socialising (residents' and tenants' association, clubs for female, youth, retired, ethnic and disabled groups). But the core of voluntary sport is the sports club movement, organised through and regulated by national governing bodies. Considering much of it has been established for over a century, however, little is known about the scale and operation of the club movement. Collins made an estimate in 1987 for the Sports Council that there were 155,000 clubs in England, 105,000 of them unaffiliated, but this has never been verified by a fuller survey, even though since 1966 the Sports Council has awarded Exchequer and Lottery grants to clubs. About 28 per cent (43,000) of these are soccer clubs. Scotland has had a more thorough survey of 3,500 of its estimated 13,000 clubs (Allison, 2001).

English sports clubs exhibit peculiar features (Collins, n.d.). They have parochial origins, in links with local villages, estates, factories, churches, women's/youth/cultural groups or (particularly) public houses. The strong links with the military, or urban or rural workers' movements found in many European states, never developed with British trade unions. This gives each a social strength – 'a community of like-minded people,' as Heinemann and Schwab (1999: 147) termed it – but also a tendency to cliquishness.

English sports clubs have an enrolment at 12 to 14 per cent of the population (perhaps less amongst adults), lower than, for example, in Germany (29 per cent), Netherlands (26 per cent) or Denmark (36 per cent). This may be because of the strong development of public sector pay-as-you-play provision in the 1960s and 1970s (a time when many continental countries saw rapid growth in clubs – Heinemann, 1999) and of commercial provision since then. Consequences of this are a lower income to the confederation, the Central Council of Physical Recreation, and a smaller credibility and influence on government since it patently does not represent all of UK sport. In contrast, the Deutsche Sportbund (German Sports Federation) is always consulted on legislation and runs its own Sports Training College in Berlin.

Single sports clubs dominate in England, and small ones at that (notably in soccer clubs), with an average estimated size of 43 members, compared with 118 in the Netherlands, 142 in Denmark, and 306 in Germany. The average size in Scotland is larger (nearer to 100, with golf clubs averaging 535). The small size means a strong social bond, but economic and organisational weakness in that there is limited scope for specialisation, a growing feature of sports organisations (Slack, 1999), and duplication of operational tasks like chairman, secretary, fixtures secretary, etc. at the cost of developmental tasks. It also makes clubs vulnerable to experienced and competent officers leaving and not being able to be replaced.

There are few large, multi-sport clubs in England, unlike in Germany and other countries. Clubs of over 1,000 members comprised only 6 per cent of Germany's 66,700 clubs in 1991, but a quarter of all affiliated members. Four out of 5 of these large clubs offered eight or more sports compared with only 4 per cent of small clubs (those with fewer than 300 members). They introduced more new competitive and leisure activities, catered three times or more often for the needs of particular groups (for example older people, children, disabled people) and were four to five times more likely to employ professional managers (Heinemann and Schubert, 1994). Thus they provide both the likelihood of having specialised skills to call on and a secure base for public investment and 'contracted' programmes. In Britain the Civil Service Sports Club and Coal Industry Welfare clubs provide some of the few examples, but many of the latter were lost in the rapid contraction of the mining industry in the 1980s and 1990s. In Scotland only 5 per cent offered two sports and 2 per cent three. This is a major structural weakness that has to be addressed in British sports policy.

Is the number of clubs or members increasing? Throughout Europe club membership grew substantially in the 1980s, but like overall participation, it has slowed down. In the UK the Sports Council produced three digests of statistics, the last in 1991. While some traditional team sports shrank, especially because of a shrinkage of the high participant 18 to 25 age group by 25 per cent, some new activities like aerobics grew; between 1975 and 1985 the numbers of affiliated clubs recorded grew by 5 per cent, but membership was substantially unchanged (Centre for Leisure Research, 1991). The English Sports Council (1997) set an (unrealistic) target for 10 per cent more club members in the very short time to 2002, but has collated no data since 1990. Yet, as the number of teenagers and early-20s in the population recovers to two-thirds of the 1980s peak, how well sport is recruiting against the manifold leisure activities competing for time and money is a vital sport and health issue.

Sport England did commission a review of sports volunteering (Sport England, 1996) that estimated that 1.49m. officials were working at club, regional and national governing body levels, a total of 88m. hours a year, equal to the

£1.5bn. turnover of the public sector and its 37,000 full time employees. It is, however, a litany repeated in Britain (Collins and Randolph, 1994; Sport England, 1996; Allison, 2001) and throughout Europe (Heinemann, 1999) that the volunteer workforce is ageing, and that it is getting more difficult to recruit volunteers. This is because some are working longer hours, want to go on playing and competing longer, and have a wider range of other leisure interests, and because quasi-professional standards of performance are increasingly expected of them.

By the same token, we know little about the distribution of sports clubs; it is taken as a truism that sports clubs (and other voluntary bodies) will be more numerous, stronger and better run in affluent, well-educated neighbourhoods than poorer ones. In Scotland, clubs in rural areas are likely to be more numer-ous but smaller than in towns (Allison, 2001: Appendix 1). Anecdotes and case studies would hint at this (Boothby et al., 1982; Bishop and Hoggett, 1986) but no definitive data exists because of the difficulty of recording the vast and shifting population of formal and particularly informal organisations. In sport, soccer is particularly fluid; perhaps only a quarter to a third of amateur soccer clubs survive a decade (Collins, n.d.). Brodie, Roberts and Lamb (n.d.: 4) wrote, 'the weakest sections of the community, the least organised and least committed, are most likely to be left without sporting provision unless some-one with the necessary power exercises *positive discrimination*' (my emphasis). The Head of Sport England's Lottery Unit, David Carpenter, admitted that 'the major asset-owning clubs have been those that have most benefited from the fund' (1999, Regeneration through Sport conference).

This brings us to the idea of sports clubs as a form of communal social capital. Putnam (2000: 40) quoted Hanigan's 1916 definition of social capital as 'those tangible substances (that) count for most in the daily life of people: namely goodwill, fellowship, sympathy, and social intercourse . . . the individual is helpless if left to himself,' and labelled it 'a kind of sociological superglue'. This has become a topic of widespread interest. Putnam outlined his idea of civic democracy as the outcome of a sequential process of social connectedness → social involvement → social engagement (Putnam et al., 1993). In *Bowling Alone* (2000) he suggested that in the competitive, selfish, individualistic society of contemporary America, communal involvement in politics (evidenced in voting and participating in party organisations), sport and the arts, churches, and trades unions has been declining since the 1950s, as have mutual ties of trust, and belief in authority figures. So, social connectedness and social capital were declining.

Other studies have begun to see whether this is happening in both Western and Eastern Europe, though the latter studies do not include sports and arts involvement (Rose, Mishler and Haerpfer, 1997; Rose and Weller, 2001). Early selected findings from a wider international study for both Britain (Hall, 1999) and Sweden (Rothstein, 2001) would refute Putnam's thesis. Indeed, trust, voting and belief in sources of authority have declined, but social participation has not done so noticeably. This was true also of sport – indeed in Sweden, if anything it had grown stronger. Elsdon et al. (1999) found about eighteen voluntary organisations per 1,000 people in Broxtowe, Nottinghamshire, of which 41 per cent were participant sport clubs and 4 per cent passive/spectating; or 8.1 per 1,000 people, with an 11.7 per cent participation rate, slightly lower than the national figures. They estimated that the national rate of involvement might be 25 per 1,000, much higher than earlier estimates for England and more than three times Putnam's estimate for the USA.

In similar vein, de Knop et al. (1996) asked whether there was a similar crisis in Flemish sports clubs and concluded that the situation is reasonably buoyant but that attention is needed to preserving the values of amateur sport while improving services. They are not 'a threatened species from another age' (Taks, Renson and Vanreusel in Heinemann, 1999: 219). (Since then there has been a move to develop an accreditation scheme to assure young people and their parents and elders of the quality of the training and care at clubs – see de Knop et al., 2001.)

Consecutive recent governments and even Sports Councils have glibly referred to the sports club movement as the *grass roots* of sport, but have not done the basic research to understand the system and its problems. Into the 1990s the Sports Council (1993) thought that the essential autonomy of clubs would be eroded as public grants and private sponsorship arrangements both made heavy calls of accountability. In 1995, the narrow youth and excellence focus of the White Paper *Sport: Raising the Game* only asked that more junior sections should be developed. The Blair Government's strategy (Department for Culture, Media and Sport, 1999: 13) saw clubs as a complement to schools and a link to high-level competition. It suggested a strengthening of the local structure, linking 'satellite' clubs in clusters to 'hub' clubs 'with the potential to develop *a number of teams* offering opportunities to progress to higher levels of competition' (para 31.8 – my emphasis: Blair was following Major in focusing on team games despite the more rapid growth of interest in individual sports). Such a two-level scheme is foreign to and, I believe, would prove anathema to the British club movement.

For all the strengths of the multi-sport club, there are dangers – that it will be beguiled by public grants and sponsorship from its self-help roots and start operating like a pay-as-you-play venue, and will seek less input than traditional members have provided; then as Horch (1998: 15) wryly commented, 'if a sport club treats its members as customers it ought not complain if they also act like customers and are no longer willing to volunteer'. But despite the power of the large clubs in Germany, it has been the small ones that have been showing the growth since (Heinemann and Schwab, 1999: 155). The same growth has been happening in Norway (Skirstad in Heinemann, 1999: 230). There seems to be a split of views about small local clubs – one as expressed here that they are individually weak and limited in capacity; and another that they are closer to their communities. Nevertheless even in the participatory society of Denmark, Ibsen opined that:

Many of the clubs are local in the sense that the activities take place within a limited geographical area (a village, town district, housing district) where most of the members are recruited. But the activities are not aimed at solving current problems in the local community and fulfilling local needs. Members' attachment to the association is little connected with the area where they are recruited and very few clubs consider themselves as a club for the local community.

(Ibsen, in Heinemann, 1999: 256)

Boessenkool (2001: 225, 229, 231) confirmed similar trends in the Netherlands, and Gratton and Taylor (2001: 141) in the UK: 'the voluntary sports club is typically independent and inward looking, not explicitly seeking to provide collective benefits'. Nor do they show much desire for cross sector collaboration with health care, or welfare.

Some conclusions can be drawn:

1   The club movement is a crucial part of the system; it is where sportspeople are contributors and not just paying customers, consuming someone else's products.
2   If it is to play a greater role in helping to meet public policy aims to increase participation of excluded groups, its structure needs strengthening; rather than hub and satellite clubs, a self-organised clustering may be feasible, where administration could be collected together to save staff, and in which particular clubs could specialise in working with particular groups or levels of performer. But this requires an unprecedented level of local co-operation, replacing the traditional situation where some clubs muddle along, just replacing members lost by natural wastage, and others compete fiercely by scouting talent in schools and competitions. Allison (2001) argued for the same process, and the Scottish Football Association is undertaking an experiment to join a cluster of twenty-seven soccer clubs in Ayrshire. Such a change needs to be espoused strongly by the Central Council of Physical Recreation to help persuade most of its members to strategically change.
3   Multi-sport clubs are not a tradition and there may be limited contexts in which new ones could be formed, where communities are developing in new private housing estates or in new programmes in redeveloped inner suburbs (analogues of the community development work undertaken in New Towns from 1950 to their handing over in the 1970s to local authorities).
4   Time is a problem in recruiting volunteers, who are expected to be better trained and more 'professional' than any previous generation. DCMS (2001: 12) committed £7m. to invest in getting 60,000 more volunteers in 2002–4 but money may not be an adequate carrot. Gratton's opinion (Ives, 2001) was that 'people haven't got the time and they would prefer to pay someone else to do [the work in clubs]'.

Much more research needs to be done on the scale, structure, distribution and capabilities of the sports club system, similar to the sample of 4,000 clubs studied every four years by the German Federal Sports Ministry. In his review of British social capital, Hall (1999) added a cautionary note that, if there was a weakness, it might well appear in working class communities. Quite simply, in Britain we don't know. Which clubs are good places to invest in as part of the Active Sports Partnerships? We don't know. The process is hit-and-miss, or first-come-first-served.

Finally, governments and agencies should understand the organisations and networks they want to partner with before intervening. The voluntary sector at national body or local club level must remain legally/constitutionally autonomous in any partnership or client relationship with government. If it does not, it loses its unique self-organised character in which the club members offer an essentially gifted relationship with its heartfelt, committed and generous support. As Horch (1998: 50) commented, 'if sport clubs are only doing the same things in the same manner as commercial sport organisations then politicians and voters will at some stage ask themselves why they should continue subsidising them'.

Gratton and Taylor (2001) likewise worried that the National Lottery might lead the sector to lose some of its independence. Without this essence of volunteering, as in interpersonal relationships, pain, distrust and disappointment are the more likely outcomes than progress towards desired objectives with either government or sponsors. The British club movement has to modernise and adapt, to avoid the mire of continued parochialism, to find its own, appropriate 'third way' and not one designed by others.

Conclusions

In the first part of the chapter I made five suggestions for improving the general effectiveness of exclusion policies in their implementation, so far as sport is concerned (though they could equally apply to other policy spheres). In the second part I highlight two major structural changes I believe are needed to make the voluntary sports club movement organisationally stronger in order for it to be able to agree to act alongside government as an active partner in tackling the cross-cutting issues of lifelong learning, community health and safety, environmental improvement, and social exclusion. It has to be said, however, that the social benefits sought by New Labour from a more active voluntary sector as part of the Third Way can scarcely be demonstrated by research, even in European countries where more is known about the form and functioning of the sports clubs.

Chapter 13

Conclusions

Summary of findings

In Chapter 2 I showed how the Victorian concept of poverty was superceded by the idea of relative poverty, as society became more affluent in the mid-twentieth century, and then of social exclusion as a process. As Lister commented

> in one of the earliest editions of *Poverty* the Child Poverty Action Group warned that rising national income would not automatically abolish poverty; on the contrary 'it may well add to the burdens of the poor as more and more things that were once luxuries have become conventional necessities.'
>
> (Lister, 1990: 51)

And so it has proved. Then I summarised a growing mountain of data on who is poor and excluded, and in what towns and country areas, and sports relationship to social class, still a reality in contemporary Britain. Finally I related this discussion to ideas about consumers and citizens.

Chapter 3 attempted to summarise two substantial literatures, one research-based, the other a mixture of research and advocacy. In the first part, constraints on people's leisure was reviewed. It is true that most individuals cannot do as much of their favourite activities nor as often or as intensely as they would like, but there are some groups who are multiply constrained, and they are often also afflicted with below-average health, diet, housing, education and job prospects; helping those of them who wish to participate may mean coherent multi-faceted interventions. In the second part I reviewed the claims made for personal, economic, social and environmental benefits flowing from playing sport.

Chapter 4 pressed home the view that poverty was the core of exclusion, notably for those without work or on low and insecure incomes on the fringes of the labour market, which includes a disproportionate share of single parents and ethnic minorities, but also several other significant groups, particularly disabled people and those pensioners without second or index-linked pensions. In common with other advanced nations, the gaps between the poorest and the richest and the rest have been growing. While for the comfortable/affluent majority the price of transport, entry or allied costs is not an issue, for the poor groups it either reduces the frequency or precludes many of the sport choices available to the majority, and their children.

Thus overall leisure facilities and services, public and voluntary, are over-used by those with above average incomes, a situation that has not changed over twenty years, not surprising since governments and their financial watch-dog have pressed for reduced subsidy, which in most cases has meant above-inflation prices rises and marketing to the groups in society most likely to re-spond. Most sports development programmes targeted at needy groups have shown a good response to effort, notably by Sports Development Officers (Hylton and Totton, 2001), but such programmes have been generally on a small, local scale that in aggregate has not shifted the balance. Leisure Cards can have a wider effect but on pages 48–50 and 58–9 I showed that most again were under-resourced in money, staff and marketing effort and produced a tokenistic take-up, made worse because many were limited to sport and hence to those already interested in it. Their potential power as a policy tool has not really been used, let alone displayed.

Exclusion and children was the focus of Chapter 5. One-third of the coun-try's children are currently in poor households, and the UK has one of the least qualified workforces in Europe. These large gaps must be closed if a large minority is not to be disadvantaged in a knowledge-based society, since co-hort studies are showing that disadvantage is reflected in adult life. Though research has not yet been done on status/income and play provision, it is clear that differences in attitudes and participation in sport are established in childhood, in that

- 'gender-appropriate' play and sports behaviour models are established by primary school time, to the detriment of girls
- girls continue to have a limited menu of sports, and drop out earlier than boys
- disabled and ethnic minority children do not have equal opportunities
- children from deprived areas take up fewer opportunities to taste and learn new sports out of school, and become club members, as the Not-tingham case study showed.

These patterns of exclusion carry into performance and elite sport. The government and sports bodies are giving focus and priority to the race and disability issues, but new youth sport programmes do not tackle the poverty issue which underlies these and is important in its own right, except by designating Sports Action Zones with some priority for investment, often covering large areas.

The view that sport was invented by men and that they are more suited to it is still alive, despite strong challenges by an increasingly empowered women's sports movement. But from childhood onwards girls and women have a narrower choice of activities, and fewer opportunities to work as administrators, managers or coaches beyond a basic level, as Tess Kay showed in Chapter 6. While many schemes have been set up and much advice has been given on enabling more participation and involvement of women in running as well as playing sport, the needs, behaviour and attitudes of the most disadvantaged and excluded have rarely been looked at. Meanwhile, general studies of the most excluded people in society have mainly ignored sport, class, poverty and gender. The conclusion is that, to be effective, future projects and programmes need to be focused more on the most deprived girls and women, and be sensitive to their individual situations, constraints and needs.

Exclusion in older age was the topic of Chapter 7. To the constraints faced by younger people are added declining physical and sometimes mental capabilities, reduced access to private transport, and an increasing fear of going out at night. Nonetheless, at this phase of life physical and mental benefits from exercise are greatest, and health and welfare expenditure increases almost exponentially. Britain certainly lags behind Scandinavian and other countries in participation, and currently has no targeted sport or health prevention policy. This is both extraordinary and perverse. Maintaining mobility and independent living would be a major social boon.

Chapter 8 clearly showed that contemporary British society shows a systematic inequality in almost all spheres of life for black ethnic minorities, arising from a lesser share of both economic and social capital, but exacerbated by a still-widespread racist set of beliefs and attitudes, that have been only weakly combated by race relations legislation, and that are reflected in both recreational and competitive sport. Football, rugby and cricket in particular are attempting to highlight the problem and mobilise their memberships to eradicate it. For access to leisure and sport the position is exacerbated by the geographical concentration in the inner parts of certain cities and the more limited public, voluntary and commercial provision that *appears* to exist there (since we do not have definitive evidence).

Chapter 9 related to sport for disabled people, and showed how, even in schools and junior clubs, there are great gaps between aspirations and participation, and that provision in mainstream schools and clubs is often poorer than that for youngsters as a whole. It is policy to 'mainstream' (assimilate) as many disabled children as possible, yet this can perversely separate them from the tailor-made system of competition set up between special schools, and replace it with much more haphazard arrangements.

Three out of 4 disabled people depend on welfare benefits and are by definition poor, and social class and gender combine to slash opportunities and participation rates compared with non-disabled adults. The Disability Discrimination Act will hopefully improve human as well as physical provision, but not overnight, and the new English Federation for Disability Sport structure is gearing up. The disabled sports movement is struggling towards empowerment and self-organisation of sport, but the attitudes of some of society are still locked into the medical or, at best, the social model of disability.

Chapter 10 was devoted to the growing political and professional interest and mountain of literature on the role of sport and adventure education in seeking to prevent at-risk young people from falling into crime, and at helping to rehabilitate those who have offended, often repeatedly. Coalter (2001c) expressed the view that there are strong theoretical grounds for believing that sport has benefits for at-risk and offending youth, but it is difficult to substantiate the claims, for three main reasons:

- In practical terms, interventions are often of a short duration and limited contact time, with little follow-up support on return to home communities, yet are seeking to combat and overturn the accumulation of years of social ills, and moreover schemes are often poorly funded because of political fright at appearing to reward crime and delinquency.
- In methodological terms, it is morally impossible to undertake the sorts of experiments common in medicine, and funding for longitudinal or before-and-after studies or adequate control groups has been rare, and incontrovertible evidence of reduced offending after treatment is difficult and laborious data to compile – anecdote, self-report and short-term measures are cheaper and expedient.
- In analysis, inadequate data and methods have not been powerful enough to unravel the programme effects from the complex of personal and community influences.

With limited resources, I became involved in and report on two case studies in Stoke and Hampshire which sought to provide evidence of

- the fragmentary socialisation into leisure of excluded young people, leading to their limited and often downright impoverished leisure lifestyles relative to middle class, settled and supported youths
- the personal benefits the at-risk youth in Stoke, and especially the offenders in Hampshire, experienced and attested to.

Chapter 11 looked at particular aspects of exclusion in country and city. Exclusion in rural areas is less obvious because of smaller numbers more thinly spread, and for the same reasons, policy instruments cost more per head to implement. But recent studies have shown no lower incidence than in towns, though some rural folk are very independent, and less likely to admit their needs; area-based policies are less easy to design and administer. Slee, Curry and Joseph (2001) produced the first study to focus on exclusion relating to countryside recreation, but avoided the issue of poverty and directly admitted to exclusion related only to factors like ethnicity and disability. Their distillation of case studies listed many of the same factors others had identified in predominantly urban studies.

The urban setting has had a long series of mainly geographically targeted policy prescriptions, both for urban regeneration and urban recreation. The Blair Government, while criticising predecessors for the number of policy initiatives, have produced as many and demanded action plans on a tight timescale, and Chapter 11 described the latest for sport and arts. Harrison (1983: 171) claimed that 'the inverse care law . . . is valid for almost all forms of public service. Private squalor and public squalor go hand in hand, accentuating each other.' Thus one gets 'postcode discrimination' in sport as much as in health, house prices, insurance, mortgages and credit (Jordan, 1996), as was clear for young people in the Nottinghamshire case study, pages 83–93.

Chapter 12 took a very initial look at some major issues around policy implementation. Firstly I looked at five practical ways to make the implementation of policy more effective:

1   giving organisations and staff a realistic chance of engendering lasting changes and of achieving desired outcomes by lengthening policy timespans, not from two or three to five years but to seven or ten, a real test in traditional British politics of political commitment
2   devoting enough resource and intellectual effort to measuring outcomes rather than being satisfied with intermediate outputs, however much they are difficult to define and slippery to measure
3   tightening the depth of focus and concentration of effort of both people and place policies, and resisting spreading finance and manpower too thin
4   resisting initiative-itis and, once convicted of the rightness of introduced policies, to stick to them long enough to give them a chance of success, despite political attack and economic pressures
5   encouraging strong partnerships in tackling cross-cutting issues, but not unwieldy ones; the test of successful outcomes and partnership management is only a means, not an end.

In the second half of the chapter, I looked at the role of sport as an expression of citizenship, both for involved individuals and as an expression of active organisations in civil society, in the form of voluntary sports clubs. The Blair Government has acknowledged some shortcomings of sports clubs, in programmes to help them improve coaching, in getting them to have the quality of their services accredited to reassure parents and relatives, and most recently at the time of writing, through suggesting that they can get indirect tax relief through registering as charities. But these actions are based on assumptions about the sector, comprised as it is of overwhelmingly small, single-sport, and in all senses parochial clubs, with little of the structural strength found in large, multi-sport clubs more common, for reasons of social history, in some European nations. I suggest two major policy changes – supporting the founding of multi-sport clubs in limited places of new development, and clustering clubs to gain economies of operation without giving up autonomy, and to provide a more secure foundation for investment of public money.

There is one neglected factor in exclusion that is mentioned in many site and user surveys, as in our case study on leisure provision for disabled people in Leicester, but to which little attention has been given by leisure research, and that is transport, or rather lack of it. The Social Exclusion Unit was undertaking a consultation on this matter in late 2001 (*SEU press notice* and consultation paper 25 July 01).

One form of exclusion on which current evidence is too scarce for it to warrant a chapter in this book, is stigmatisation and prejudice on the grounds of sexuality. Homosexuality and lesbianism is a site of social exclusion that extends beyond leisure. Despite the growing acceptance of the gay community in life generally, there are as yet few studies of the issue in sport. Griggin and Genasci (1990) said, 'because of the extreme negative stigma attached to homosexuality in our culture, many, perhaps most, gay and lesbian people live double lives and are invisible members of our communities.' The first Gay Games were held in the US in 1992 and that is where most studies have been done; the same event did not happen again until 2000 in the UK. More studies have focused on lesbian than homosexual sport (e.g., Lenskyj, 1990; Squires and Sparkes, 1996; Clarke, 1998). Homophobia was seen in that many women playing in 'men's' sports like rugby in particular were labelled 'dykes,' accurately or otherwise. But King and Thompson (2001) interviewed officials of ten gay clubs in London and five other cities. The clubs (affiliated with some forty others to the British Gay and Lesbian Sports Federation) were open to men and women but were predominantly male. The reasons given for forming them was that gays 'felt out of place' in mainstream clubs, and wanted to have somewhere to play that felt safe, and where they could meet other gays. Both sexes had experienced prejudice in mainstream sport, but little or none in their competitive encounters with 'straight' clubs.

Clarke (1998) criticised both the English Sports Council and DCMS for not identifying in their respective national strategies gays as a group suffering from social exclusion, and like the Dutch and other governments, there has been little recognition, let alone encouragement or support for separate gay sports organisations, for fear of social splintering. Nonetheless the Dutch Ministry of Welfare, Public Health and Culture commissioned Hekma (1998) to undertake an ethnographic review of the situation in the Netherlands. A third of women and a quarter of men in Hekma's sample had experienced some incident, but only a few had received verbal harassment, threats of physical abuse, or expulsion from a mainstream club. But the low incidence was a result of gay men and lesbians keeping quiet about their sexuality. The Dutch National

Table 13.1 The extra impact of social class on other factors affecting sports participation

Indexed against males without a disability (60.3% participation = 100)

All DE male	75	DE age 16–19	84
DE without disability	65	DE age 25–29	64
White majority, all ages	56	DE age 30–44	50
DE ethnic minority	46	DE age 45–59	30
DE female	45	DE age 60–69	24
DE adult with disability	35		

Olympic Committee has included sexuality in its anti-discrimination code since 1994. This is an area deserving and needful of more research before policy can be soundly developed. Examination of sexual abuse and predation in sport is just being recognised, in research (for example, Brackenridge, 2001) and policy (for example, by the setting up in Leicester of a Centre for the Protection of Young People in Sport jointly by Sport England and the National Society for the Prevention of Cruelty to Children).

My conclusion is that exclusion is real; that at the core of most of it is poverty, though for evidence of its manifestations in leisure and sport, we generally have to rely on the approximate surrogate measures of socio-economic or social groups. But the pattern of coincident deprivations that add up to exclusion for millions of adults and children are irrefutable. One way of looking at this is to measure the extra impact on participation of social class to other factors like gender, age, ethnicity and disability. Table 13.1 does this, using Sport England's Sports Equity Index, and demonstrates the extent of the effect.

Equity, non-participation and exclusion

As Coalter (2000) pointed out, non-participation does not equal exclusion. Since leisure activities are inherently those of choice, and the choice is ever-widening, non-participation may, for many leisure activities, be the norm (Slee, Joseph and Curry, 2001: 17). People choose not to take part in most forms of leisure activity because they are not attracted by it or its pro-ponents, or are not motivated to train and find no achievement in it, or they have a profound disinterest. Coalter took Le Grand's argument that exclusion can be said to occur when people want to take part but cannot, or when society may suffer, or not gain communal benefits, if people cannot participate (for example in greater costs to the health service, or social cohesion damaged by obvious unfairness). In a similar way, shared amenities – the economist's 'merit goods', like parks – may not get sufficient use or popular support to be sustained without the central or local state intervening.

In Chapter 3 and Table 3.4 (page 33), I have already shown the great dispar-ity of participation in sport in general, and in the use of the main forms of public sports provision, sports halls and swimming pools. In the case of the former, the gap between the top and bottom of the social spectrum had returned in the recession of the mid-1990s to the level of the mid-1980s, and in the case of the latter the participation of the poorer and less-educated had not improved over more than twenty years.

Harland et al. (n.d.) listed factors affecting non-participation as:

- a general attitude that something is 'boring/not interesting/rubbish' – common amongst young people towards sport, the arts, museums, and libraries until they are taken and introduced to them by someone with charisma and skill
- a perceived talent barrier, especially in sport and the arts
- lack of relevance to them, or of feeling comfortable in particular settings
- negative affective outcomes – embarrassment, anxiety, intimidation (demonstrated by girls' views on PE and sport in Chapter 5, and by many with lower educational attainments with respect to museums and galleries or theatres)
- image barriers – just not seeing something as appropriate. Thirty-eight per cent of adult respondents to the Allied Dunbar National Fitness Survey (Sports Council/Health Education Authority, 1992) and a higher proportion of the women did not see themselves as 'sporty.' Partly as a consequence, the Health Education Authority has since focused on more everyday accessible forms of exercise with no connotations of fitness and excellence – walking, dancing, stair climbing, with only cycling and swimming included, more as recreations than sports, and as sources of moderate rather than vigorous exercise.

Data is, of course, needed: it is almost non-existent for tourism and arts (for example, in Selwood, 2001) and sparse for countryside visiting. A burst of activity had occurred regarding libraries and museums (MORI, 2001; Muddiman et al., 2000) and this has led to policy statements (Resource, 2001a, b; Department for Culture, Media and Sport, 2001b), arguing that these leisure subsectors can make a major contribution to social inclusion. The DCMS has accepted a working party's proposals for more investment in regional and local museums with £2.5m. in 2000–3 rising to £28m. in 2006–7, devoted specifically to social inclusion work. The report exemplified the Tyne and Wear museums service which, while doubling overall attendances during the 1990s, had increased the share by people in groups C2, D and E from 20 to 52 per cent.

Providers can do something to change some of the attitudes listed above by product modification, enticements to improve access and better promotional methods, but as shown in Chapter 3 many people are constrained from taking part in multiple ways. The argument has been mounted that in a market-based, if regulated, economy, they can choose from a wide range of other leisure activities. But the fallacy of this can be shown in that there is little evidence of this

happening on any scale. There is no one survey covering the full range of leisure and so evidence has to be pieced together from a wide variety of sources
(Table 13.2). Unfortunately, only one survey of tourism contains social strati-
fication data, but of the eight types of leisure activity listed most show a marked
social disparity of up to 30 per cent or more, with only coach holidays, pop
concerts and pub visiting showing small differences, and countryside day trips
which show skilled manual workers as the largest group, with slightly more Ds
and Es than As and Bs making visits; tourists to the countryside, on the other
hand, show a strong gradient, in line with Smith's (2001) findings below. Not
surprisingly, in general, people in higher status groups with higher incomes
also take part more frequently, thus extending the differences. For example, in
visiting museums and galleries:

	% visitors/players	*annual frequency*	*% all visits*
AB	36	3.19	40
DE	16	2.62	14

Smith (2001) reported that 4 in 10 British people take no form of holiday, a
figure that has not reduced since 1989 (English Tourist Board, 1989). Collins
(2003 forthcoming) pointed out that the same social gradient is found in
sport, visiting theatres, museums and galleries, and even cinema and public
libraries. The same issue has been raised in the USA by More (1999), challenging the middle class bias of the planners and managers of its National
Parks Service. The DCMS made the same argument in abolishing entry fees
to the national museums of Britain. This is not evidence of choosing different options in the 'supermarket' of away-from-home leisure; it is a repeat of
limited choice for those with poorer economic and social capital. Sport
England has done virtually no research on non-participants in over thirty
years, but neither have other sectors (see Muddiman, et al., 2000 for libraries). Slee et al. (2001) cited a Gallup 1998 survey where 28 per cent of people
regarded access to the countryside as a priority for government but the
gradient was the reverse of that shown in Table 13.2, with the greatest desire
to access the countryside amongst the DE groups:

% suggesting greater access is very important	
AB	15
C1	24
C2	30
DE	41

Table 13.2 Inequalities in participation across the leisure spectrum by social class (per cent)

%	Holidays					Pubs	Library	Theatre	Pop	Museum/ gallery	Books		Cinema	Day visits	Tourist	GB population
	GB	Abroad	Airline charter	Coach	Adventure						Buy	Read				
AB	76	65	31	7	63	24	79	34	26	47	32	69	17	23	32	22
Cl	73	51	36	10	59	29	75	33	34	31	31	61	19	30	33	27
C2	70	41	40	9	54	38	51	18	22	23	18	44	11	21	20	23
D	69	36	47	8	49	34	57	16	18	15	19	41	10	26	15	28
E	60	26	37	9	33	24	49					46	2			
Difference AB–DE	16	35	+2	+2	30	0	30	18	8	32	13	23	15	–3	17	n/a

Sources:
Col 2, 3 GB and foreign holidays1995, Mintel, 1996b
Col 4 Airline charter holiday in last 3 years, Mintel, 2000b
Col 5 Inclusive UK coach holidays in last 3 years, Mintel, 2001
Col 6 Adventure holidays, Mintel, 1999
Col 7 Visiting pubs, Mintel, 1996a
Col 8 Library users, Muddiman et al., 2000
Col 9 and 10 Attenders at any form of theatre, pop concerts 1996–97, Arts Council of England, 2000
Col 11 Visitors to museums and galleries 1999, MORI, 2001
Col 12 All books bought 1999, Book Marketing Ltd, 2000
Col 13 Reading books in last week 1996, Mintel, 1996a
Col 14 Cinema visitors once a month or more often 2000, Mintel, 2000a
Col 15 Day visits 1998, Social and Community Planning Research, 1999
Col 16 Tourist trips to countryside including villages, Countryside Agency, 2001: 69

Muddiman et al. (2000: xi) described libraries as 'at present, only superficially open to all'. They spoke of two models of social inclusion by public library authorities – a 'weak' one of *voluntary inclusion*, where infrastructure and informational change are made and a general invitation to take part issued, and much stronger policies involving targeting, outreach, community development and other interventions. They concluded that 'overwhelmingly, the public library service has adopted the first, and weaker of these alternatives' (2000, 57–8), and all their good practice examples came from places using the latter approach. They showed (2000: 23, 28) that only one in three library authorities had strategic inclusion policies, and that fewer than this targeted the most needy or excluded – the unemployed, prisoners and their families, the homeless, lesbians/homosexuals, refugees, travellers or working class people. Moreover, nearly 1 in 2 had no community outreach projects.

While I would be marginally less critical of policies for sport centrally and locally, I would say that they have focused disproportionately on disabled and ethnic minority people (who, with women, have statutory support), and have played down the poverty issue (except in some geographical pockets), and the lack of good transport for non-car owners. In the same way as for libraries, the strong model has costs: it involves affirmative action in 'intervention, the targeting of resources, outreach work, and positive action to fulfil individual needs' (Muddiman et al., 2000: 60). These are conclusions shared by Slee et al. (2001) for countryside recreation, Coalter et al. (2001c) for sport, and Smith (2001) for tourism.

Finally, it is worth pointing out that other researchers in Europe are finding social class gradients in their sport. Van der Meulen, Kraylaar, and Utlee (2001), using a life history approach with a large sample, showed that people with a higher level of final education were less likely to drop out of sport, having been more likely to take it up in the first place, as in Table 2.3 illustrated (page 13). In elite sport, Nagel and Nagel (2001) reported on the social status of 310 athletes in (west) Germany; the proportion of high level athletic competitors from high status backgrounds from 1981 to the present was 40 per cent compared with 30 per cent from low status backgrounds. This difference was statistically significant for participants in track and field, hockey, swimming, fencing, riding, rowing and sailing (the latter having 80 per cent high status). Only wrestling, Alpine/Nordic skiing, and cycling showed significant number of low status participants. This is a noticeably less skewed distribution than for Britain, as outlined on pages 82–3.

Evaluation and future lines of research

Virtually every piece of research calls for further research and better understanding. Tiresome though some may see it, this book repeats the litany. Previous work has been too descriptive, atheoretical, short-term, output-related, short on in-depth understanding and users' or managers' perceptions, dependent on recall and self-report, and often not realistically grounded in

Table 13.3 Relationships between evaluation criteria and stakeholder interests

	Those who pay	Intended beneficiaries	Professionals	Managers	Politicians
Effectiveness		*	*	*	*
Efficiency	*	*	*	*	*
Equity		*		*	*
Acceptability	*		*		*
Accessibility	*		*	*	
Appropriateness	*	*		*	
Responsiveness	*	*	*	*	*
Accountability		*	*	*	*
Ethical considerations		*	*		
Choice	*	*		*	

Source: Thomas and Palfrey, 1996

context. Thomas and Palfrey (1996) argued that as wells as seeking effectiveness and efficiency, any public sector programme should be scrutinised for the following factors:

- equity (treating people with equal needs equally)
- acceptability (approximating to customer/consumer satisfaction)
- accessibility (of information, resources and services)
- appropriateness (relevance to each person's need)
- accountability (to citizens and any other investors)
- ethical considerations (be explicit about values and how conflicts will be resolved)
- responsiveness to consumers (in speed, accuracy and empathy)
- choice (which is a real issue in free-time activities like sport and leisure).

They also relate these criteria in an interesting way to the different stakeholders in any policy (Table 13.3); such an analysis has yet to be done in any full sense for a sport or leisure policy.

The research agenda is broad, long and will be costly if taken seriously, reflecting any form of affirmative policy action for excluded people. It has been best summarised as this book goes to print by Coalter (2001h), thus:

1   *Measuring outputs*
    - social effectiveness in terms of what kinds of people use facilities and services, and how often
    - common data for comparisons across the leisure sub-sectors (to provide better data than that in Table 13.2!)
    - the nature and extent of non-use, with evidence on the reasons for not taking part, and the barriers to use, leading to an ability to assess the potential for particular services to address inclusion.

2   *Measuring outcomes,* a more complex and contentious issue to define and evaluate than outputs, going beyond enjoyment to the development of personal social capital, evidence of evolving confidence and self-esteem (as in the delinquency case study in Chapter 10), impacts on educational performance, local economic benefits and health promotion.
3   *Understanding organisational factors,* including the experiences of customers and providers.
4   *Demonstrating the development of various forms of communal social capital,* which Coalter said will be time-consuming and expensive.

Apart from my own endorsement, Long and Sanderson (2001: 201) and Rowe (2001) support several of these aspects, the former speaking of the need to capture any negative side-effects.

Endnote

The Salvation Army/Henley Centre (1999), prognosticating on the period to 2010, argued that society will:

- see living standards for the majority rise by a third in real terms
- have a widening poverty gap, with the top tenth having ten times the income of the bottom tenth
- see greater work pressures on all groups, 'less able to withdraw from this rat race due to the increasing need to make private provision for their old age' (p. 6).
- have fewer family households
- have a vulnerable middle-aged group in a 'care sandwich' responsible for dependent children and older people, while trying to ensure their own pensions.

Collating data on how people spend their time, from thirty-five time budget diary studies from twenty nations, Gershuny (2000) argued that, over the long run, three convergent processes can be perceived, between:

- the volumes of (paid and unpaid) work, which is reducing, and leisure, which is increasing
- work and leisure for both genders, though women still do more work than men
- class/status groups, though for high-status, information-based workers, work may be increasing because of the demand for their services and because much is intrinsically enjoyable. This is the group who are 'running out of time,' and may purchase their leisure in short, capital- and labour-intensive bursts (Becker, 1965), whereas other groups have more time and less money, and consume in other ways.

Thus Veblen's (1953) case that access to free time was the main means of social differentiation, is substantially weakened – what may distinguish future generations is *how* they use that time. Gershuny contended that the relationship between leisure and citizenship is that shorter working hours 'frees time for education and self-improvement, for political participation and for cultural activities' (2000: 60). Greater out-of-home activity generates service employment. Contending that the demand for labour is not fixed, he strongly suggested (Gershuny, 2000: 242–8) that public policy should make some major shifts, so as to promote:

- reduced working hours through lumps of time for maternity leave, training, sabbaticals (as proposed by Martin and Mason, 1998), that is, more flexible time, rather than previously suggested work-sharing within tightly regulated hours when leisure cannot be shared and enjoyed with others, like the current limited leisure style of shift workers
- more flexible hours of operation of public and other leisure provision to enable the extra consumption to occur
- related strongly to this, better quality and more flexible (i.e. evening and weekend) public transport services, crucial for non-car owners and reduced environmental damage
- better education, for consumption by both adults and children (a point strongly made also by Martin and Mason), including via TV-related media
- provision of support services to facilitate this lifestyle, which might have been unpaid in earlier times – care for children, sick and older people. The affluent have started to pay for these already, but although recent governments' policies have been willing to develop child care to enable more women to work, they have sought to cut back, privatise or transfer the costs of ill health and care of older people.

Gershuny concluded:

A fraternal concern to improve standards of consumption among even the poorest members of society, in part through public regulations and provisions which directly affect the daily pattern of activities, could serve to stimulate the economy in ways that also benefit a substantial proportion of the better-off. And the more the society's consumption consists of services that embody high-value labour, the smaller is the category of 'the poor' to be concerned about.

(Gershuny, 2000: 248)

As was made clear in Chapter 8, the Blair Government believes that participation in culture and leisure activity makes a contribution towards 'the building and maintenance of social capital' (Department for Culture, Media

Table 13.4 Projects being evaluated by DCMS for contributions to social inclusion

Scheme	Sponsor	Aims	Funding
Sports Coach qualifications	Charlton Athletic Race Equality	Develop skills and self-esteem in a wide range of ethnic groups	SRB, Greenwich Dev Ag, A for E
Leeds Football Community Link Project	Leeds City Council NACRO	Divert 5- to 16-year-olds from antisocial behaviour, gain business sponsorship	SRB 4
Police and Youth Encouragement Scheme	Mersey Police, Brathay Hall Trust	Discourage 12- to 14-year-olds from involvement in crime through outdoor activities	Profits from management development courses
Youth Charter for Sport	YCS	Involving youth in sport and arts in Manchester/Merseyside	SRB, sponsors
Aiming Higher	Birmingham Outdoor Education Centre	Raise potential for learning among children with poor school attendance	NOF, Tudor Trust

Key to funding: SRB = Single Regeneration Budget; Greenwich Dev Ag = Greenwich Development Agency; A for E = Arts for Everyone, part of NOF; NOF = New Opportunities Lottery Fund.

and Sport, 2001b: 115) and is 'a powerful influence . . . on social exclusion' (Department for Culture, Media and Sport, 2001a: 8). The DCMS has made valiant attempts to improve access to sport, arts and culture, most directly through abolishing some national museum charges, but also through encouraging inclusion policies in cultural strategies for its Lottery funding bodies, regional cultural consortia and local authorities, and investing in training for sports development officers and volunteers (Department for Culture, Media and Sport, 2001a: 8). In 2001 it commissioned research into fourteen projects to be evaluated over a two-year period, selected from over 200 submitted; six focused on the arts, one each on broadcasting, museums and libraries, and five on sport (as shown in Table 13.4 – see www.culture.gov.uk/role/research_projects,html accessed 1 October 2001). Whether the recent increases in child benefits and pensions and the area redistribution programmes are enough to reduce the exclusion gap remains to be seen.

Hylton and Totton (2001: 63) concluded that 'sport and society both reproduce inequality but they can both also challenge it'. Sport is on the periphery of social exclusion rather than at its core. It is substantially a self-help movement or a consumer product and, apart from some local authorities, largely has kept itself aloof from social problems while partly reflecting them. If sportspeople do not become more involved it will go on being a mirror rather than an agent of change. Being concerned about the efficiency of the sports delivery process and the effectiveness of programmes is not enough. Social change needs enablers, not just in the public sector. Sport has grown to be a larger part of people's lives and social life in the last fifty years. Yet Chapters 4 to 11 show that the gaps in opportunities for sport have been slowly closing for most women and some older people, are still large for Asian groups, and huge for most disabled people, one parent families, and many other poor people: opportunities are inequitable in the Sport England or Rawlsian senses described in Chapter 2 (page 10).

To be an agent of change means working with people and institutions in other sectors with other values, styles of operation and perspectives, and involves compromises and negotiations. Sport can bring joy and achievement for many people who have not had much of either in other spheres of their lives so far – the 'flow experiences' described by Csikszmentmihalyi, 'finding delight in what the body can do' (1992: 94–116). Other countries demonstrate to Britain that extending participation and its many benefits *is* possible, even if they still suffer a lesser degree of exclusion.

The messages from this book are simple but profound: sport can be a policy partner and a tool for combating social exclusion. To be effective, it has to be much more people-focused, and if area programmes are politically necessary, they need to be more tightly focused for cost-effectiveness. Programmes need to be longer term, better led, and designed *with* and not just *for* the people and organisations intended to benefit. Sport must be knit with many other aspects of citizenship.

Sport *for all who want it* is still a worthy and worthwhile objective for anyone who believes in a just society and equal opportunities of citizenship, and, I believe, a feasible one. As Donnelly wrote:

> Although sport has been an important agent in the production and reproduction of social inequality, democratising actions on the part of individuals and organisations have sensitised us to sport's potential to be an equally important agent of social transformation for the production of social equality, [and has] the potential to transform individuals and communities in ways that seriously reduce inequalities.
>
> (Donnelly, 1996: 237)

With its values of shared experience and mutual support, the sports world can leave inclusion to others and be part of the problem of an unequal society, or it can take the hard decisions and demanding steps to be part of the moves to inclusion, and become part of solutions.

References

Chapter 1 Introduction

Power, A. (1999) Social exclusion RSA lectures 7.12.99 accessed from <www.rsa.org.uk> 8 April 02

Slee, W., Curry, N. and Joseph, D. (2001) *Removing barriers, creating opportunities: Social exclusion in countryside leisure in the UK* Cardiff: Countryside Recreation Network

Chapter 2 From absolute poverty to social exclusion

Adonis, A. and Pollard, S. (1997) *A class act: The myth of a classless society* London: Hamish Hamilton

Alcock, P. (1997) *Understanding poverty* London: Macmillan

Alcock, P. and Craig, C. (1998) *Mapping local poverty: Monitoring and evaluation of anti-poverty strategy in Britain* Discussion paper 3 Sheffield: Sheffield Hallam University

Atkinson, R. (2000) Combating social exclusion in Europe: The new urban policy challenge *Urban Studies* 37, 5–6 1037–55

Audit Commission (1999) *The price is right* London: Audit Commission

Barclay, J. (1995) *Inquiry into income and wealth* 2 vols York: Joseph Rowntree Foundation

Beck, U. (1992) *Risk society: Towards a new modernity* London: Sage

Berghman, J. (1995) Social exclusion in Europe: Policy context and analytical framework in Room, G. et al. (eds) *Beyond the threshold: The measurement and analysis of social exclusion* Bristol: Policy Press

Beveridge, W. (1942) *Social insurance and allied services* Cm6404 London: HMSO

Booth, C. (1882) *Life and labour of the people in London* London: Macmillan

Bourdieu, P. (1978) Sport and social class *Social Science Information* 18.6, 821–30

Bourdieu, P. (1985) *Distinction: A social critique of the judgement of taste* London: Routledge

Brown, A. and Madge, J. (1982) *Despite the welfare state* London Heinemann Education

Burgess, E. (1967) The growth of the city in Burgess, E.W., Park, R.E. and McKenzie (eds) *The city* Chicago: Chicago University Press

Byrne, D. (2001) *Social exclusion* Buckingham: Open University Press

Coalter, A., Duffield, B. and Long, J. (1986) *The rationale for public sector invest-ment in leisure* London: Sports Council

Coalter, F. (1989) Leisure policy: an unresolvable dualism? in Rojek, C. (ed) *Leisure for leisure* Basingstoke: Macmillan

Coalter, F. (1990) The politics of professionalism: Consumers or citizens? *Leisure Studies* 9, 107–19

Coalter, F. (1998) Leisure studies, leisure policy and social citizenship: The failure of welfare or the limits of welfare? *Leisure Studies* 17.4, 21–36

Coalter, F. (2000) Public and commercial leisure provision: Active citizens and pas-sive consumers *Leisure Studies* 19, 163–81

Commins, P. (ed) (1993) *Combating social exclusion in Ireland 1990–94: A midway report* Brussels: European Commission

Department of Social Security (1998) *A new contract for welfare: New ambitions for our country Cm3805* London: The Stationery Office

Department of Social Security (1999) *Opportunity for all: Tackling poverty and social exclusion, 1st Annual Report 1999 Cm4445* London: The Stationery Office

Department of Social Security (2001) *Households below average income 1994–5, 1999–2001* London: DSS

Department of the Environment (1975) *Sport and recreation White Paper* London

Department of the Environment, Transport and the Regions (1998) *Index of local deprivation* <www.detr.gov.uk> accessed 10 Jan 1999

Donnison, D. (1982) *The politics of poverty* Oxford: Martin Robertson

Duffy, K. (1995) *Social exclusion and human dignity in Europe* Brussels: Council of Europe

Dustin, D.L., More, T.A. and McAvoy, L.H. (2000) The faithful execution of our public trust: Fully funding the National Parks through taxes *Journal of Park and Recreation Administration* 18.4, 92–103

Esping-Anderson, G. (1990) *The three worlds of welfare capitalism* London: Princeton University Press

European Commission (1994) *European social policy: A way forward for the Union* Brussels: European Commission

European Foundation for the Improvement of Living and Working Conditions (1995) *For citizens and against exclusion: The role of public welfare services* Dublin: EFILWC

Fenwick, J. (1995) *Managing local government* London: Chapman and Hall

Field, F. (1990) *Losing out: The emergence of Britain's underclass* Oxford: Basil Blackwell

Giddens, A. (1991) *Modernity and self-identity: Self and society in the late modern age* Cambridge: Polity Press

Giddens, A. (1998) *The Third Way* Cambridge: Polity Press

Glennerster, H., Lupton, R., Noden, P. and Power, A. (1999) *Poverty, social exclu-sion and neighbourhood: Studying the area bases of social exclusion* CASE paper 22, London: London School of Economics

Glyn, D. and Miliband, D. (eds) (1994) *Paying for inequality: The economic cost of social inequality* London: Rivers Oram Press

Glyptis, S. (1989) *Leisure and unemployment* Milton Keynes: Open University Press

Goodin, R. (1996) Inclusion and exclusion *European Journal of Sociology* 37(2)

Hobcraft, J. (1998) *Intergenerational and life-course transmission of social exclusion: Influences of childhood poverty, family disruption, and contact with the police* CASE paper 15, London: London School of Economics

Holman, R. (1978) *Poverty* London: Martin Robertson

Horne, J., Tomlinson, A. and Whannel, G. (1999) *Understanding sport: An introduction to the sociological and cultural analysis of sport* London: E&F Spon

Hurst, C. (2001, 4th ed) *Social exclusion: Forms, causes, consequences* Boston: Allyn and Bacon

Jargowsky, P.A. (1996) *Poverty and place: Ghettos, barriers and the American city* New York: Russell Sage Foundation

Jarvie, G. and Maguire, J. (1994) *Sport and leisure in social thought* London: Routledge

Kempson, E. (1997) *Life on a low income* York: York Publishing Services for the Joseph Rowntree Foundation

Kennett, C.R. (2002) *Leisure poverty and social exclusion: An analysis of leisure cards schemes in Great Britain* unpublished PhD thesis Loughborough: Loughborough University

Kew, F. (1997) *Sport: Social problems and issues* Oxford: Butterworth Heinemann

Layard, R. (1997) Preventing long term unemployment in Snower, D.J., and de la Dehasa, G. (eds) *Unemployment policy* Cambridge: Cambridge University Press

Levitas, R. (1996) The concept of social exclusion and the new Durkheimian hegemony *Critical Social Policy* 16, 5–20

Levitas, R. (1998) *The inclusive society? Social exclusion and New Labour* Basingstoke: Macmillan

Lilley, P. (1996) letter to Paul Coggins, chair of the UK International Year against Poverty Coalition *Guardian* 15 May

Lister, R. (1990) *The exclusive society: Citizenship and the poor* London: Child Poverty Action Group

Lister, R. (1998) From equality to social inclusion: New Labour and the welfare state *Critical Social Policy* 18.2, 215–25

McGregor, S. (1981) *The politics of poverty* London: Longman

McIntosh, P. and Charlton, V. (1985) *The impact of Sport for All programmes 1966–84, and a way forward* London: Sports Council

Mack, J. and Lansley, S. (1985) *Poor Britain* London: Allen and Unwin

Marger, M. (2001, 2nd ed) *Social exclusion: Patterns and processes* Mountain View, CA: Mayfield

Marshall, G. (ed) (1997) *Repositioning class: Social inequality in industrial societies* London: Sage

Marshall, T.H. (1950) *Citizenship and social class and other essays* Cambridge: Cambridge University Press

Martin, J. and White, A. (1998) *OPCS' surveys of disabled people in GB, Report 2 Financial circumstances of disabled adults in private households* London: HMSO

Murray, C. (1990) *The emerging British underclass* London: Institute of Economic Affairs

Murray, C. (1994) *Underclass: The crisis deepens* London: Institute of Economic Affairs

Nankivell, O. (1988) *Market morality* Audenshaw Research Paper 118 Oxford: The Hinksey Centre

Oatley, N. (ed) (1998) *Cities, competition and urban policy* London: Paul Chapman

Oppenheim, C. and Harker, L. (1996) *Poverty: The facts* London: Child Poverty Action Group

Osberg, L. (1995) The equity/inefficiency trade-off *Canadian Business Economics* Spring 5

Palfrey, C. et al. (1992) *Policy evaluation in the public sector* Aldershot: Avebury

Park, R.E. (1952) *Human communities* New York: Free Press

Parker, S. (1997) Leisure and culture: Consumers or participants? Paper to *Leisure, Culture and commerce* LSA conference Roehampton, London, July

Parks and Recreation Federation of Ontario (1997) *The benefits catalogue* Ottawa: CPRA

Penney, D. (2000) Physical Education . . . in what and whose interests? in Jones, R.L. and Armour, K.M. (eds) *Sociology of sport: Theory and practice* London: Pearson Education

Powell, M. (ed) (1999) *New Labour, new welfare state? The 'Third Way' in British social policy* Bristol: Policy Press

Power, A. (1997) *Estates on the edge: The social consequences of mass housing in Northern Europe* Basingstoke: Macmillan

Ravenscroft, N. (1993) Public leisure provision and the good citizen *Leisure Studies* 12, 33–44

Ravenscroft, N. (1996) Leisure, Consumerism and active citizenship in the UK *Managing Leisure* 1, 163–94

Ravenscroft, N. (1998) The changing regulation of public leisure provision *Leisure Studies* 17, 138–54

Rawls, J. (1971) *A theory of justice* Cambridge, Mass: Harvard University Press

Roberts, K. (1978) *Contemporary society and the growth of leisure* London: Longmans

Roberts, K. (1996) Young people, schools, sport, and government policies *Sport Education and Society* 1.1, 47–57

Roberts, K. (1999) *Leisure in Contemporary Society* Wallingford, Oxon: CABI Publishing

Robinson, P. and Oppenheim, C. (1998) *Social exclusion indicators* London: Institute of Public Policy Research for the Social Exclusion Unit

Roche, M. and Annesley, C. (1998) *Comparative social inclusion policy in Europe: Report 1 Contexts* Sheffield: SEDEC Coordination Centre, Sheffield University

Roll, J. (1992) *Understanding poverty* London: Family Policy Studies Centre

Room, G. et al. (1993) *Anti-poverty research in Europe* Bristol: School for Advanced Urban Studies

Room, G. et al. (eds) (1995) *Beyond the threshold: The measurement and analysis of social exclusion* Bristol: Policy Press

Rowntree, B. (1901) *Poverty: A study of town life* London: Macmillan

Savage, M. (2000) *Class analysis and social transformation* Buckingham: Open University Press

Scott, J. (1994) *Poverty and wealth: Citizenship, deprivation and privilege* London: Longman

Smith, A. (1812) *The wealth of nations* Harmondsworth: Penguin, 1979

Social Exclusion Unit (1998) *Bringing Britain Together* London: Cabinet Office

Sport England (2001) *Making English sport inclusive: Equity guidelines for governing bodies* London: SE

Stebbins, R. (1997) Casual leisure: A conceptual framework *Leisure Studies* 16.1, 17–25

Stedman-Jones, G. (1971) *Outcast London: A study in the relationship between the classes in Victorian society* Oxford: Oxford University Press

Sugden, J. and Tomlinson, A. (2000) Theorising sport and social class in Coakley, J. and Dunning, E. (eds) *Handbook of sports studies* London: Sage

Taylor, P. and Page, K. (1994) *The financing of local authority sport and recreation: A service under threat?* Melton Mowbray: ISRM

Tomlinson, A. (1986) 'Playing away from home': Leisure, access and exclusion. In: Golding, P. (ed) *Poverty and exclusion* London: Child Poverty Action Group

Tomlinson, A. (1991) Leisure as consumer culture in Botteril, D. and Tomlinson, A. (eds) *Ideology, leisure policy and practice* Publication 45, Eastbourne: Leisure Studies Association

Townsend, P. (1979) *Poverty in the UK: A survey of household resources and standards of living* London: Penguin

Townsend, P. (1987) Disadvantage *Journal of Social Policy* 16, 125–46

Veal, A. (1998) Leisure studies, pluralism and social democracy *Leisure Studies* 17, 249–67

Veit-Wilson, J. (1998) *Setting adequacy standards* Bristol: Policy Press

Walker, A. and Walker, C. (eds) (1997) *Britain divided: The growth of social exclusion in the 1980s and 1990s* London: Child Poverty Action Group

Walker, R. (1995) the dynamics of poverty and social exclusion in Room, G. et al. (eds) *Beyond the threshold: The measurement and analysis of social exclusion* Bristol: Policy Press

Walker, R. and Park, J. (1997) Unpicking poverty in Oppenheim, C. (ed) *An inclusive society* London: Institute of Public Policy Research

Wilkinson, R. (1998) What health tells us about society *Institute of Development Studies Bulletin* 29.1, 77–84

Wilson, W.J. (1997) *When work disappears: The world of the new urban poor* New York: Alfred Knopf

Chapter 3 Constraints on and benefits of playing sport

Allen, L. et al. (1998) *Benefits based management: Demonstration project technical report* Clemson, Ar: Clemson University

Bovaird, T., Nichols, G. and Taylor, P. (1997) *Approaches to estimating the wider economic and social benefits resulting from sports participation* Birmingham: Aston Business School

Brodie, D. and Roberts, K. (1992) *Inner city sport: Who plays, what are the benefits?* Culembourg: Giordano Bruno

Brodie, D., Roberts, K., and Lamb, K. (nd) *Citysport Challenge* Cambridge: Health Promotion Research Trust

Coalter, F. (2001a) *Realising the potential of cultural services: The case for libraries* London: Local Government Association

Coalter, F. (2001b) *Realising the potential of cultural services: The case for museums* London: Local Government Association

Coalter, F. (2001c) *Realising the potential of cultural services: The case for sport* London: Local Government Association

Coalter, F. (2001d) *Realising the potential of cultural services: The case for the arts* London: Local Government Association

Coalter, F. (2001e) *Realising the potential of cultural services: The case for urban parks, spaces and the countryside* London: Local Government Association

Coalter, F. (2001f) *Realising the potential of cultural services: The case for play* London: Local Government Association

Coalter, F. (2001g) *Realising the potential of cultural services: The case for tourism* London: Local Government Association

Collins, M.F. (2002) Sport for All as a multi-faceted product of domestic and international influences, in Da Costa, L. and Miragaya, A-M. (eds) *Worldwide trends in Sport for All* Oxford: Meyer and Meyer Sport

Collins, M.F., Henry, I.P. and Houlihan, B.M.J. (1999) *Sport and social exclusion* report to Policy Action Team 10 London: DCMS

Dorricott, O. (1998) *Social cohesion and sport* paper 98/14: Strasbourg: Council of Europe, Committee for the Development of Sport

Driver, B.L., Brown, P. and Peterson, G. (1991) *Benefits of leisure* College Station, PA: Venture Publishing

Driver, B.L. and Bruns, D.H. (1999) Concepts and uses of the benefits approach to leisure, in Jackson, E.L. and Burton, T.L. (eds) *Leisure studies: Prospects for the 21ˢᵗ century* State College, PA: Venture Publishing

Goodale, T.L. and Witt, P.A. (1989) Recreation, non-participation and barriers to leisure in Jackson, E.L. and Burton, T.L. (eds) *Understanding leisure and recreation: Mapping the past, charting the future* State College, PA: Venture Publishing, Inc.

Harland, J. et al. (nd) *Attitudes to participation in the arts, heritage, broadcasting and sport: A review of recent research*, unpublished report to Dept of National Heritage Slough: National Foundation for Educational Research

Health Education Authority (1999) *Physical Activity and inequalities* London: HEA

Huertes, K. et al. (2000) Benefits-based programming: Making an impact on youth *Journal of Leisure Research* 32,1

Jackson, E. (1988) Leisure constraints: A review of past research *Leisure Sciences* 10, 203–15

Jackson, E. (1990a) Variations in the desire to begin a leisure activity: Evidence of antecedent constraints? *Journal of Leisure Research* 22, 55–70

Jackson, E. (1990b) Recent developments in leisure constraint research *Proceedings of the 6ᵗʰ Canadian Congress on Leisure Research* Waterloo: Canadian Leisure Studies Association

Jackson, E.L. (1991) Leisure constraints/constrained leisure Introduction *Journal of Leisure Research* 23.4, 279–85

Jackson, E.L. and Scott, D. (1999) Constraints to leisure pp 299–321 in Jackson, E.L. and Burton, T.L. (eds) *Leisure studies: Prospects for the 21ˢᵗ century* State College, PA: Venture Publishing

Kay, T.A. and Jackson, G.A.M. (1990) Leisure Constraints in Williams, T., Almond, L. and Sparkes, A. (eds) *Sport and physical activity* London: E&F Spon

Kay, T.A. and Jackson, G.A.M. (1991) Leisure despite constraint *Journal of Leisure Research* 23, 301–13

Long, J. and Sanderson (2001) The social benefits of sport: Where's the proof? in Gratton, C. and Henry, I. (eds) *Sports in the City* London: Routledge

Patrickkson, G. (1995) *The significance of sport for society: Health, socialisation, economy: A scientific review* Strasbourg: Council of Europe Press

Purdy, M. and Banks, D. (1999) *Health and exclusion* London: Routledge

Social Exclusion Unit (1998) *Bringing Britain Together* London: Cabinet Office

Sport England (1999a) *The value of sport* London: SE

Sport England (1999b) *The value of sport to local authorities* London: SE

Sport England (1999c) *The value of sport to regional development* London: SE

Sport England (1999d) *The value of sport to health* London: SE

Sullivan, C. (1998) *The growing business of sport and leisure: An update* Wellington, NZ: Hillary Commission

Vuori, I. et al. (eds) (1995) *The significance of sport for society: Health, socialisation, economy* Strasbourg: Council of Europe Press

Waddington, I. (2000) Sport and health: A sociological perspective in Coakley, J. and Dunning, E. (eds) *Handbook of sports studies* London: Sage Publications

Walker, R. (1995) The dynamics of poverty and social exclusion in Room, G. et al. (eds) *Beyond the threshold: The measurement and analysis of social exclusion* Bristol: Policy Press

Wilkinson, R. (1998) What health tells us about society. *Institute of Development Studies Bulletin* 29.1, 77–84

Witt, P. and Crompton, J. (1996b) *Recreation programs that work for at risk youth: The challenge of shaping the future* Pennsylvania: Venture Publishing

Chapter 4 Poverty: The core of exclusion

Alcock, P., Craig, G., Dalgleish, K. and Pearson, S. (1995) *Combating local poverty: The management of anti-poverty strategies by local government* Luton: Local Government Management Board

Alcock, P. and Craig, G. (1998) Monitoring and evaluation of local authority anti-poverty strategies in the UK *International Journal of Public Sector Management*, 11.7, 553–65

Audit Commission (1989) *Sport for whom?* London: HMSO

Audit Commission (1999) *The price is right* London: Audit Commission

Balloch, S. and Jones, B. (1990) *Poverty and anti-poverty strategy: The local government response* London: Association of Metropolitan Authorities

Barclay, J. (1995) *Inquiry into Income and Wealth* 2 vols York: Joseph Rowntree Foundation

Campbell, H. (1993) *The impact of variations in charges on, usage levels at local authority sports facilities: Summary and policy implications* Information Digest FM23 Edinburgh: Scottish Sports Council

Centre for Leisure Research (1993) *Survey of concession cards in Scotland: Final report* CLR: Edinburgh

Chartered Institute of Public Finance (1999) *Leisure and Recreation Statistics: Estimates 1998–99* London: CIPFA

Chartered Institute of Public Finance (2000) *Charges for Leisure Services Statistics 2000–01* London: CIPFA

Coalter, F. (1989) Leisure policy: an unresolvable dualism? pp 115–29 in Rojek, C.(ed) *Leisure for leisure* Basingstoke: Macmillan

Coalter, F. (1991) Sports Participation: Price or Priorities? *Leisure Studies* 12, 171–82

Coalter, F. (2000) Public and commercial leisure provision: active citizens and passive consumers *Leisure Studies* 19, 163–81

Collins, M.F. (1996) Sights on sport *Leisure Management* 15.9, 26–8

Collins, M.F. (1997) Does a new philosophy change the structures? Compulsory Competitive Tendering and local authority leisure services in Midland *England Managing Leisure* 2.4, 204–16

Collins, M.F. and Kennett, C.R. (1998) Leisure poverty and social exclusion: the growing role of leisure cards *Local Governance* 24.2, 131–42

Collins, M.F. and Kennett, C. (1999) Leisure, poverty and social exclusion: the growing role of passports in leisure in Great Britain *European Journal for Sports Management* 6.1, 19–30

Dawson, D. (1988) Leisure and the definition of poverty *Leisure Studies* 7, 221–31

Department of Culture Media and Sport (1999) *Sport and Arts* report of Policy Action Team 10 London: DCMS

Department of the Environment Transport and the Regions (1999) *Index of Local Deprivation* London: DETR

Department of the Environment, Transport and the Regions (2000) *Index of deprivation* Regeneration research summary 31 London: DETR

Department of National Heritage (1995) *Sport: Raising the game* London: DNH

Eady, J. (1994) *Leisure Card Schemes* Recreation Management factfile 37 London: Sports Council

English Sports Council (1997) *England, the sporting nation: A strategy* London: ESC

Frisby, W., Crawford, S., and Dorer, T. (1997) Reflections on participatory action research: The case of low income women *Journal of Sports Management* 11, 8–28

Galvin, A. et al. (2000) *How much? A project to investigate the impact of programmes, prices and promotion on young people's theatre attendance* Sheffield: Sheffield Theatre Trust

Gordon, D. and Forrest, R. (1995) *People and places 2: Social and economic distinctions in England* Bristol: School for Advanced Urban Studies

Gratton, C. and Taylor, P. (1985) *Sport and recreation: an economic analysis* London: E&F Spon

Gratton, C. and Taylor, P. (1994) *The impact of variations in charges on usage levels in local authority facilities* Research Digest 34 Edinburgh: Scottish Sports Council

Grimshaw, P. and Prescott-Clarke, P. (1978) *Sport school and community* Research Working Paper 9 London: Sports Council

Harvey, D. (1994) Flexible accumulation through urbanisation: Reflections on 'postmodernism' in American cities in Amin, A. (ed) *Post-Fordism: A reader* London: Blackwell

Henry, I.P. (1993) *The politics of leisure policy* Basingstoke: Macmillan

Higgins, V. and Ball, R. (1999) Local authority anti-poverty strategies in Scotland *Public Policy and Administration* 14:1, 60–75

Holt, R. (1990) *Sport and the British: A modern history* Oxford: Oxford University Press

Horne, J., Tomlinson, A. and Whannel, G. (1999) *Understanding sport: An introduction to the sociological and cultural analysis of sport* London: E&F Spon

Houlihan, B.M.J. (1991) *The policy and politics of sport* London: Routledge

Jessop, B. (1992) Fordism and post-Fordism: Critique and reformulation in Scott, A. and Stopper, M. (eds) *Pathways to regionalism and economic development* London: Routledge

Kaplan, M. (1975) *Leisure: Theory and policy* New York: John Wiley

Kay, T.A. and Jackson, G.A.M. (1991) Leisure despite constraint *Journal of Leisure Research* 23, 301–13

Kennett, C.R. (2002) *Leisure poverty and social exclusion: An analysis of leisure cards schemes in Great Britain* Loughborough: Loughborough University

Kew, F. (1997) *Sport problems and issues* Oxford: Butterworth Heinemann

Leicester City Council (unpublished, 1985) *Leisure pass: Annual report* Leicester: LCC

Leicester City Council (unpublished, 1996) *Leisure Pass customer survey* Leicester: LCC

Leicester City Council (unpublished, 1998) *Leisure Pass report* to Arts and Leisure Committee Leicester: LCC

Local Government Association (1994) *Anti poverty matters* London: Local Government Management Board

Local Government Association (2001) *All together now? A survey of local authority approaches to social inclusion and anti-poverty* Research Report 20 London: LGA

Local Government Management Board (1997) *Linking anti-poverty and equalities strategies* Notes from a seminar 11.6.97 *mimeo* Luton: LGMB

Macdonald, I. (2001) Splashing out for young people *Leisure Manager* 8, 26–7

McCabe, M. (1993) Family leisure budgets: Experience in the UK *World Leisure & Recreation* 35.3, 30–4

McCabe, M. (1994) Family leisure budgets: Bringing body and soul together in Brackenridge, C. (ed) *Body Matters* LSA conference proceedings 47, 150–61

McCabe, M. (1995) *Modest but adequate: Summary budgets for 16 households* York: Family Budget Unit

Mack, J. and Lansley, S. (1985) *Poor Britain* London: Allen and Unwin

Mayer, M. (1994) Post-Fordist city politics in Amin, A. (ed) *Post-Fordism: A reader* London: Blackwell

More, T. and Stevens, T. (2000) Do user fees exclude low income people from resource-based recreation? *Journal of Leisure Research* 32.3, 341–57

Oxford City Council (1998) *Reports on Flex Card* to Leisure Services Committee 12 Jan and 1 July Oxford: OCC

Peters, T. (1992) *Liberation management* London: Macmillan

PIEDA (1991) *The economic significance and impact of sport in Scotland* Reading: PIEDA

Polley, M. (1997) *Moving the goalposts: A history of sport and society since 1945* London: Routledge

Puranaho, K. (2000) *Why only the rich can play* Paper to 8th Congress of the European Association of Sports Management, San Marino

Sleap, M. (1998) *Social issues in sport* Basingstoke: Macmillan

Social Exclusion Unit (1998) *Bringing Britain together* London: Cabinet Office

Social Exclusion Unit (2000a) *Bridging the gap* London: SEU

Social Exclusion Unit (2000b) *Policy Action Team 18: Better information* London: SEU

Social Exclusion Unit (2001a) A *national strategy of neighbourhood renewal: Policy action team audit* London: SEU

Social Exclusion Unit (2001b) *A new commitment to neighbourhood renewal: National strategy action plan* London: SEU

Sport England (2000) *The use and management of sports halls and swimming pools in England 1997* London: Sport England

Sports Council (1981) *Annual report and accounts 1980–81* London: SC

Sports Council (1988) *Annual report 1987–88* London: SC

Sports Council/Health Education Authority (1992) *Allied Dunbar national fitness survey, main report* London: SC/HEA

Summerson, T. (2000) Youth Card: Background and aims: Paper to launch conference, St Ermins Hotel, London 12.2.2000 <www.dfee.gov.uk> accessed 6 Feb 2000

Telford and Wrekin Partnership (1998) *A strategy for combating poverty and social exclusion in Telford and Wrekin* Telford: T and W District Council

Walker, R. (1997) Poverty and social exclusion in Europe in Walker, A. and Walker, C. (eds) *Britain divided: The growth of social exclusion in the 1980s and 1990s* London: Child Poverty Action Group

Walker, R. and Park, J. (1997) Unpicking poverty in Oppenheim, C. (ed) *An inclusive society* London: Institute of Public Policy Research

Wilkinson, R. (1998) What health tells us about society *Institute of Development Studies Bulletin* 29.1, 77–84

Chapter 5 Exclusion, education and young people's sport

Allison, M. (1999) Play for tomorrow *Leisure Manager* 17.5, 19–22

Allison, M., Coalter, F. and Taylor, J. (1999) *Young people and sport* Research Report 70, Edinburgh: Scottish Sports Council

Allison, M. and Taylor, J. (1997) *Team Sport Scotland 1994–97 Evaluation* Research report 53 Edinburgh; Scottish Sports Council

Alstead, A. (1996) Developing youth sports *Proceedings* 4th European Congress on Sports Management, Montpellier, 2–8

Anders, G. (1982) Sport and youth culture *International Review of Sports Sociology* 1.17, 49–60

Anstett, M. and Sachs, B. (1995) *Sports, jeunesse et logique d'insertion* [Sports, youth and the logic of insertion] Paris: Documentation Francaise

Baker, D. and Witt, P.A. (1996) Evaluation of the impact of two after school recreation programs *Journal of Park and Recreation Admin* 14.3, 23–44

Becker, P. et al. (2000) *Sport as a tool for the social integration of young people* Hamburg: GOPA Consultants

Blair, A. (1999) The Beveridge lecture. Speech at Toynbee Hall, London 18 Mar 99 on <www.number-10.gov.uk/public/info/index.html> accessed 25 Nov 99

Bradshaw, J. (2001) *Poverty: The outcomes for children* London: Family Policy Studies Centre

Brettschneider, W-D. (1990) Adolescents, leisure, sport and lifestyle in Williams, T., Almond, L. and Sparkes, A. (eds) *Sport and physical activity: Moving towards excellence* London: E&F Spon

Brodie, D. and Roberts, K. (1992) *Inner city sport: Who plays, what are the benefits?* Culembourg: Giordano Bruno

Brown, G. (1999) Speech to Surestart conference 7 July 1999 <www.hm-treasury.gov.uk/speech/cx70799.html>

Buller, J. (1998) *Bridging the gap? An evaluation of Champion Coaching and Performance Squads in Nottinghamshire* unpublished MSc Thesis Loughborough: Loughborough University

Buller, J.R. and Collins, M.F. (2000) Bridging the post-school institutional gap: Champion Coaching in Nottinghamshire *Managing Leisure* 5, 200–21

Bundrick, D. and Witt, P.A. (1998) *College Station after-school programme* paper on <wwwrpts.tamu.edu/rpts/faculty/pubs/wittpub9.htm> accessed 12 July 00

Bynner, J. (1999) Poverty in the early years: Evidence from the 1958 and 1970 British Birth Cohort studies in *Persistent poverty and lifetime inequality: The evidence* CASE report 5 London: London School of Economics

Campbell, S. (2000) Change through sport *Recreation* 59.8, 21–3

Candler, P. (1999) *Cross-national perspectives on the principles and practice of children's play provision* unpublished PhD, Leicester: De Montfort University

Central Council for Physical Recreation (1960) *Sport in the community* (The Wolfenden Report) London: CCPR

Centre for Leisure Research (1999) *Notes on youth and sport* unpublished Edinburgh: Centre for Leisure Research

Charlton Athletic Racial Equality (1998) *Annual report* London: CARE

Charrier, D. (1997) *Activites physiques et sportives et d'insertion des jeunes* [Physical and sporting activities and insertion of youth] Paris: Documentation Francaise

Child, E. (1985) *General theories of play* London: Playboard

Children's Play Council (2000) *Best play – what play provision should do for children* London: CPC

Coalter, F. (1999) Sport and recreation in the UK: Flow with the flow or buck the trends? *Managing Leisure* 4, 24–39

Coalter, F., Allison, M. and Taylor, J. (2000) *The role of sport in regenerating deprived urban areas* Edinburgh: Scottish Executive Central Research Unit

Collins, M.F. (1994) Children's play: 'Little orphan Annie' in the British leisure system in Leslie, D. (ed) *Leisure and tourism: Towards the millennium* vol 2 Leisure Studies Association publication 52, Eastbourne: LSA

Collins, M.F. and Buller, J.R. (2002 in press) Social exclusion from high performance sport? *Social Issues in sport*

Crompton, J. and Witt, P.A. (1997) The roving leader program in San Antonio *Journal of Park and Recreation Administration* 15.2, 84–92

Day Care Trust (2001) *Thinking big: Childcare for all* London: DCT

Department for Education and Employment (2000) *Connexions – the best start in life for every young person* Nottingham: DfEE publications

de Knop, P. et al. (1995) Towards a sound youth policy in the club *European PE Review* 1.1, 6–14

de Knop, P. et al. (1996) *Youth-friendly sports clubs: Developing an effective youth sport policy* Brussels: VUB Press

de Knop, P. et al. (1997) *Sports stimulation initiatives for underprivileged youth and immigrant youth in Flanders* Paper to European Network of Sports Sciences in Higher Education meeting, Bordeaux 117–27

de Knop, P. and de Martelaer, K. (2001) Quantitative and qualitative evaluation of youth sport in Flanders and the Netherlands: A case study *Sport, Education and Society* 6.1, 35–51

Department for Education and Employment (2000) *Sure Start* London: DfEE

Department for Culture Media and Sport (1999) *A sporting future for all* London: DCMS

Durham County Council (1999) *Deerness Valley Gym Club* unpublished report Durham: DCC

English Sports Council (1997) *Local authority support for sports participation in the younger and older age groups* Policy briefing London: ESC

English Sports Council (1998) *The development of sporting talent, 1997* London: ESC

Flintoff, A. and Scraton, S. (2001) Stepping into active leisure? Young women's perceptions of active lifestyles and their experiences of school PE *Sport, Education and Society* 6.1, 5–21

Gibson, A. and Asthana, S. (1999) Local markets and the polarisation of public sector schools in England and Wales *Trans Inst Br Geogr NS* 25, 303–19

Gratton, C. (1996) *Position paper on sporting performance and excellence* unpublished paper Sheffield: Sheffield Hallam University

Gregg, P., Harkness, S. and Machin, S. (1999) *Child development and family income* York: York Publishing Services for the Joseph Rowntree Foundation

Hardman, K. and Marshall, J. (2000) *A worldwide survey of the state and status of school PE* Manchester: Manchester University

Health Education Authority (1998) *Young and active?* London: HEA

Heinemann, K. and Schwab, M. (1999) Sports clubs in Germany in Heinemann, K. (ed) *Sports clubs in various European countries* Cologne: Club of Cologne

Heinila, K. (1989) The sports club as a social organisation in Finland *International Review of the Sociology of Sport* 24.3, 225–46

Hendry, L. (1992) Sport and Leisure: The not-so-hidden curriculum? in Coleman, J.C. and Adamson, C.W. (eds) *Youth policy in the 90s – The way forward ?* London: Routledge

Hendry, L.B., Shucksmith, J.S., Love, J. and Glendinning, A. (1993) *Young people's leisure and lifestyles* London: Routledge

Higher Education Funding Council for England (1997) *The influence of neighbourhood type on participation in Higher Education, Interim report* London: HEFCE

Hill, M.S. and Jenkins, S.P. (2000) Poverty among British children: chronic or transitory in Micklewright, J. (ed) *Poor children in Europe* London: Family Policy Studies Centre

Hill-Tout, J., Lindsell, S. and Pithouse, A. (1995) *Evaluation of venture play, Caia Park, Wrexham* Cardiff: University of Wales College

Hindermeyer, O. (ed) (1998) *Les actions de solidarite Bilan 1997* [Actions of solidarity: Review 1997] Paris: Union Nationale des Centres Sportifs de Plein Air

Hobcraft, J. (2000) *The roles of schooling and adult education in the emergence of adult social exclusion* Centre for Analysis of Social Exclusion paper 43 London: London School of Economics

Houlihan, B. (1997) *Sport, policy and politics* London: Routledge

Houlihan, B. (1999) *Sporting excellence, schools and sports development: The politics of crowded policy spaces* unpublished paper to CRSS-EPER conference on PE and Excellence Leicester September

Hutson, S., Thomas, J. and Sutton, M. (1995) *Why boys and girls come out to play: Sport and school age children at the transition from primary to secondary education* Cardiff: Sports Council for Wales

Institute of Sport and Recreation Management (2000) *Couch kids* Information sheet 201 Melton Mowbray: ISRM

Jones, S.G. (1988) *Sport, politics and the working class: A study of organised labour and sport in inter-war Britain* Manchester: Manchester University Press

Kay, T.A. (2000) Sporting excellence: A family affair? *European Physical Education Review* 6.2, 151–69

Kennett, C.R. (1997) *How can social exclusion through poverty be overcome in the Olympic movement?* unpublished paper to 5th International postgraduate seminar, Olympia

Kirk, D. et al. (2000) *Towards girl-friendly PE: The Nike/YST Girls in Sport partnership project* Loughborough University: Institute of Youth Sport

Kremer, J., Ogle, S. and Trew, K. (eds, 1997) *Young people's involvement in sport* London: Routledge

Lobo, F. (1998) Young people, employment and leisure behaviour *World Leisure and Recreation* 1.98, 4–8

MacDonald, R. (1997) *Youth and social exclusion* London: Routledge

McDonald, D. and Tungatt, M. (1991) *National demonstration projects – major lessons for sports development* London: Sports Council

MacPhail, A., Eley, D. and Kirk, D. (2001 unpublished) Listening to young people's voices: Youth sport leaders' advice on facilitating participation in sport Loughborough: Institute of Youth Sport

Mason, V. (1995) *Young people and sport in England* London: Sports Council

Martinek, T. and Hellison, D.R. (1997) Fostering resiliency in underserved youth through physical activity *Quest* 49.1, 34–49

Mathieson, J. and Summerfield, C. (eds) (2000) *Social focus on young people* London: Stationery Office

Mizen, P. et al. (2000) *Work, labour and economic life in late childhood* Children 5–16 Research Briefing 4, Coventry: University of Warwick

Moore, R. (1986) *Childhood's domain* London: Croom Helm

MORI (2000) *Nestle Family Monitor 2000 – Sport and the Family* London: MORI

MORI (2001) *Young people and sport in England, 1999* London: Sport England

National Association for the Care and Resettlement of Offenders (1998) Annual *report 1997–98: Towards a safer future* London: NACRO

National Coaching Foundation (1996) *Champion Coaching – the guide* Leeds: Sports Council

Nottinghamshire County Council (1993) *Proposal for the re-launch of STS* Nottingham: Leisure Services Dept

Nottinghamshire County Council (1994) *Social Need in Nottinghamshire* Nottingham: Planning and Economic Development Dept

Oakley, B. and Green, M. (2000) *Elite sport development systems and playing to win: Uniformity and diversity in international approaches* paper to Leisure Studies Association conference Glasgow, July 2000

Office for Standards in Education (2000) *Sports colleges: The first two years* London: OFSTED

Penney, D. and Evans, J. (1999) *Policy, politics and practice in physical education* London: E&F Spon

Penney, D. and Harris, J. (1997) Extra-curricular PE: More of the same for the more able? *Sport, Education and Society* 2.1, 41–54

Piachaud, D. and Sutherland, H. (2000) *How effective is the British government's attempt to reduce child poverty?* CASE paper 38 London: London School of Economics

Poinsett, A. (ed) (1996) *The role of sports in youth development* Report of Carnegie Corporation meeting 18.3.96 New York: CC of New York

Qualifications and Curriculum Authority (1999) *Analysis of educational resources: Resources for PE 5–16* London: QCA

Rees, C.R. and Miracle, A.W. (2000) Education and sports in Coakley, J. and Dunning, E. (eds) *Handbook of sports studies* London: Sage

Rigg, M. (1986) *Action sport: An evaluation* London: Sports Council

Riordan, J. and Kruger, A. (1996, eds) *The story of worker sport* Champaign, Ill: Human Kinetics

Roberts, K. (1983) *Youth and leisure*, London: George Allen and Unwin

Roberts, K. (1996) Young people, schools, sport, and government policies *Sport Education and Society* 1.1, 47–57

Roberts, K. and Fagan, C. (1999) Young people and their leisure in former communist countries: Four theses examined *Leisure Studies* 18, 1–17

Roberts, K. and Parsell, G. (1994) Youth cultures in Britain: The middle class takeover *Leisure Studies* 13, 33–48

Rowe, N., Moore, S. and Mori, K. (1999) *General Household Survey: Participation in sports in GB, 1996* London: Sport England

Rowley, S. (1992a) *TOYA: TOYA and Lifestyle* London: Sports Council.

Rowley, S. (1992b) *TOYA: Identification of Talent* London: Sports Council

Rudd, P. and Edwards, K. (1998) Structure and agency in youth transitions: Student experiences of vocational FE training *Journal of Youth Studies* 1.1, 39–62

Schweinhart, L. and Weikart, D. (1997) *Lasting differences: The High/Scope pre-school curriculum project through age 23* High/Scope Press

Searle, C. (1993) *The BOA athlete report: 25 ways to put the Great back into sporting Britain* London: British Olympic Association

Seppanen, P. (1982) Sports clubs and parents as socialising agents in sport *International Review of Sports Sociology* 1.17, 79–90

Sharp, C. et al. (1999) *Playing for Success: An evaluation of the first year* RR167 London: Department for Education and Employment

SMC Management Services Inc (1998) *Developing a recreation framework for children and youth* Toronto: Ontario Ministry of Citizenship, Culture and Recreation

Smith, F. (2000) *Child-centred after school and holiday childcare* Children 5–16 Research Briefing 10 Uxbridge: Brunel University

Smith, F. and Barker, J. (2001) Commodifying the countryside: The impact of out-of-school care on rural landscapes of children's play *Area* 33.2, 169–76

Sparkes, J. (1999) *Schools, education and social exclusion* CASE Paper 29 London: London School of Economics

Sport England (2000) *The use and management of sports halls and swimming pools in England 1997* London: Sport England

Sport England (2001) *Sport equity index on* <www.sportengland.co.uk> accessed 10 Aug 01

Sports Council (1990) *Norwich Activities Promoter for women: Final evaluation report* London: Sports Council

Sports Council (1993) *Young people and sport: Policies and frameworks for action* London: Sports Council

Sports Council (1995) *Running sport: Starting a junior section* London: Sports Council

Sports Council/Coventry City Council (1989) *Active lifestyles: An evaluation of the project's work* Coventry: CCC

Sports Council for Wales (nd) *Time out: Is PE out of time and out of resources?* Cardiff: SCW

Stassen, B. (ed) (1996) Sports de proximite et d'aventure, outils d'insertion sociale [Neighbourhood and adventure sports, useful in social insertion] *Sport* no.155 Brussels: Ministere de la Culture et des Affaires sociales

Stead, D. and Swain, G. (eds, 1987) *Youth work and sport* London: Sports Council/ NYB/NCVYS

Stone, E.J. et al. (1998) Effects of physical activity interventions in youth: Review and synthesis *Am J. Prev.Med.* 15.4, 298–315

Thomson, I. (1998) *Sport in Denmark* Edinburgh Scottish Sports Council:

Thomson, R. and Beavis, N. (1985) *Talent identification in sport* Otago, NZ: Faculty of PE

UK Sport (2000) *Annual report* London: UKS <www.uksport.gov.uk> accessed 3 Mar 00

UK Sport (2001) *World class: The athlete's view* London: UKS

Wade, E. (1987) *Bridging the gap: A scheme to stop school leavers dropping out of sport* London: Sports Council

Waterville Children's project (1998) *Waterville projects 1997* North Shields: WCP

White, A. and Rowe, N. (1996) England in de Knop, P. et al. (eds) *World-wide trends in youth sport*, Champaign, Ill: Human Kinetics

Witt, P. (1999) Evaluation of the 1998–99 Neighborhood Teen Program of Austin Parks and Recreation Department <pwitt@rtps.tamu.edu> accessed 17 July 00

Witt, P. (2000) *Differences between after-school programme participants and non-participants* <wwwrpts.tamu.edu/rpts/faculty/pubs/wittpub12.htm> accessed 17 July 00

Youth Charter for Sport (1998) *Youth Charter for Sport as a contributor to social regeneration* Brochure Manchester: YCS

Chapter 6 Gender, sport and social exclusion

Birrell, S. and Theberge, N. (1994) Ideological control of women in sport in Costa, D.M. and Guthrie, S.R. (eds) *Women and sport: Interdisciplinary perspectives* Champaign, Ill: Human Kinetics

Campbell, K. (1999) *Women-friendly sports facilities* Facilities Factfile 1 Recreation Management London: Sport England

Central Council for Physical Recreation (1960) *Sport in the community* (The Wolfenden Report) London: CCPR

Collins, M.F. (1996) Getaway girls and wild outdoor women, in Etchell, C. (ed) *Today's thinking for tomorrow's countryside* Cardiff: Countryside Recreation Network

Coventry Women in Sport Group (1991) *Opening doors for women in sport: Report on work undertaken 1990/1991* Coventry: Coventry City Council

Deem, R. (1986) *All work and no play? The sociology of women and leisure* Milton Keynes: Open University Press

Department of Social Security (1998) *A new contract for welfare: New ambitions for our country Cm3805* London: The Stationery Office

Duquin, M.E. (1982) The importance of sport in building women's potential *Journal of Physical Education, Recreation and Dance* 53.3, 18–36

Fasting, K. (1993) *Women and sport: Monitoring progress towards equality* Oslo: The Norwegian Confederation of Sports Women's Committee

Glyptis, S., Kay, T. and Murray, M. (1985) *Working with women and girls* Birmingham: Sports Council, West Midland Region

Greendorfer, S. (1983) Shaping the female athlete: The impact of the family in Boutilier, M.A. and San Giovanni, L. (eds) *The sporting woman* Champaign Ill: Human Kinetics

Griffin, P.S. (1989) Homophobia in Physical Education *CAHPER Journal* 55.2, 27–31

Hargreaves, J. (1994) *Sporting females: Critical issues in the history and sociology of women's sports* London: Routledge

Horne, J. and Bentley, C. (1989) Women's magazines, 'Fitness chic' and the construction of lifestyles in Long, J. (ed) *Leisure, health and well being* Publication 44, Eastbourne: Leisure Studies Association

Kay, T.A. (1996a) Women's work and women's worth: The leisure implications of women's changing employment patterns *Leisure Studies* 15.1, 49–64

Kay, T.A. (1996b) Just do it? Turning sports policy into sports practice *Managing Leisure* 1.4, 233–47

Kay, T.A. (1999) Gender ideologies in magazine portrayals of sport: King Eric v. the Billion $ Babe *Journal of European Area Studies* 7.2, 157–76

Kay, T.A. (2000) Leisure, gender and the family: The influence of social policy context *Leisure Studies* 19.4, 247–65

Land, H. (1999) The changing worlds of work and families in Watson, S. and Doyal, L. (eds) *Engendering Social Policies* Buckingham: Open University Press

McDonald, D. and Tungatt, M. (1990) *National demonstration projects: Activities promoter for women Norwich City Council* Final Evaluation Report. Manchester: Sports Council, Research Unit North West

McKay, J. (1997) *Managing gender: Affirmative action and organisational power in Australian, Canadian and New Zealand sport* Albany, NY: State University of New York Press

North Tyneside Council (1990) *Women's sports development* Durham: Sports Council, Northern Region

Office for National Statistics (1998) *Living in Britain: General Household Survey 1996* London: The Stationery Office

Oppenheim, C. (1998) *An inclusive society: Strategies for tackling poverty* London: Institute for Public Policy Research

Pascall, G. (1997) *Social policy: A new feminist analysis* London: Routledge

Research Unit, North West (1996) *Activities promoter for women, City of Norwich Council* Phase 2 Monitoring Report Manchester: Sports Council

Rowe, N.F. (1995) *Young people and sport* unpublished discussion paper London: Sports Council

Southern Council for Sport and Recreation (1989) *Strategy for sport 1990–93: Women in Sport* Reading: SCSR

Sports Council (1993) *Policy and frameworks for Action* London: Sports Council

Sports Council (1994) *The Brighton Declaration on women and sport* London: Sports Council

Talbot, M. (1989) Being herself through sport in Long, J. (ed) *Leisure, health and well being* Publication 44, Eastbourne: Leisure Studies Association

Taylorson, D. and Halfpenny, P. (1991) *Women and sport in the North West* Manchester: University of Manchester, Centre for Applied Social Research

West Midland Council for Sport and Recreation (1988) *A regional strategy topic study on women and sport* Birmingham: WMCSR

Willis, P. (1982) Women in sport and ideology in Hargreaves, J.A. (ed) *Sport, culture and ideology* London: Routledge and Kegan Paul

Chapter 7 Exclusion and older people in sport

Age Concern/Commission for Racial Equality (1998) *Age and race: Double discrimination – Life in Britain today for ethnic minority elders* London: AC/CRE

Armstrong, J., Midwinter, E. and Wynne-Harley, D. (1987) *Retired leisure: Four ventures in post-work activity* London: Centre for Policy on Ageing

Bernard, M. (ed) (1988) *Positive approaches to ageing: Leisure and lifestyle in older age* Stoke on Trent: Beth Johnson Foundation

Boyle, M. and McKay, J. (1995) 'You leave your troubles at the gate': A case study of exploitation of older women's labour and leisure in sport *Gender and Society* 9.5, 556–75

Clarke, A. (1993) Leisure and the elderly: A different world? Paper to LSA conference *Leisure in different worlds* Loughborough UK 14–18 July

Collins, M.F. (2002) Sport for All as a multi-faceted product of domestic and international influences in Da Costa, L. and Miragaya, A-M. (eds) *Worldwide trends in Sport for All* Oxford: Meyer and Meyer Sport

Department of Social Security (nd) *Opportunity for all: Tackling poverty and social exclusion: Indicators of success* London: DSS

Department of Social Security (1999) *Opportunity for all: Tackling poverty and social exclusion Cm4445* London: The Stationary Office

Department of Social Security (2000) *The changing welfare state: Social security spending* London: DSS <www.dss.gov.uk/hq/spending> accessed 11 Nov 00

English Sports Council (1997) *Policy briefing: Local authorities support for sports participation in the younger and older age groups* London: ESC

Finch, H. (1997) *Physical activity 'at our age'* London: Health Education Authority

Freysinger, V.J. (1999) Life span and life course pressures on leisure in Jackson, E.L. and Burton, T.L. (eds) *Leisure studies: Prospects for the 21st century* State College, PA: Venture Publishing

Gant, R. (1997) Elderly people, personal mobility and the environment *Geography* 82.3, 207–17

Govaerts, F. (1993) Sports and aging paper to *Sports Sciences in Europe in 1993* congress Cologne 8–12 Sept

Harada, M. (1999) Ageing and leisure in Japan *World Leisure and Recreation* 41.3, 30–2

Harahousou, Y. (1999) Elderly people, leisure and physical recreation in Greece *World Leisure and Recreation* 41.3, 20–4

Hawkins, B. (1999) Population ageing: Perspectives from the United States *World Leisure and Recreation* 41.3, 11–14

Heinila, K. (1989) The sports club as a social organisation in Finland *International Review of the Sociology of Sport* 24.3, 225–46

Hirvensalo, M., Lampinen, P. and Rantenen, T. (1998) Physical exercise in old age: An eight-year follow up study on involvement, motives and obstacles among persons aged 65–84 *Journal of Ageing and Physical Activity* 6, 157–68

Kelly, J. and Ross, J-E. (1989) Later-life leisure: Beginning a new agenda *Leisure Sciences* 11, 47–59

Law, C.M. and Warnes, A.M. (1976) The changing geography of the elderly in England and Wales *Transactions, Institute of British Geographers* New Series 11.4, 453–71

Long, J. and Wimbush, E. (1979) *Leisure around retirement* London: Sports Council/ ESCRC

McGuire, F. (2000) What do we know? Not much: The state of leisure and ageing research *Journal of Leisure Research* 32.1, 97–100

McPherson, B. (1991) Ageing and leisure benefits: A life cycle perspective in Driver, B, Brown, P. and Peterson, G.L. (eds) *Benefits of leisure* State College, PA: Venture Publishing

McPherson, B.D. (1999) Population ageing and leisure in a global context: Factors influencing inclusion and exclusion within and across culture *World Leisure and Recreation* 41.3, 5–10

Midwinter, E. (1992) *Leisure: New opportunities in the third age* Dunfermline: Carnegie UK Trust

Nicholl, J.P., Coleman, P. and Williams, B.T. (1993) *Injury in sport and exercise* London: Sports Council

O'Brien Cousins, S. (1995) Social support for exercise among elderly women in Canada *Health Promotion International* 10.4, 273–82

O'Brien Cousins, S. (1999) Cross-cultural studies on physical activity, sport and ageing in North America *World Leisure and Recreation* 41.3, 15–19

Povlsen, J. and Larsen, K. (1999) Ageing and leisure in Denmark *World Leisure and Recreation* 41.3, 25–9

Rodgers, H.B. (1977) *Rationalising sports policy* Strasbourg: Council of Europe

Scase, R. and Scales, J. (2000) *Fit and fifty?* Swindon: Economic and Social Research Council

Scraton, S., Bramham, P. and Watson, B. (2000) 'Staying in' and 'going out': Elderly women, leisure and the postmodern city pp 101–20 in Scraton, S. (ed) *Leisure, time and space: Meanings and values in people's lives* Leisure Studies Association publication 57 Eastbourne: LSA

Seigenthaler, K.L. and Vaughan, J. (1998) Older women in retirement communities: Perceptions of recreation and leisure *Leisure Sciences* 20, 53–66

Seppanen, P. (1982) Sports clubs and parents as socialising agents in sport *International Review of Sports Sociology* 1.17, 79–90

Sport England (2000) *The use and management of sports halls and swimming pools in England 1997* London: Sport England

Sports Council/Health Education Authority (1992) *Allied Dunbar national fitness survey, main report* London: SC/HEA

Stead, M., Wimbush, E., Eadie, D.R. and Teer, P. (1997) A qualitative study of older people's perceptions of ageing and exercise: The implications for health promotion *Health Education Journal* 56, 3–16

UK Sport/Sport England/CONI (1999) *Compass 1999: Sports participation in Europe* London: UK Sport

Chapter 8 Social exclusion and sport in a multicultural society

Arnaud, L. (1996) *Sports policies, ethnic minorities and democracy: A comparative analysis of Lyons and Birmingham* paper to 4th EASM congress, Montpellier

Baas, J.M., Ewert, A. and Chavez, D.J. (1993) Influence of ethnicity on recreation and natural environment use patterns: Managing recreation sites for ethnic and racial diversity *Environmental Management* 17.4, 523–9

Bayliss, M. (1989) PE and Racism: Making changes *Multicultural Teaching* 7, 19–22

Brownhill, S. and Thomas, H. (1998) Ethnic minorities and British urban policy: A discussion of trends in governance and democratic theory *Local Government* 24.1, 43–55

Burnett, C. and Hollander, W. (1999) *'Sport for All' versus 'All for Sport:' Empowering the disempowered in South Africa* paper to Sport for All congress Barcelona November

Cabinet Office (2000) *Minority ethnic issuers in social exclusion and neighbourhood renewal* London: Cabinet Office

Cabinet Office (2001) *Improving labour market achievements for ethnic minorities in British society: A scoping* note <www. Cabinet-office.gov.uk/info/2001/ethnicity/scope. shtml> accessed 13 Aug 01

Carrington, B. and McDonald, I. (2001) *Race, sport and British society* London: Routledge

Carrington, B. and McDonald, I. (forthcoming 2003) The politics of race and sports policy in Houlihan, B.M.J. (ed) *Sport and society* London: Sage

Carroll, R. and Hollinshead, G. (1993) Equal opportunities: Race and gender in PE: A case study in Evans, J. (ed) *Equality, education and Physical Education* London: Falmer Press

Cashmore, E. (1982) *Black sportsmen* London: RKP

Cashmore, E. (1989) *United Kingdom? Race, class and gender since the war* London: Unwin Hyman

Cashmore, E. (2nd ed, 1996) *Making sense of sports* Routledge: London

Centre for Leisure and Sport Research (2001) *Part of the Game? An examination of racism in grassroots football* Leeds: Leeds Metropolitan University

Chisti, M. (1991) Birmingham Pakistan Sports Forum *Sport and Leisure* 32:28

Collins, M.F., Jackson, G.A.M. and Buller, J.R. (1999, unpublished) *Leisure for disabled people in Leicester* report to City Council Loughborough: Loughborough University

Collins, T. (1998) Racial minorities in a marginalized sport: Race, discrimination and integration in British Rugby League football in Cronin, M. and Mayall, D. (eds) *Sporting nationalisms: Identity, ethnicity, immigration and assimilation* London: Frank Cass

Commission for Racial Equality/Age Concern (1998a) *Age and race: Double discrimination – an overview of life for ethnic minority elders in Britain today* London: CRE/AC

Commission for Racial Equality/Age Concern (1998b) *Age and race: Double discrimination – education and leisure* London: CRE/AC

Daniel, W. (1968) *Racial discrimination in England* Harmondsworth: Penguin

Deane, J. and Westerbeek, H. (1999) De-ethnicisation and Australian soccer: The management dilemma in *Proceedings* 7th European Congress of Sports Managers 16–19th September Thessaloniki: EASM

de Knop, P., Theeboom, M., Van Engeland, E., Van Puymbroek, L., de Martelaer, K., Wittock, H. and Verlinden, T. (1994) Islamic immigrant girls and sport in Belgium *Proceedings* 2nd European Congress on Sport Management 241–56

de Knop, P., Theeboom, M., Wittock, H. and de Martelaer, K. (1996) Implications of Islam on Muslim girls' sport participation in Western Europe: Literature review and policy recommendations for sport promotion *Sport, Education and Society* 1.2, 147–64

Elling, A., de Knop, P. and Knoppers, A. (2001) The integrating and differentiating significance of sport in de Knop, P. and Elling, A. (eds) *Values and norms in sport* Aachen: Meyer and Meyer Sport

English Sports Council (1997a) *England, the sporting nation: A strategy* London: ESC

English Sports Council (1997b) *Working towards racial equality – a good practice guide for local authorities* London: ESC

Fleming, S. (1991) Sport, schooling and Asian male youth culture in Jarvie, G. (ed) *Sport, racism and ethnicity* London: Falmer Press

Floyd, M.F. (1998) Getting beyond marginality and ethnicity: the challenge for race and ethnic studies in leisure research *Journal of Leisure Research* 30.1, 3–22

Floyd, M.F., Gramann, J.H., and Saenz, R. (1993) Ethnic factors and the use of public outdoor recreation areas *Leisure Sciences* 15, 83–98

Glyptis, S.A., Collins, M.F. and Randolph, L. (1995) *Place and pleasure: The sporting claim vol 2 Good practice case studies* Leeds: Yorkshire & Humberside Council for Sport and Recreation

Gramann, J.H. and Allison, M. (1999) Ethnicity, race and leisure in Jackson, E.L. and Burton, T.L. (eds) *Leisure Studies: Prospects for the 21st century* State College, PA: Venture Publishing, Inc.

Hillary Commission (1998) *Task force report on Maori sport* Wellington, NZ: The Hillary Commission

Home Office (2001) *Community cohesion* Report of the Review Team chaired by Ted Cantle London: Home Office

Horne, J., Tomlinson, A. and Whannel, G. (1999) *Understanding sport: An introduction to the sociological and cultural analysis of sport* London: E&F Spon

Hylton, K. (1999) Where are the black managers? *Leisure Manager* September, 32–4

Johal, S. (2001) Playing their own game in Carrington, B. and MacDonald, I. (eds) *Race, Sport and British society* London: Routledge

Johnson, C.Y., Bowker, J.M., English, D.B.K. and Worthen, D. (1998) Wildland recreation in the rural South: An examination of marginality and ethnicity theory *Journal of Leisure Research* 30.1, 101–20

Jones, L. (1998) Inequality in access to local environments: The experiences of Asian and non-Asian girls *Health Education Journal* 57, 313–28

Leaman, O. and Carrington, B. (1985) Athleticism and the reproduction of gender and ethnic marginality *Leisure Studies* 4, 205–17

Long, J. (2000) No racism here? A preliminary examination of sporting innocence *Managing Leisure* 5, 121–33

Long, J. and Hylton, K. (2000) *Shades of white: An examination of whiteness in sport* paper to Leisure Studies conference Glasgow

MacGowan, H. (1997) The accessibility of Australian Aboriginal people to sport and recreation in Collins, M.F. and Cooper, I.S. (eds) *Leisure management: Issues and applications* Wallingford: CAB International

Maguire, J. (1988) Race and position assignment in English soccer: A preliminary analysis of ethnicity and sport in Britain *Sociology of Sport Journal* 5.3, 257–69

Maguire, J. (1991) Sport, racism and British society: A sociological study of male Afro-Caribbean soccer and rugby union players in Jarvie, G. (ed) *Sport, racism and society* London: Falmer Press

Melnick, M. (1988) Racial segregation by playing position in the English football league: A preliminary analysis *Journal of Sport and Social Issues* 12.2, 122–30

Merkel, U. (1999) Sport in divided societies – the case of the old, the new, and the 're-united' Germany in Sugden, D. and Bairner, A. (eds) *Sport in divided societies* Brighton/Aachen: Meyer and Meyer

Merrett, C. (1996) 'In nothing else are the deprivers so deprived': South African sport, apartheid and foreign relations 1945–71 *International Journal of Sport History* 13.2, 146–65

Ouseley, H. (1995, October) *Let's kick racism Newsletter* 2, London: Advisory Group against racism and intimidation

Platt, L. and Noble, M. (1999) *Race, place and poverty: ethnic groups and low income distributions* York: York Publishing Services for the Joseph Rowntree Foundation

Polley, M. (1998) *Moving the goalposts: A history of sport and society since 1945* Routledge: London

Ravenscroft, N. and Markwell, S. (2000) Ethnicity and the integration and exclusion of young people through park and recreation provision *Managing Leisure* 5, 135–50

Rowe, N. and Champion, R. (2000) *Sports participation and ethnicity in England: National survey 1999–2000 Headline findings* London: Sport England

Scott Porter Research and Marketing Ltd (2001) *Sport and ethnic minorities: Aiming at social inclusion* Research Report 78 Edinburgh: SportScotland

Sleap, M. (1998) *Social issues in sport* Basingstoke: Macmillan

Sport England (2000) *The use and management of sports halls and swimming pools in England 1997* London: Sport England

Sport England/Commission for Racial Equality (1999) *Cash for black and ethnic minority sport* leaflet Leeds: SE/CRE

Sporting Equals (2001) *Achieving racial equality: A standard for sport* information sheet Melton Mowbray: Institute of Sport and Recreation Management

Sports Council (1994) *Black and ethnic minorities in sport: Policy and objectives* London: Sports Council

Sports Council NW (1991) *Sport and racial equality* Factfile 3 Manchester: Sports Council

Sports Council Y&H (1995) *Sharing good practice: Sport and black and ethnic minorities: 'Is it cricket?'* Leeds: Sports Council

Stodolska, M. and Jackson, E.L. (1998) Discrimination in leisure and work experienced by a white ethnic minority group *Journal of Leisure Research* 30.1, 23–46

Taylor, D.E. (1992) *Identity in ethnic leisure pursuits* San Francisco: Mellen Research University Press

Taylor, T. and Toohey, K. (1996) Sport, gender and ethnicity: An Australian perspective *World Leisure and Recreation* 38.4, 35–7

Taylor, W., Baronowski, T. and Rohm Young, D. (1998) Physical activity interventions in low income ethnic minority and populations with disability *American Journal of Preventative Medicine* 15.4, 334–43

Thompson, G. (1999) Wicked issues in Best Value in *Proceedings* 1998 ISRM conference Melton Mowbray: ISRM

Travis, A. and Rowan, D. (1997) Ethnic equality: A beacon burning darkly *Guardian* 2 October, 17

Verma, G.K. and Darby, D.S. (1994) *Winners and losers: Ethnic minorities in sport and recreation* Brighton: Falmer Press

Wilson, G.D.H. and Hattingh, P.S. (1992) Environmental preferences for recreation within deprived areas: The case of black townships in South Africa *Geoforum* 34.4, 477–86

Chapter 9 Sport and disability

Anderson, E.M., Clarke, L. and Spain, B. (1982) *Disability in adolescence* London: Methuen

Barnes, C., Corker, M., Cunningham-Burley, S., Davis, J., Priestley, M., Shakespeare, T. and Watson, N. (2000) *Lives of disabled children* Children 5–16 briefing Stirling: ESRC

Barnes, C., Mercer, G. and Shakespeare, T. (1999) *Exploring disability: A sociological reader* Cambridge: Polity Press

Beresford, P. (1996) Poverty and disabled people: Challenging dominant debates and policies *Disability and Society* 11.4, 553–67

Borrett, N., Kew, F. and Stockham, K. (1996 unpublished) *Disability, young people, sport and leisure* paper to WLRA 4th World Congress Cardiff July 18–20

BSAD (1994) *Short guide to the design of sports buildings* London: British Sports Association for the Disabled

Cavet, J. (1995) Leisure provision in Europe in Hogg, J. and Cavet, J. (1995) *Making leisure provision for people with profound learning and multiple disabilities* London: Chapman and Hall

Centre for Leisure Research (1995) *Sport for people with disabilities in the East Midlands* Nottingham: East Midland Council for Sport and Recreation

Collins, M.F., Jackson, G.A.M. and Buller, J.R. (1999, unpublished) *Leisure for disabled people in Leicester* report to City Council Loughborough: Loughborough University

Collins, M.F., Randolph, L. and Sellars, C. (1994) *Service to voluntary sport: Nurturing or starving the grass roots* Nottingham: East Midland Council for Sport and Recreation

Community Consultants (1989) *Survey of people with disabilities: Recreational, community and leisure needs* London: Community Consultants

Countryside Agency (2000) *Sense and accessibility* CAX26 Cheltenham: CA

Dattilo, J. and Williams, R. (1999) Inclusion in leisure services delivery in Jackson, E.L. and Burton, T.L. (eds) *Leisure studies: Prospects for the 21st century* State College PA: Venture Publishing

Denyer, D. (1997) *Peak Park guided walks* unpublished BSc dissertation, Loughborough: Loughborough University

Department of Social Security (1997) *Social security statistics* London: DSS de Pauw, K. and Gavron, S. (1995) *Disability and sport* Champaign, Ill: Human Kinetics

Disability Rights Task Force on Civil Rights for Disabled People (1999) *From exclusion to inclusion* London: Department for Education and Employment

Dishman, R.K. (1995) Physical activity and public health: Mental health *Quest* 47, 362–85

Doll-Tepper, G. et al. (1994) *The future of sport science in the Paralympic movement* Berlin: IPC

Drake, R.F. (1994) The exclusion of disabled people from positions of power in British voluntary organisations *Disability and Society* 9, 461–90

English Federation of Disability Sport (2001 draft) *Building a fairer sporting society – Sport for disabled people in England: A four year development plan 2000–2004* London: EFDS

English Sports Council (1998) *Working towards racial equality in sport: A Good Practice guide for local authorities* London: ESC

French, D. and Hainsworth, J. (2001) 'There aren't any buses and the swimming pool is always cold!' Obstacles and opportunities in the provision of sport for disabled people *Managing Leisure* 6, 35–49

Glyptis, S.A.G., Collins, M.F. and Randolph, L. (1995) *Good practice vol 3 of Regional Strategy for Water and Countryside Sport* Leeds: Yorkshire and Humberside Council for Sport and Recreation

Greenfield, B.J. and Senecal, J. (1995) Recreational multifamily therapy for troubled children *American Journal of Orthopsychiatry* 65.3, 434–9

Healey, P. (1998) Institutionalist theory, social exclusion and governance in Allen, J., Madanipour, A. and Cars, G. (eds) *Social exclusion in European cities: Processes, experiences and responses* London: Jessica Kingsley Publishers

Health Education Authority (1999) *Physical activity and inequalities* London: HEA

Heiser, B. (1995) The nature and causes of transport disability in Britain and how to remove it in Zarb, G. (ed) *Removing disabling barriers* London: Policy Studies Institute

Hogg, J. and Cavet, J. (1995) *Making leisure provision for people with profound learning and multiple disabilities* London: Chapman and Hall

Hums, M.A., Moorman, A.M., and Wolff, E.I. (2000) *Paralympic athletes' inclusion into National Sports Organisations* paper to 8th European Sports Management Congress Sept San Marino

Institute for Leisure and Amenity Management (1997) *Disability Discrimination Act: Issues and guidelines Factsheet 97/5* Reading: ILAM

Kent Sports Development Unit (1999) *Sportslink projects in Kent* (mimeo) Canterbury: KSDU

Kitchen, R. (1998) 'Out of place', 'Knowing one's place': Space, power and the exclusion of disabled people *Disability and Society* 13.3, 343–56

Leicester City Council (1998) *Access to leisure facilities: A guide for disabled people* Leicester: LCC

Leicester City Council (1999) *Services for disabled people* Leicester: LCC

Leishman, M. (1996) Gaining access: Disability Discrimination Act *Leisure Management*

Levitt, L. (1991) Recreation for the mentally ill in Driver, B.L., Brown, P.J. and Peterson, G.L. (eds) *Benefits of leisure* State College, PA: Venture Publishing

McConkey, R. and McGinley, P. (1990) *Innovations in leisure and recreation for people with a mental handicap* Chorley: Lisieux Hall

Martin, J. and White, A. (1998) *OPCS' surveys of disabled people in GB, Report 2 Financial circumstances of disabled adults in private households* London: HMSO

Messent, P., Long, J. and Cooke, C. (1996, unpublished) *Care, choice and leisure opportunities in the community for people with learning disabilities* 4th WLRA congress Free time and the quality of life in the 21st century, Cardiff/Leeds: Leeds Metropolitan University

Modell, S.J. (1997) An exploration of the influence of educational placement on the community recreation and leisure patterns of children with developmental disabilities *Perceptual & Motor Skills* 85, 695–704

Morris, J. (1989) *Able lives: Women's experience of paralysis* London: The Women's Press

Mowl, G. and Edwards, C. (1995 unpublished) *Leisure space and disability* paper to Recreation and the City conference Staffordshire University 8 Sep 95, Newcastle upon Tyne: University of Northumbria

Newman, I. (1988) The integration of people with disabilities in countryside recreation and outdoor pursuits in Williams, T. and Newman, I. (eds) *Initial research on integration and community involvement in community sport and recreation* Working paper 4 EveryBody Active project Sunderland: Sunderland Polytechnic.

Nixon, H.L. II (2000) Sport and disability in Coakley, J. and Dunning, E. (eds) *Handbook of Sports Studies* London: Sage

Oliver, M. (1996a) *Understanding disability: From theory to practice* Basingstoke: Macmillan

Oliver, M. (1996b) A sociology of disability or a disability sociology in L. Barton (ed) *Disability and society: Emerging issues and insights* London: Longman

Paterson, K. and Hughes, W. (2000) Disabled bodies in Hancock, P. et al. (eds) *The body, culture and society* Milton Keynes: Open University Press

Phillips, D. (1996) Access to facilities *Leisure Opportunities* 28 Oct 96

Riordan, J. and Kruger, A. (1999) *The international politics of sport in the 20th century* London: E&F Spon

Rowe, N. (2001) *The social landscape of sport: Recognising the challenge and realising the potential* paper to CRN conference Countryside recreation and social exclusion London Sept 01

Scott Porter Research and Marketing Ltd (2001) *Sport and people with a disability: Aiming at social inclusion* Research Report 77 Edinburgh: SportScotland

Sharkey, P. (1996) Equal Rights *Recreation* Nov

Sly, F. (1996) Disability and the labour market *Labour Market Trends* Sept 413–24

Smith, R. (2001) Including the forty per cent: Social exclusion and tourism policy in G. McPherson and M. Reid (eds) *Leisure and social inclusion: Challenges to policy and practice* Publication 73 Eastbourne: Leisure Studies Association

Sport England (1999) *Planning policies for sport* London: SE

Sport England (2000) *The use and management of sports halls and swimming pools in England 1997* London: SE

Sport England (2001) *Young people with a disability and sport: Headline findings* London: SE

Sports Council (1994) *Guidance Notes: Access for disabled people* London: SC

Sports Council Y&H (1995) *Sharing good practice: Sport for people with Disabilities* Leeds: Sports Council

Stoneham, J. (2001) Making connections for accessible greenspaces *Countryside Recreation* 9.1, 14–16

Taylor, W., Baronowski, T. and Rohm Young, D. (1998) Physical activity interventions in low income ethnic minority and populations with disability *American Journal of Preventative Medicine* 15.4, 334–43

Thomas, N. (2001 unpublished) Sports policy for disabled people Stafford: Staffordshire University

Thomas, N. and Houlihan, B. (2000) The development of sports policies for disabled people in England: issues for the new Millennium, paper to Paralympic conference Sydney

Thomas, T. and Green, K. (1992) *Children today in Lancashire: Diverse opportunities* London: National Children's Play and Recreation Unit

Thomson, N. (1984) *Sport and recreation provision for disabled people* London: Architectural Press

Townsend, P. (1979) *Poverty in the UK* Harmondsworth: Penguin

Tungatt, M. (1990) Everybody Active project in Williams, C., Almond, L. and Sparkes, A. (eds) *Sport and physical activity* London: E&F Spon

Voluntary Action Leicester (1998) *Directory of Voluntary Groups in Leicester* Leicester: VAL

Walker, A. (1982) *Unqualified and underemployed* Basingstoke: Macmillan

Watson, N., Shakespeare, T., Priestley, M., Barnes, C., Davis, J., Cunningham-Burley, S. and Corker, M. (2000) *Life as a disabled child: A qualitative study of young people's experiences and perspectives* Edinburgh: University of Edinburgh

Wetherby, A. (1998) *Disability Discrimination Act* Facilities Factfile London: English Sports Council

West, P.C. (1984) Social stigma and community recreation participation by the mentally and physically handicapped *Therapeutic Recreation Journal* 18.1, 40–9

Williams, T. (1988) *Issues of integration, participation and involvement in physical education and sport* Working Paper 1 EveryBody Active project Sunderland: Sunderland Polytechnic

Chapter 10 Sport and youth delinquency

Allen, L. and Paisley, K. (1998) Top 10 ways to impact at-risk youth in recreation programming *Parks and Recreation* 33.3, 80–6

Anstett, M. and Sachs, B. (1995) *Sports, jeunesse et logiques d'insertion* [Sports, youth and the logic of insertion] Paris: Ministere de la Jeunesse et des Sports

Audit Commission (1996) *Misspent youth: Young people and crime* Abingdon, Oxon: Audit Commission

Bacon, W. (1981) *Leisure and learning in the 1980s* LSA conference report Eastbourne: Leisure Studies Association

Badenoch, D. (1998) *Wilderness adventure programs for youth at risk* paper to 21st biennial ACHPER conference, Adelaide

Bailey, P. (1987) *Leisure and class in Victorian England: Rational recreation and the contest for control 1830–85* London: Methuen

Baker, D. and Witt, P.A. (1996) Evaluation of the impact of two after school recreation programs *Journal of Park and Recreation Administration* 14.3, 23–44

Barrett, J. and Greenaway, R. (1995) *The role and value of outdoor adventure in young people's personal and social development* Coventry: Foundation for Outdoor Adventure

Base Camp (1994) conference papers Ambleside

Begg, D.J. et al. (1996) Sport and delinquency: An examination of the deterrence hypothesis in a longitudinal study *British Journal of Sport Medicine* 30, 335–41

Brantingham, P. and Faust, F. (1976) A conceptual model of crime prevention *Crime and Delinquency*, 22, 248–96

Brodie, D., Roberts, K., and Lamb, K. (nd) *Citysport challenge* Cambridge: Health Promotion Research Trust

Bundrick, D. and Witt, P.A. (1998) *College Station after-school programme* paper <wwwrpts.tamu.edu/rpts/faculty/pubs/wittpub9.htm>

Burt, C. (1925) *The young delinquent* London: London University Press

Bynum, J. (1996) *Juvenile delinquency: A sociological approach* Boston: Allyn and Bacon

Central Statistical Office (1991) *Social trends* London: CSO

Clarke, J. and Critcher, C. (1985) *The devil makes work* Basingstoke: Macmillan Education Ltd

Coalter, F. (1989) *Sport and anti-social behaviour: A literature review* Edinburgh: Scottish Sports Council

Coalter, F. (1996) *Sport and anti-social behaviour: A policy-related review* Edinburgh: Scottish Sports Council

Coalter, F. (2001c) *Realising the potential of cultural services: The case for sport* London: Local Government Association

Coalter, F., Allison, M. and Taylor, J. (2000) *The role of sport in regenerating deprived urban areas* Edinburgh: Scottish Executive Central Research Unit

Cohen, A.K. (1955) *Delinquent boys: The culture of the gang* New York: Collier Macmillan

Cohen, S. (1980, 2nd ed) *Folk devils and moral panics* London: Martin Robertson

Coleman, J.C. (1979) *The school years* London: Methuen

Cook, D. (1997) *Poverty, crime and punishment* London: Child Poverty Action Group

Cooper, B. (1989) *The management and prevention of juvenile crime problems* London: Home Office

Coopers and Lybrand (1994) *Preventative strategy for young people in trouble* unpublished report London: C and L

Crime Concern (no date) *Splash – A guide for scheme organisers* Swindon: Crime Concern

Crown Prosecution Service (1996) *Statistics* London: CPS

de Knop, P. et al. (1997) *Sports stimulation initiatives for underprivileged and immigrant youth in Belgium* unpublished paper to conference European Network of Sports Sciences in Higher Education, Bordeaux, 117–23

Downes, D. (1966) *The delinquent solution* London: Routledge and Kegan Paul

Duck, R.A. (1998) *A report on youth at risk* Toronto: Ontario Ministry of Citizenship, Culture and Recreation

Duret, P. and Augustini, M. (1993) *Sports de rue et insertion sociale* [Street sports and social insertion] Paris: National Institute of Sport and PE

Farrington, D. (1996) Understanding and preventing youth crime *Social Policy Research* 93, 1–6

Faulkner, D. (1987) *Community based sentencing – the use of Outdoor Challenge* Manchester: Sports Council North West

Giddens, A. (1982) *Profiles and critiques in social theory* Basingstoke: Macmillan

Giddens, A. (1997) *Sociology* Cambridge: Polity Press

Graham, J. and Bowling, B. (1995) *Young people and crime* London: Home Office

Greenaway, R. and Barrett, J. (1995) *Why adventure: The role and value of outdoor adventure in young people's personal and social development: A review of research* Coventry: Foundation for Outdoor Education

Hampshire Probation Service (1993) *Hants sports counselling annual report 1992–3* Winchester: HPS

Hampshire Probation Service (1997) *Hants sports counselling annual report 1996–7* Winchester: HPS

Hedges, B. (1986) *Personal leisure histories* London: ESRC/Sports Council

Hendry, L.B., Shucksmith, J., Love, J. and Glendinning, A. (1993) *Young people's leisure and lifestyles* London: Routledge

Hindermeyer, O. (1998, ed) *Les Actions de solidarité 1997 edition* [Actions for solidarity] Montreuil: Union Nationale des Centres Sportifs de Plein Air

Home Office (1992) *Criminal statistics* London: Home Office

Home Office (1993) *Statistical bulletin 1992* London: Home Office

Hopkins, D. and Putnam, R. (1993) *Personal growth through adventure* London: David Fulton Press

Jason-Lloyd, L. (1993) *The criminal justice acts: A basic guide* Huntingdon: ELM

Kelly, F.J. and Baer, D.J. (1968) *Outward bound schools as an alternative to institutionalisation for adolescent delinquent boys* Boston: Fandel

Long, J. and Dart, J. (nd) *Youth, leisure, sport, crime and community: An annotated bibliography* unpublished Leeds: Leeds Metropolitan University

Long, J. and Sanderson (2001) The social benefits of sport: Where's the proof? in Gratton, C. and Henry, I. *Sport in the City* London: Routledge.

Lundman, R. (1993, 2nd ed) *Prevention and control of juvenile delinquency* Oxford: Oxford University Press

McCormack, F. (2000) *Leisure exclusion? Analysing interventions using active leisure with young people offending or at-risk* unpublished PhD thesis, Loughborough: Loughborough University

McCormack, F. (2001) The policy of outreach interventions for young people to achieve community development and social inclusion through leisure in McPherson, G. and Reid, G. (eds) *Leisure and social exclusion* publication 73 Eastbourne: Leisure Studies Association

Mackay, S. (1993) Research findings related to the potential of recreation in delinquency prevention *Trends* 30.4, 27–30, 46

Martin, J.P. and Webster, D. (1994) *Probation motor projects in England and Wales* Manchester: Home Office

Marshall, A. (1994, unpublished) *Young people and crime* Leicester: National Youth Agency

Matza, D. (1969) *Becoming deviant* Englewood Cliffs: Prentice Hall

Mays, J. (1972) *Juvenile delinquency, the family and the social group* London: Longman

Mays, J.B. (1954) *Growing up in the city: A study of juvenile delinquency in an urban neighbourhood* Liverpool: Liverpool University Press

Mirrlees-Black, C. and Maung, N.A. (1994) *Fear of crime: Findings from the 1992 British Crime Survey* Research Findings 9, London: Home Office

Morgan, D. (1998a) Youth crime and sport in *ISRM conference report*, Melton Mowbray: Institute of Sport and Recreation Management

Morgan, D. (1998b) Sport off the streets: A preliminary analysis of the impact of Recreation Zones in *Sport in the city conference proceedings* vol 2 Sheffield: Sheffield Hallam University

Muncie, J. (1984) The trouble with kids today in *Youth and crime in post war Britain* London: Hutchinson

Muncie, J. (1999) Institutionalised intolerance: Youth justice and the 1998 Crime and Disorder Act *Critical Social Policy* 59, 147–75

Nichols, G. (2001) A realist approach to evaluating the impact of sports programmes on crime reduction in McPherson, G. and Reid, G. (eds) *Leisure and social exclusion* publication 73 Eastbourne: Leisure Studies Association

Nichols, G. and Booth, P. (1999) *Programmes to reduce crime and which are supported by local authority leisure departments* Melton Mowbray: Institute for Sport and Recreation Management

Nichols, G. and Taylor, P. (1996) *West Yorkshire Sports Counselling: Final evaluation* Sheffield

Office for National Statistics (2000) *Living in Britain: The General Household Survey* London: ONS

Parks and Recreation Federation of Ontario (1997) *The benefits catalogue* Ottawa: CPRA

Pitts, J. (1988) *The politics of juvenile crime* London: Sage

Potas, I., Vining, A. and Wilson, P. (1990) *Young people and crime: Costs and prevention* Canberra: Australian Institute of Criminology

Purdy, D. and Richard, S. (1983) Sport and juvenile delinquency: An examination and assessment of four major theories *Journal of Sport Behavior*, 6.4, 179–93

Roberts, K. (1983) *Youth and leisure*, London: George Allen and Unwin

Roberts, K. (1996) Young people, schools, sport, and government policies *Sport Education and Society* 1.1, 47–57

Robins, D. (1990) *Sport as prevention* Oxford: Centre for Criminological Research, University of Oxford

Scarman, Lord (1982) *The Scarman Report* London: Penguin

Segrave, J. and Hastad, D.N. (1985) Three models of delinquency *Sociological Focus* 18.1, 1–17

Sharp, C., Mawson, C., Pocklington, K., Kendall, L. and Morrison, J. (1999) *Playing for success: An evaluation of the first year* RR167 London: Department for Education and Employment

Shaw, P. (1999) *Policy Action Team 10: Arts and neighbourhood renewal* London: Department for Culture, Media and Sport

Smith, M. (1992) *The changing position of young people* conference notes, London: City Challenge

Sports Council (1989) *A policy for young people and sport* London: SC

Stoke on Trent City Council (1994) *Sport and recreation – towards the millennium: A strategy for leisure provision in Stoke on Trent* Stoke: STCC

Sugden, J. and Yiannakis, A. (1982) *Sport and juvenile delinquency: A theoretical base* Storrs-Mansfield, Conn: University of Connecticut

Sullivan, C. (1998) *The growing business of sport and leisure: An update* Wellington, NZ: Hillary Commission

Taylor, P., Crow, I., Irvine, D. and Nichols, G. (1999) *Demanding physical programmes for young offenders under probation supervision* Research Findings 91 London: Home Office

Taylor, P. and Nichols, G. (1996) *West Yorkshire Probation Service sports counselling project final evaluation report* Sheffield: Sheffield University

Thorpe, D., Smith, D., Green, C.J. and Paley, J.H. (1980) *Out of care: The community support of juvenile offenders* London: George Allen and Unwin Ltd

Torkildsen, G. (1992) *Leisure and recreation management* London: E&F Spon

Trulson, M. (1986) Martial arts training: A 'novel' cure for juvenile delinquency *Human Relations* 39.12, 1131–40

Tsuchiya, M. (1996) Recreation and leisure programmes for delinquents: The non-custodial option in Collins, M.F. (ed) *Leisure in industrial and post-industrial societies* Eastbourne: Leisure Studies Association

Tungatt, M. (1991) *Solent sports counselling final evaluation report* Manchester: Sports Council, Research Unit North West

Twemlow, S.W. and Sacco, F.C. (1998) The application of traditional martial arts practice and theory to the treatment of violent adolescents *Journal of Leisure Research* 30.3, 356–79

Utting, D. (1997) *Reducing criminality among young people: A sample of relevant programmes in the UK* London: Home Office

Webb, B. and Laycock, G. (1992) *Tackling car crime: The nature and extent of the problem* London: Home Office

West, D. (1967) *The young offender* London: Penguin Books

Witt, P. (1999) Evaluation of the 1998–99 Neighborhood Teen Program of Austin Parks and Recreation Department <pwitt@rtps.tamu.edu> accessed 17 July 00

Witt, P. (2000) Differences between after-school programme participants and non-participants <wwwrpts.tamu.edu/rpts/faculty/pubs/wittpub12.htm> accessed 17 July 00

Witt, P.A. and Crompton, J. (1997) The protective factors framework: A key to programming for benefits and evaluating for results *Journal of Park and Recreation Administration* 15.3, 1–18

Witt, P.A. and Crompton, J. (1996a) The at-risk youth recreation project *Journal of Park and Recreation Administration* 14, 1–9

Chapter 11 Rural and urban perspectives on exclusion and sport

Alcock, P., Craig, G., Pearson, S., Lawless, P. and Robinson, D. (1998) *Inclusive regeneration: The impact on regeneration of local authorities' corporate strategies for tackling regeneration* Sheffield: Centre for Regional Economic and Social Research

Bailey, N., Barker, A. and MacDonald, K. (1995) *Partnership agencies in British urban policy* London: UCL Press

Bennett, K., Hudson, R. and Beynon, H. (2000) *Coalfields regeneration: Dealing with the consequences of industrial decline* Bristol: Policy Press

Bianchini, F. (1998) Culture, economic development and the locality in Hardy, S., Malbon, B. and Taverner, C. (eds) *The role of art and sport in local and regional economic development* London: Regional Studies Association/Jessica Kingsley

References 283

Blowers, A. and Young, S. (2000) Britain: Unsustainable cities in Low, N., Gleeson, B., Elander, I. and Lidskog, R. (eds) *Consuming cities: The urban environment in the global economy after the Rio declaration* London: Routledge

Boardman, B. (1998) Travel and poverty *Rural Focus* 10–11

Boothby, J., Tungatt, M., Townsend, A.R. and Collins, M. (1982) *A sporting chance? Family, school and environmental influences on taking part in sport* Study 22 London: Sports Council

Bramley, G. (1998) *Where does public spending go?* London: Department of the Environment, Transport and the Regions

Brodie, D., Roberts, K., and Lamb, K. (nd) *Citysport Challenge* Cambridge: Health Promotion Research Trust

Brown, D. (1999) *Care in the country: Inspection of community care in rural areas* London: Department of Health

Byrne, D. (1998) Public policy and social exclusion (review article) *Local Economy* 13.1, 81–3

Cartmel, F. and Furlong, A. (2000) *Youth employment in rural areas* York: York Publishing Services for the Joseph Rowntree Foundation

Chapman, P., Phimister, E., Shucksmith, M., Upward, R. and Vera-Toscano, E. (1998) *Poverty and exclusion in rural Britain: The dynamics of low income and employment* York Publishing Services for the Joseph Rowntree Foundation

Cloke, P., Milbourne, P. and Thomas, C. (1994) *Lifestyles in rural England* Rural Research report 18 Rural Development Commission: Salisbury

Coalter, A., Allison, M. and Taylor, J. (2000) *The role of sport in regenerating deprived urban areas* Edinburgh: Scottish Central Research Unit

Collins, M.F. and Jackson, G.A.M. (1998) Economic impacts of sport and tourism in de Knop, P. and Standeven, J. (eds) *Sports Tourism* Champaign, Ill.: Human Kinetics.

Commins, P. (ed) (1993) *Combating social exclusion in Ireland 1990–94: A midway report* Brussels: European Commission

Countryside Agency (2001) *The state of the countryside 2001* Cheltenham: Countryside Agency

Department for Culture, Media and Sport (1998) *Creative industries: Report of the Creative Industries Task Force* London: DCMS

Department for Culture, Media and Sport (2001) *Building on PAT10 progress report on social inclusion* London: DCMS

Department of the Environment (1977) *Recreation and deprivation in inner urban areas* London: HMSO

Department of the Environment (1989) *Sport and active recreation provision in the inner cities: Report of the Minister for Sports Review Group* London: DOE

Department of the Environment, Transport and the Regions (1996) *Town centres and retailing* Planning policy guidance note 6 London: DETR

Department of the Environment, Transport and the Regions (1998) *The 1998 index of local deprivation: Patterns of deprivation and 1991–6 change* Regeneration Research Summary 21 <www.regeneration.detr.gov.uk> accessed 14 Dec 98

Department of the Environment, Transport and the Regions (2000) *Our towns and cities: The future – delivering an urban renaissance* <www.regeneration.detr.gov.uk/policies> accessed 29 Nov 00

Department of Transport and the Regions (2000a) *Social exclusion and the provision and availability of public transport* <www.mobility-unit.detr.gov.uk> accessed 2 Oct 00

Department of Transport and the Regions (2000b) *Our countryside: The future: A fair deal for rural England* White Paper <www.detr.gov> accessed 7 Mar 01

Department of Transport and the Regions (2001a) *Rural White Paper implementation plan* <www.detr.gov.uk> accessed 2 Apr 01

Department of Transport and the Regions (2001b) *Rural England: A discussion document* <www.detr.gov.uk> accessed 1 Mar 99

Duffy, R. (2000) *Satisfactions and expectations: Attitudes to public services in deprived areas* CASE paper 45 London: London School of Economics

Dunn, J., Hodge, I., Monk, S. and Kiddle, C. (1998a) *Developing indicators of rural disadvantage* Salisbury: Rural Development Commission

Dunn, J., Hodge, I., Monk, S. and Kiddle, C. (1998b) *Rural disadvantage: Understanding the processes* Salisbury: Rural Development Commission

Evans, G. (1998) Urban leisure: Edge city and the new leisure periphery in Collins, M.F. and Cooper, I.S. (eds) *Leisure management: Issues and applications* Wallingford: CAB Intertnational

Fitzpatrick, S., Hastings, A. and Kintrea, K. (2000) Youth involvement in urban regeneration: Hard lessons, future directions *Policy and Politics* 28.4, 493–509

Forrest, R. and Kearns, A. (1999) *Joined up places? Social cohesion and neighbourhood regeneration* York: York Publishing Services for the Joseph Rowntree Foundation

Francis, D. and Henderson, P. (1994) *Community development and rural issues* London: Community Development Foundation/ACRE

Geddes, M. (1997) *Partnership against poverty and exclusion? Local regeneration strategies and excluded communities in the UK* Bristol: Policy Press

Glyptis, S.A., Collins, M.F. and Randolph, L. (1995) *Place and pleasure: The sporting claim Vol 2: Good practice case studies* Leeds: Yorkshire & Humberside Council for Sport and Recreation

Gore, A., Dabinett, G. and Breeze, J. (1999, 2000) *The coalfields and the lottery phase 1, phase 2* Sheffield: Centre for Regional Economic and Social Research, Sheffield Hallam University

Gratton, C., Dobson, N. and Holliday, S. (1998) *Football came home: The impact of Euro '96* Sheffield: Leisure Industries Research Centre

Greater London and South East Council for Sport and Recreation (1983) *Special needs, special measures: Sport and recreation in London's inner city* London: GLSECSR

Hall, P. (1998) Creative cities in Hardy, S., Malbon, B. and Taverner, C. (eds) *The role of art and sport in local and regional economic development* London: Regional Studies Association/Jessica Kingsley

Hall, P. (2000) Creative cities and economic development *Urban Studies* 37.4, 639–49

Harrison, C. (1991) *Countryside recreation in a changing society* London: TMS Partnership

Healey, P., Cameron, S., Davoudi, S., Graham, S. and Mandipour, A. (eds, 1995) *The new urban context* Chichester: John Wiley & Sons

Hedges, A. (1999) *Living in the countryside: The needs and aspirations of rural populations CAX 28* Cheltenham: Countryside Agency

Kelly, O. and Wojdat, E. (1997) *Creative bits: The social impact of arts programmes* London: Comedia

Lee, P. and Murie, A. (1998) Targeting deprivation through housing tenure is flawed *New Economy* 5.2, 89–93

Linadio, M. (1996) *Car culture and countryside change* London: The National Trust

Local Government Association (1998) *Tackling rural poverty and social exclusion: The role of local authorities* London: LGA

McCulloch, A. (2001) Ward level deprivation and wider social and economic outcomes in British Household Panel Study *Environment and Planning A* 33, 667–84

Matthews, H. et al. (2000) Growing up in the countryside: Children and the rural idyll *Journal of Rural Studies* 16, 141–53

Milbourne, P. (ed) (1994) *Revealing rural 'others': Representation, power and identity in the British countryside* London: Pinter

National Council of Voluntary Organisations (1994) *Not just fine tuning: A review of community care plans for rural areas* London: NCVO

New Policy Institute (2000) *Indicators of poverty and social exclusion in rural England CAX41* Cheltenham: Countryside Agency

Oatley, N. (2000) New Labour's approach to age-old problems *Local Economy* 15.2, 86–97

Pavis, S., Platt, S. and Hubbard, G. (2000) *Young people in rural Scotland: Pathways to social inclusion and exclusion* York: York Publishing Services for the Joseph Rowntree Foundation

Price, P. (1999) *New sports facilities as the catalyst for urban regeneration* Institute of Sport and Recreation Management 1998 conference proceedings 261–70 Melton Mowbray; ISRM

Robinson, T. (nd) *The City Challenge programme in South Newcastle* Newcastle on Tyne: Newcastle University

Robson, B.T. et al. (2001) *Slim pickings for the cities of the north* email file from author 2 Mar 01

Rural Media Company (2000) *Not seen, not heard? Social exclusion in rural areas* CA 49, Cheltenham: Countryside Agency

Scott, J. (1994) *Poverty and wealth: Citizenship, deprivation and privilege* London: Longman

Scottish Poverty Information Unit (2000) *Briefing 10: Rural poverty in Scotland* <www.spiu.gcal.ac.uk/Povscot.html> accessed 14 Mar 00

Shucksmith, M. and Chapman, P. (1998) Rural development and social exclusion *Sociologica Ruralis* 38. 2, 225–42

Slee, W., Curry, N. and Joseph, D. (2001) *Removing barriers, creating opportunities: Social exclusion in countryside leisure in the UK* Cardiff: Countryside Recreation Network

Social Exclusion Unit (2000) *Report of PAT 13 on Shops* London: SEU

Social Exclusion Unit (2001a) A *national strategy of neighbourhood renewal: Policy Action Team Audit* London: SEU

Social Exclusion Unit (2001b) *A new commitment to neighbourhood renewal: National Strategy Action Plan* London: SEU

Speak, S. and Graham, S. (2000) *Service not included: Social implications of private sector restructuring in marginalised neighbourhoods* Bristol: Policy Press

Spilsbury, M., and Lloyd, N. (1998) *1997 survey of rural services* Salisbury: Rural Development Commission

Sport England (1999) *Regeneration through sport: Sport's contribution to community development* conference notes London: Sport England.

Stewart, M. et al. (1999) *Cross-cutting issues affecting local government* report to DETR Bristol: University of West of England

Streich, L. (1999) *Alternatives to the bus shelter: Imaginative ways to make it happen for young people in rural areas* Leicester: Youth Work Press

Todorovic, J. and Wellington, S. (2000) *Living in urban England: Attitudes and aspirations* London: Department of the Environment, Transport and the Regions

UK Sport (1999) *Major events: The economics* London: UK Sport

UK Sport (2000) *Major events blueprint: Measuring success* London: UK Sport

White, S. and Higgs, G. (1997) *The application of deprivation measures at the community level in Wales: A statistical and GIS approach* Papers in Planning Research 165 Cardiff: University of Wales

Whyatt, A. (nd) *The creative capital: Cultural industries, young people and regeneration in London* London: TS2K Trafalgar Square 2000 and others

Chapter 12 Policy implementation: Stronger citizenship and communal social capital through sport?

Allison, M. (2001) *Sport clubs in Scotland* Research Report 75 Edinburgh: SportScotland

Allison, M.T. (1991) Leisure, sport and the quality of life: Those on the fringes in Oja, P. and Telama, R. (eds) *Sport for all* Amsterdam: Elsevier Science

Atkinson, R. (2000) Combating social exclusion in Europe: The new urban policy challenge *Urban Studies* 37. 5–6, 1037–55

Baubock, R. (2001) Social and cultural integration in civil society in McKinnon, C. and Hampsher-Monk, I. (eds) *The demands of citizenship* London: Continuum

Bishop, J. and Hoggett, P. (1986) *Organising around enthusiasms: Patterns of mutual aid in leisure* London: Comedia

Boessenkool, J. (2001) Constructing viable sports clubs in Steenbergen, J., de Knop, P. and Elling, A. (eds) *Values and norms in sport* Oxford: Meyer and Meyer Sport

Boothby, J. et al. (1982) *A sporting chance? Family, school and environmental influences on taking part in sport* Study 22 London: Sports Council

Brodie, D. and Roberts, K. (1992) *Inner city sport: Who plays, what are the benefits?* Culembourg: Giordano Bruno

Brodie, D., Roberts, K., and Lamb, K. (nd) *Citysport Challenge* Cambridge: Health Promotion Research Trust

Bryant, P. (2001) *Social exclusion and sport: The role of training and learning* Report to Sport England London: SPRITO TCL

Carley, M., Chapman, M., Hastings, A., Kirk, K. and Young, R. (2000) *Urban regeneration through partnership* Bristol: Policy Press

Centre for Leisure Research (1991) *A digest of sports statistics for the UK*, 3rd edition London: Sports Council

Chanan, G. (1999) *Local community involvement: A handbook for good practice* Dublin: European Foundation for Living and Working Conditions

Coalter, F. (2001) *Realising the potential of cultural services: The case for sport* London: Local Government Association

Coalter, F., Allison, M. and Taylor, J. (2000) *The role of sport in regenerating deprived urban areas* Edinburgh: Scottish Executive Central Research Unit

Church, A. et al. (2002) *Identifying social, economic and environmental outcome indicators relevant to sport* Brighton: University of Brighton

Collins, M.F. (nd) Fragmentation, stability and turnover in British sports clubs, and clubs as social capital unpublished paper Loughborough: Loughborough University

Collins, M.F. and Reeves, M. (1995) *From coal industry welfares to community welfares* unpublished paper for CISWO Loughborough: Loughborough University

Conway, M. (ed) (1999) *Partnerships, participation, investment, innovation: Meeting the challenge of distressed areas* Dublin: European Foundation for the Improvement of Living and Working Conditions

de Knop, P., Van-Meerbeek, R., Vanreusel, B., Laporte, W., Theeboom, M., Wittock, H. and De-Martelar, K. (1996) Sports clubs in crisis: The Flemish *situation European Journal of Sport Management* 2.2, 36–52

Department for Culture, Media and Sport (2001) *Building on PAT 10: Progress report on social inclusion* London: DCMS

Department of the Environment, Transport and the Regions (1998) *Building partnerships for prosperity* London: DETR

Ellison, N. (1997) Towards a new social politics: Citizenship and reflexivity in late modernity *Sociology* 31.4, 697–717

Elsdon, K., Reynolds, J. and Stewart, S. (1999) *Studying local voluntary organisations* London: National Council for Voluntary Organisations

English Sports Council (1997) *England: The Sporting Nation* London: English Sports Council

European Commission (2000) *Inclusive cities: Building capacity for development* Luxembourg: European Commission

Fukuyama, F. (1999) *The great disruption: Human nature and the reconstitution of social order* London: Profile Books

Geddes, M. (1997) *Partnership against poverty and exclusion?* Bristol: Policy Press

Giddens, A. (1994) *Beyond left and right: The future of radical politics* Cambridge: Polity Press

Glyptis, S. (1992) *Sport and unemployment* Milton Keynes: Open University Press

Gratton, C. and Henry, I. (2001) *Sport in the city* London: Routledge

Gratton, C. and Taylor, P. (2001) *The economics of sport and recreation* London: Routledge

Hall, P.A. (1999) Social capital in Britain *British Journal of Politics* 29, 417–61

Hambleton, R., Purdue, D., Razzaque, K. and Stewart, M. with Huxham, C. and Vangen, S. (2000) *Community leadership in area regeneration* Bristol: Policy Press

Heinemann, K. and Schubert, M. (1994) *Die Sportverein* [Sports clubs] German Federal Sports Institute Publication 80. Schorndorf: Verlag Kasl Hofman

Heinemann, K. and Schwab, M. (1999) Sports clubs in Germany in Heinemann, K. (ed) *Sports clubs in various European countries* Cologne: Club of Cologne

Henry, I. (1999) Social inclusion and the leisure society *New Political Economy* 4.2, 283–8

Horch, H.D. (1998) Self-destroying processes of sports clubs in Germany *European Journal of Sports Management* 5.1, 46–58

Houlihan, B. (2001) Citizenship, civil society and the sport and recreation professions *Managing Leisure*, 1–14

Ives, J. (2001) Finance: Sports funding (interview with Chris Gratton) *Leisure Manager* 19.3, 25–6

Jordan, B. (1996) *A theory of poverty and social exclusion* Cambridge: Polity Press

Kearns, A. and Forrest, R. (2000) Social cohesion and multilevel urban governance *Urban Studies* 57. 5–6, 995–1017

Marshall, T.H. (1992) Citizenship and social class in Marshall, T.H. and Bottomore, T. *Citizenship and social class* London: Pluto Press

Martin, W.H. and Mason, S. (1998) *Transforming the future: Rethinking work and leisure* Sudbury: Leisure Consultants

Matarasso, F. (1998) *Poverty and oysters: The social impact of local arts development in Portsmouth* Stroud: Comedia

Patrickkson, G. (1995) *The significance of sport for society: Health, socialisation, economy: A scientific review* Strasbourg: Council of Europe Press

Pierre, J. and Peters, B.G. (2001) *Governance, politics and the state* Basingstoke: Macmillan

Powell, M., Boyne, G. and Ashworth, G. (2001) Towards a geography of people poverty and place poverty *Policy and Politics* 29.3, 243–58

Putnam, R.D. (2000) *Bowling alone* New York: Simon and Schuster

Putnam, R.D., Leonard, R., and Nanetti, R.Y. (1993) *Making democracy work* Princeton: Princeton University Press

Rhodes, R.A.W. (2000) *Transforming British government. Volume 1: Changing Institutions* Basingstoke: Macmillan/ESRC

Rigg, M. (1986) *Action sport: An evaluation* London: Sports Council

Robinson, T. (nd) *The City Challenge programme in South Newcastle* Newcastle on Tyne: Newcastle University

Rose, R., Mishler, W. and Haerpfer, C. (1997) *Getting real: Social capital in post-Communist societies* Studies in Social Policy 278 Glasgow: University of Strathclyde

Rose, R. and Weller, C. (2001) Coping with organisations: Networks of Russian social capital <www.socialcapital.strath.ac.uk/catalog31_0.html> accessed 11 July 01

Rossi, P.H., Freeman, H.E., and Lipsey, M. (1999, 6th edition) *Evaluation: A systematic approach* Thousand Oaks, CA: Sage

Rothstein, B. (2001) Social capital in the Social Democratic welfare state *Politics and Society* 29.2, 207–41

Selwood, H.J. and Jones, R. (1993) The Americas Cup in retrospect: The aftershock in Fremantle in Veal, A.J. et al. (eds) *Leisure and tourism: Social and environmental change* Sydney: University of Technology

Slack, T. (1999) *Understanding sports organisations* Champaign, Ill.: Human Kinetics

Smith, D.M. (1985) *Geography, inequality and society* Cambridge: Cambridge University Press

Sport England (1996) *Valuing volunteers in the UK* London: SE

Sport England (1999) *Regeneration through sport: Sport's contribution to community development* conference papers London, 11 Feb 99 London: Sport England

Sport England (2001a) *The sports partnerships: Building for the future – a discussion paper* <www.sportengland.co.uk> accessed 8 Aug 01

Sport England (2001b) *Sport Action Zones: Summary report on the establishment of the first 12 zones* <www.sportengland.co.uk> accessed 22 Nov 01

Sport England (2001c) *Performance indicators for the development of sport: A guide for local authorities* London: SE

Sports Council (1993) *Sport in the 90s: New horizons* London: SC

Taylor, A. (1997) 'Arm's length but hands on' – Managing the new governance: The Department of National Heritage and cultural policy in Britain *Public Administration* 75, 441–66

Taylor, M. (1992) *Signposts to community development* London: Community Projects Foundation

Taylor, P. (2001) Forecasting in Gratton, C. and Henry, I. (eds) *Sport in the city* London: Routledge

Witt, P. and Crompton, J. (1996) *Recreation programs that work for at risk youth: The challenge of shaping the future* Pennsylvania: Venture Publishing

Chapter 13 Conclusions

Arts Council of England (2000) *Arts Statistics 1986–87, 1997–98* London: ACE

Becker, G. (1965) A theory of the allocation of time *Economic Journal* 75, 493–517

Bemelmans-Videc, M-L., Rist, R.C. and Vedung, E. (eds) (1998) *Carrots, sticks and sermons: Policy instruments and their evaluation* New Brunswick, NJ: Transaction Publishers

Book Marketing Ltd (2000) *Bookfacts 2000* London: BML

Boothby, J., Tungatt, F.M., Townsend, A. and Collins, M. (1982) *A sporting chance? Family, school and environmental influences on taking part in sport* Study 22 London: Sports Council

Brackenridge, C. (2001) *Spoilsports* London: Routledge

Clarke, G. (1998) Queering the pitch and coming out to play: Lesbians in physical education and sport *Sport, Education and Society* 3.2, 145–60

Coalter, F. (2001a) *Realising the potential of cultural services: The case for sport* London: Local Government Association

Coalter, F. (2001b) *Realising the potential of cultural services: Research agenda* London: Local Government Association

Coalter, F. and Allison, M. (1996) *Sport and community development* Edinburgh: Scottish Sports Council

Cohen, C. and Pate, M. (2000) Making a meal of arts evaluation: Can social audit offer a more balanced approach? *Managing Leisure* 5, 103–20

Collins, M.F. (1990) The economics of sport, and sports in the economy in C.P. Cooper (ed) *Progress in Tourism, Recreation and Hospitality Management* 3

Collins, M.F. (2003, forthcoming) Sport and social exclusion in Houlihan, B.M.J. (ed) *Sport and society* London: Sage

Countryside Agency (2001) *The state of the countryside 2001* Cheltenham: Countryside Agency

Csikszmentmihalyi, M. (1992) *Flow: The psychology of happiness* London: Rider

Department for Culture, Media and Sport (2001a) *Libraries, museums, galleries and archives for all: Co-operation across the sectors to tackle social exclusion* London; DCMS

Department for Culture, Media and Sport (2001b) *Building on PAT 10: Progress report on social inclusion* London: DCMS

Donnelly, P. (1996) Approaches to social inequality in the sociology of sport *Quest* 48, 221–42

English Tourist Board (1989) *Tourism for all* London: ETB

Gershuny, J. (2000) *Changing times: Work and leisure in post industrial society* Oxford: Oxford University Press

Griggin, P. and Gensasci, J. (1990) Addressing homophobia in physical education: Responsibilities for teachers and researchers in Messner, M.A. and Szabo, D.F. (eds) *Sport, men and the gender order: Critical feminist perspectives* Champaign, Ill: Human Kinetics

Harland, J. et al. (nd) *Attitudes to participation in the arts, heritage, broadcasting and sport: A review of recent research,* unpublished report to the Department of National Heritage Slough: National Foundation for Educational Research

Harrison, P. (1983) *Inside the inner city* Harmondsworth: Penguin

Hekma, G. (1998) 'As long as they don't make an issue of it'. . . . Gay men and lesbians in organised sports in the Netherlands *Journal of Homosexuality* 35.1, 1–23

Henry, I. (2001) Postmodernism and power in urban policy: Implications for sport and cultural policy in the city *European Sport Management Quarterly* 1, 5–20

Hylton, K. and Totton, M. (2001) Community sports development in Hylton, K. et al. (eds) *Sports development: Policy, processes and practice* London: Routledge

Institute of Leisure and Amenity Management (1999) *Contribution of the arts and sports to neighbourhood renewal and reducing social exclusion* Reading: ILAM

Jordan, B. (1996) *A theory of poverty and social exclusion* Cambridge: Polity Press

King, L. and Thompson, P. (2001) 'Limp-wristed, Kylie Minogue-loving, football-hating, fashion victims' Gay sports clubs – providing for male members, challenging social exclusion? in McPherson, G. and Reid, G. (eds) *Leisure and social exclusion* publication 73 Eastbourne: Leisure Studies Association

Lenskyj, H.J. (1990) Power and play: Gender and sexuality issues in sport and physical activity *International Review of Sociology of Sport* 25.3, 235–43

Linder, S. (1970) *The harried leisure class* New York: Columbia University Press

Lister, R. (1990) *The exclusive society: Citizenship and the poor* London: Child Poverty Action Group

Long, J. and Sanderson, I. (2001) The social benefits of sport: Where's the proof? in Gratton, C. and Henry, I. (eds) *Sport in the city* London: Routledge

Martin, W.H. and Mason, S. (1998) *Transforming the future: Rethinking work and leisure* Sudbury: Leisure Consultants

Mintel (1996a) Leisure trends *Leisure Intelligence* Jan

Mintel (1996b) The British on holiday at home *Leisure Intelligence* Feb

Mintel (1999) Adventure holidays *Leisure Intelligence* Jan

Mintel (2000a) The UK cinema market *Leisure Intelligence* Sept

Mintel (2000b) Budget holidays *Leisure Intelligence* Nov

Mintel (2001) Coach holidays *Leisure Intelligence* Jan

More, T.A. (1999) Reconceiving recreation policy in an era of growing social inequality *Proceedings of 1999 NE Recreation Research Symposium* US Forest Service, 415–19

MORI (2001) *Visitors to museums and galleries in the UK* London: Resource

Muddiman, D. et al. (2000) *Open to all? The public library and social exclusion* London: Resource

Nagel, M. and Nagel, S. (2001) *Social background and top performance sports* paper to ECSS Congress 24–28 July, Cologne

National Playing Fields Association (1998) *Regeneration through recreation* London: NPFA

Palfrey, C. and Thomas, P. (1996) Ethical issues in policy evaluation *Policy and Politics* 24.3, 277–85

Resource (2001a) *Using museums, galleries, archives and libraries to develop a learning community: A strategic plan for action* London: Resource

Resource (2001b) *Renaissance in the regions: A new vision for England's museums* London: Resource

Room, S. (2001) Participation in sport in Hylton, K., Bramham, P., Nesti, M. and Jackson, D. (eds) *Sports development: Policy, processes and practice* London: Routledge

Rowe. N. (2001) *The social landscape of sport: Recognising the challenge and realising the potential* paper to regional conferences London: Sport England

Salvation Army/Henley Centre (1999) *The paradox of prosperity* London: Henley Centre for Forecasting

Selwood, S. (2001) *The UK cultural sector: Profile and policy issues* London: Policy Studies Institute

Slee, W., Curry, N. and Joseph, D. (2001) *Removing barriers, creating opportunities: Social exclusion in countryside leisure in the UK* Cardiff: Countryside Recreation Network

Smith, R. (2001) Including the forty per cent: Social exclusion and tourism policy in G. McPherson and M. Reid (eds) *Leisure and social inclusion: Challenges to policy and practice* Publication 73 Eastbourne: Leisure Studies Association

Social and Community Planning Research (1999) *UK Day Visits Survey 1998* London: SCPR

Sports Council/Health Education Authority (1992) *Allied Dunbar National Fitness Survey, main report* London: SC/HEA

Squires, S.L. and Sparkes, A.C. (1996) Circles of silence: Sexual identity in physical education and sport *Sport, Education and society* 1.1, 77–101

Thomas, P. and Palfrey, C. (1996) Evaluation: Stakeholder-focused criteria *Social Policy and Administration* 30.2, 125–42

Van der Meulen, R., Kraylaar, G. and Utlee, W. (2001) *Lifelong on the move: An event analysis of attrition in on-elite sport* paper to ECSS Congress, 24–28 July Cologne

Veblen, T. (1953) *The theory of the leisure class* New York: American Library

Young Mens' Christian Association (1999) *Contribution of the arts and sports to neighbourhood renewal and reducing social exclusion* London: YMCA

Author Index

Subject Index